**JOHN HOWEY & ASSOCIATES** selected and current works

THE MASTER ARCHITECT SERIES

# JOHN HOWEY & ASSOCIATES selected and current works

images
Publishing

Published in Australia in 2006 by

The Images Publishing Group Pty Ltd

ABN 89 059 734 431

6 Bastow Place, Mulgrave, Victoria 3170, Australia

Tel: +61 3 9561 5544  Fax: +61 3 9561 4860

books@images.com.au

www.imagespublishing.com

National Library of Australia Cataloguing-in-Publication entry:

John Howey Associates: selected and current works.

ISBN 1 86470 133 1.

1. John Howey Associates.  2. Architectural firms – United States – Florida.
3. Architecture, American – Pictorial works.  4. Architecture – United States – Pictorial works.
I. John Howey Associates.  (Series: Master architect series. VII).

720.9759

Edited by Robyn Beaver

Designed by The Graphic Image Studio Pty Ltd, Mulgrave, Australia
www.tgis.com.au

Film by Mission Productions Limited, Hong Kong
Printed by Everbest Printing Co Ltd. in Hong Kong/China

# Con
# tents

In his four decades of practice in Florida, John Howey has received acclaim for his indigenous approach to architecture distinguished by his consistency of thoughtfulness and diversity of expression. In addition to his array of master plans, office buildings, and commercial projects, his Tampa-based firm has planned, built or remodeled more than fifty houses. By synthesizing experiences from the east coast of Florida to the western shores of California he has created, as he describes, "a new way of thinking about housing and lifestyle. Florida architecture in the new millennium is the result of strong influences from both within and without. Architecture is the process of layering these influences."

Howey has been blessed with intuitive skill and sensitivity, which reach beyond the places he has been before. His work expresses the timeless principles of contemporary architecture while drawing upon his cultural experiences and the architects he admires—Paul Rudolph, Victor Lundy, Craig Elwood, Irving Gill, and John Lautner, to name a few. "My work is a collective lesson of experiences with each project becoming more complex and sophisticated, responding to site, climate, and context while expressing a deeper personal journey," he explains. Together, they demonstrate how an intelligent and thoughtful reinterpretation of contemporary architectural ideas can enrich everyday living, captivating all those who experience his work. He focuses with skill on how people will experience the building as they pass through and around it.

In the modernist tradition, Howey remains devoted to rigorous geometry and the use of simple, often sculptural, form. This aesthetic cannot be defined by any simple categorization. The key to his process is his willingness to examine a commission for what it has to offer rather than to impose upon it a rigid formal preconception. Howey looks first at what exists, studies the site and seeks to relate what he puts upon it to the adjacent landscape or urban context. The result may not resemble the natural setting or its neighboring structures, but it is always calculated to fit into the larger context of the landscape or urban setting.

Fore word

Lawrence Scarpa

Impressive as Howey's professional achievement may be, his personal accomplishments are no less compelling. He has authored numerous articles and books including *The Sarasota School of Architecture* (MIT Press, 1995), which arguably is credited with creating the revolution that continues to save the most important period of 20th-century modern architecture in Florida. His unbridled optimism continues to shepherd Howey into new areas of discovery. His energy and enthusiasm for architecture continues to be amazing. After forty years of success one would think, "It's time to smell the roses." On the contrary, Howey continues to explore new avenues and add greater depth to his already impressive career. *John Howey & Associates Selected and Current Works* showcases a formidable personal collection of Howey's most compelling projects spanning his career from the early 1960s to the present.

**Lawrence Scarpa**
**Santa Monica, California**

Florida needs an Esther McCoy. Chronicler of the modern architecture of Southern California through its several generations, McCoy cemented both relationships and individual importance, founding the *idea* of a tradition and situating it in the larger world of ideas. McCoy was not alone in this collaborative act of creation, which hit kismet during the days of John Entenza's legendary *Arts and Architecture* magazine, sponsor of the renowned Case Study Houses. Writing was crucial to this architectural invention and the symbiosis continues in the flourishing and incisive Los Angeles School of urbanists. And then there's Mike Davis, Joan Didion, Reyner Banham, Roger Starr, Raymond Chandler, Christopher Isherwood, not to mention Hollywood, pulling successive utopias and dystopias from the streets of the city. All help everyone to see both place and practice more clearly.

Florida has long had the architecture but not the culture to back it up, not enough writing to support the building, notwithstanding Elmore Leonard, Carl Hiassen, and re-runs of *Miami Vice*. Too bad. The state is amazing, marked by thick and variegated traditions extending back centuries, by a set of landscapes that architecture constantly engages, by numerous communities seeking their special bliss, by the omnipresent beach, by a political culture that is often laughable in its extremes (think Schwarzenegger and Jeb, think hanging chads … ), by the presence of a shifting collection of utopias, dramatically various. And, like California, Florida has its myths and nightmares, its dark side, its secret narratives, fuel for infinite legend, plenty of bad news for Native Americans, for African Americans, for the environment. California and Florida are two troubled paradises with problem destinies, beleaguered by maniacal ecologies constantly poised at catastrophe, full of friction.

But let's focus on the sense of hope, the wildly varied intentionality of the state's settlements. The patchwork of golf and shore communities, balm for those with a foot in the grave seeking a leg-up on the afterlife, saturates the landscape with an even more improbable green. Such affinity groups, whether the elderly deployed with demographic precision in their appropriately luxurious or threadbare camps, the vivid community-out-of-exile of the Miami Cubans, the Haitian ghetto, the tropical discipline of Cocoanut Grove, the faded louche of Key West, the new money paradise on

Intro
duction

Michael Sorkin

Brickell, the Truman Show, nothing-can-go-wrong nightmare of Celebration and Seaside, Orlando's theme-park sprawl, the technopolis of Cape Canaveral—beyond Fellini—the instant-city youth rites of Fort Lauderdale, the high deco Jewish leisure utopia of Miami Beach (the twin of labor fixated, "Bauhaus" Tel Aviv), and on it goes.

Within this maelstrom of fabricated identities, there's something else, arguably the state's greatest artistic achievement: Sarasota, a still-vital architectural convergence that now far exceeds the confines of its town of origin. Let us, then, replace the academic sounding Sarasota "School" with some more capacious language … and call it Florida Modern. At its headwaters the amazing group that descends from Paul Rudolph (FLW and the circus lurking in the background) and includes, among many others, Victor Lundy, Ralph Twitchell, Tim Seibert, Carl Abbott, William Rupp, Gene Leedy, and many more, fatefully aligned.

The work they produced, at once breezy and tectonic, beautifully composed, immersed in landscape and views, free in form (sometimes in plan), precisely but lightly detailed, has inspired an ongoing architectural investigation that remains true to these roots. This "second generation" includes William Morgan, Don Singer, Spillis, Candela, and John Howey, as well as the younger Sarasotans still at it. All pursue the gentle clarity of their predecessors and all enjoy the same prismatic verve, the same deep respect for the singularity of site. Against the background of hurricane-hardened dryvit chateaux that forms the state's architectural default, these brave poets still search for their truth.

John Howey has drawn and built work of elegance and directness that continues to engage and enlarge the tradition. In his Shell Point house of 1989, a triangular section raised on stilts buffers its interiors behind great flapped gables that rise to air and view. The Longboat Key house of 1995, the Trocke House of 1976, and the Bierley house of 1970 use elegantly complex roofscapes to sectionally modulate clear plans and to bring a missing topographic to Florida's endless flatscape. Most dramatic is the Gallery House of 2000 with its commanding roof in the form of an inverted, truncated pyramid, a beacon above its wing-flanked central pavilion.

Howey is a great aggregator, and assembler of forms, with a mastery that flows from Rudolph. At the Bay Villa townhouses of 1970, the rhythm of standing seam roofs, walled terraces, and light monitors is elegant and lively. At a much larger scale, Howey's project for the Iran National Library of 1977 is a dazzling assemblage of cubes, at once controlled, exuberant, and rich in dialogue with Persian geometries. Howey works his way up and down the scales with complete confidence. His ongoing "sky-tower" project takes this rhythm into the vertical, the skyscraper as a kind of Nogouchi lamp, a lantern on the horizon. The tower's base, covered in foliage, dives past existing low buildings to meet the street, a strange and winning transition.

The street—an endangered species in so much of Florida—is dear to Howey, whose projects for plazas, including the lushly sculptural 1980 City Hall Plaza in Tampa, are welcoming and concise, a gift to the public. He lavishes equal attention of such quotidian items of streetscape as the ingenious bus shelters of St. Petersburg (with Carl Abbott) and tiny serpentine mechanical equipment screens for Tampa. This, like the rest of John Howey's work, finds its grace through both formal dexterity, and ease of inhabitation. It is architecture meant for life well-lived and John Howey's long and artistic pursuit of these subtle pleasures is the measure of his marvelous achievement. This architecture is alive.

Bring on the bards!

**Michael Sorkin**
**New York**

## Architecture

Imagine how the first person felt when he or she stacked loose stones in a field to make a wall, or used tree limbs to make a roof or floor that led to the idea of shelter. From essence—"to be"—comes "what is", or the idea of "wall" in this case. Without preconceptions, a state of being within one's mind is necessary, much like the first wall-creator had, with a blank panorama of possibilities from which to choose. This absolute reduction to nothingness affords the opportunity for one to arrive at a timeless idea, like the first wall that was made from loose stones scattered about the landscape. To me, recognition of this is the instance of creation—or architecture.

## Architecture is

*"… architecture is a thoughtful making of spaces."*

Louis Kahn

Whatever your beliefs, we were formed in darkness and nothingness. Light appeared. There was no longer just darkness. With light, sky, land, and water, man and his habitation were revealed. Light, or its absence, is always with us. This is a constant.

To again quote Louis Kahn:

*"An architectural space must reveal the evidence of its making by the space itself. It cannot be a space when carved out of a greater structure meant for greater space, because the choice of a structure is synonymous with the light, which gives image to that space. Artificial light is only a single, tiny, static moment in light and is the light of night and never can equal the nuances of mood created by the time of day and the wonder of the seasons.*

*A plan of a building should read like a harmony of spaces in light. Even a space intended to be dark should have just enough light from some mysterious opening to tell us how dark it really is. Each space must be defined by its structure and the character of its natural light …"*

# Philos ophy

John Howey

## Architecture is action

Architecture is not static. Again, consider "wall", a most fundamental part of architecture. Wall itself implies action: it can keep people in or people out. Large openings through walls can order movement of people and goods back and forth. Smaller openings—windows—create specific views to or from. Walls can become seats to sit on. They can be inscribed with names or thoughts to be read. Wall is one of many elements of action in space making that architects possess on their journey to creating dynamic architecture.

**John Howey**

SKY

1

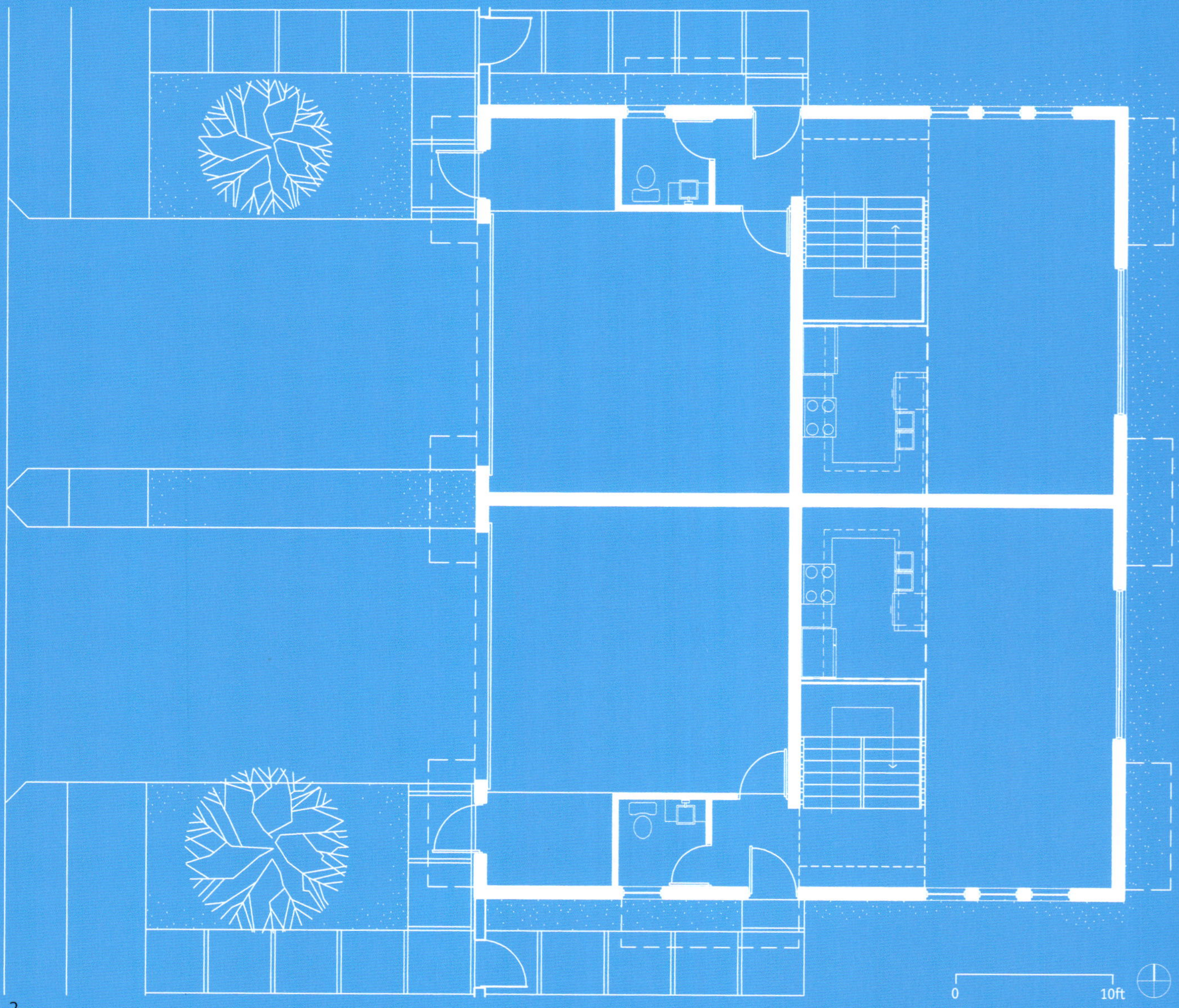

2

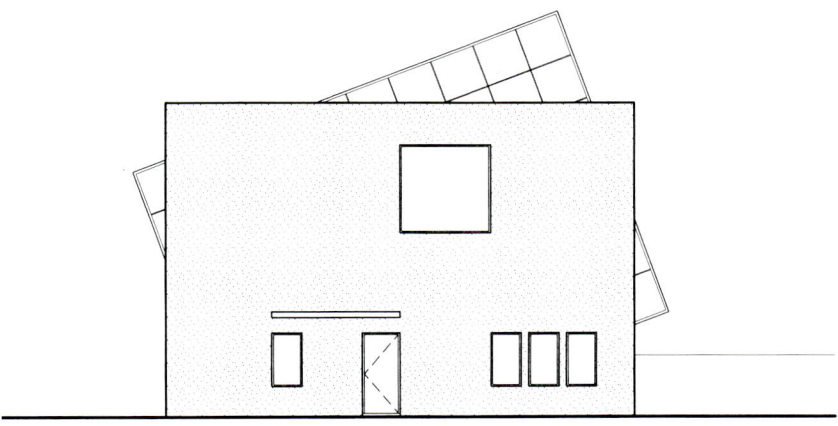

3

**Design 2004**

Tampa, Florida
Mr and Mrs Henry Fernandez
8,400 square feet
Concrete footings, masonry
walls, metal frame construction,
stucco, and translucent
fiberglass skylights

Designed for a developer, this four-unit loft apartment complex is planned as a stand-alone or as a project that can be repeated on adjacent lots of the same size. The site's narrow footprint, with street and alley access at its ends, led Howey to focus each unit's living space inward to a private landscaped court in the middle.

## Loft Apartments

Gated access to each unit is from walled side yards, with front garages buffering each unit from street and alley noise. Inside, the upper floors become split-level above the garage, affording 13 foot-6 inch ceilings in the living, kitchen, and dining spaces. Access to bedrooms, loft, and roof deck is from a steel stair suspended from the townhouse walls and ceilings, with a continuous, central spine support from entry to roof. Front-to-rear sloping fiberglass skylights illuminate the floors and stairs of each loft apartment.

1 Model
2 Entry level floor plan
3 Side elevation
4 Section rendering

4

5

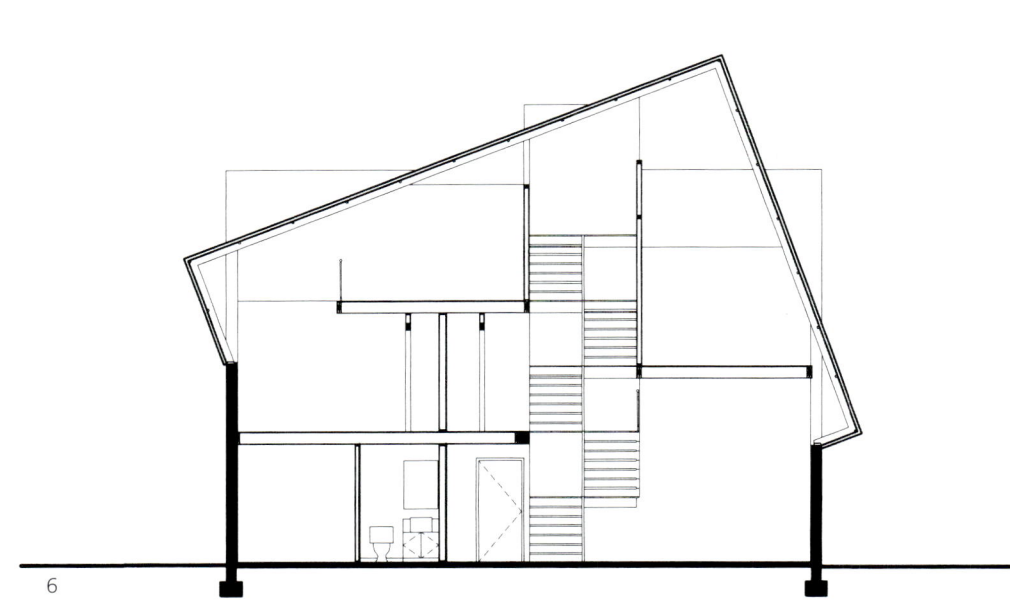

6

7

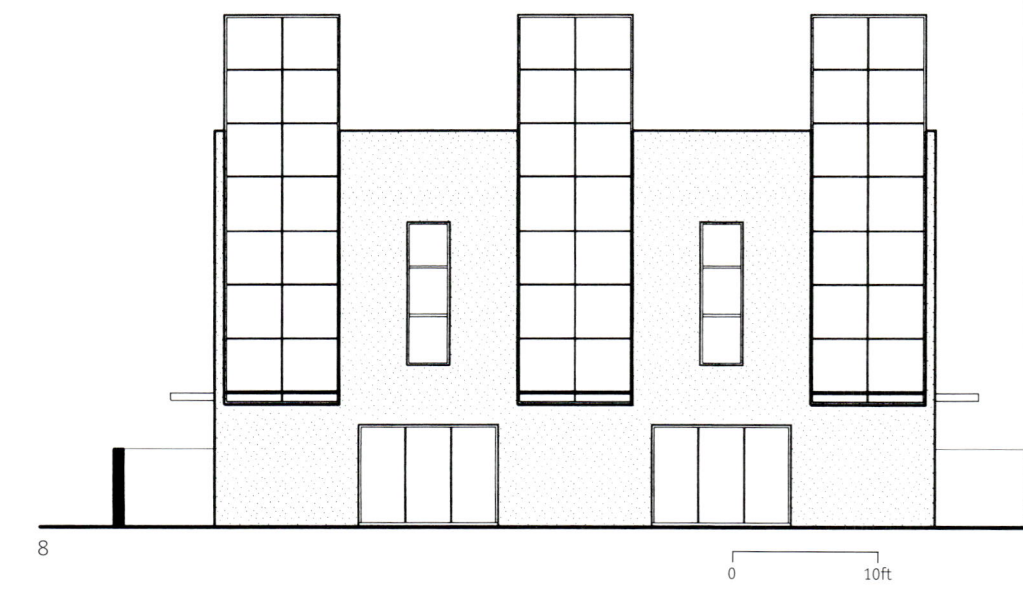

8

0          10ft

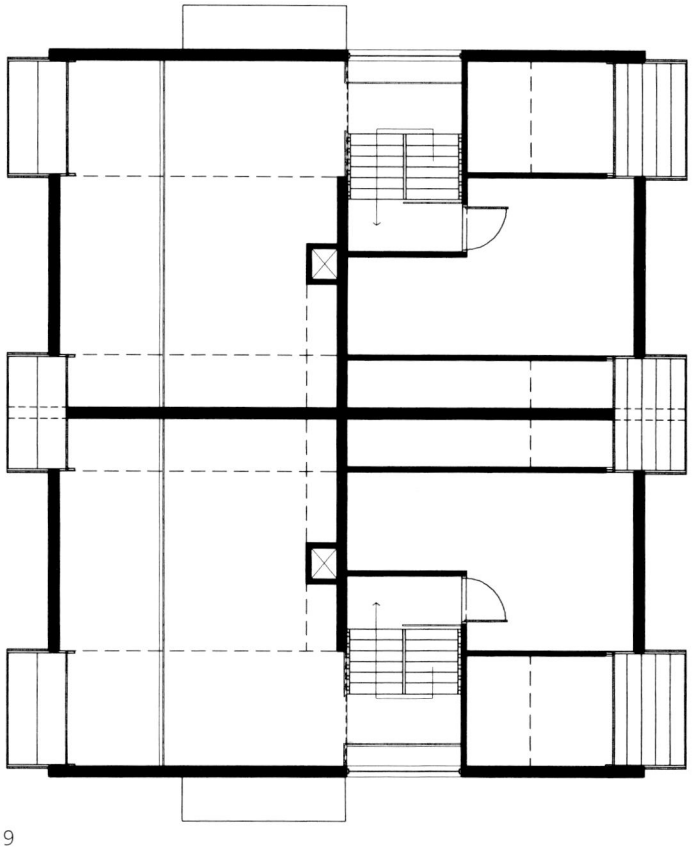

9

5&7 Stair detail rendering
  6 Section
  8 Rear elevation
  9 Mezzanine/roof level plan
 10 Second floor plan

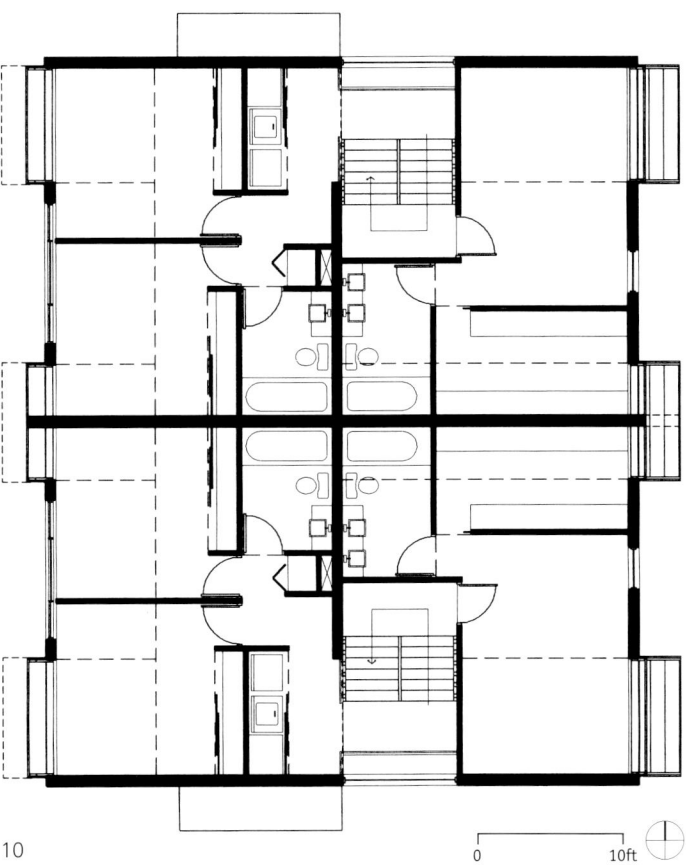

10

0                    10ft

1

2

3

4

1  Rendering (view looking north)
2  Rendering (view looking west)
3  Rendering (view from south)
4  Rendering (view from southeast)
5  Pinnacle ideas

# 02

**Tower 101**

Ascending more than fifty stories, Howey's signature tower is certain to define Tampa's skyline. Incorporating sophisticated technology that will power, illuminate, and shade the building by solar energy, the structure gracefully marries ecologically efficient engineering with visually arresting design. The central location of the tower preserves the existing sidewalk character of the city block by retaining the perimeter historic brick buildings for retail use. One of the two major entries is through these buildings to the hotel and its lobby. The other entrance is on a main street with walks and a trolley system connecting it to the Tampa Convention Center and sports arena to the south. Within the lobby are two floors of retail connected by escalators. The building's central core of elevators and stairs serve condominium offices above retail, a boutique hotel with a sky-lobby at mid-height, and condominium apartments at the top. Hotel concierge service will be available to the apartments; parking is underground.

### Design 2001

Tampa, Florida
Tampa Tower LLC
1,140,000 square feet total
900,000 square feet
above grade
Trussed tube concept with
diagonal structural members
placed at outer walls,
reinforced concrete building
core, steel deck or post-
tensioned concrete floors

At the tower's peak—the highest point in central Florida—a sky-deck and penthouse prism will offer 360-degree views. The tower owes its unusual sculptural silhouette to a series of undulating sloped walls that are the key to the building's climate control. The façade encases a textured glass curtain "scrim", incorporating a system of solar panels connected to a central computer "brain". In addition to providing the building's air conditioning and electricity, the solar technology enables the transfer of heat from warm areas to cold areas and is sophisticated enough to independently climatize each of the tower's facets. The ethereal scrims appear opaque from the exterior but transparent from the interior, simultaneously affording views and privacy. A spire atop the tower's crown, along with its frame and tensile cables, provides wireless communication resources as well as a potential broadcast transmission site for the military or media.

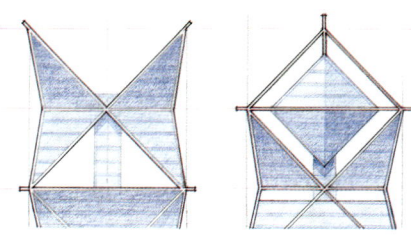

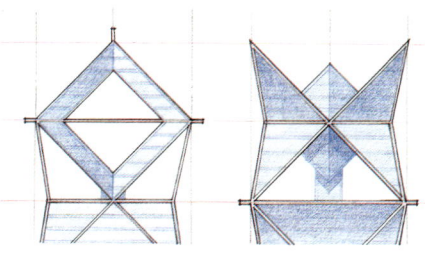

5

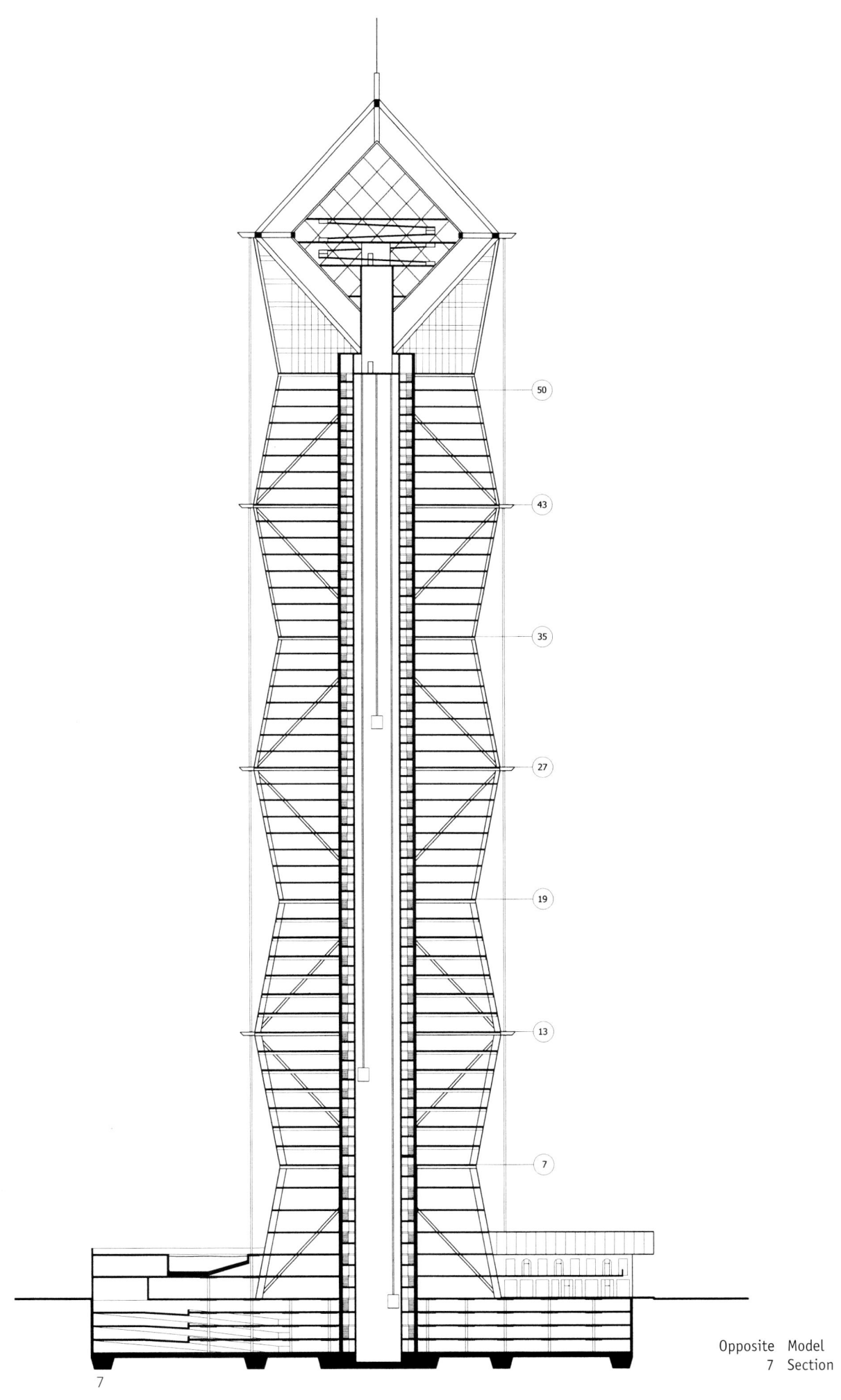

50

43

35

27

19

13

7

7

Opposite Model
7 Section

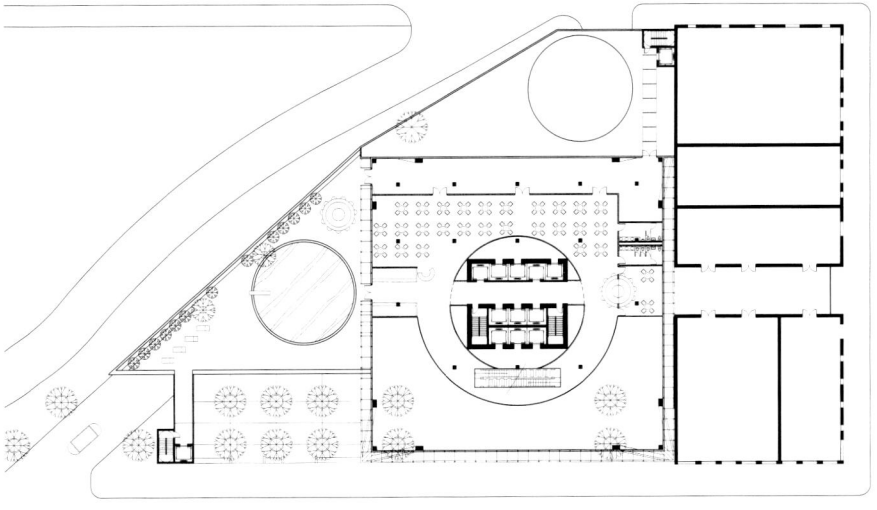

8

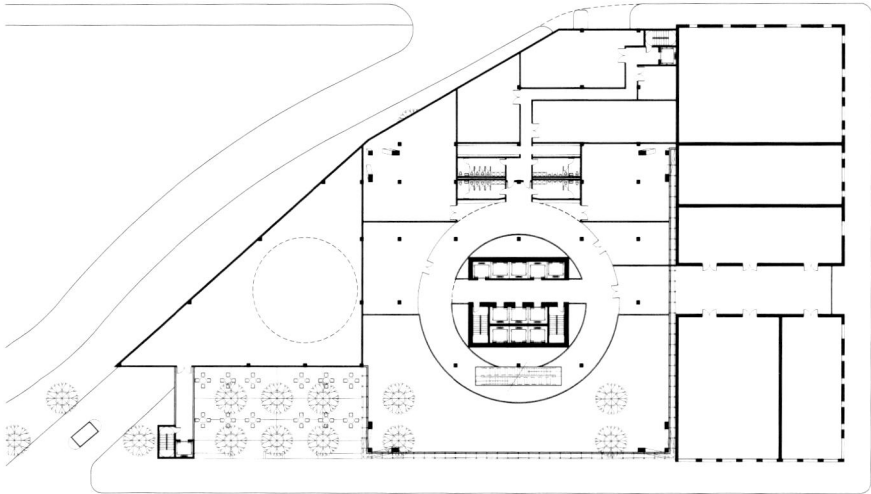

9

8  Third floor plan
9  Second floor plan
10  Lobby floor plan
11  Typical apartment floor plan
12  Typical hotel floor plan
13  Sketch of lobby

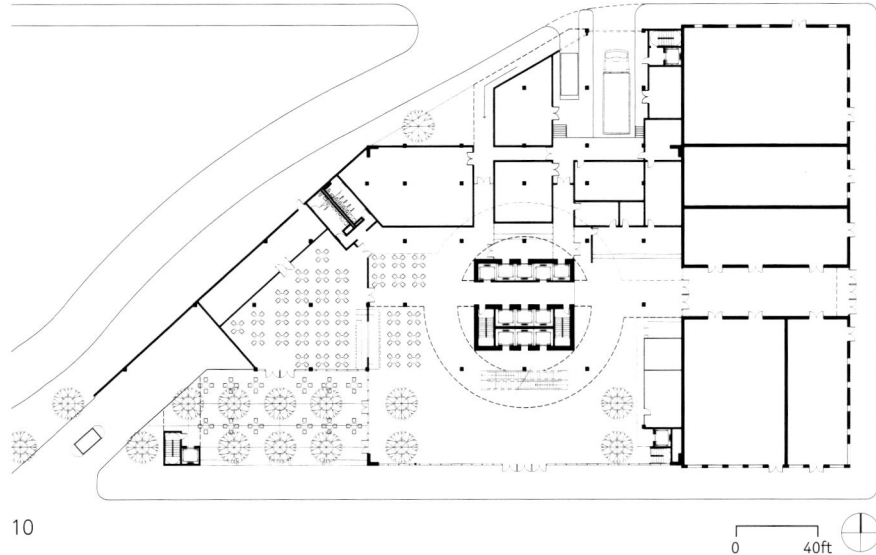

10

0    40ft

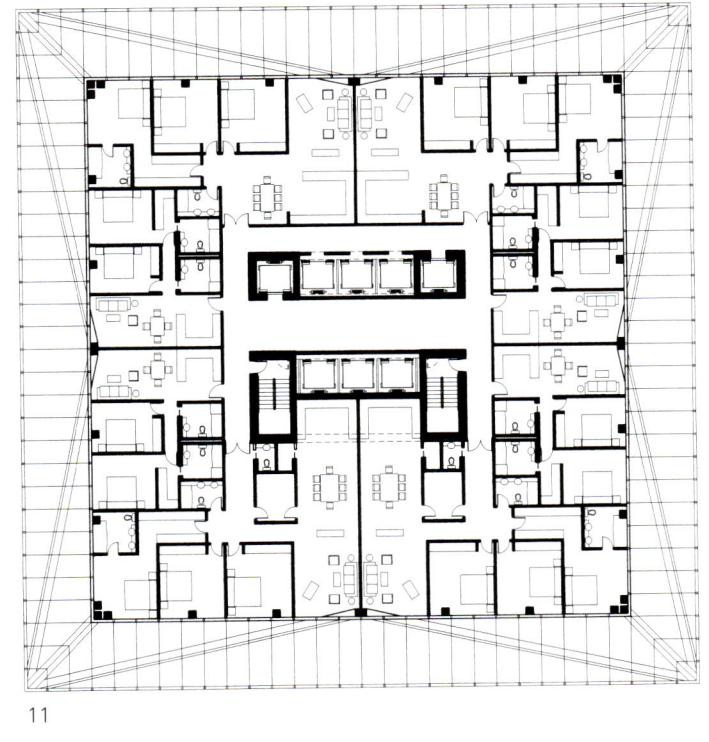

11

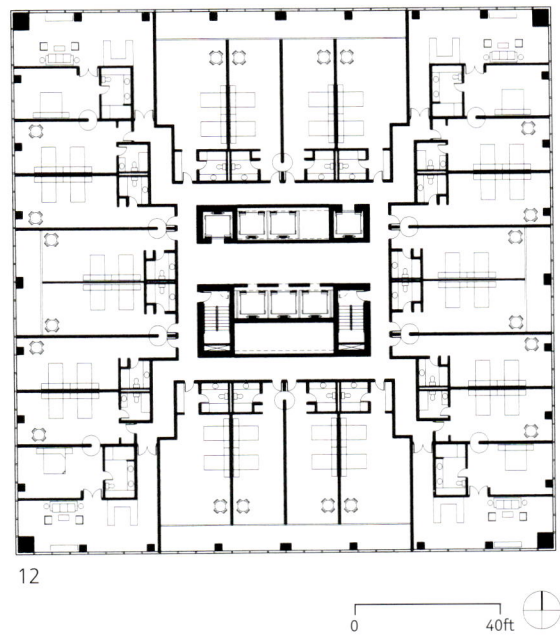

12

0              40ft

13

1,3&4 Model
2 Section
5 Floor plan

1

2

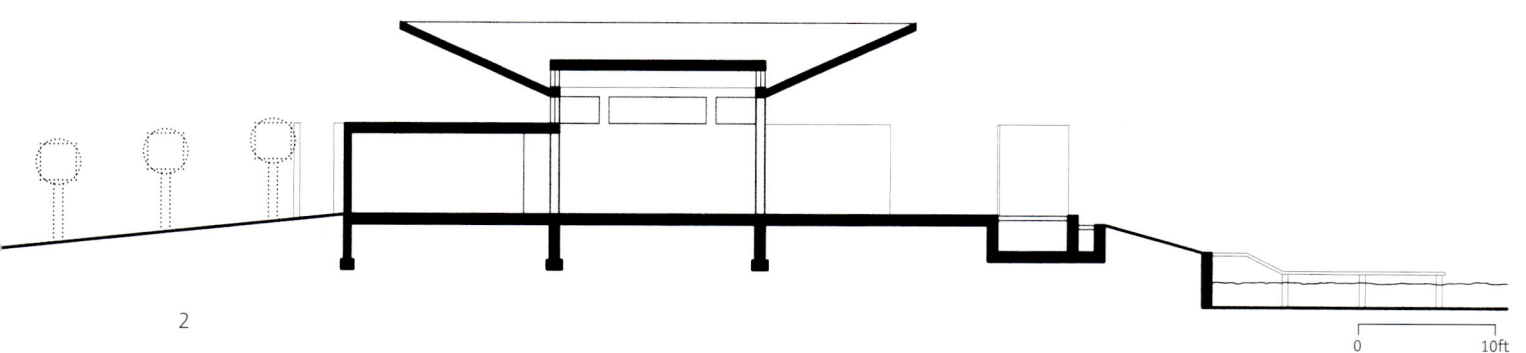

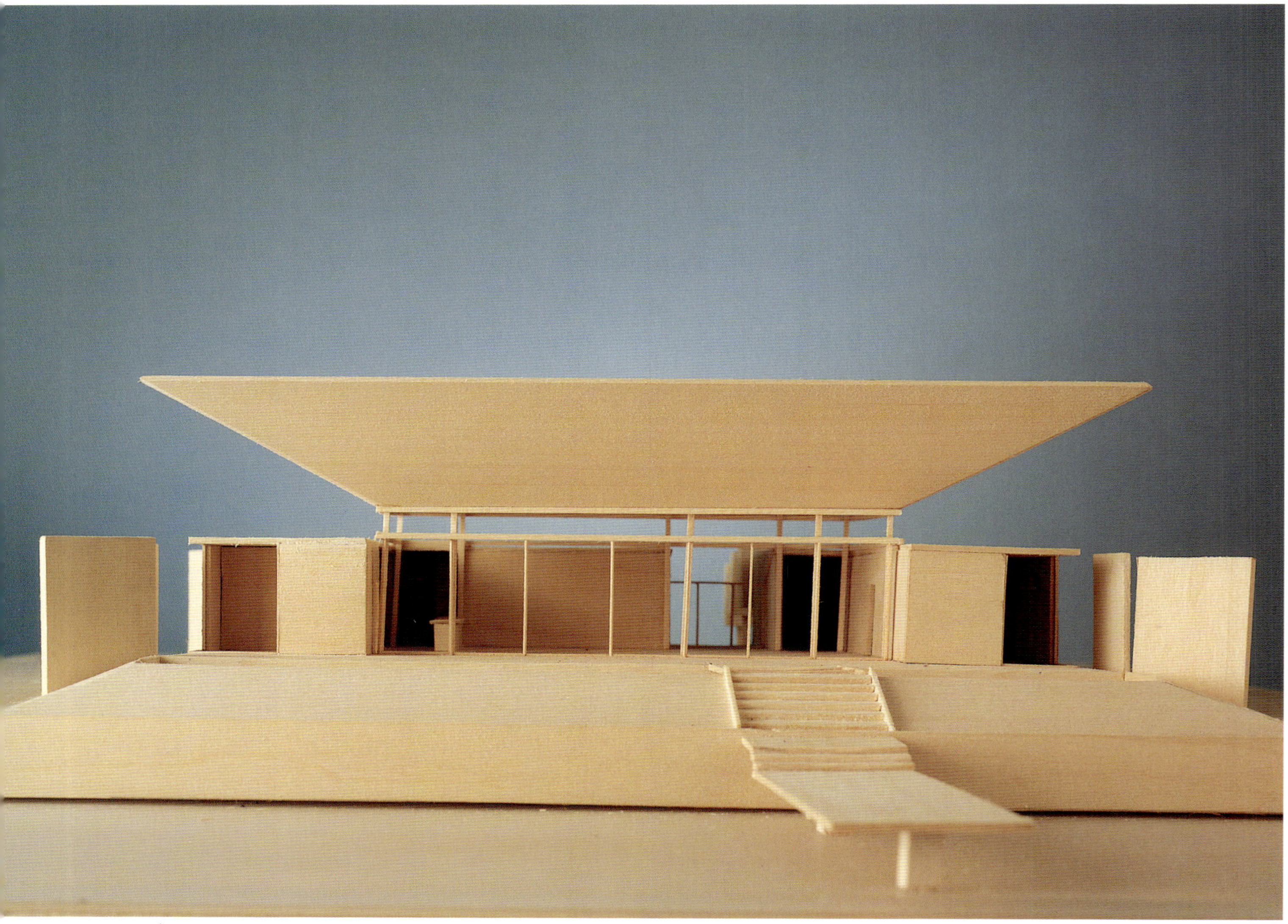

## Design 2000

Bayway Isles, Florida
Mr and Mrs Jerry Houlton
3,400 square feet
Elevated precast concrete floor
system, masonry walls, cast-
in-place concrete roof, stucco,
marble, aluminum, and glass

3

4

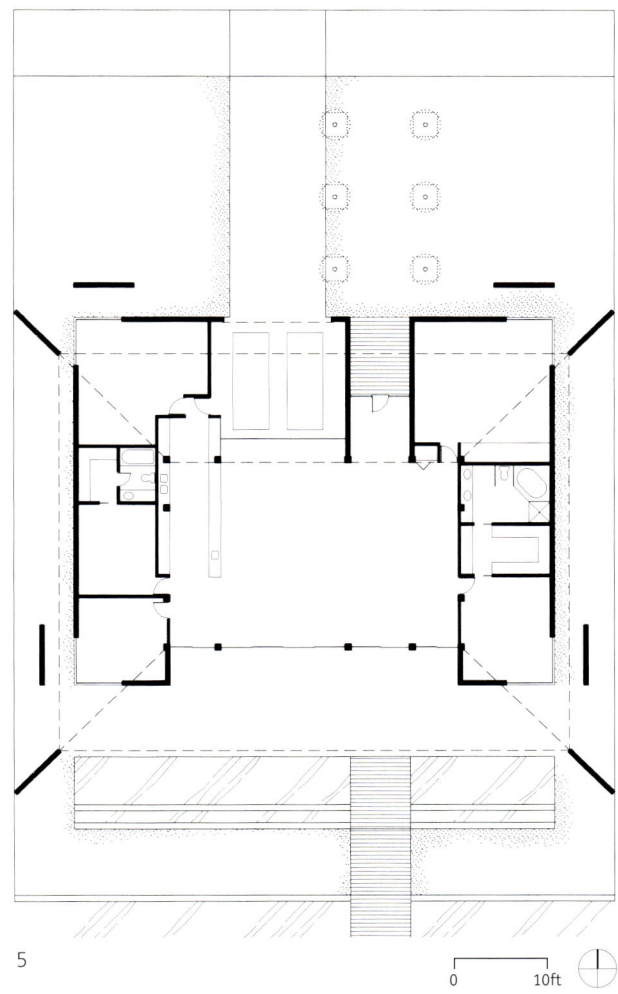

5

0          10ft

# 03

## Gallery House

A retired executive and his wife desired a live-in art museum for their modern art, sculpture, and ikebana, all on one level. The site, on a man-made island in Boca Ciega Bay, faces south, with views of the Sunshine Skyway Bridge. The main level is elevated for enhanced views and flood protection, with the living/gallery space placed at the center. The personal and service spaces surround the gallery on three sides, affording perimeter column support for the high sculptural, concrete roof under which horizontal strips of indirect natural light illuminate the gallery. The higher roof appears to float over the lower flat-roofed elements, whose corner windows are shielded from the sun and view by angled freestanding walls that also define individual landscaped areas. A linear lap pool rests at the bay boundary and makes a water edge with the bay beyond.

1

2

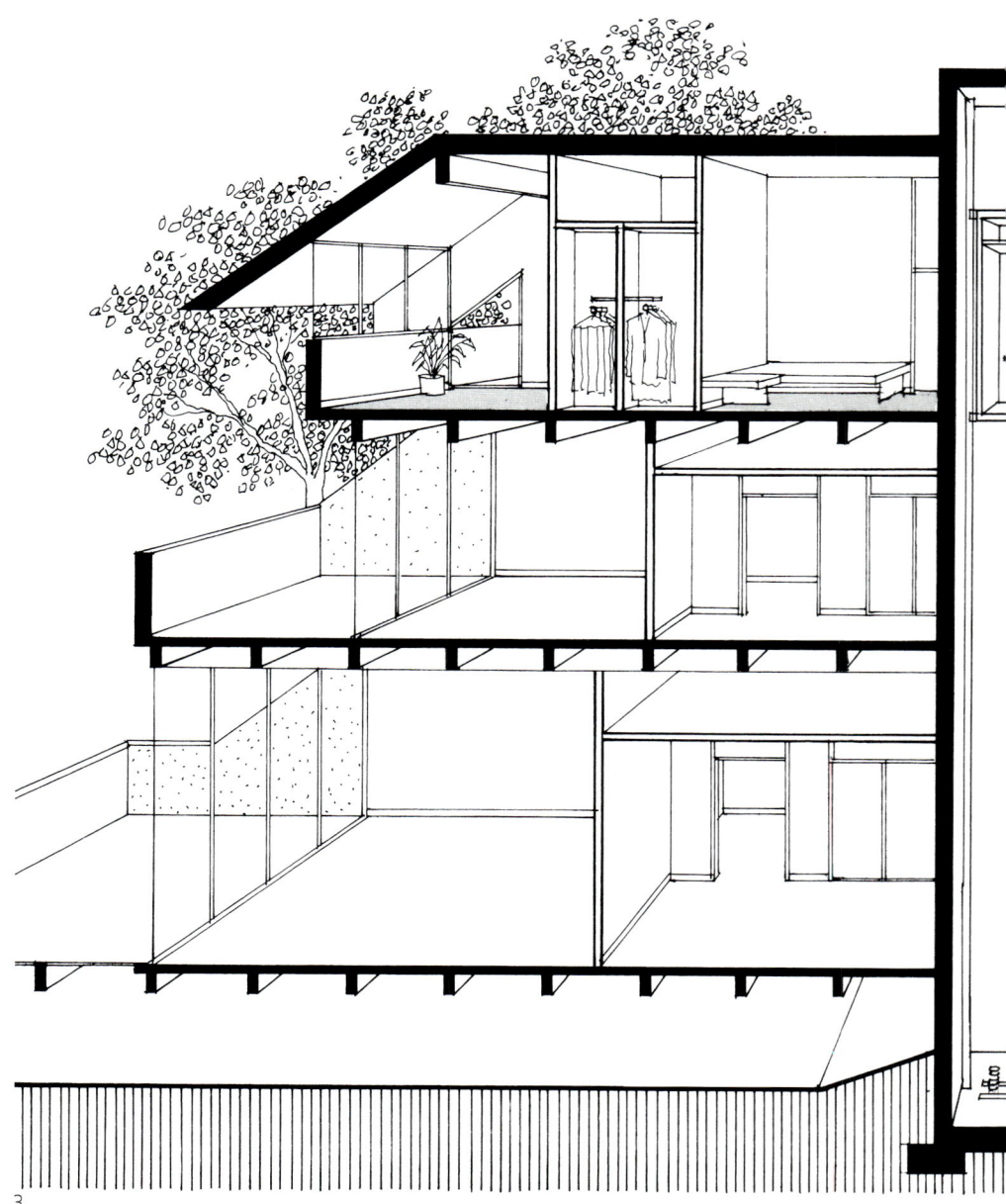

3

## Design/Construction
## 1989/1991

Tampa, Florida
Mark Molenda
1,750 square feet
Metal studs, drywall, seashell
stucco, carpet, marble, and
ceramic tile flooring

One of two top-level penthouse units, this apartment was designed for a sports representative. The unit serves as both his residence and office. Many of the owner's activities with his clients are centered here, and he required seating for audiovisual displays, a fireplace, a large aquarium, and adjacent dining. The living–dining area opens to a balcony overlooking a city park and Hillsborough Bay beyond. Ceilings are 11 and 12 feet high. Perimeter walls have side strip windows affording views of sky and trees. Perched among treetops, this penthouse emanates privacy and intimacy; access to the unit from the public entry and garage is by elevator or stairs.

04

**2548 Bay Park Place**

1 Building exterior
2 Dining area leading to balcony
3 Section perspective

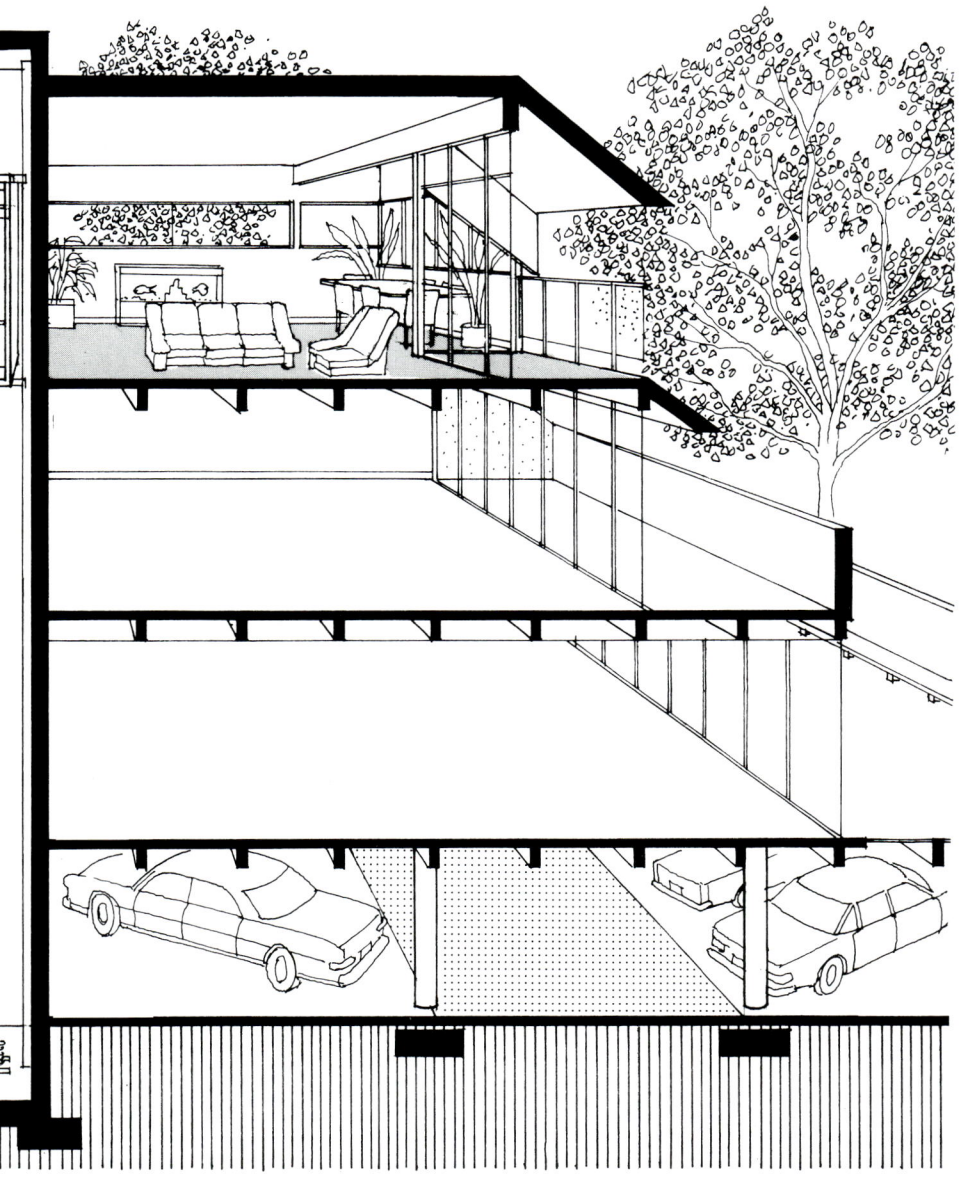

Opposite Living area
5 Floor plan

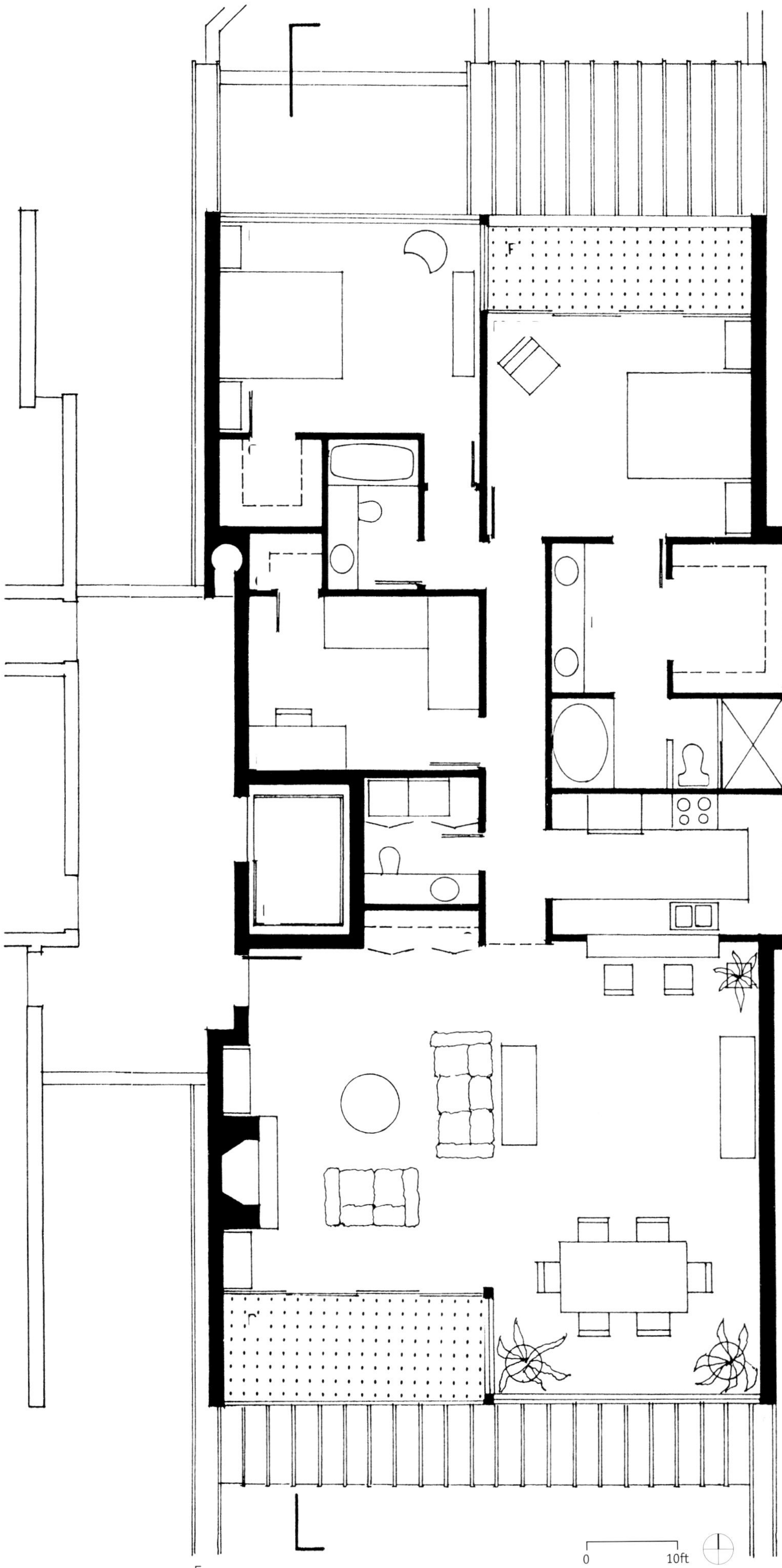

5

1

2

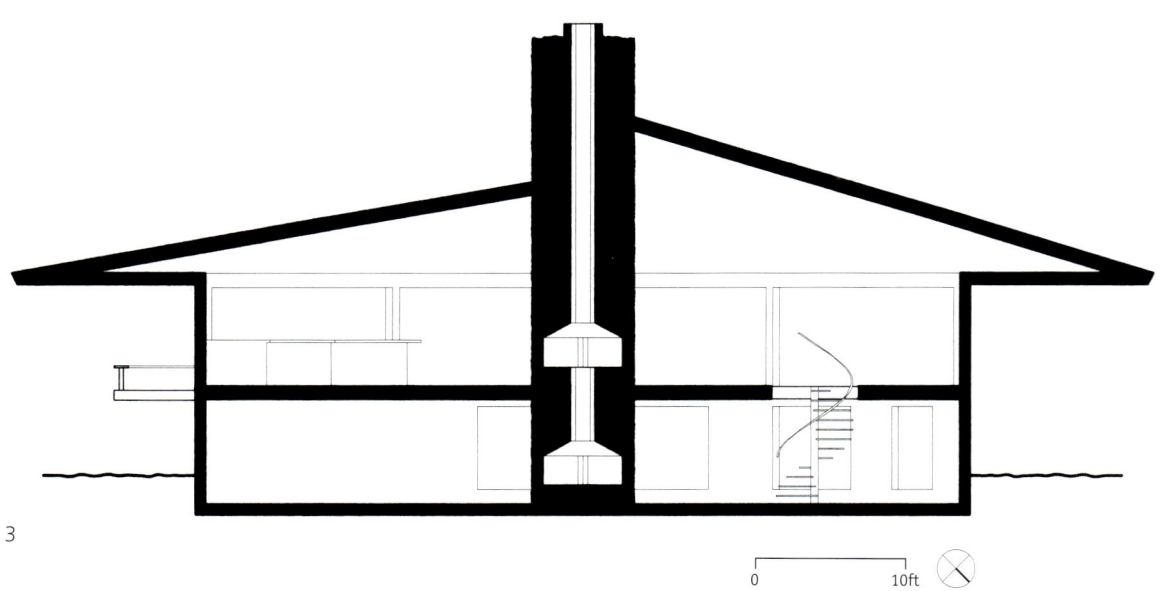

3

0          10ft

1 Model side elevation
2 Model rear elevation
3 Section
4 Entry level floor plan
5 Lower level floor plan

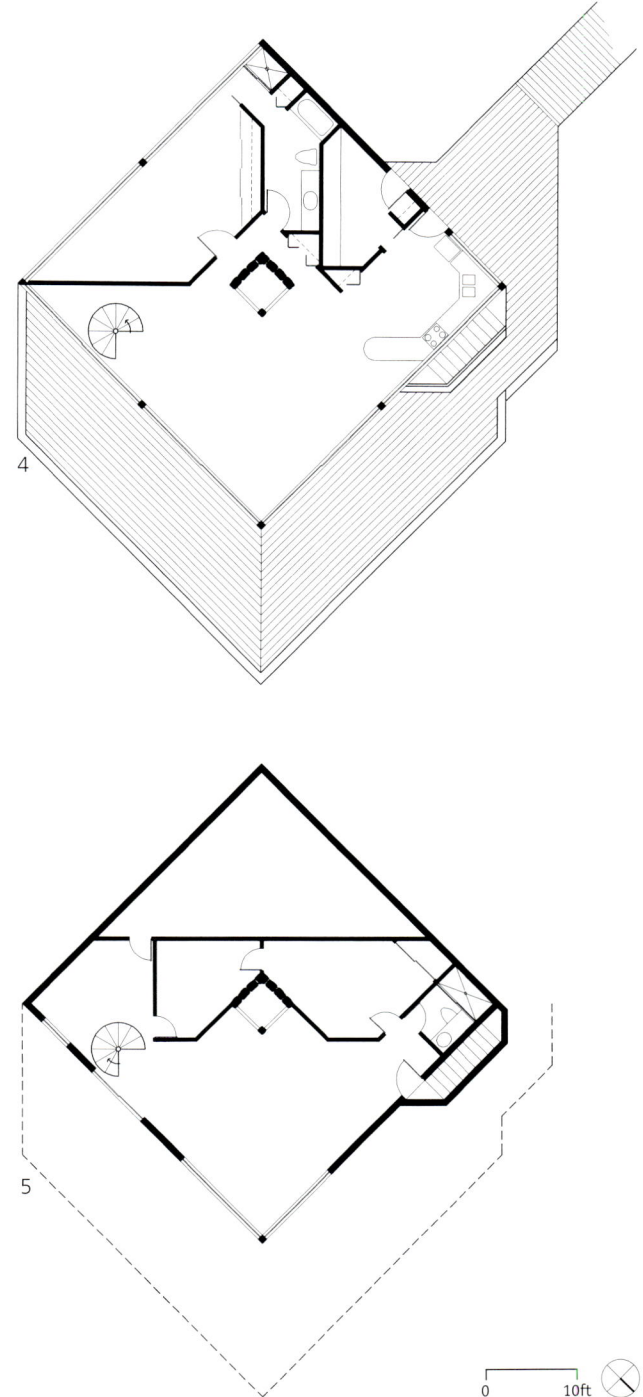

4

5

0          10ft

# 05

## Mountain Residence

Anchored on the side of a mountain, accessible only by four-wheel drive vehicles, this residence is planned for year-round living. The original concept shown here sets the lowest level of the structure into the site slope; the top entry at grade provides access to the living, dining, kitchen, and the master bedroom suite, which has a cantilevered wood deck wrapping around its two view-sides.

Beneath, the additional bedrooms, recreation room, and storage space, have their own lower at-grade patio, facing the view. Using the two-story central stone fireplace as generator for the hipped roof, Howey rotated the entire structure 45 degrees to grade for optimum access, lighting and views. By slicing the four roof ridges to allow clerestory lighting to the interior, indirect lighting was provided to the major interior spaces on the top floor.

### Design 1985
Alarka, North Carolina
Mr and Mrs David Allison
2,880 square feet
Concrete, masonry, wood
frame floors and roof, local
stone, vertical siding, and
Galvalume

1

2

This multipurpose project contains medical offices on the main level and bachelor living quarters above. Located on a corner site, the building is bound by two active streets and an interior alley, with views over a small city park to Boca Ciega Bay. The medical offices are entered from a textured-stone parking area. The alley provides access to the second-level apartment, which also serves as evening seminar space for medical presentations. To satisfy the client's interest in Asian architecture and to deflect street noises, a grid of curved roof sections was devised for the project. The sloping roofs form a cruciform plan over the apartment and rectangular offices below. The resultant corner voids become outdoor balconies for apartment leisure and viewing, and the solid balcony railings create an acoustical buffer for the building.

# 06
## Medical Offices and Residence

### Design/Completion
### 1974/1976

St. Petersburg, Florida
Dr Albert Davis
4,500 square feet
Concrete slab and footings, with steel tube columns and beams to secure the wood frame construction; cedar roof decking on curved laminated wood beams, ceramic roof tiles, cedar siding, and copper trim

1  Front exterior
2  Front entry
3  Interior
4  Section

3

4

0            10ft

5

5 Exterior detail
6 Living area
7 Interior leading to balcony
8 Second level floor plan
9 Main level floor plan

6

7

8

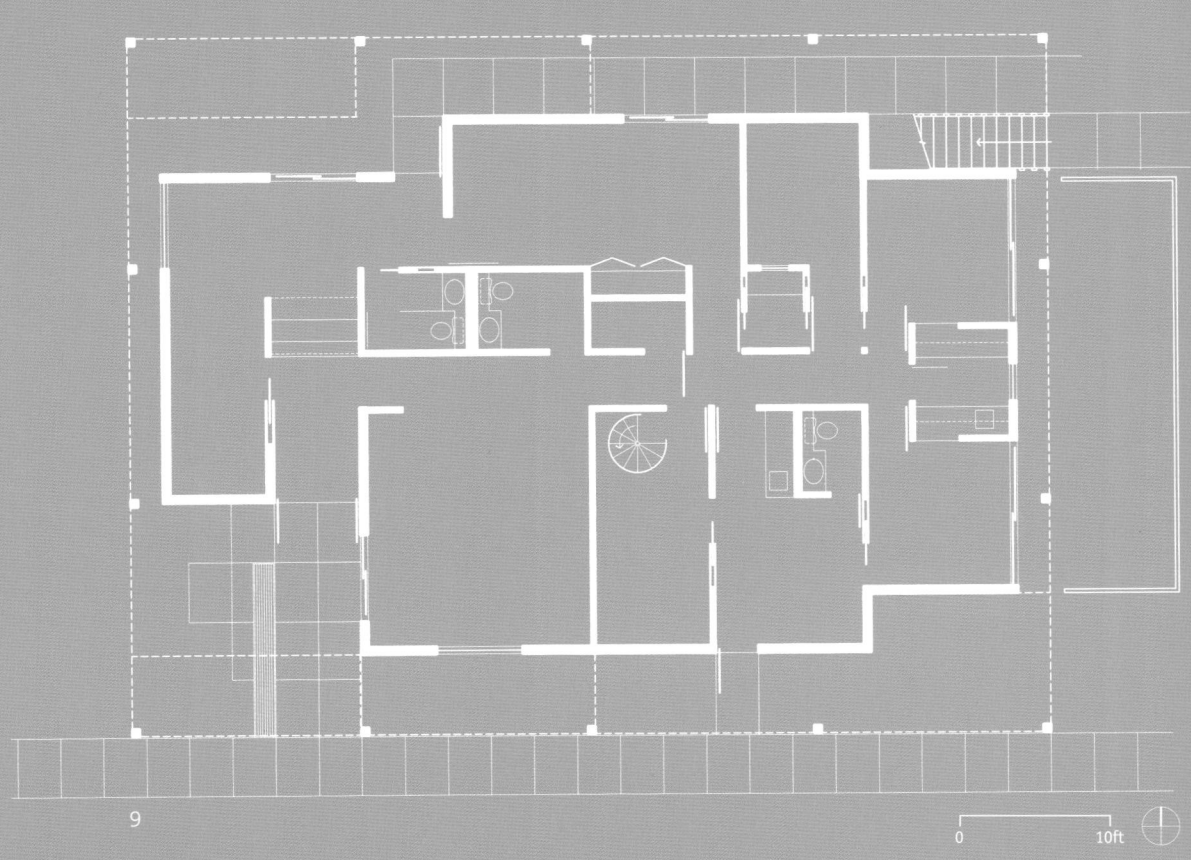

9

0          10ft

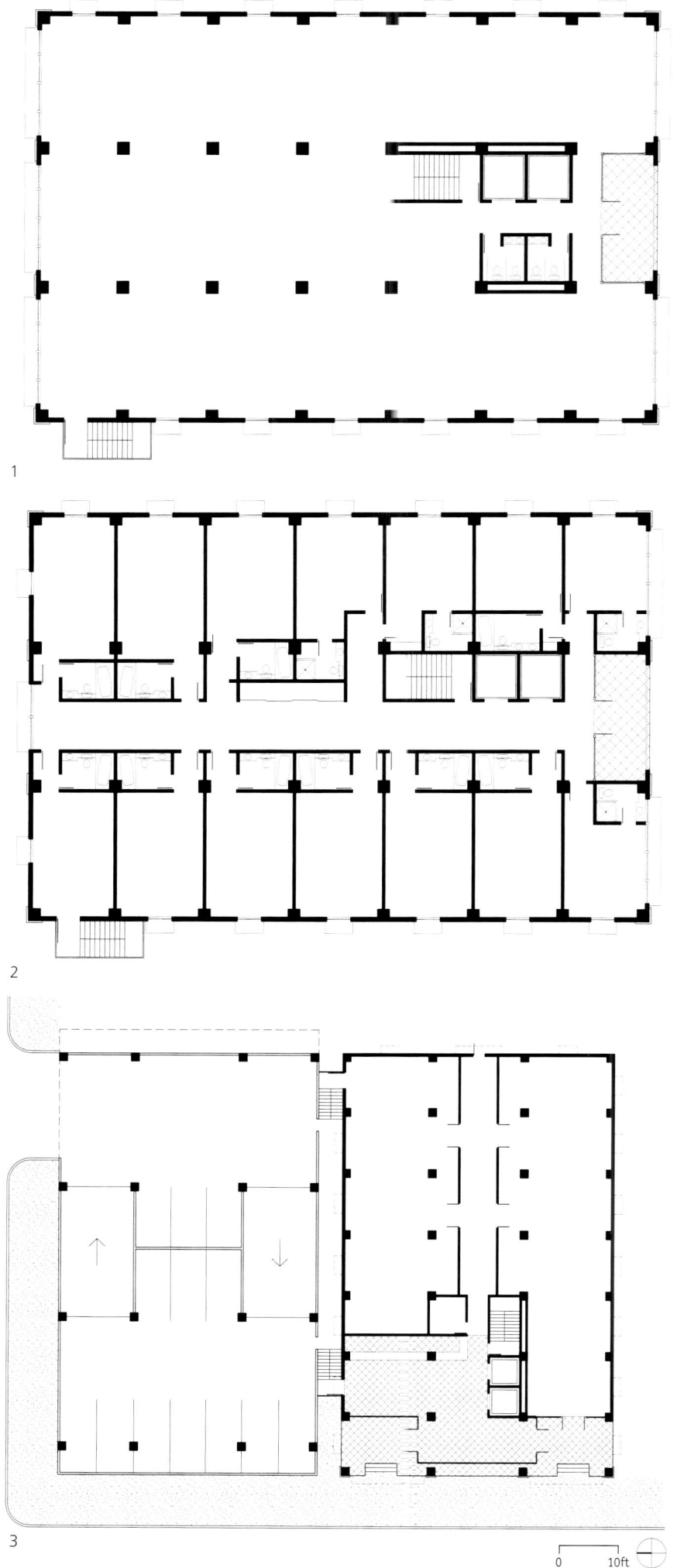

1

2

3

0    10ft

# 07

## Bayview Hotel

4

### Design 1966

Tampa, Florida
Lykes Brothers
114,200 square feet
Existing concrete foundations, building frames, floors and roof; new glass façade, balcony rails, canopies, stucco, carpet, and clay tile

This renovation project began with the installation of a required second stair exit for a 10-story economy hotel owned by Lykes Bros. Shipping Lines. Seeing the opportunity to upgrade the building into a better hotel with more profit potential, the owners commissioned Howey to design a new building envelope with interior amenities to complement the new exterior design. The exterior masonry walls were removed to expose the contemporary proportions of the 55-year-old concrete frame. New floor-to-ceiling, exterior reflective glass panels were extended from each frame opening. Concrete columns, floors, and ceilings were to be sandblasted throughout. Inside, drywall, color, acoustical ceiling panels, and textured carpet were selected to contrast with the concrete surfaces. While carpet was used on the upper hotel levels, a more durable clay tile and area rugs became the main-floor lobby and restaurant surfaces. New concrete entrance canopies were to be hung and cantilevered from the building frame at street level. Landscaping was planned to complete this mid-rise makeover.

1 Optional office floor plan
2 Typical hotel floor plan
3 Entry level hotel/parking floor plan
4 Original building façade
5 Front elevation rendering

5

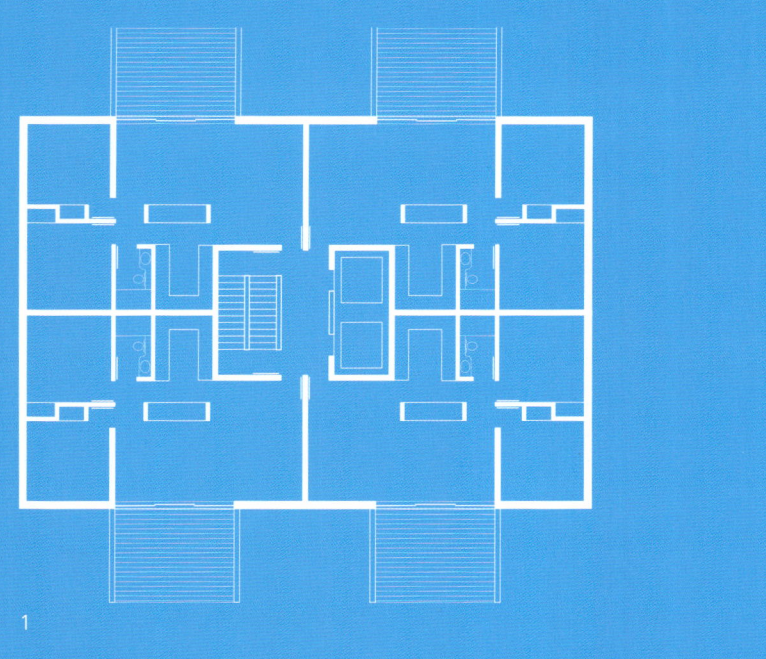

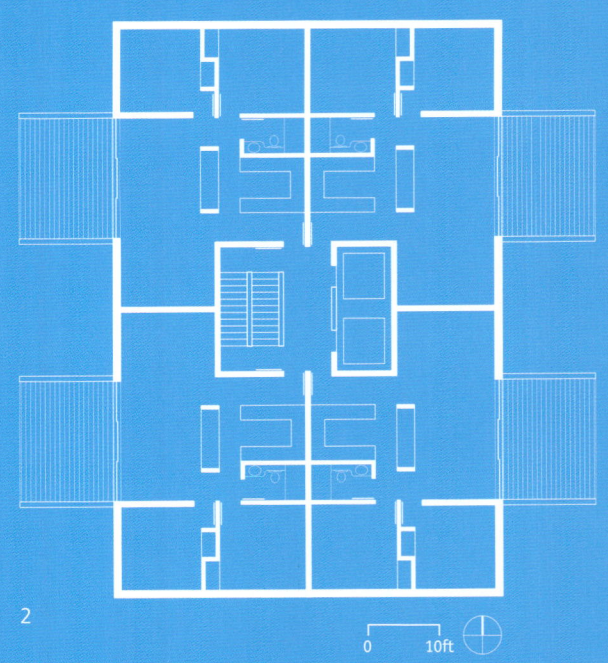

1

2

0    10ft

3

0    10ft

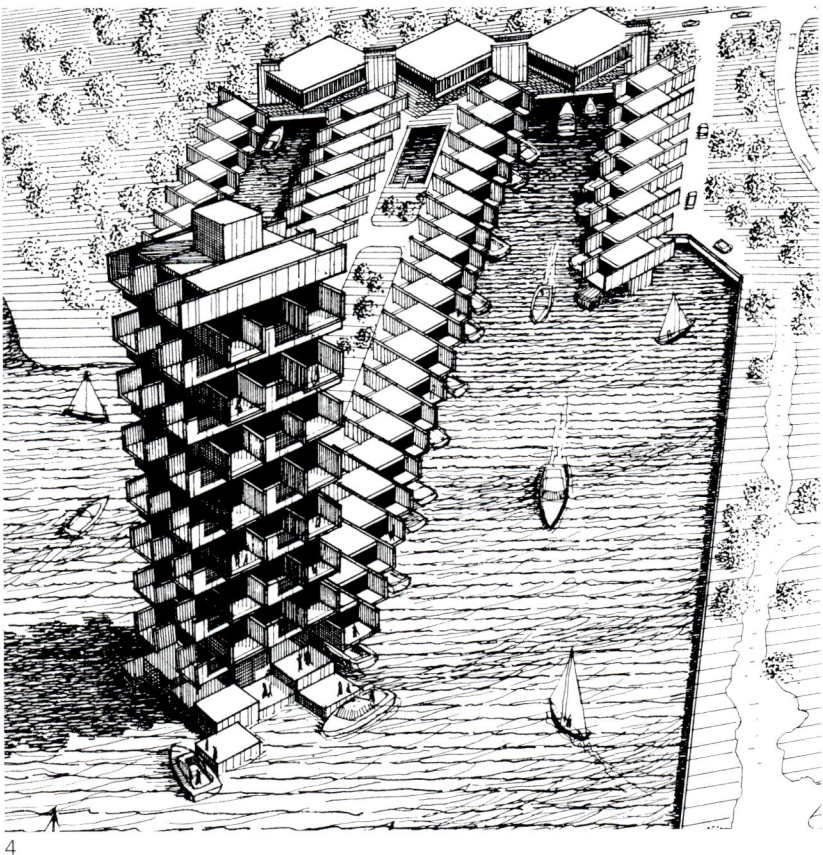

4

## Modular Apartments

This client wished to build waterfront apartments on a 3-acre parcel edging the Hillsborough River. He was interested in the possibility of prefabricated housing units, shipped for assembly on site. Due to the property shoreline configuration, it was possible to create two narrow inlets with a spit of land made from earth that had been removed to cut the inlets. At water level, boat-ports were created for 61 low-rise units. At grade, carports were designed to accommodate parking for both low-rise units and for a 17-story tower that would be built at the land's tip. The high-rise building contains two units per floor, serviced by a central elevator/stair core.

### Design 1966

Tampa, Florida
Charles Wishart
170,000 square feet
Concrete piling, grade beams,
precast concrete floor and
wall units, concrete block,
stucco, glass, aluminum,
built-up roofs

The construction concept began with the establishment of sea walls, in-place foundations, and the erection of the central concrete tower that would receive the modular, concrete wall-and-floor units of several sizes for both low- and high-rise apartments. The off-site manufactured units were to be shipped as needed for installation. A clubhouse, harbormaster, and restaurant were to flank the entrance to the complex.

1   Tower east/west plan – four units
2   Tower north/south plan – four units
3   Tower/low rise plan at entry level
4   Rendering

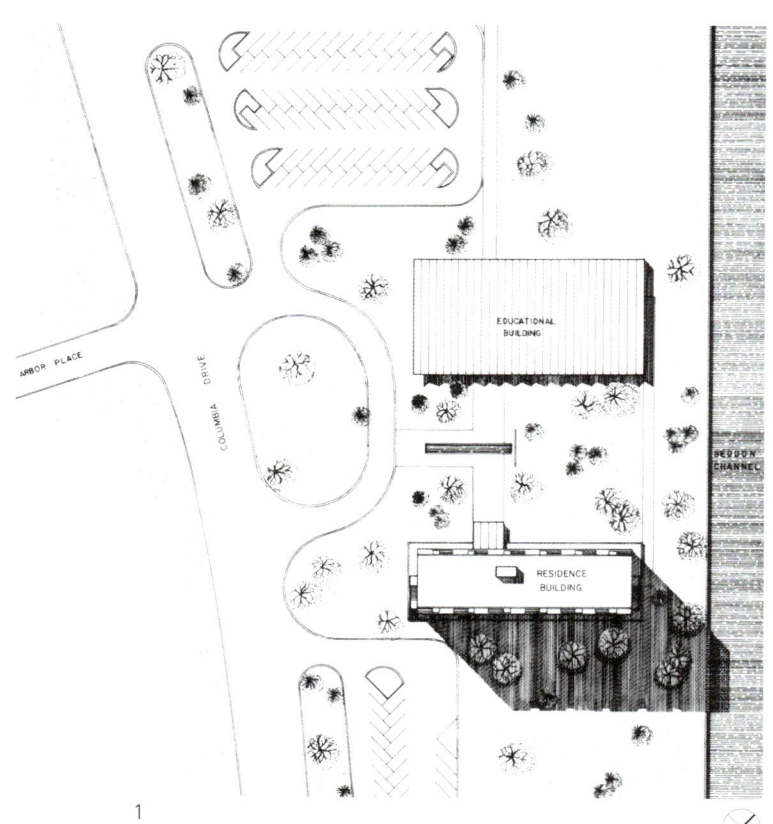

1

2

3

4

1 Site plan
2 Section perspective
3 South façade
4 Exterior detail
5 Exterior stair
6 North façade

**09**

## School of Nursing Dormitory

**Design/Completion**
**1960/1961**

Tampa, Florida
68,000 square feet
Precast concrete pilings, cast-in-place concrete footings, T columns, concrete pan system, precast Travertine-faced panels, concrete railings, glass, and aluminum

Supported on concrete pilotis, the seven-floor, student-nurse dormitory rises above the main administration/reception lobby level. The double-loaded corridor floors are interconnected with central elevators and stairs at each end. Residence suites are either single or double. The voids of each T-shaped column accommodate a shower and toilet with a vanity between each two suites. Lounge, laundry, snack bar, and sewing and ironing spaces are situated in the center of each floor. The interior spaces are arranged to create undulating walls and balconies on the north and south exteriors. The textured Travertine walls were selected to interplay with the smooth, cast concrete balcony and sunscreen system. A folded-plate concrete canopy at the ground-level main entry repeats the roof silhouette of the adjacent single-story classroom building.

*James H. Kennedy, AIA*
*John Howey, Project Designer*

5    6

## 7 Second floor plan

TRUNK STORAGE

MAID'S STORAGE

MECHANICAL EQUIPMENT

RECREATION

ELECTRICAL

MECH. EQUIP.

MACHINE ROOM

MACHINE ROOM

MECH. EQUIP.

CORRIDOR

UP

ISOLATION

ISOLATION

EXAM EXAM

HOUSE MOTHER

HOUSE MOTHER

HOUSE MOTHER

GUEST

GUEST

DOUBLE

W

ST

7

7 Second floor plan
8 Façade detail
9 Ground floor plan
10 North façade
11 Exterior detail
12 Exterior stairwell

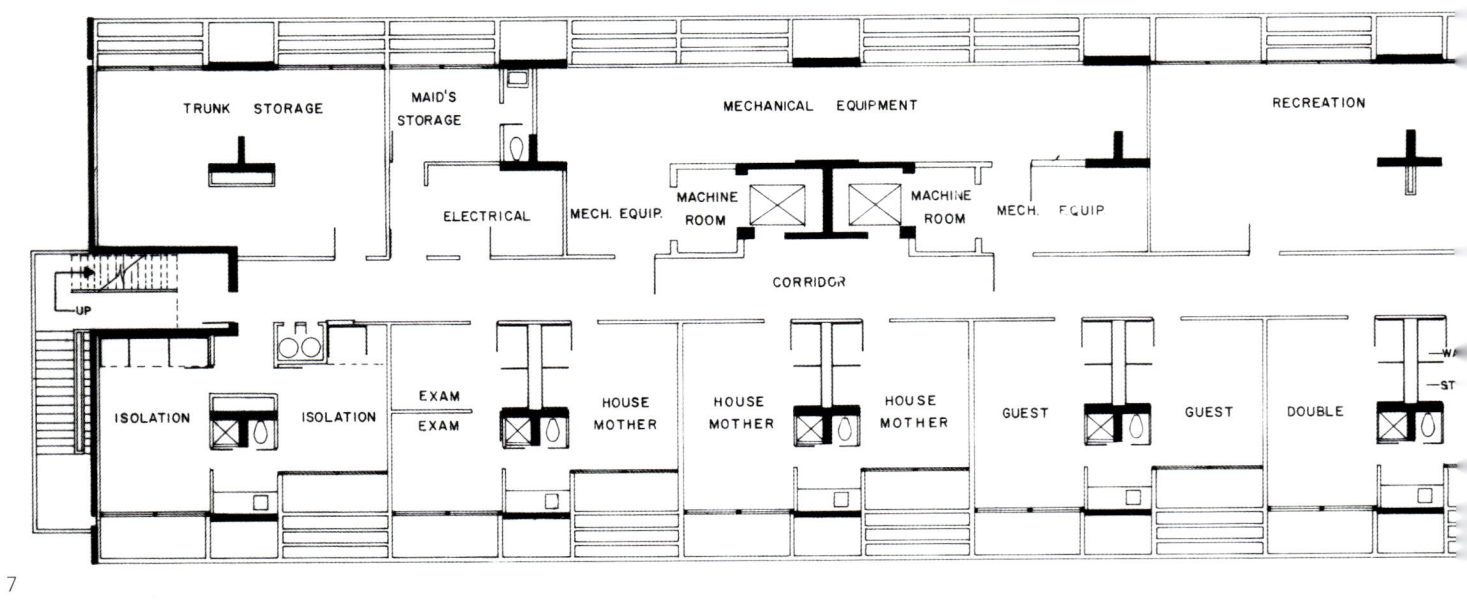

8

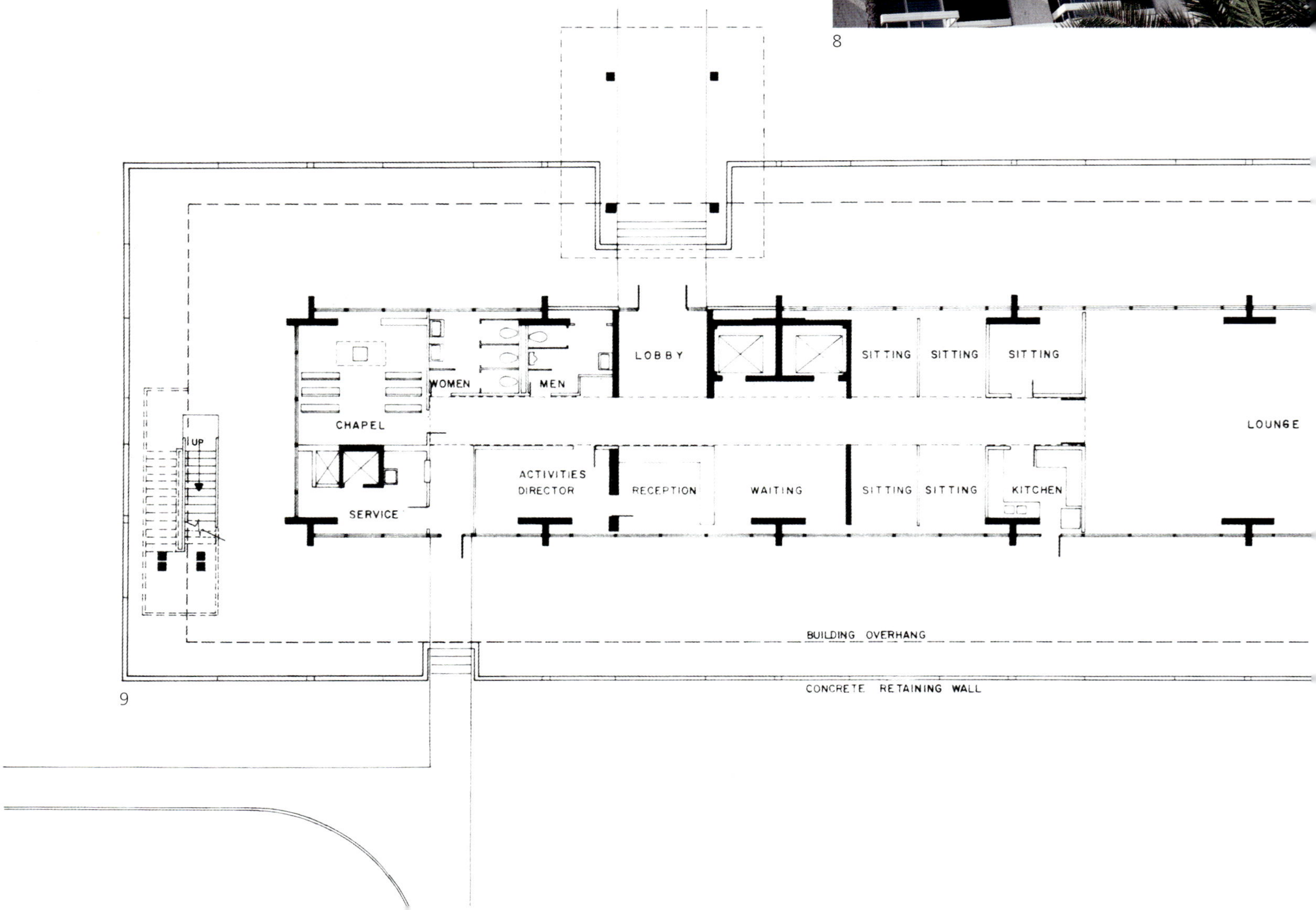

## 9 Ground floor plan

UP

CHAPEL

WOMEN

MEN

LOBBY

SITTING SITTING SITTING

LOUNGE

SERVICE

ACTIVITIES DIRECTOR

RECEPTION

WAITING

SITTING SITTING

KITCHEN

BUILDING OVERHANG

CONCRETE RETAINING WALL

9

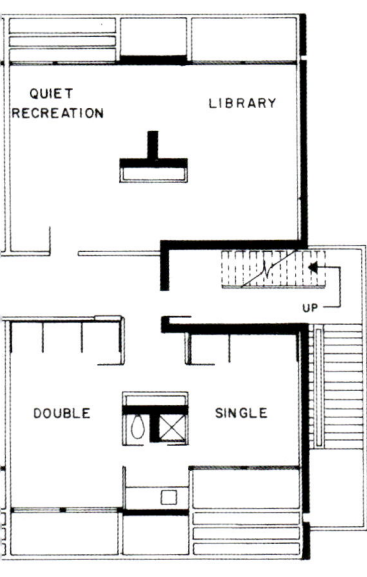

10

11

12

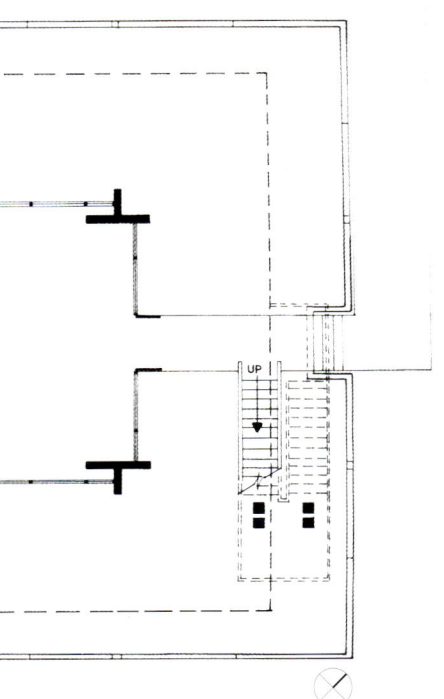

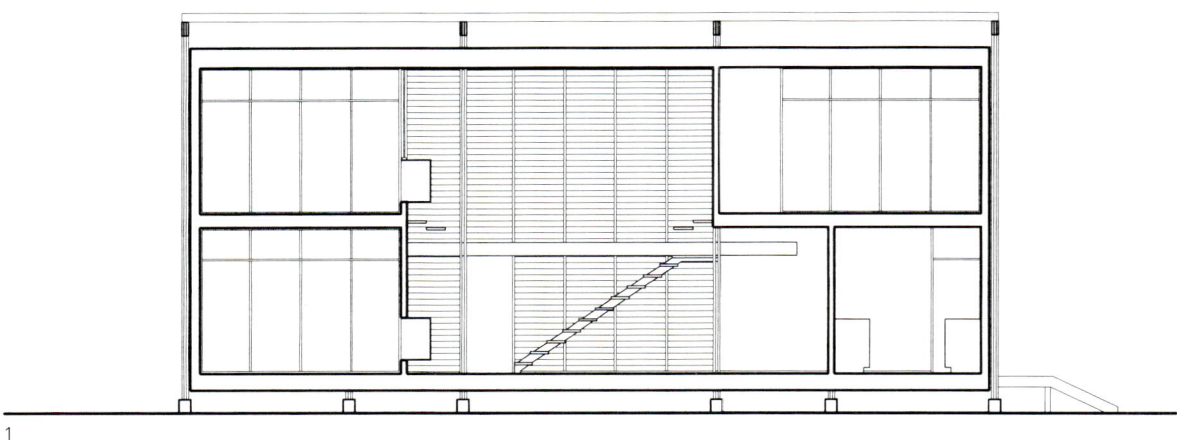

1

2

3

1 Section
2 Model of south elevation
3 Model from southeast
4 West elevation
5 Aerial view of pool model

4

5

**Design/Completion**
**1952/1953**

Interior restoration 1998
Lido Shores, Florida
1,800 square feet
Concrete column footings,
wood space columns, floor and
roof framing, cypress siding,
oak flooring, gypsumboard,
and tile

In 1952 Architect Paul Rudolph designed the Umbrella House for developer Phil Hiss "to attract attention from the road" for Hiss. Soon after, the completed house gained national and international attention. Today it remains an icon of mid-twentieth century modern (Florida) architecture. When it was purchased in 1997, the new owners contacted Howey to assist them in restoring the interior to its original condition.

# 10

## Umbrella House Restoration

Poorly added interior items were removed. Original cabinetwork, hardware, floors, walls, and ceilings were refinished to original condition. Original color schemes and period furniture were selected to complete the interior. The structure's most important feature, the slat umbrella roof, which shaded the house and pool area, was lost in a hurricane in the 1960s. This monumental canopy remains to be restored. The second owners intend to rebuild the umbrella using Howey's ideas for an improved structural design.

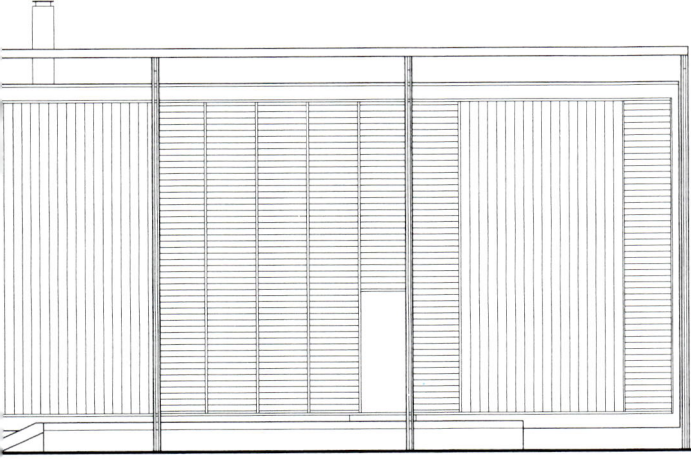

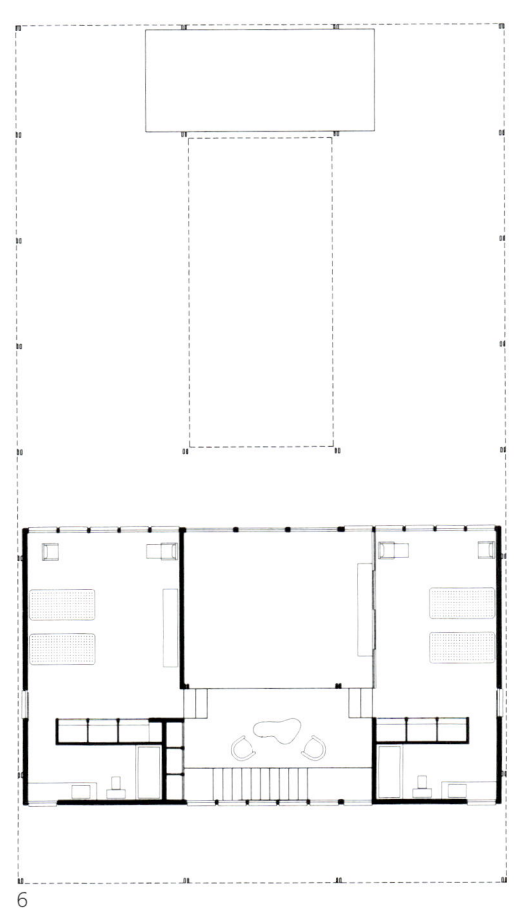

6

7

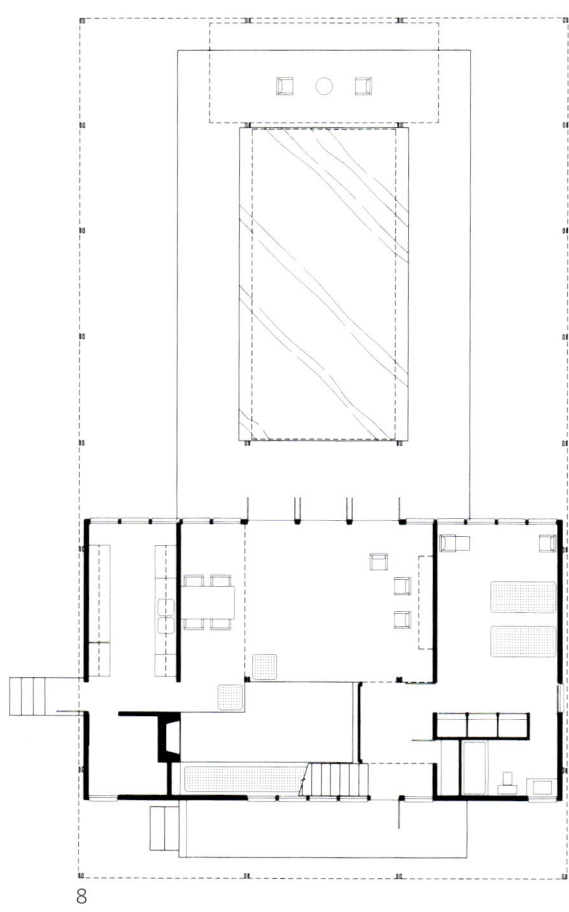

8

9

6  Upper level floor plan
7  House exterior
8  Lower level floor plan
9&11  Upstairs living area
10  Exterior detail
12&13  Living area

10

11

12

13

WATER

1 Site elevation
2 Site plan
3 Rendering of bridge
4 Rendering of pool corner
5 Rendering of pool from above

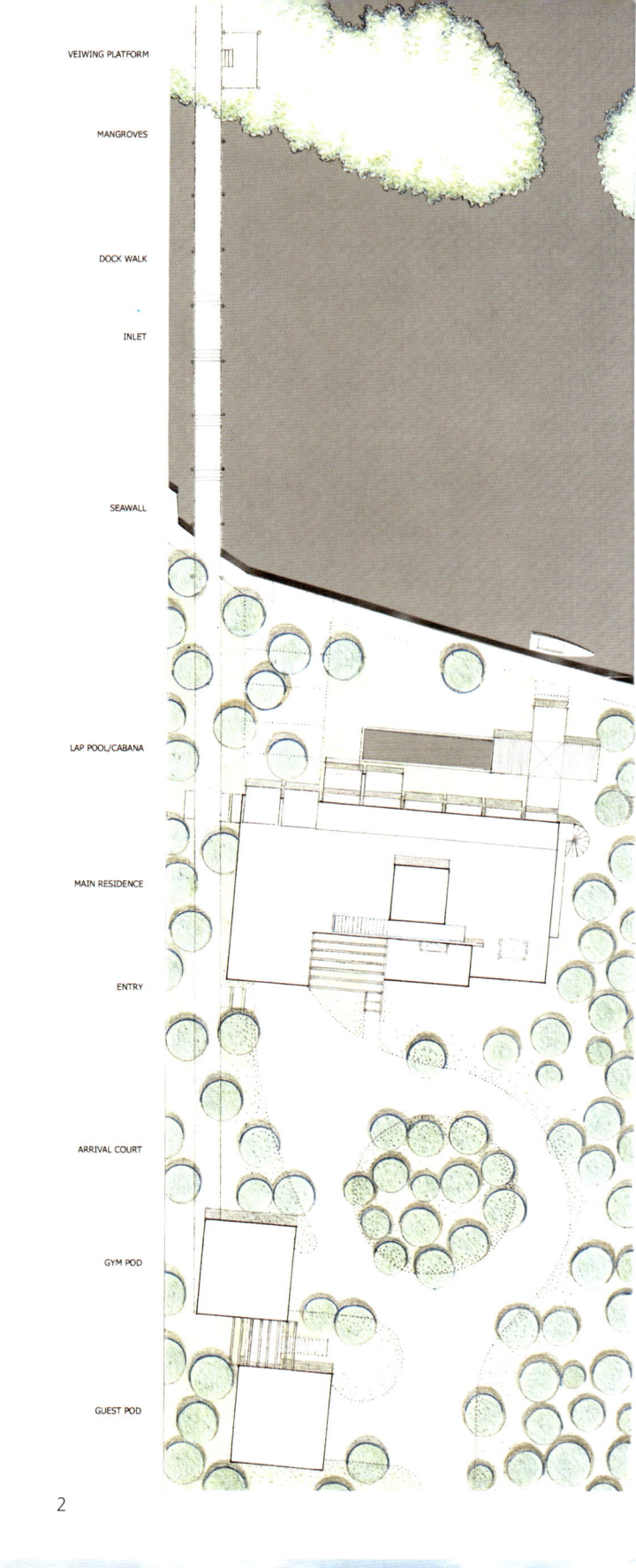

VEIWING PLATFORM

MANGROVES

DOCK WALK

INLET

SEAWALL

LAP POOL/CABANA

MAIN RESIDENCE

ENTRY

ARRIVAL COURT

GYM POD

GUEST POD

2

1

MANGROVES

DOCK WALK

INLET

SEAWALL

CABANA

MAIN RESIDENCE

ENTRY

# 11

## Florida Bayfront Residence

This existing 1950s Florida Keys residence is to be doubled in size while retaining and extending the modernist character of the original building. The site, of more than two acres, gradually slopes from the road to Florida Bay. Its lush tropical growth and shell driveway from the street to the residence will be retained and improved to accommodate new, separate, raised guest quarters and a small gymnasium. In a similar manner, the additions to the main house will be elevated to minimize site intrusion. Bedrooms, formal dining, a rooftop eagle's nest, decks, and a trophy room to display antique fishing gear are all included in the second floor expansion. On the bay side, the owners specified a small cabana with a lap pool near the seawall where small boats will be moored. A long dock stretching from the seawall through the mangrove flats to deepwater anchorage is included for larger boats.

### Design 2003

Islamorada, Florida
6,000 square feet
Concrete, stucco, stainless
steel, laminated glass, metal
fold-up hurricane panels,
drywall, tile, and keystone

3

4

ARRIVAL COURT GYM POD GUEST POD

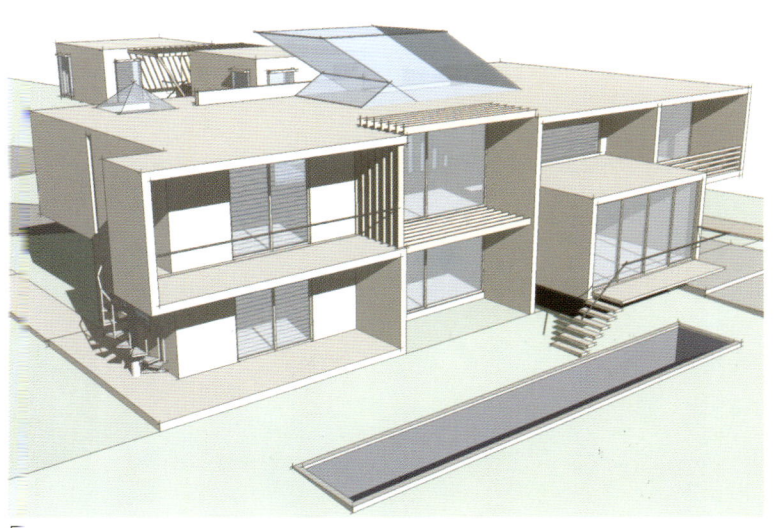

5

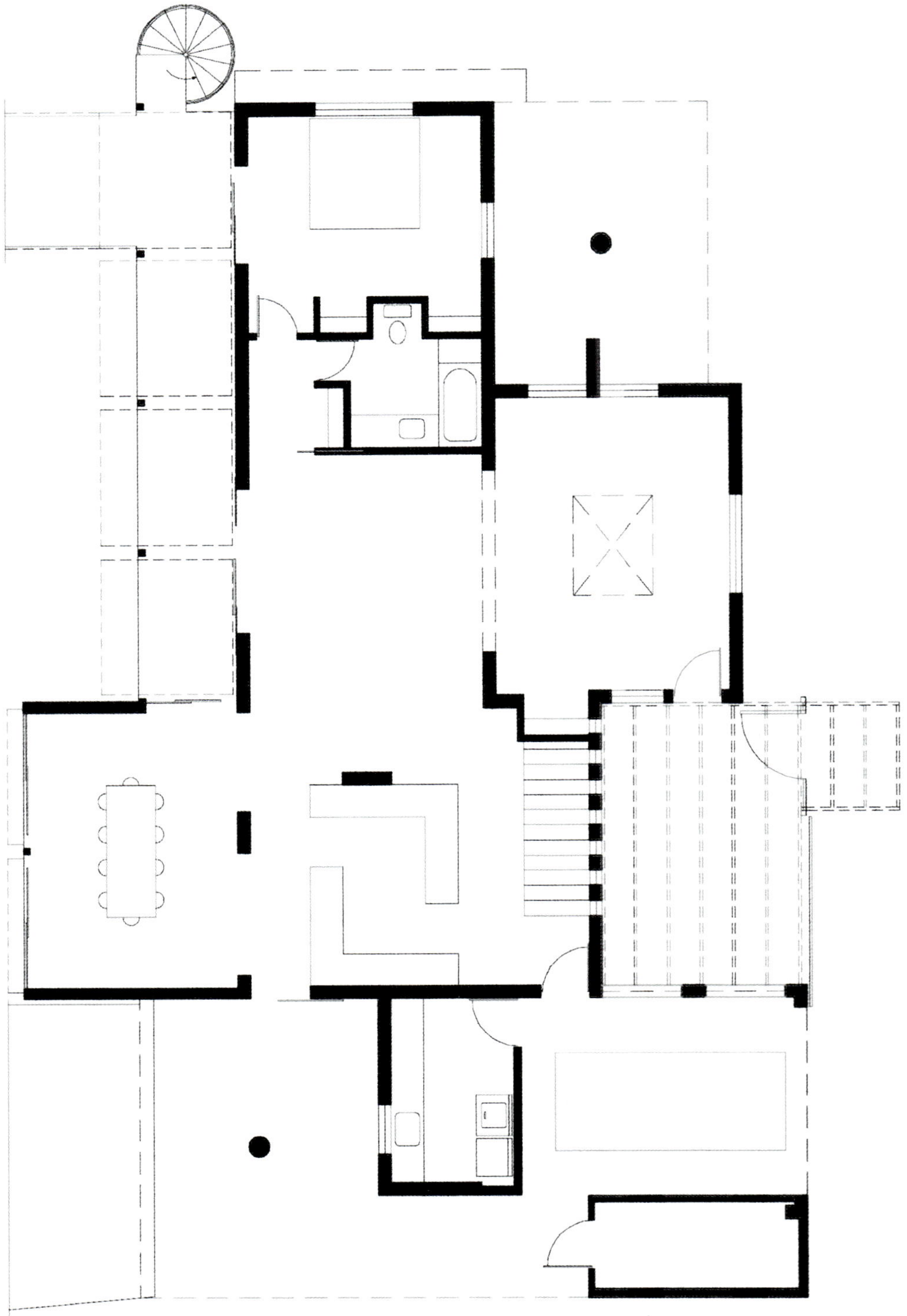

6

7

6   Lower level floor plan
7   Entry elevation
8   Upper level floor plan
9   Longitudinal section

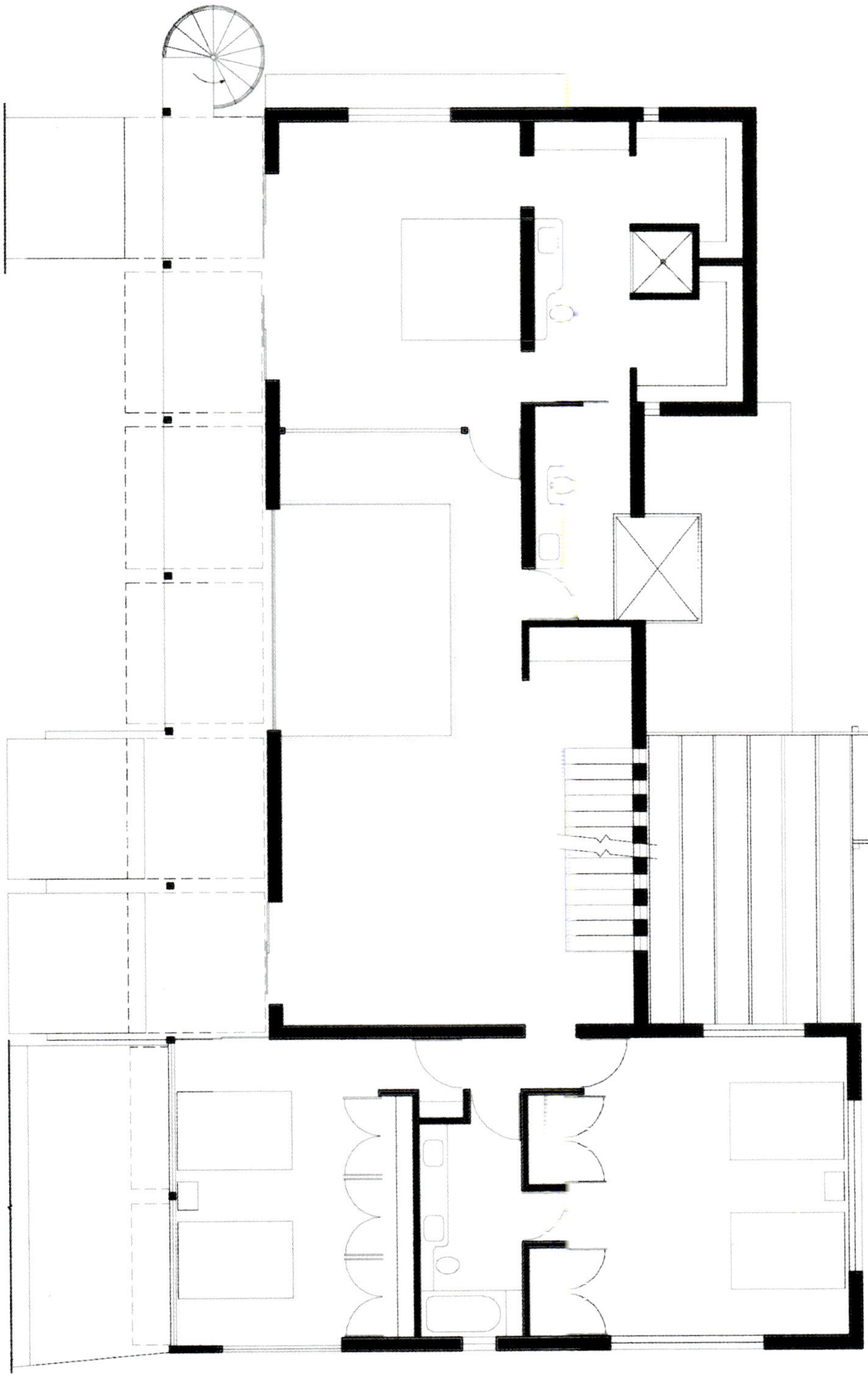

8

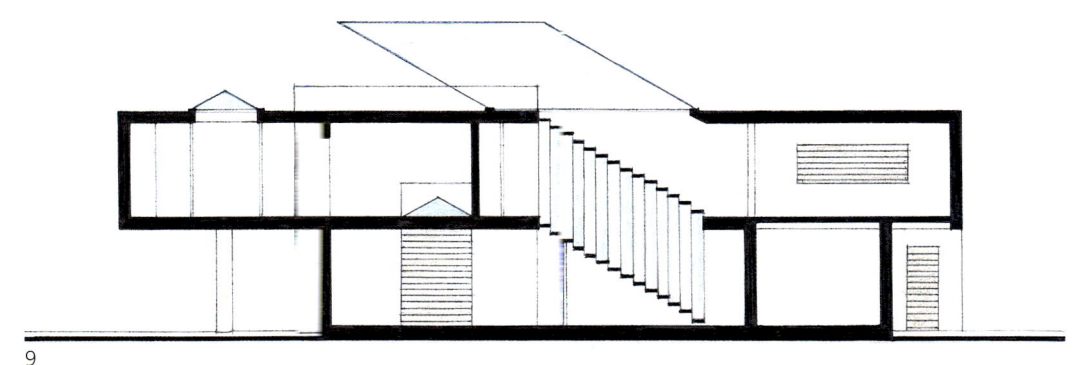

9

1                                          2                                                         3

1–3   Model views
  4   Ground floor plan
  5   Second level plan
  6   View of sand dunes

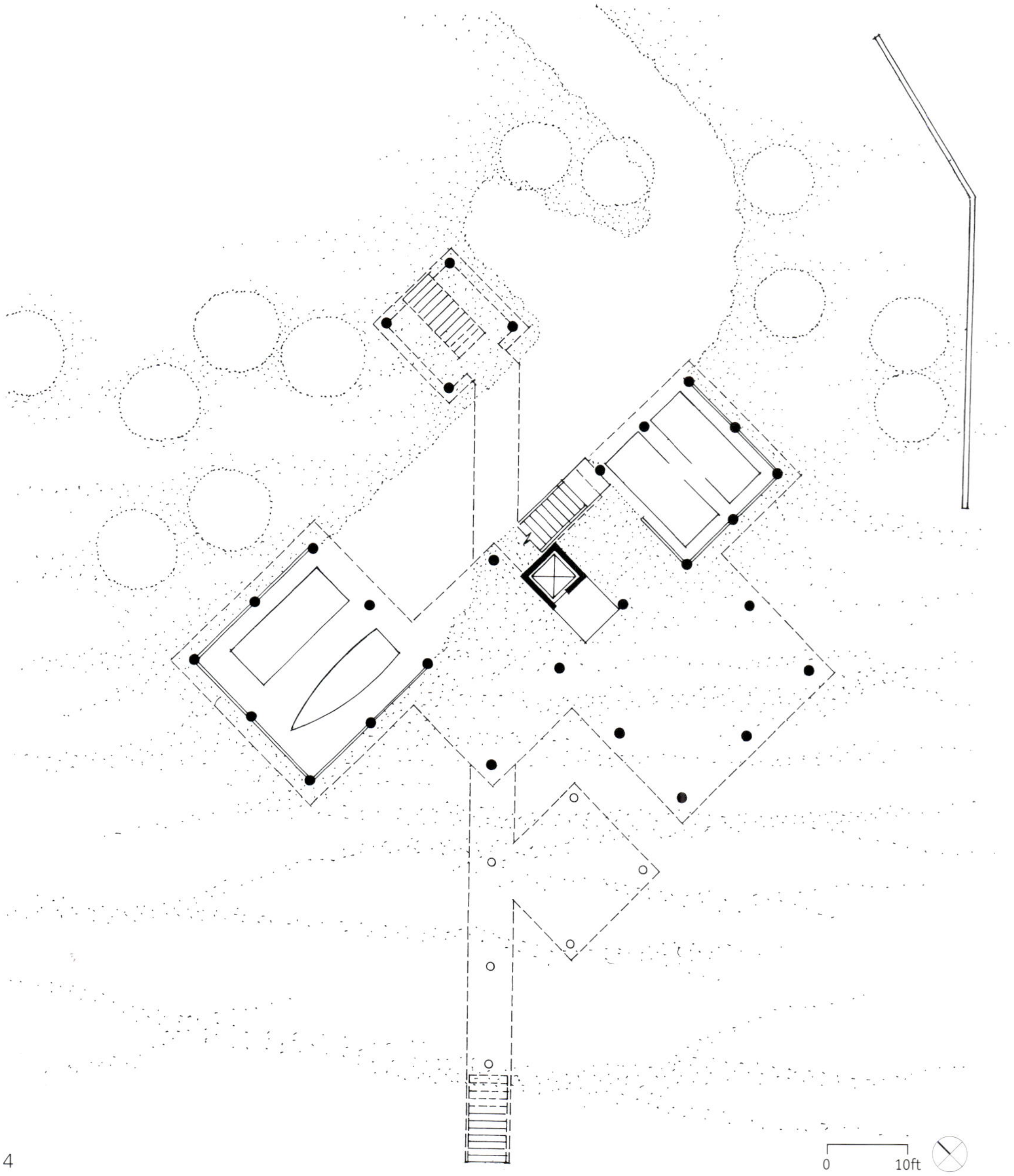

4

0        10ft

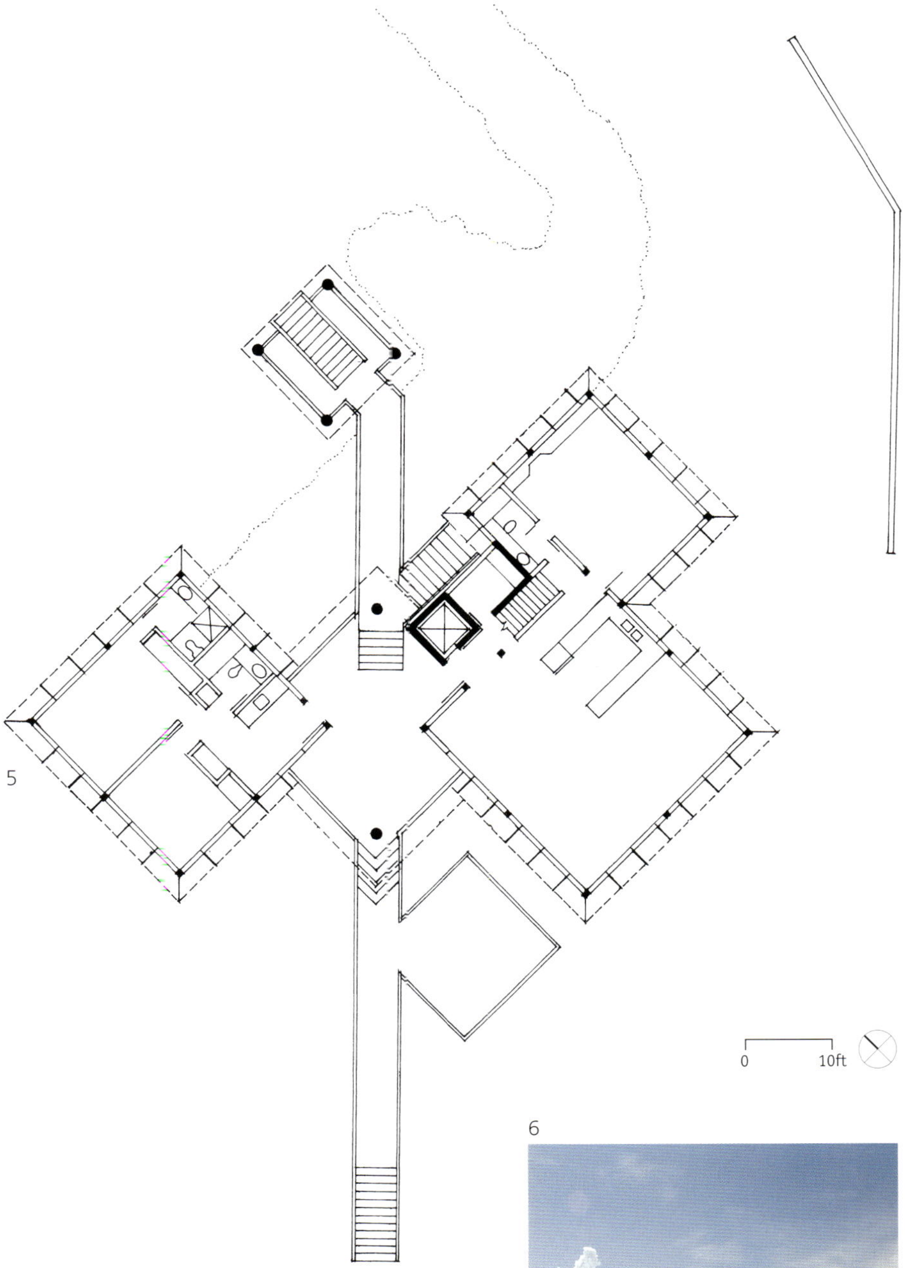

# 12

## Gulf Front Residence

### Design/Completion
#### 1995/1997

Longboat Key, Florida
Mr and Mrs Paul Whiting
3,500 square feet
Concrete pilings, columns, and
beams; wood and steel frame
construction; cypress siding;
galvalume standing seam
roofs; Palope decking

0      10ft

5

6

The clients, who live an hour's drive away from their beach property, wanted to create an informal retreat for their family and weekend guests. A system of individual, interconnected, raised pods with metal hip roofs was devised, to accommodate the family's activities, provide privacy, and preserve as much of the sand dunes and natural vegetation on site as possible.

The site, on one of the few remaining open stretches of beach on Longboat Key, is fan-shaped and opens to the Gulf of Mexico with 180-degree views to the south and west. An elevated dune walkover was designed, stretching from the pods to the beach trail. Upper structural outriggers on the pods act as roof tie-downs and support the installation of hurricane/sunscreen shutters.

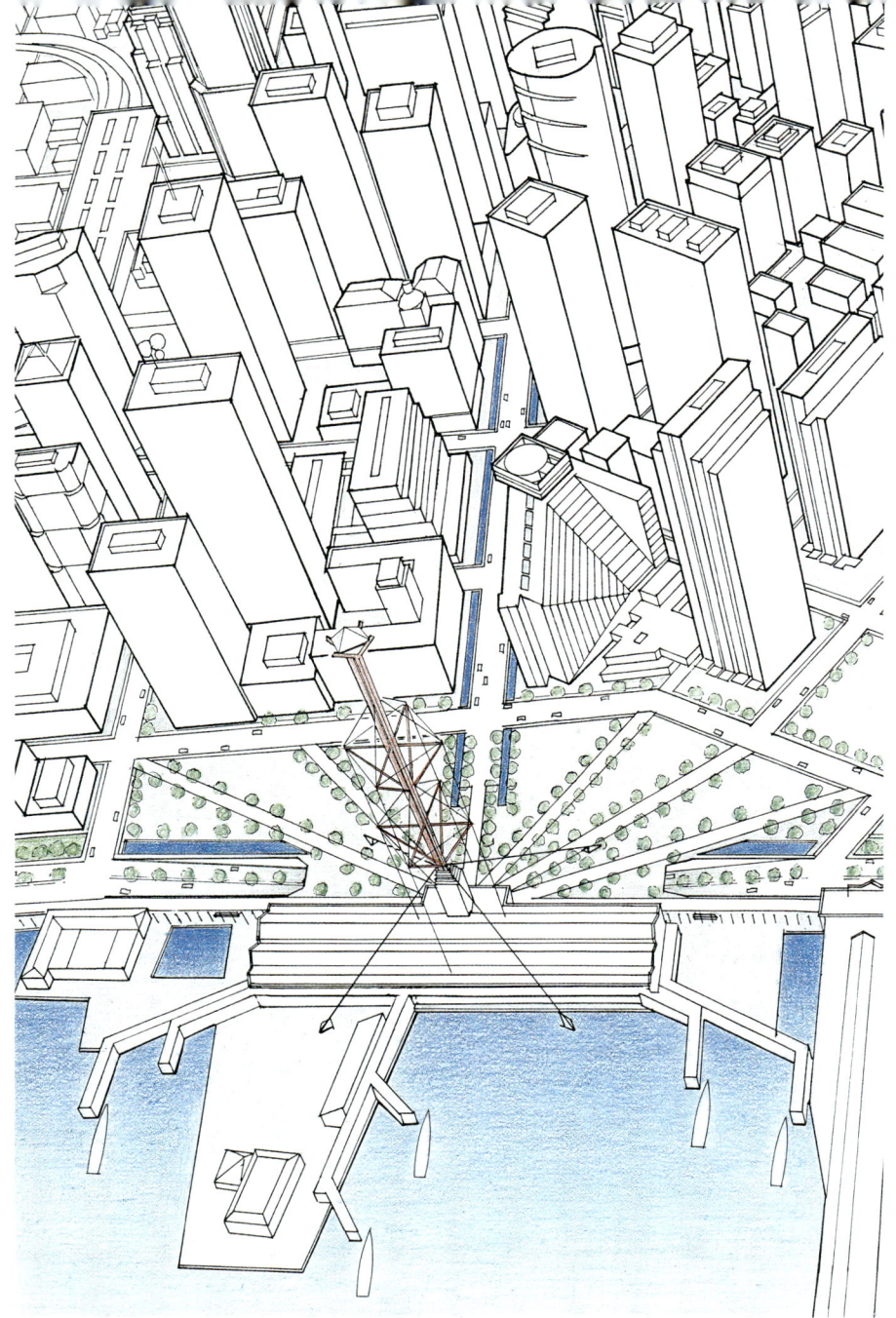

1

2

3

4

San Francisco, California
30 acres
Piling supported precast and
cast-in-place concrete, pavers,
and light rail construction

1  Aerial view of tower
2  Rendering of Embarcadero Boulevard
3  Development model
4  Aerial view of San Francisco

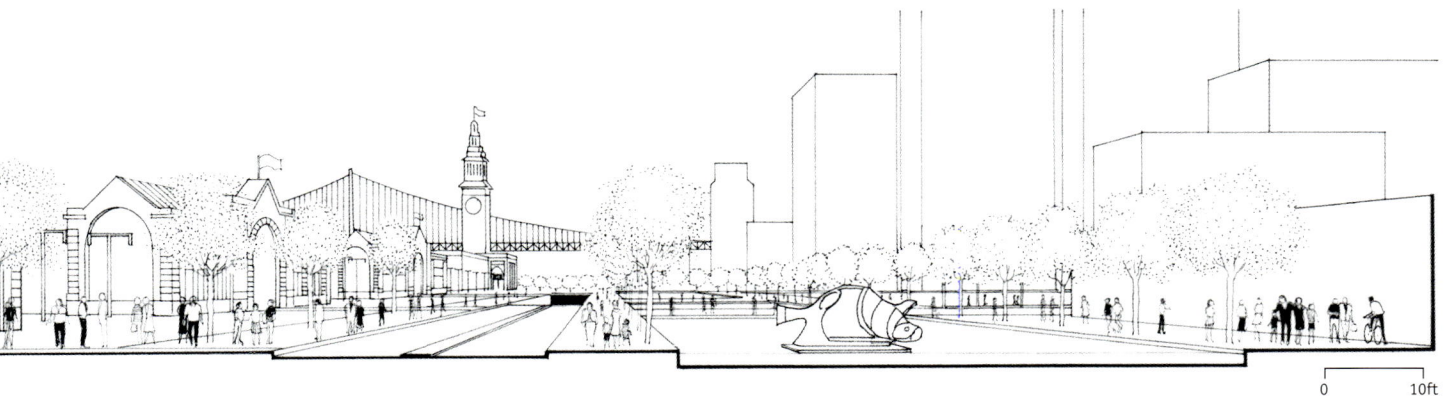

By 1990, the Embarcadero, San Francisco's aging waterfront edge, was doomed to become an unsightly elevated concrete expressway strip, destroying scenic views and its use as historic landmark. Concerned citizens stopped construction and initiated demolition of this political boondoggle. A group called "Vision San Francisco Embarcadero" organized an international competition to elicit new ideas for the waterfront. Howey's competition entry responded with a linear, landscaped, light rail system, connecting China Basin to the south with the central Ferry Building, Telegraph Hill, and Fisherman's Wharf to the north. On the western side, a continuous canal was envisioned with connecting city streets crossing as bridges over this waterway to the Embarcadero. Existing pocket parks would be interconnected with new strip parks. In this way, the waterfront would be revitalized with a continuous pedestrian-way encouraging new residential, office, retail, and tourist areas to intermix with the historic dock and maritime structures.

13

**Embarcadero Competition**

5

5 Aerial view of development
6 Pier section rendering
7 Ferry tower section
8 Coit Tower section
9 Axonometric view of development

6

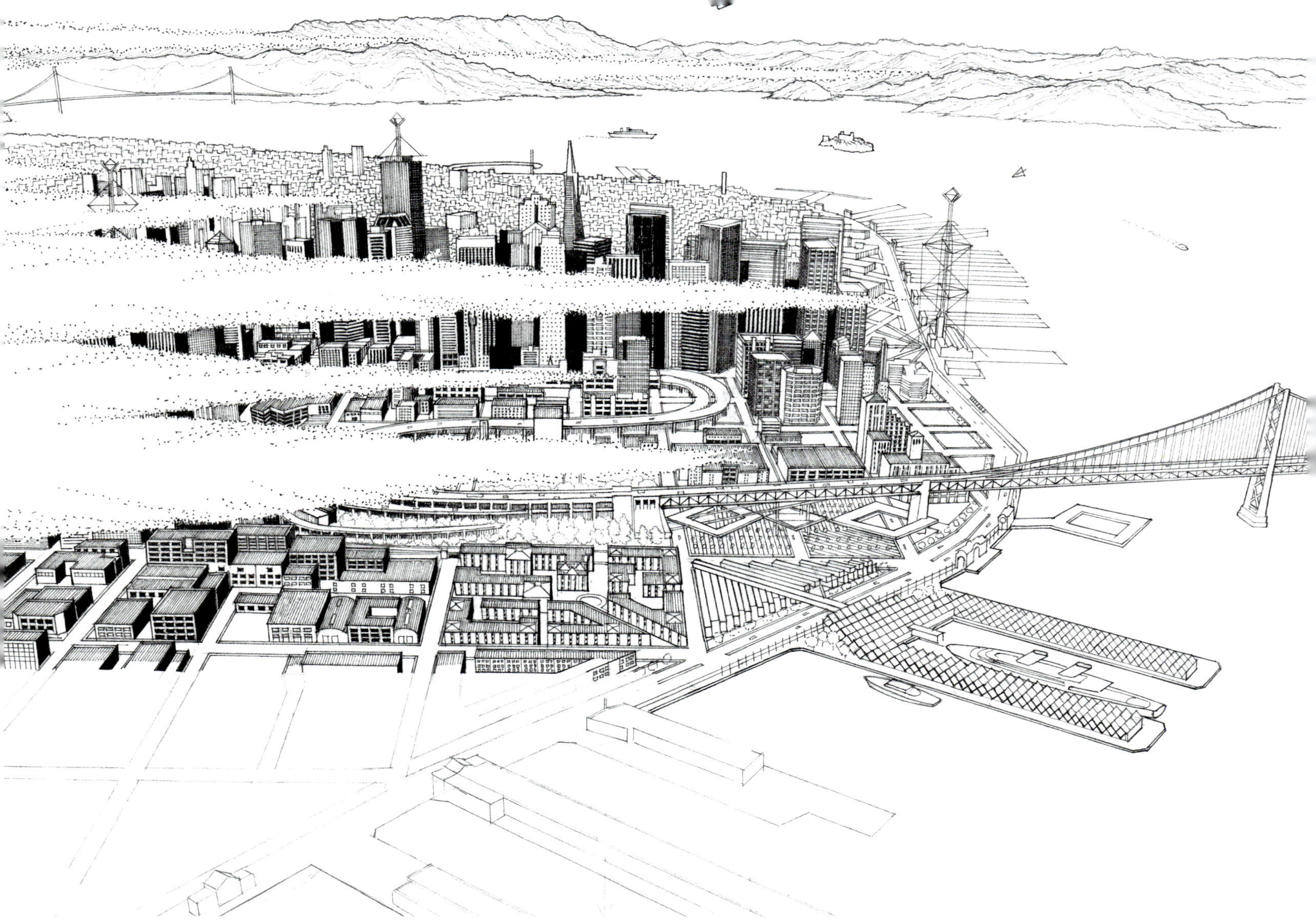

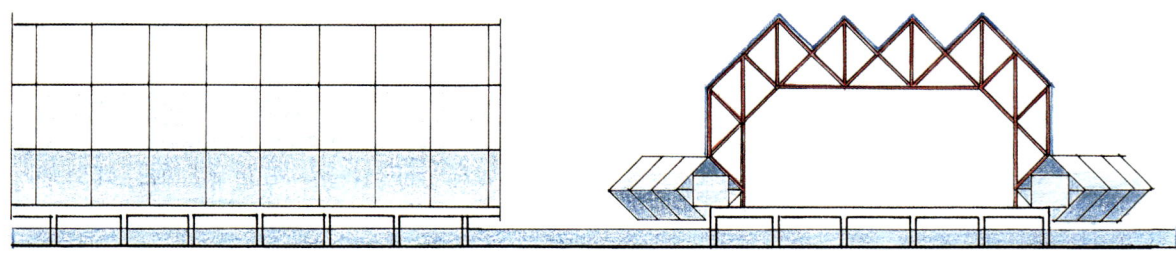

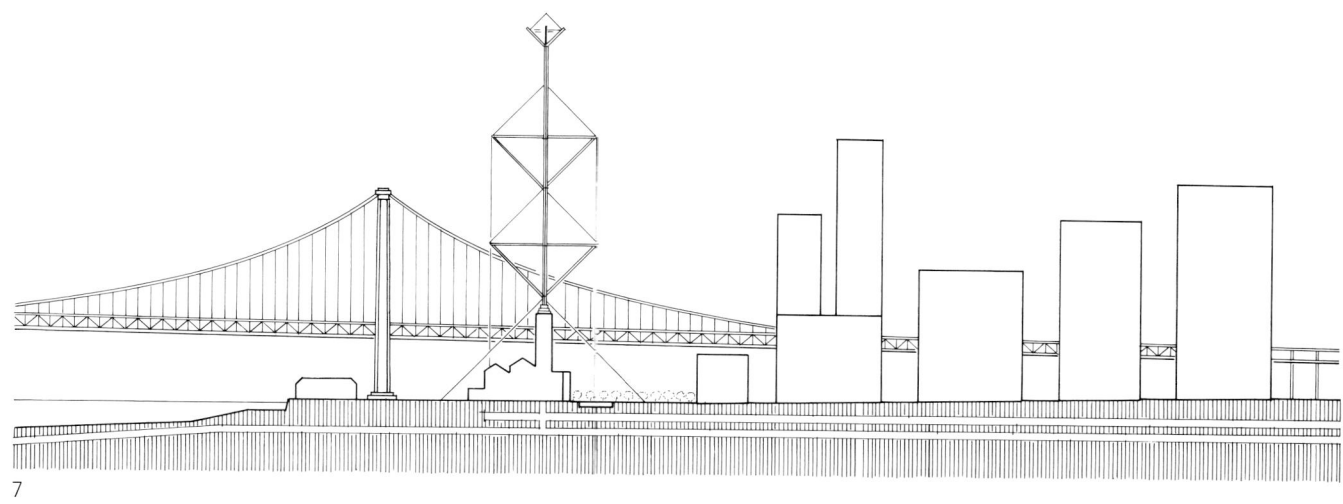

7

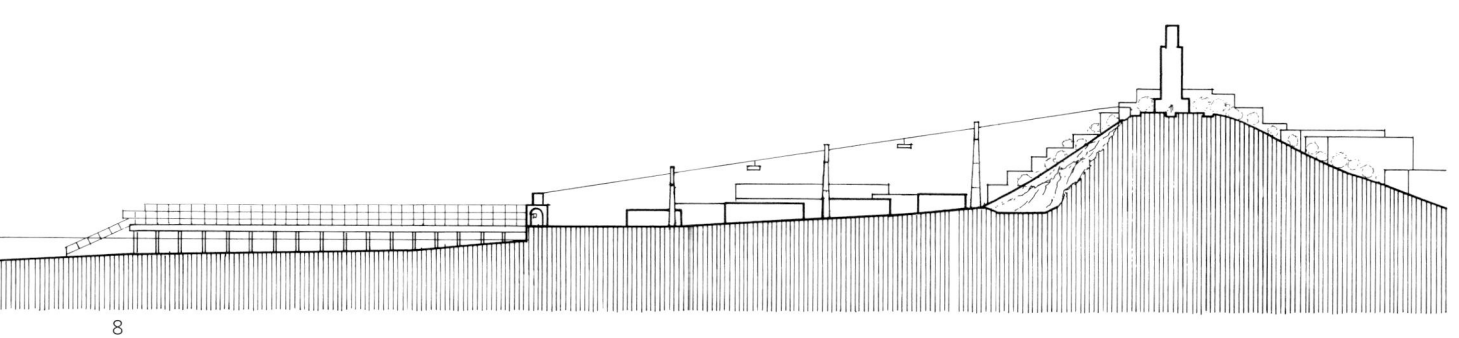

8

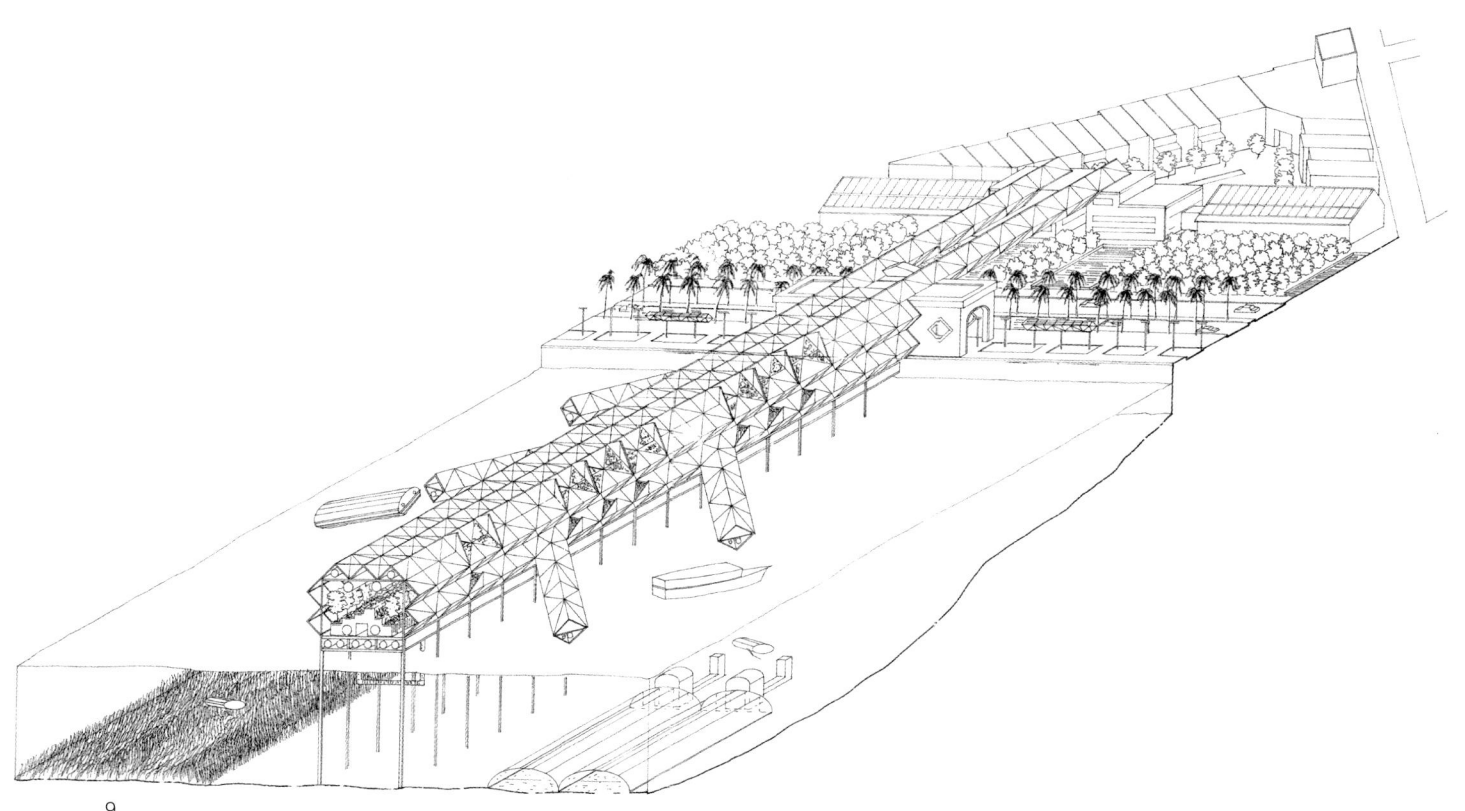

9

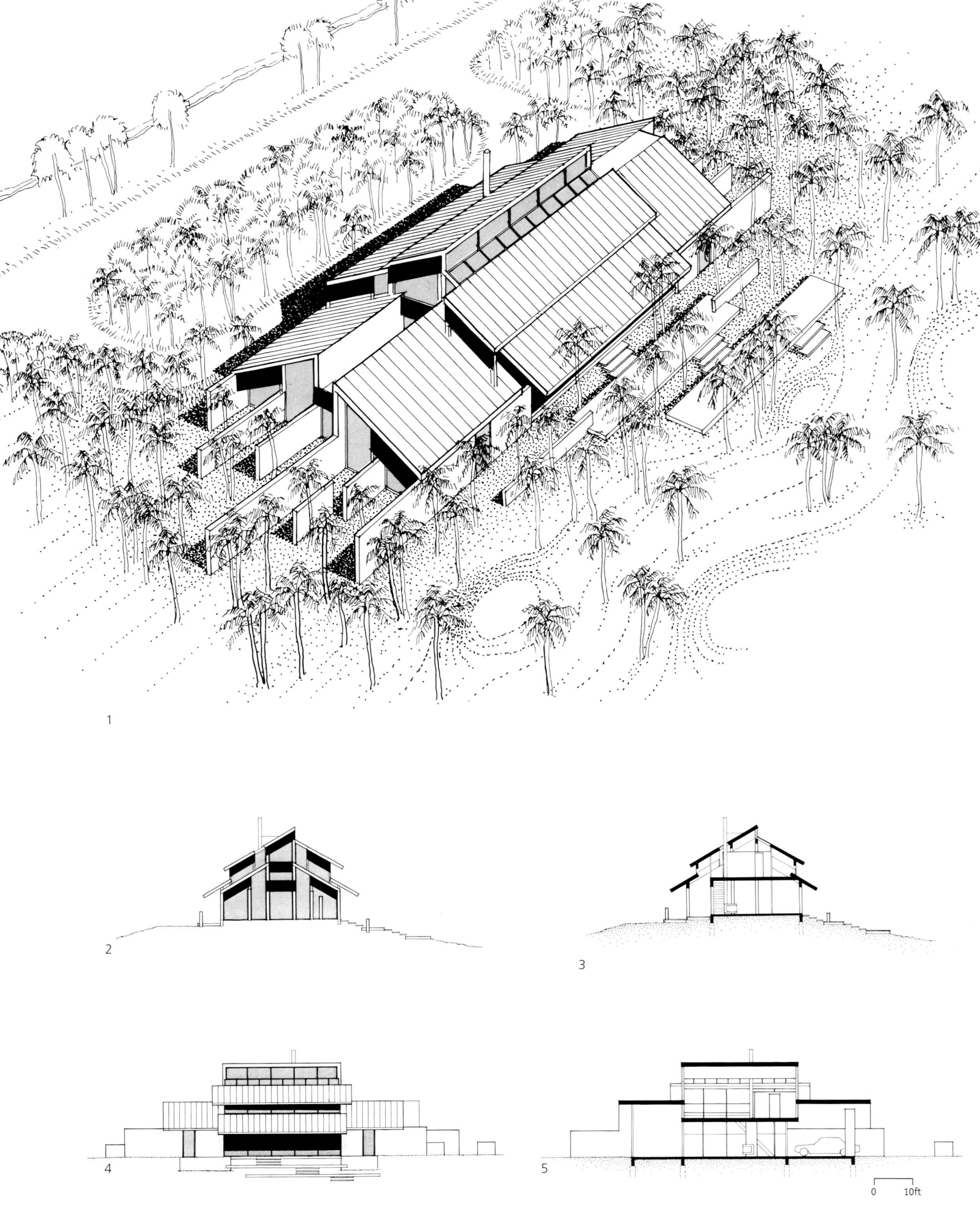

1

2

3

4

5

0    10ft

## Design 1990

Manasota Key, Florida
Mr and Mrs James Wallace
2,500 square feet
Concrete piling and grade
beams, and slabs on grade,
masonry walls with seashell
textured stucco, galvalume
roofs, wood tongue-and-
groove flooring, carpet,
and tile pavers

This island site straddles a 19-foot-high ridge facing the Gulf of Mexico. More than 100 pygmy palms dot this arid site, which slopes to a dune and sea oat beach at the Gulf. Entry is from a shell road on the Lemon Bay side. Howey's two-story design accommodates a young couple, their daughter, and three Alaskan Huskies. Their program called for active inside and outside spaces, with courtyards and fenced areas for the family and their pets. Inside, the first level contains living and dining rooms, kitchen, children's wing, carport, and canine quarters. The highest level is the master bedroom suite located to catch bay and Gulf breezes and views. Walls run parallel with the site contours, creating the outside linear courtyards for adults, children, and pets.

# 14

## Island House

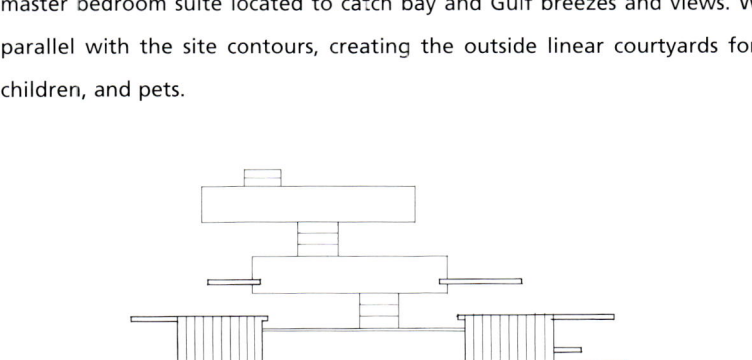

6
0  10ft

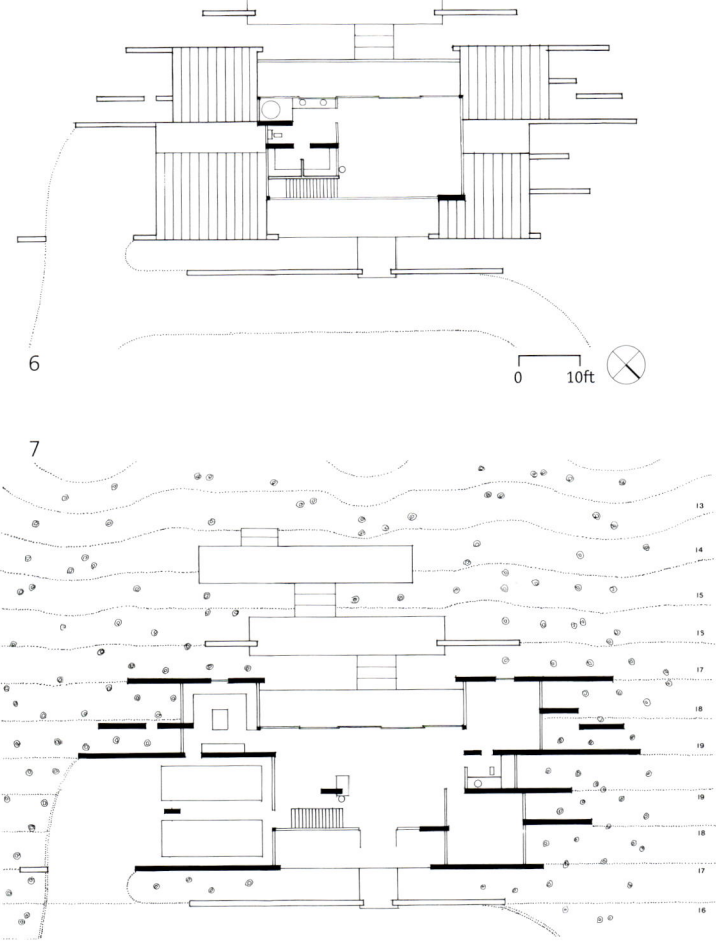

7

1

2

# 15

## Coastal Residence

This vacation house is located on the Gulf of Mexico in the Florida Panhandle. The owners, who are boating enthusiasts, wanted to incorporate an existing structural frame on the site into their new house. To this end, wood floor framing is secured to new and existing concrete pilings that are driven to the limerock base. There are full wood trusses at the building ends for lateral support. Inside, partial trusses support stairs, partitions, and roofs. The owners also wanted a house that could be completely open while they were there, then made secure for long periods of time when unoccupied. A system of lift-up roof panels was devised to achieve this. In addition to the living area, there are two bedrooms, a loft, and three baths. Third-floor viewing decks are accessible by ladder, and various decks at different levels take advantage of the views of the Gulf and the prevailing breezes. The directness of a modest frame structure raised above the earth for views and breezes is particularly appealing.

### Design 1988

Shell Point, Florida
Mr and Mrs Frank Seco de Lucena
2,400 square feet
New and existing concrete pilings, wood trusses with wood floor and roof framing, hinged lift-up panels, vertical wood siding, and metal roofs

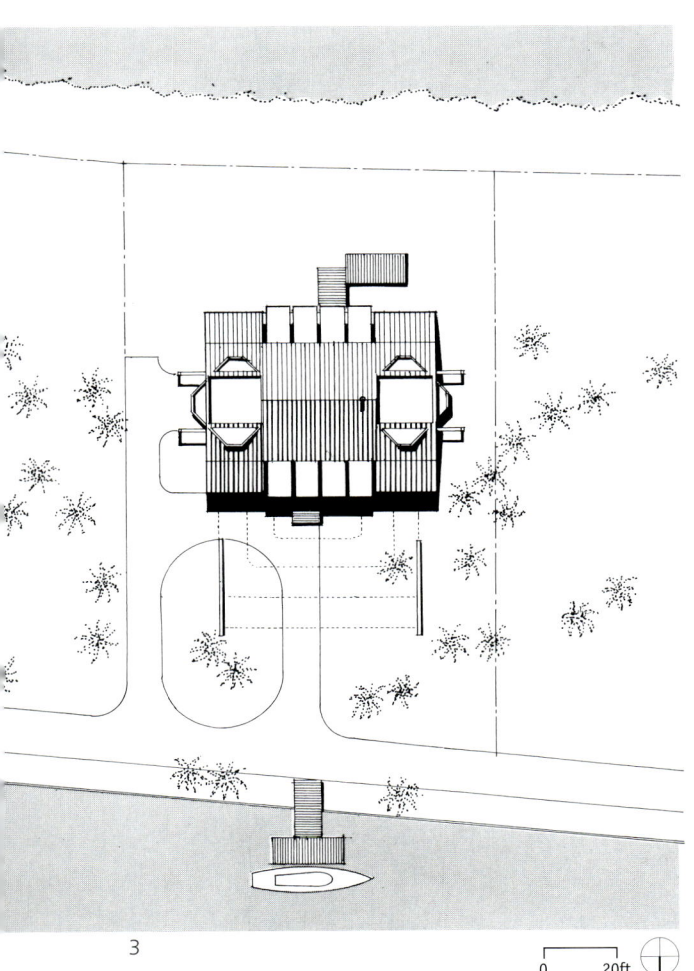

3

0    20ft

1  Model views
2  Aerial rendering
3  Site plan

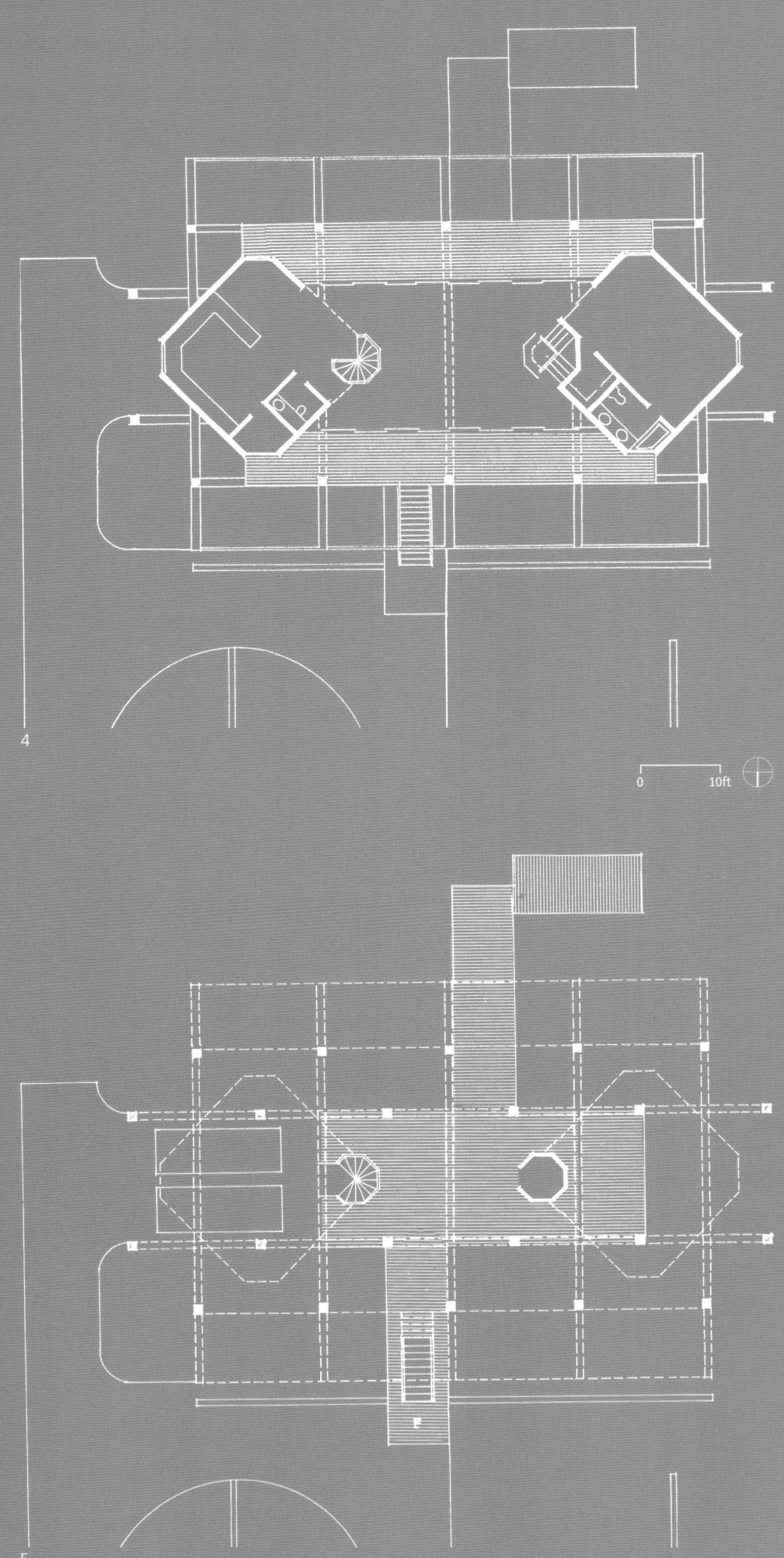

4

0        10ft

5

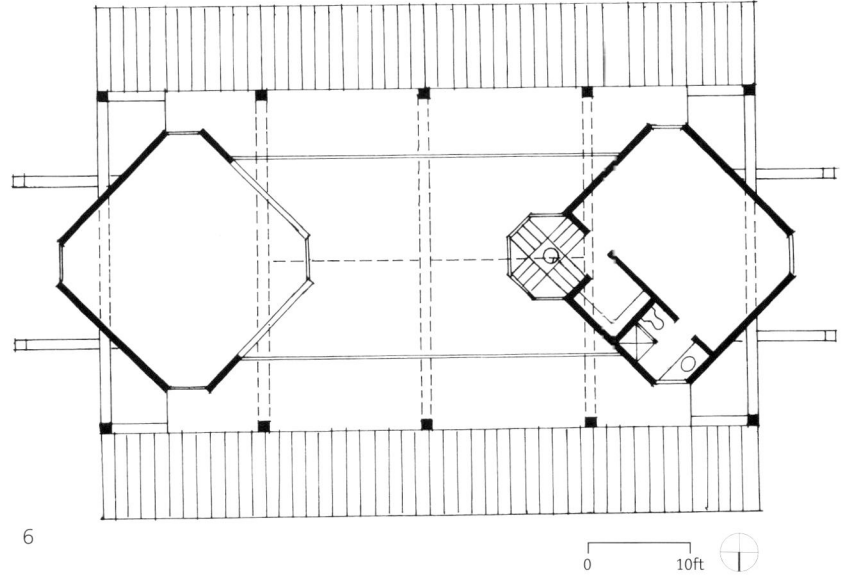

4  Main living level floor plan
5  Lower level floor plan
6  Upper level floor plan
7  Longitudinal section

6

0        10ft

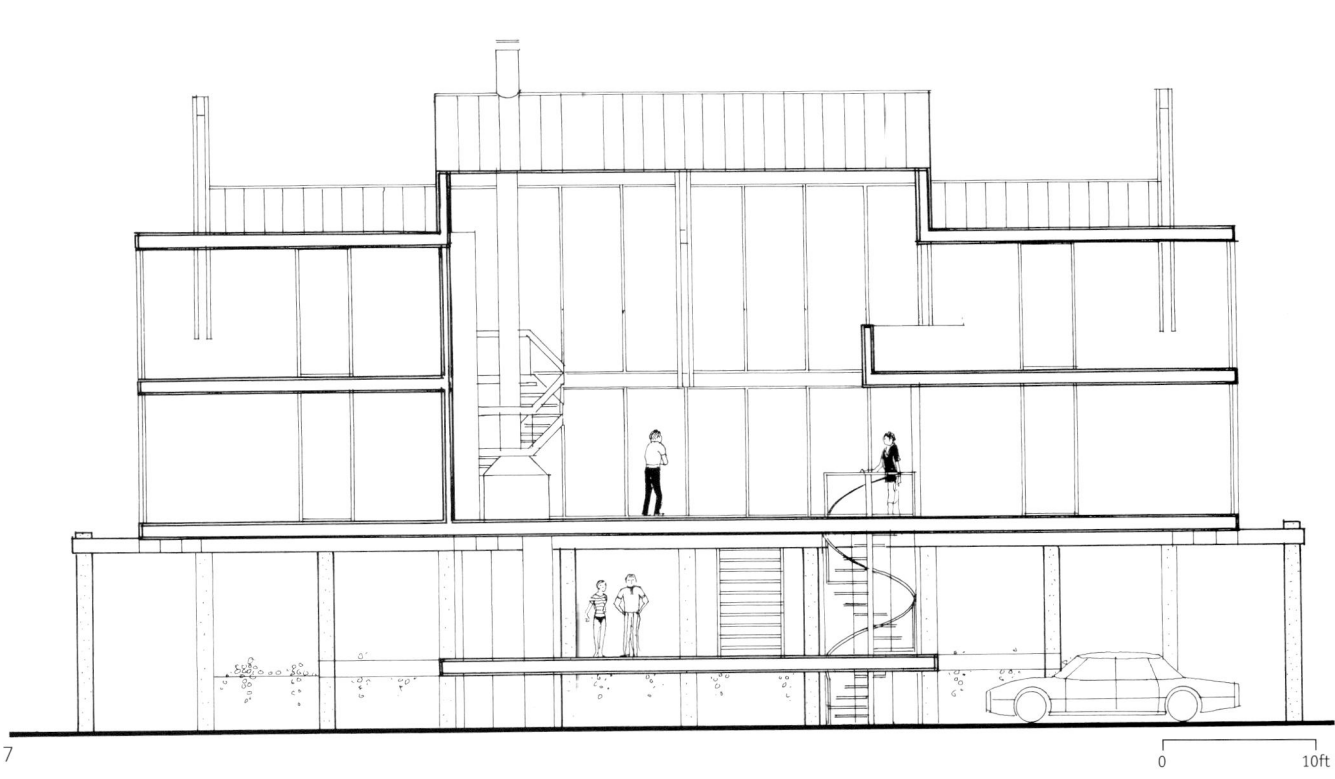

7

0                    10ft

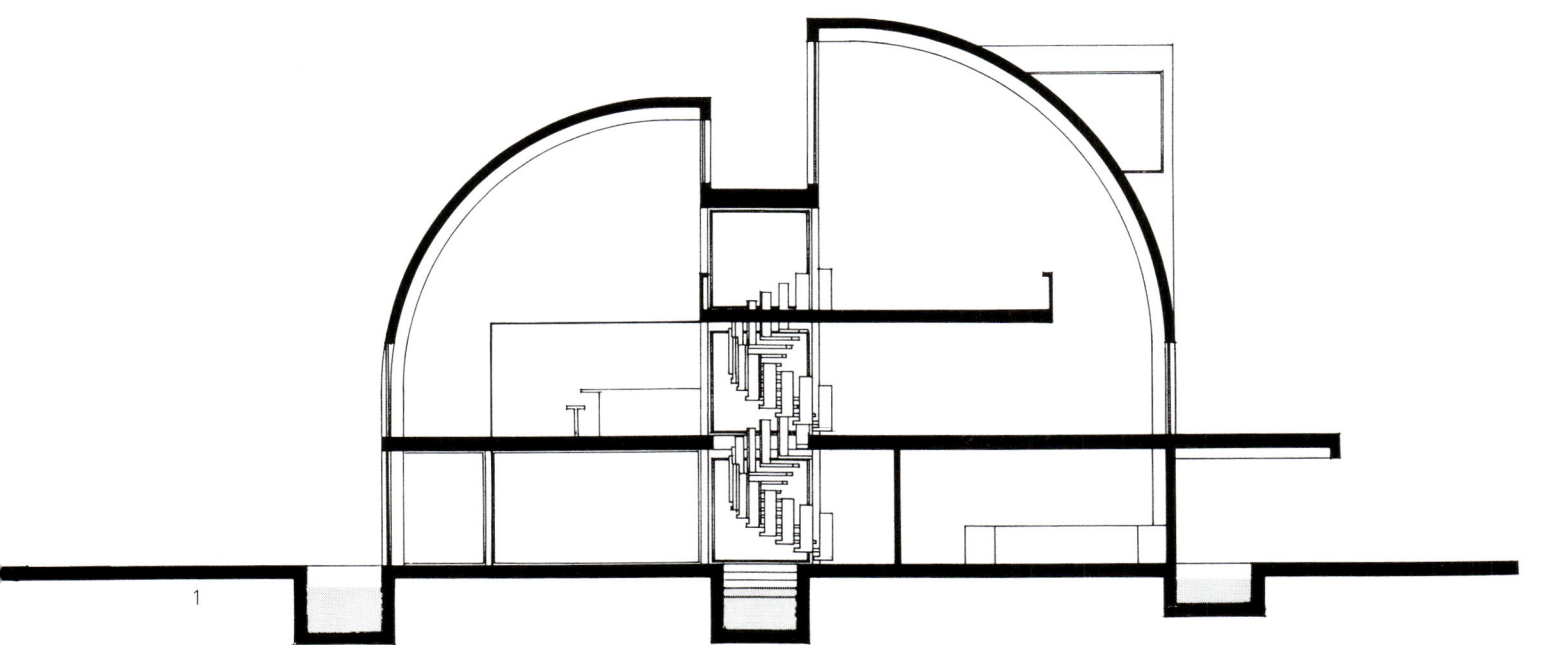

1

2

3

4

1 Section
2–4 Model views
5 Site plan

## Design 1988

Longboat Key, Florida
Mr and Mrs Charles Hay
3,200 square feet
Grade beams on concrete
pilings, masonry walls to
second level, wood framing
above; stained concrete floors,
tile, carpet, gypsum walls
and ceilings

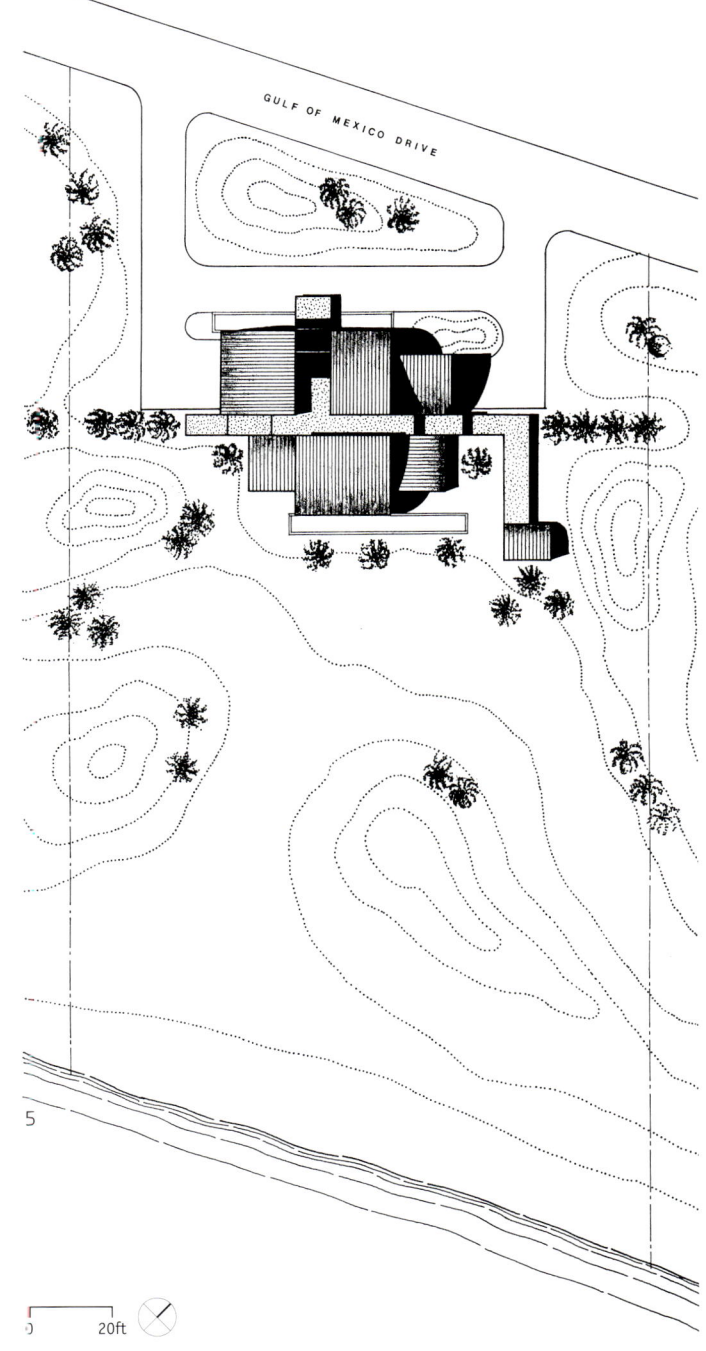

# 16

## Beach Front Residence

This unrealized design was to be a weekend house for a husband and wife who needed a retreat, as well as space to entertain guests when required. To meet these needs, the house was divided into three levels: the top level is the wife's artist loft with separate guest bedrooms; the second level consists of the main living, kitchen, dining, and master bedroom suites; and the beach level, which accommodates five automobiles, informal living/recreation with food service, a lap pool, and a beach gazebo facing the Gulf of Mexico. The interior spaces are ordered around a central spine, with a common stair from the entry that connects the three levels. The rooftops are curved to allow in light and breezes from windows located at the top of the wall. The structure and landscaping span the width of the lot and create privacy between road and beach.

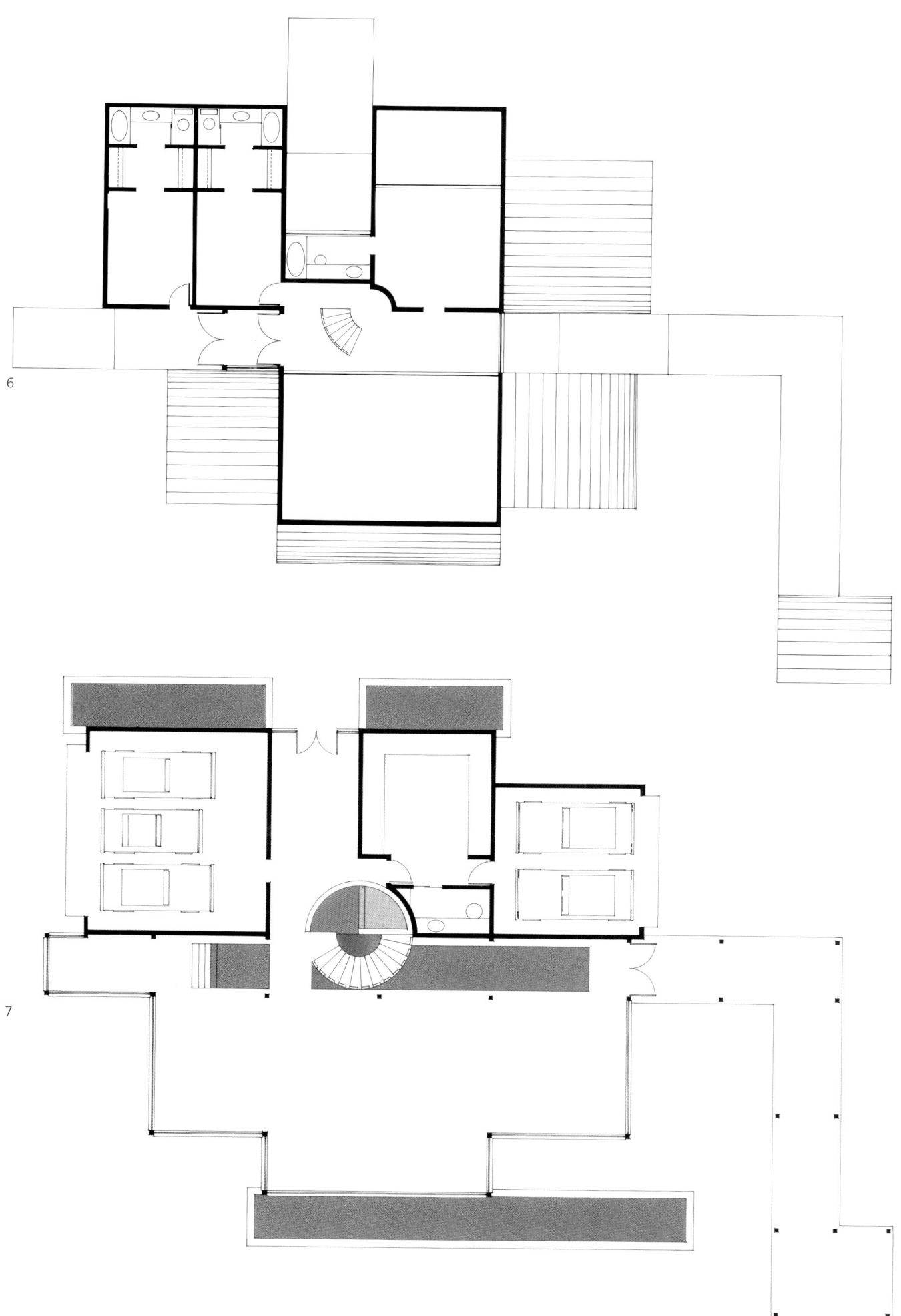

6

7

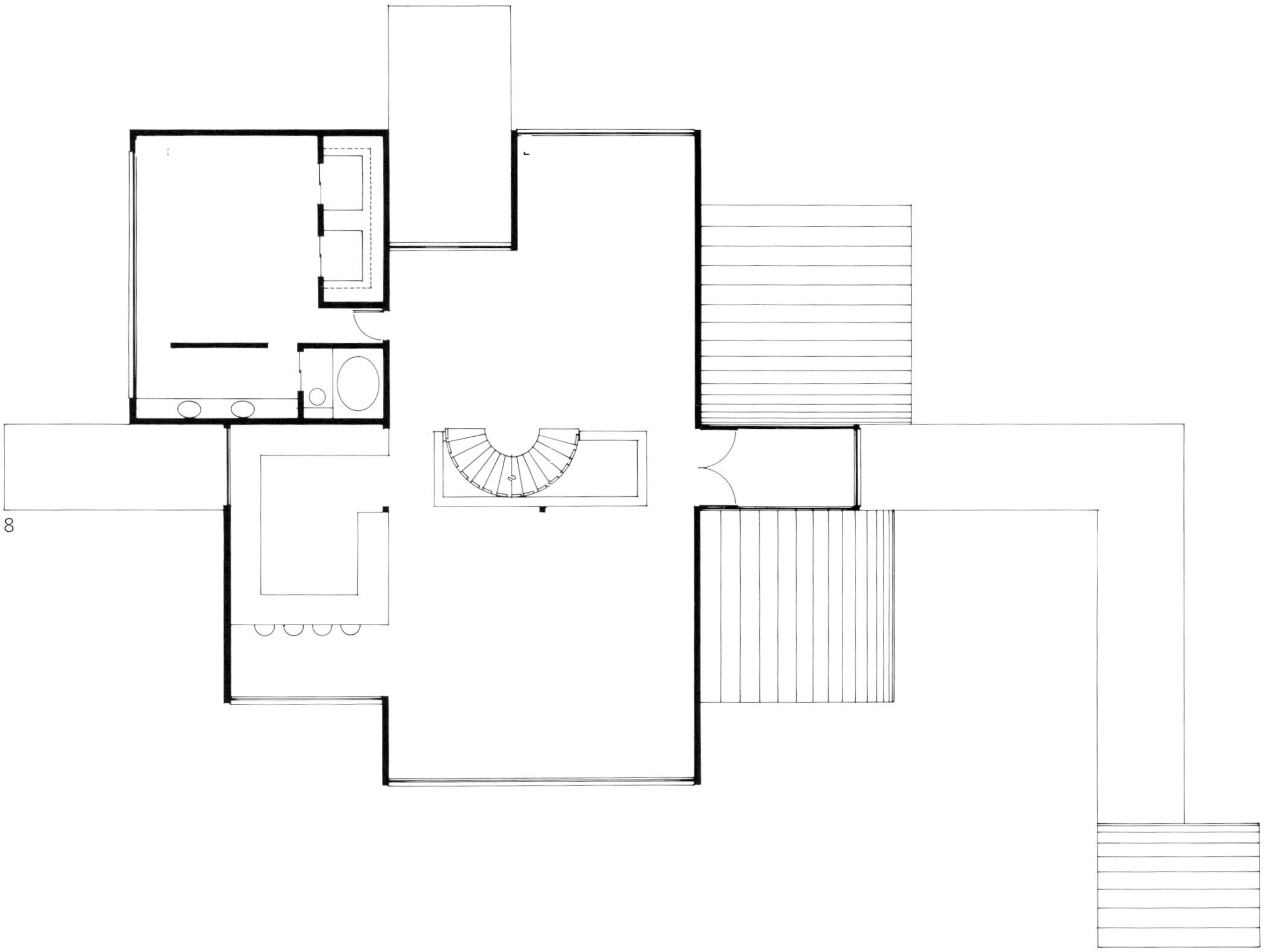

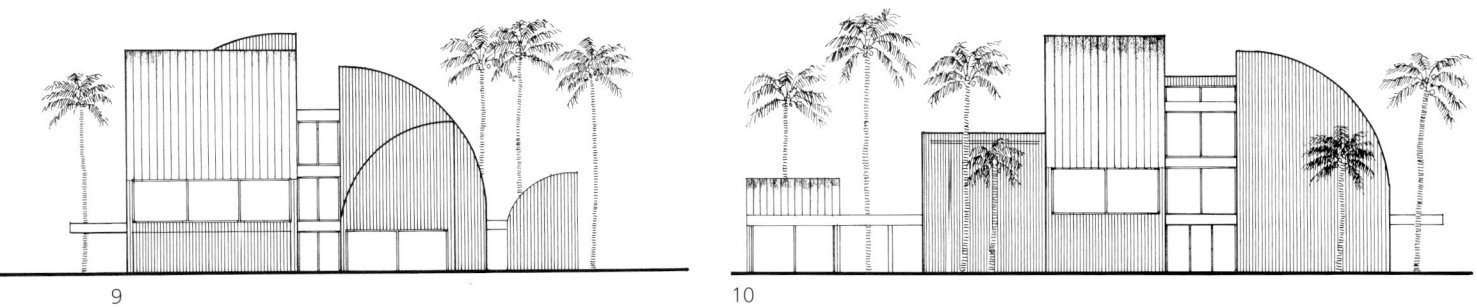

8

9

10

6   Second level floor plan
7   Ground level floor plan
8   Third level floor plan
9   Southwest elevation
10  Northwest elevation

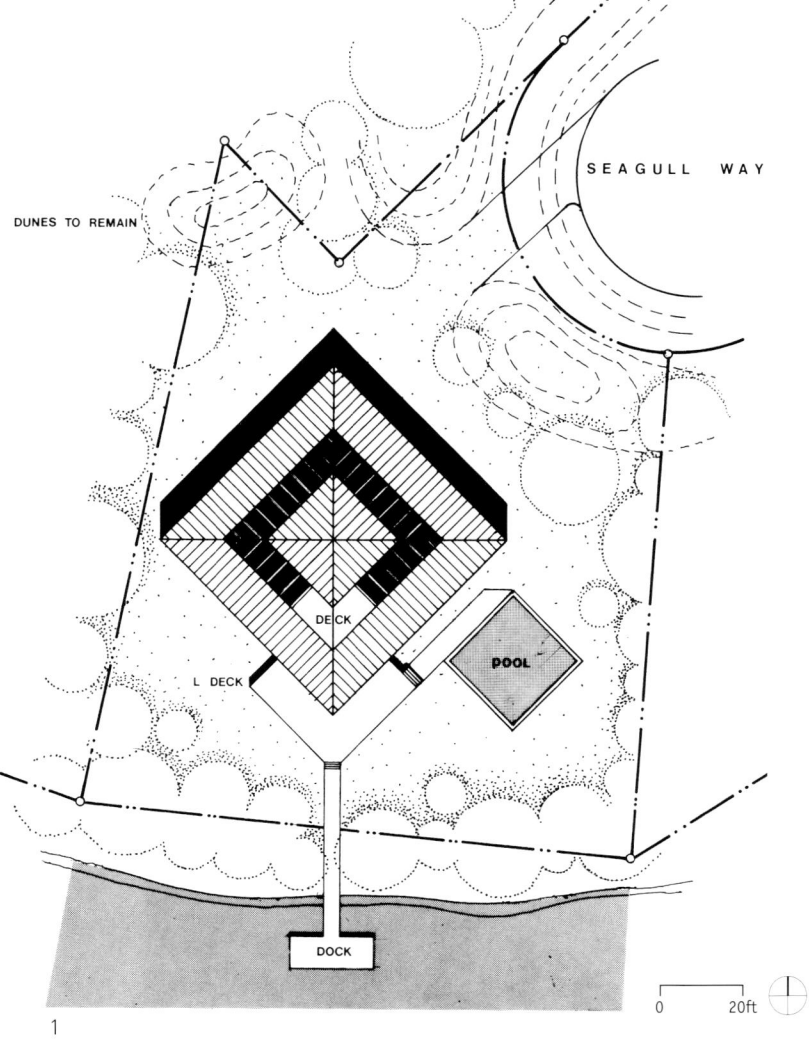

SEAGULL WAY

DUNES TO REMAIN

DECK

L DECK

POOL

DOCK

0        20ft

1

1  Site plan
2  Northeast elevation
3  Southeast elevation
4  Lower level floor plan
5  Entry level floor plan
6  Upper level floor plan

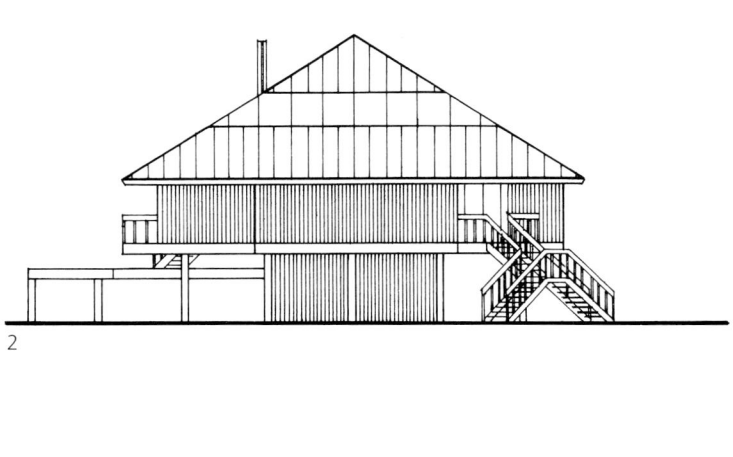

2

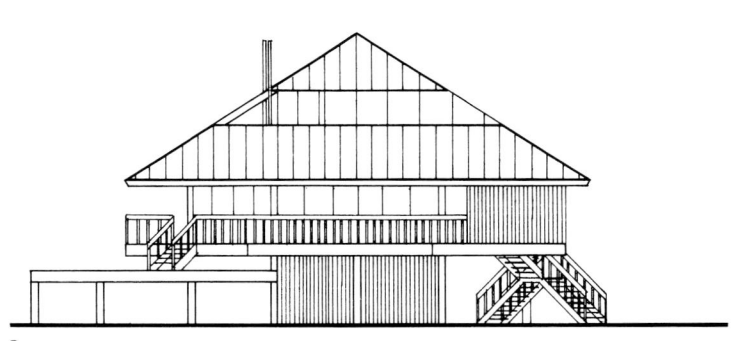

3

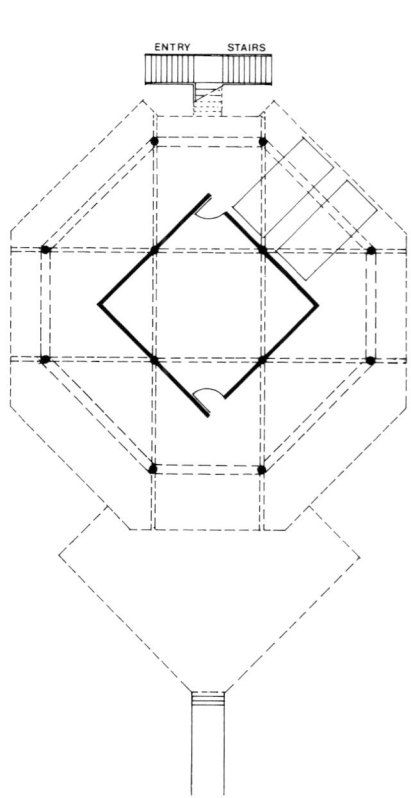

ENTRY    STAIRS

4

## Design/Completion
## 1984/1986

Anna Maria Island, Florida
Mr and Mrs Jack Whiteside
3,500 square feet
Poured concrete columns on
pilings with grade beams,
wood and steel framing,
vertical cedar siding, carpet,
ceramic tile, and terne metal

This three-level vacation home, perched next to a small inlet, fitted this family of five so well that it soon turned into their permanent residence. The main living and children's bedroom level forms an octagonal plan within its square, overhanging roof. The top center part of the roof becomes the upper master bedroom level with deck views across the inlet. Under the living level, Howey placed the entry stair, auto parking, and storage, tucked between the concrete piers extending to the roof. All windows are operable for natural ventilation. An outside, main-level deck connects swimming pool and living areas that face the inlet. Site sand dunes and natural landscaping were preserved and enhanced.

**17**

## Island Residence

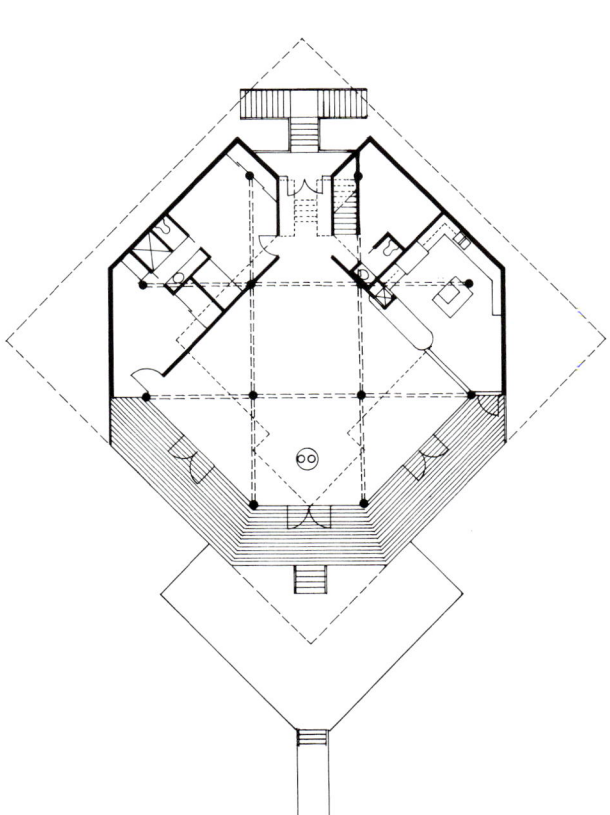

5

TO DOCK

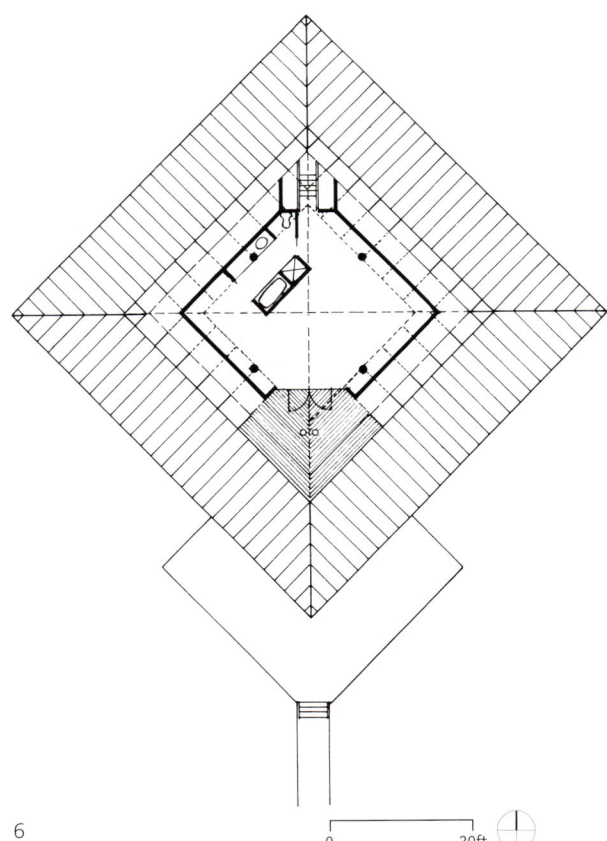

6

0          20ft

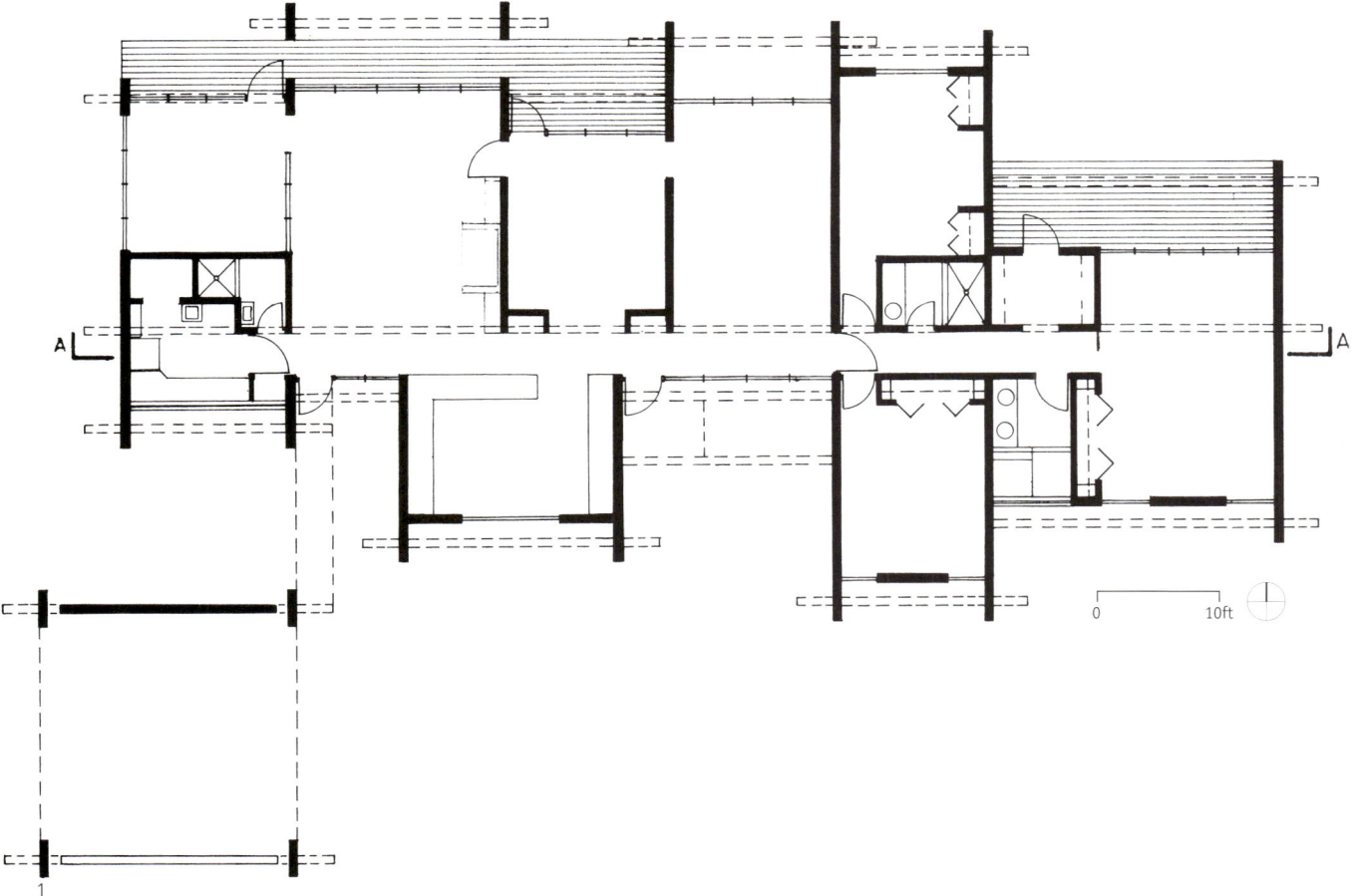

1  Floor plan
2,3,5,6  Exterior views
4  West elevation

0          10ft

2

3

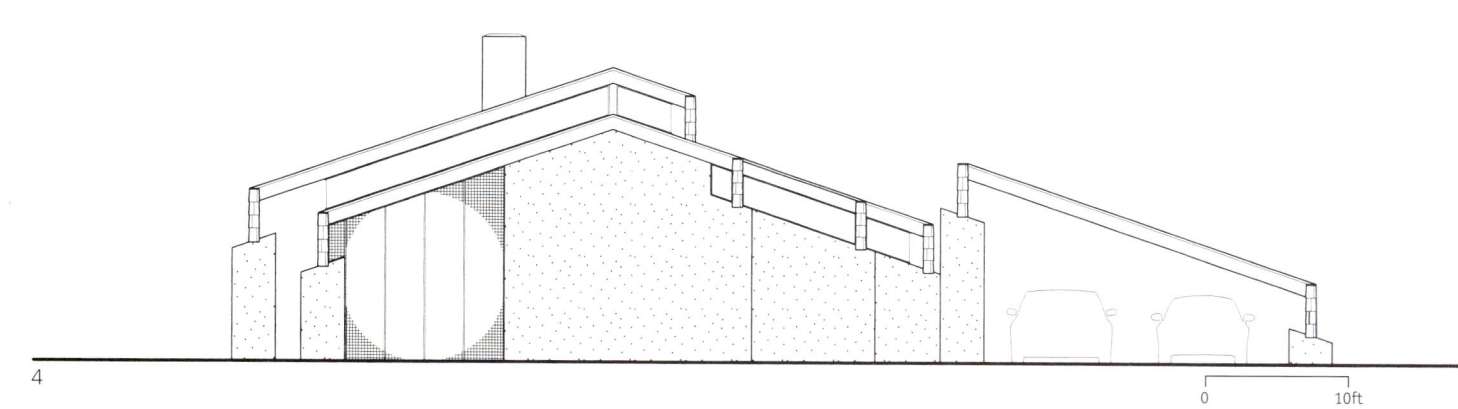

4

0          10ft

5

6

# 18

## Lake Residence

Set on an earth podium with views through a cypress stand to Lake Keystone, this residence is typical of Howey's gallery schemes. In this case, the gallery allows spaces of varying sizes and heights to grow out of either side of its central spine. The living, dining, bedroom and porch face the lake. Garage, utility, kitchen, and den are on the entry side. As in the earlier McPherson residence, the gallery ceiling becomes the horizontal air-conditioning duct to supply all rooms. Roofs on either side of the gallery become individual shed roofs of varying heights sloping to the exterior. The extended end of each lower roof is folded to provide a sunshade. The high ends of the roofs over the gallery become horizontal glass windows allowing light into each space.

### Design/Completion
### 1976/1977

Lake Keystone, Florida
Mr and Mrs Michael Trocke
3,600 square feet
Concrete footings, block
pilasters and walls, plywood
diaphragm beams, wood
framing, asphalt shingles,
stucco, aluminum, and glass

1

2

3

4

Inspired by the whitewashed cubic architecture of Greek Island residences, Howey used this geometric ideal of space and surfaces in his design for Pappas Restaurant. Pappas, established by the late Louis Pappas and carried on by his three sons, is nationally known for its Greek cuisine. The sons decided to simplify their operations from three smaller bay area restaurants to one large restaurant in Tarpon Springs. A site adjacent to the Anclote River at the entrance to the 70-year-old Greek sponge docks was selected. Requirements were to seat 800: 100 in the bar, 500 in the dining room, and 200 in the banquet room. Other items desired were a large basement, a dock on the river to receive boating patrons, and a spacious auto valet parking entrance. A drop in grade of 12 feet from the major street to the river seawall allowed the main level of the restaurant to be placed above the river, affording the best views to the sponge docks and the handsome Florida sunsets. Below, shops line the dock area, with basement space behind for laundry facilities and storage. The top level houses the banquet room with a roof deck view. By using a 20-foot x 20-foot grid, Howey subdivided the exterior into smaller stuccoed cube units, and the interior into units with wood ceilings suspended at varying heights to achieve either intimate or open dining areas.

# 19

## Louis Pappas Restaurant

### Design/Completion
### 1973/1975

Tarpon Springs, Florida
Michael, Lucas, and Jackie Pappas
42,000 square feet
Concrete pilings and foundation
walls, concrete block, steel frame,
bar joists, metal studs, stucco,
glass, aluminum, cedar, drywall,
tile, and carpet

1&2  Exterior viewed from river
3&4  Exterior entrance

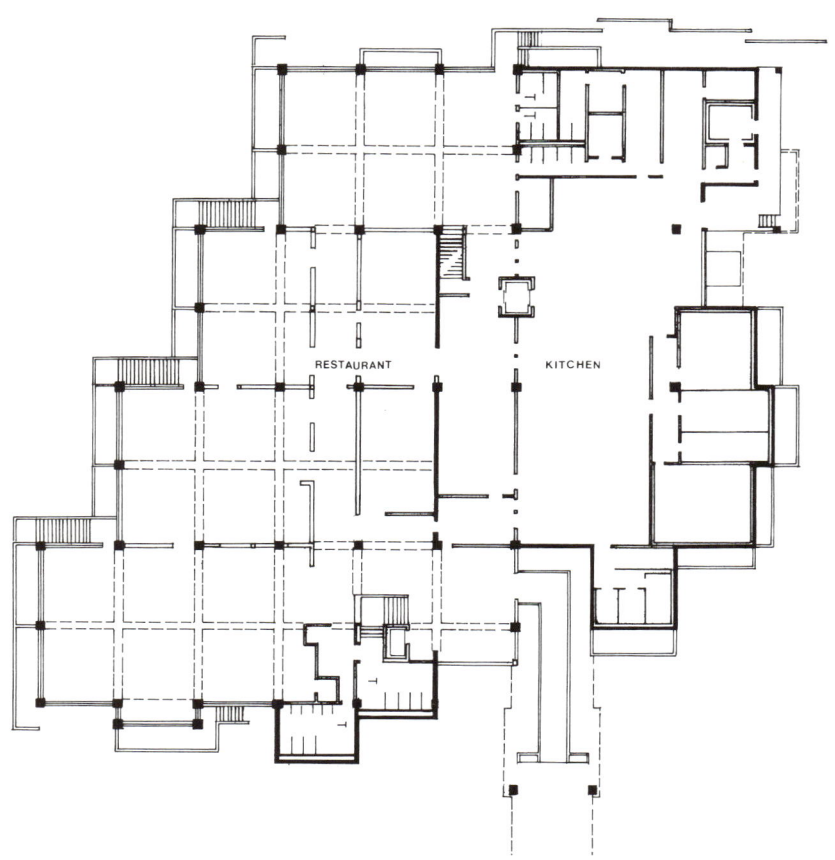

5

RESTAURANT    KITCHEN

0          20ft

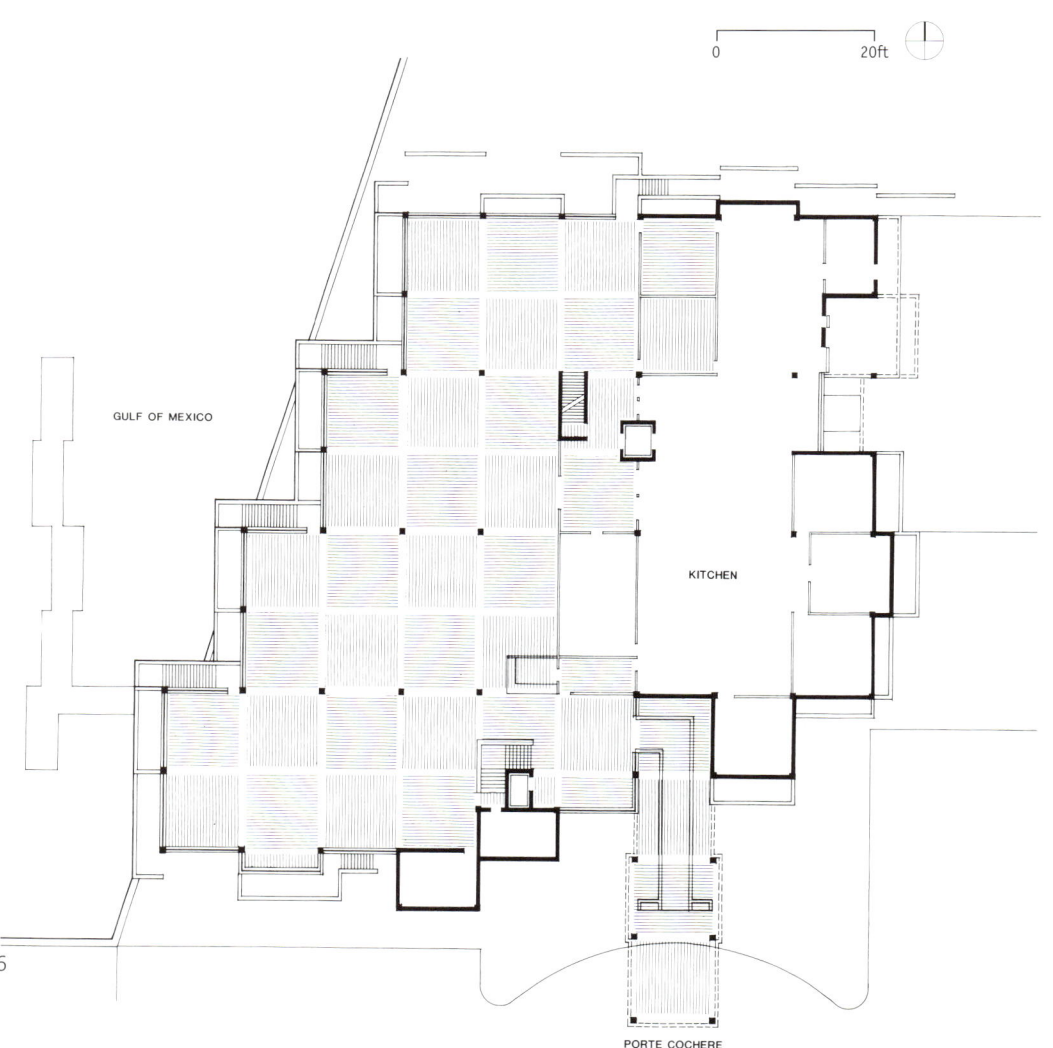

GULF OF MEXICO

KITCHEN

6

PORTE COCHERE

7

8

9

5  Main floor plan
6  Reflected ceiling
7–9  Interior views

1

1–4  Exterior views
5&6  Interior views

2

3

4

# 20

## Bierley Residence

Design/Completion
1969/1970

Tampa, Florida
Mr and Mrs John Bierley
3,000 square feet
Concrete slab on grade, post
and beam construction, with
load bearing wood stud walls
sheathed with plywood and
finished in vertical cypress
boards

Located on the site of a former landscape nursery, this two-story wood residence was designed for a husband and wife who planned to have a family. The area abounds in plants, shrubs, and a variety of trees that buffer the sides and rear of the house. A pond with cattails separates the structure from a main road at the front. Privacy, and retaining the natural setting of the property were the major requirements of the owners. The living areas of the residence all face the pond, with the second-level bedrooms accessed by a gallery open to the spaces below. Underneath are entry, living room, den, and kitchen. At each end are screened porches. An area where three palm trees stood was chosen as the construction site, and these trees were transplanted to the front of the house. A private auto entrance from an existing access road was created at the rear of the property, and the reed growth around the perimeter of the pond was retained to provide additional privacy.

5

6

1   Site plan
2   View from river
3   Floor plans

1

2

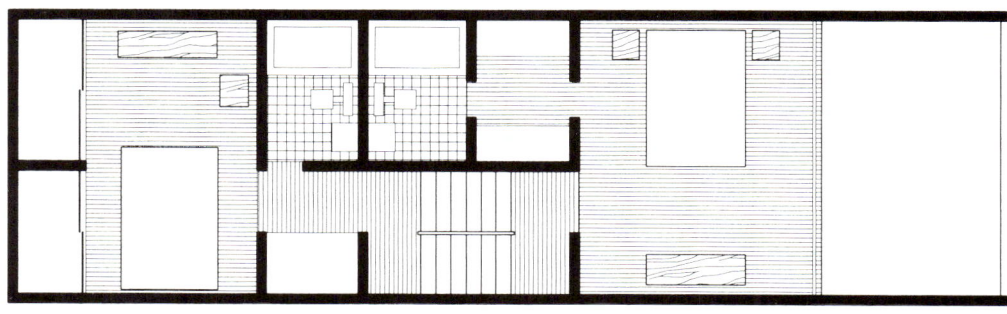

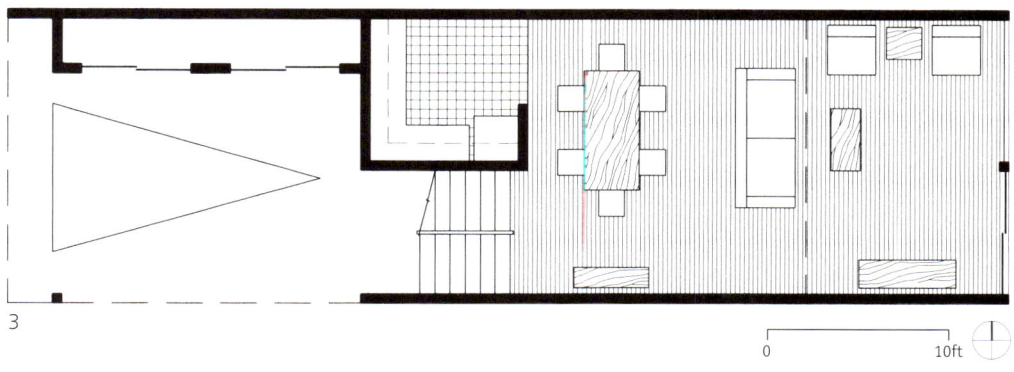

3

```
0          10ft
```

## Garden Apartments

**Design 1966**
Tampa, Florida
Charles Wishart
103,000 square feet
Concrete footings, pilings,
concrete block, precast
concrete floor and roof panels,
concrete pavers, stucco, glass,
aluminum, built-up roofs

The second of two multi-family sites owned by this client (see also Modular Apartments, p. 38) consists of 7 acres covered with clusters of mature oak trees. From its entrance street, the site slopes gently to its other major boundary, the Hillsborough River. At the property's lowest point along the river, Howey proposed that an inlet be cut to provide a sheltered boat basin at its end. The concept here is a loop road crossing over the inlet, connecting with fingers of staggered two- and three-level garden apartments that stretch from road to water. Vistas between the apartment rows allow multiple views of the river. General docking and boat-ports for bordering units are within the boat basin. Apartment interiors are split-level, with one-and-a-half-story living spaces in the larger units. A total of 140 low-rise apartment units were planned for this site.

1

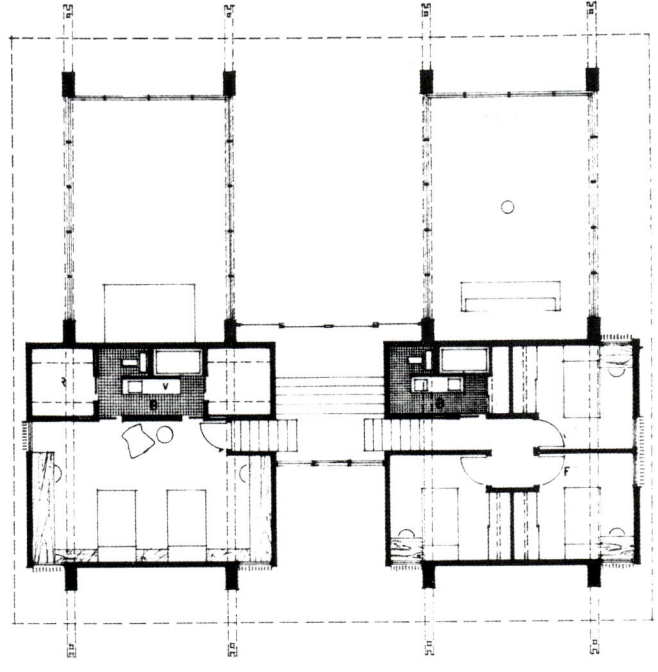

2

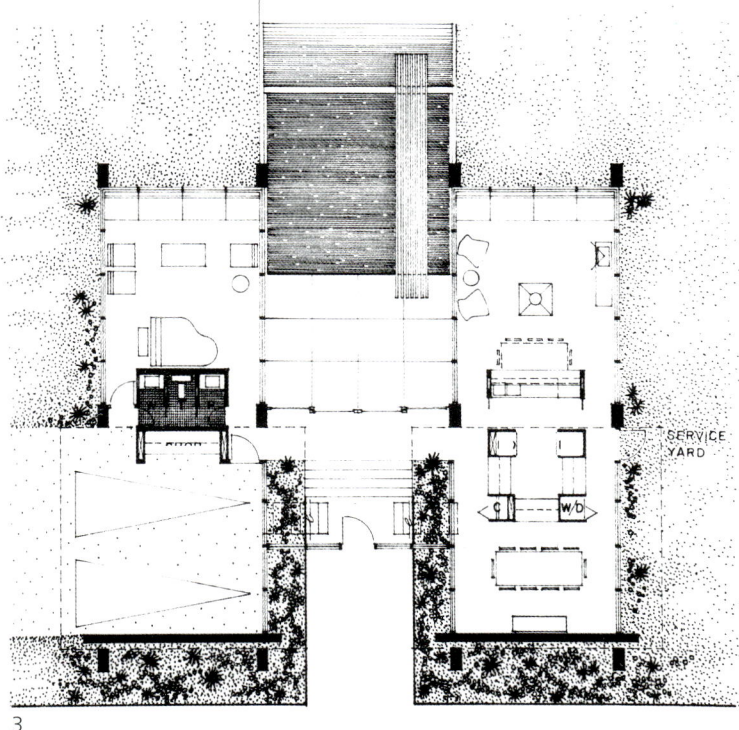

3

## Residence Design Competition

4

This winning design was a house for a family of five, located on Tampa Bay. The dominant feature was a land cut-and-fill, which provided a water inlet from the bay for boat mooring and a future swimming pool. The fill from the cut was to be used to raise the first floor level of the house and to provide an elevated ramp at the street-side entry. The client brief was that the master bedroom, children's bedrooms, entry, kitchen, living, dining, family rooms, and seawall surrounding the residence be built for $30,000. The bedrooms were elevated to catch the prevailing breezes. The two living spaces beneath the bedrooms were separated by a screened porch, which provided for ventilation on three sides. At the conclusion of the competition, the family was transferred from St. Petersburg to California, and the design was not built.

### Design 1964

St. Petersburg, Florida
Mr and Mrs Richard Duval
2,800 square feet
Concrete footings, slab on grade with stacked concrete block columns; second floor walls and roof are wood framed to columns

FLORA

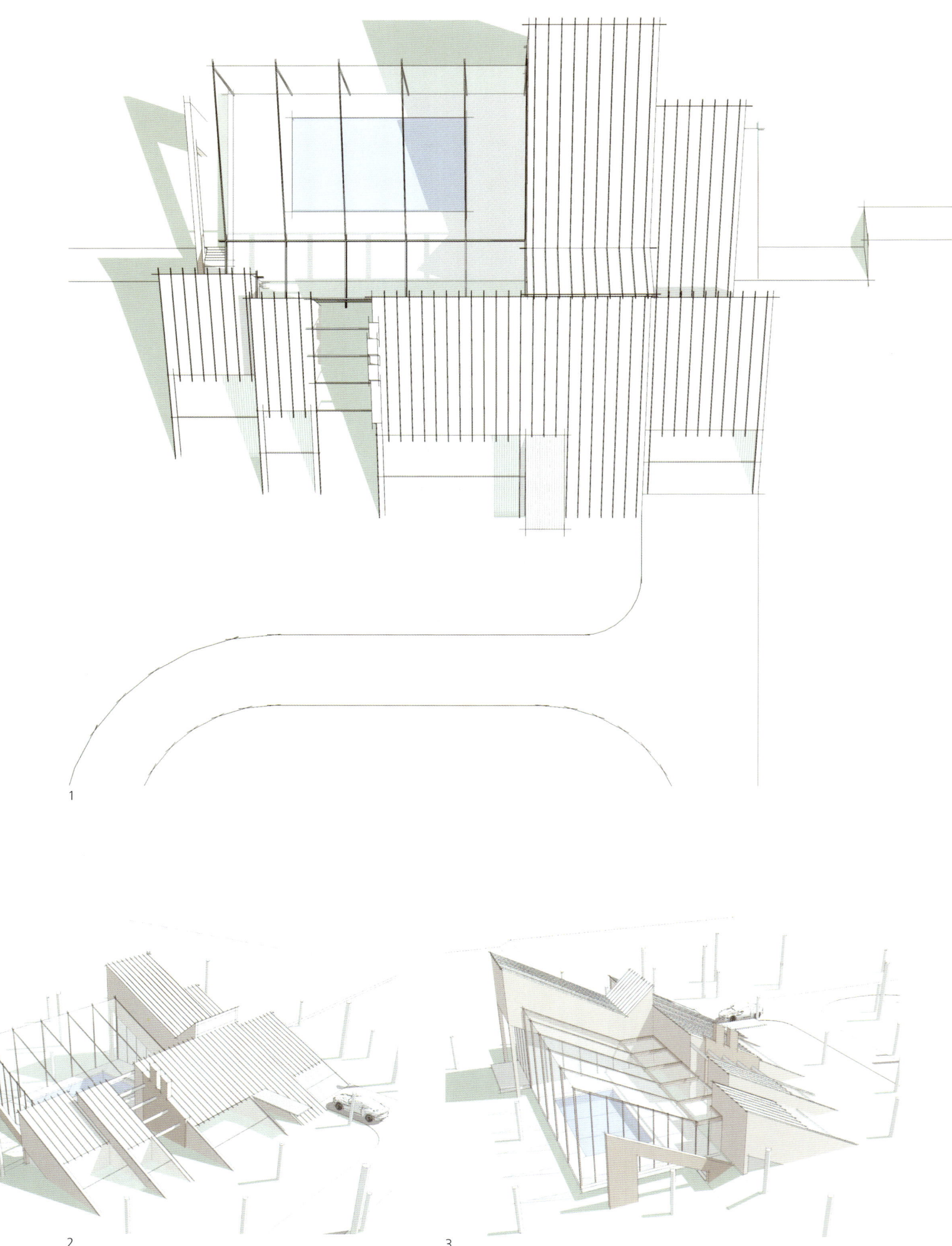

1

2                                                          3

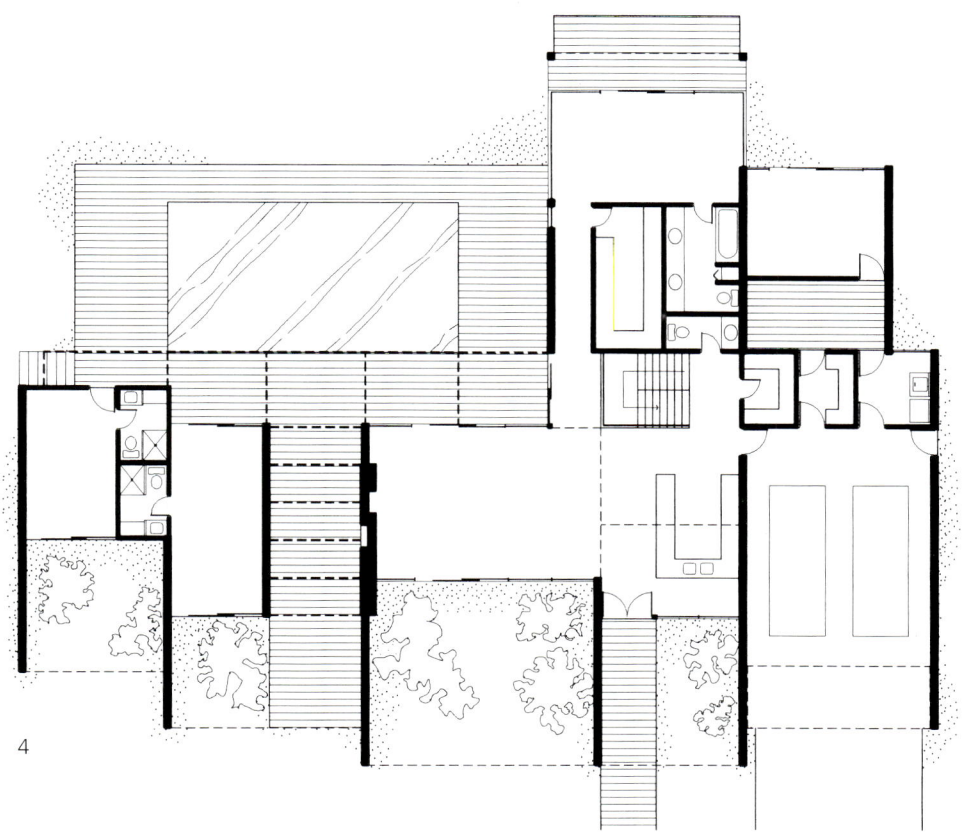

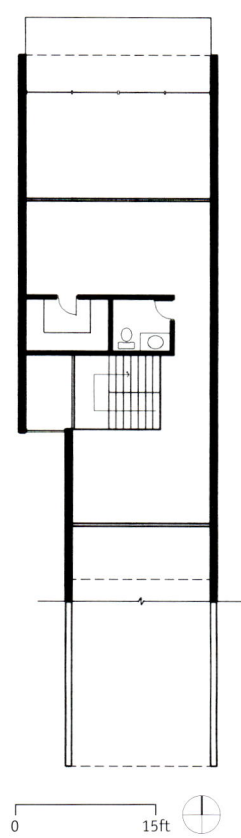

4

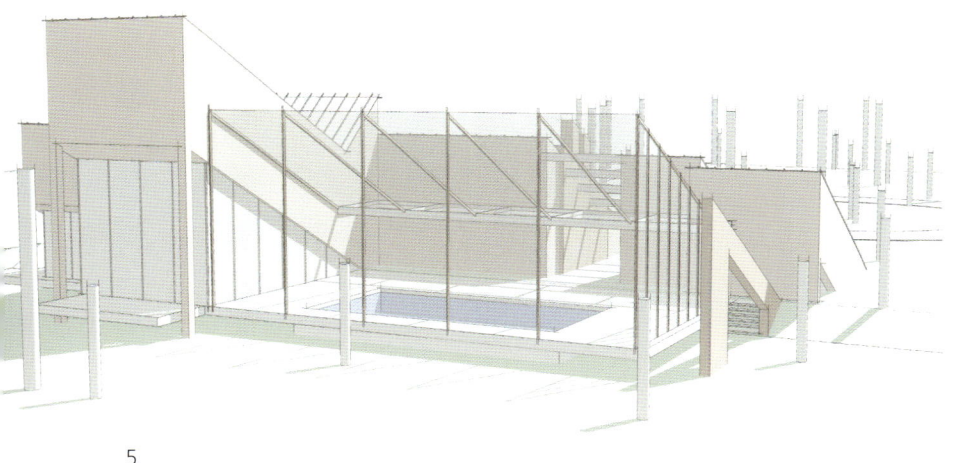

5

1  Site plan
2  Front aerial view
3  Side aerial view
4  Floor plan
5  Corner aerial view

## Design 2005

Springhill, Florida
Mr and Mrs Bill Roth
5 acres
Concrete piers, masonry, wood
framing, stucco or cypress siding,
copper standing-seam roofs

This central Florida site was originally part of a large horse farm. The land is populated by a stand of oak trees, which also line the access road on the south. To the north, the ground slopes gently to grassland and a small lake in the distance. The clients wanted Howey to place their house within the trees in such a way that views of the lake and rolling hills would still be possible. An elevated swimming pool and deck front the central living spaces. To the west are two guest pods. To the east are the personal spaces, kitchen, garage, and a pottery work-space. A second-level office and exercise room are over the master bedroom suite. The house, with its shed roofs, appears to grow out of the ground toward the views. At grade, movable kevlar screen panels serve as security and hurricane protection when closed.

## Country Residence

1

2

3

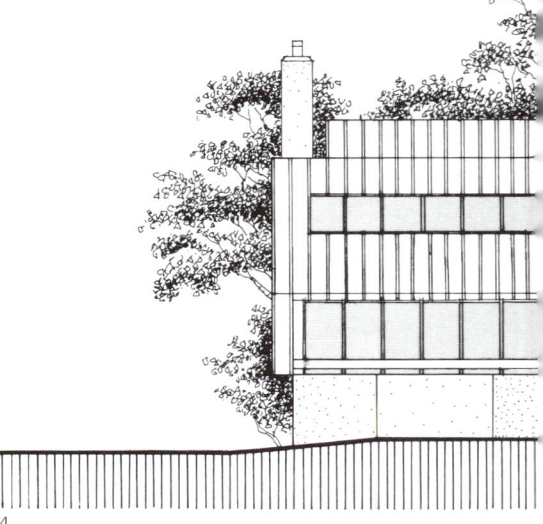

4

1&3  Model exterior
  2  Exterior
  4  South elevation
  5  Seashell stucco

# 24
## Bay Park Place

Located in a large oak hammock, this site borders a city park with views to Hillsborough Bay. The clients wished to develop the site with luxury homes to take advantage of both the site and the view. Howey's design solution places the parking at the lowest site elevation, with three levels of paired, mid-rise units above. Concealed water retention ponds lie next to the parking area. At each end of the site are multi-level town-homes with their own entrances, making a total of eight units in the complex.

The main pedestrian entry is through a three-story middle slot that allows for views to the park upon arrival at the first level lobby. The sloped copper roofs are compatible with the neighborhood character. A pattern of voids and solids is created through the alternating open balconies within the roofs. Undulating ribbons of roof copper enclose the town-home ends. In order to keep the complex within residential height requirements, the parking garage was placed a half-level below the elevation of the city park. This project was designed for suburban privacy within walking distance of downtown Tampa.

### Design/Completion
### 1988/1989

Tampa, Florida
Bay Park, Inc.
17,500 square feet
Spread concrete footings, reinforced masonry bearing walls, precast concrete joists and poured decks, copper roofs, seashell stucco walls, ceramic tile, carpet, and wood decking

5

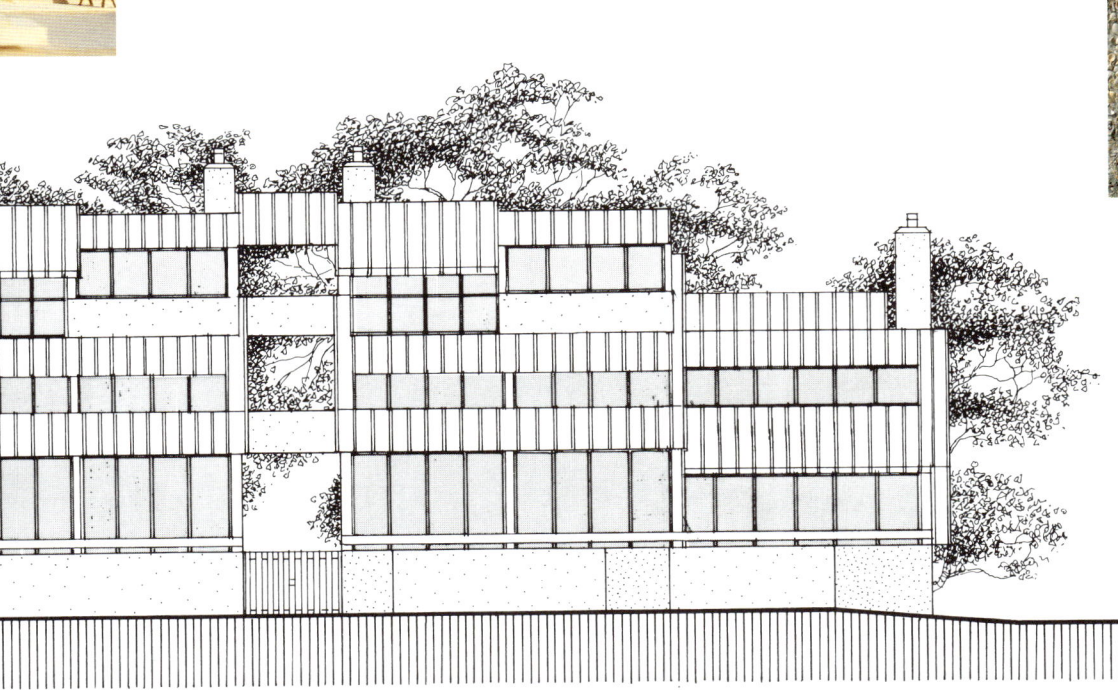

0          10ft

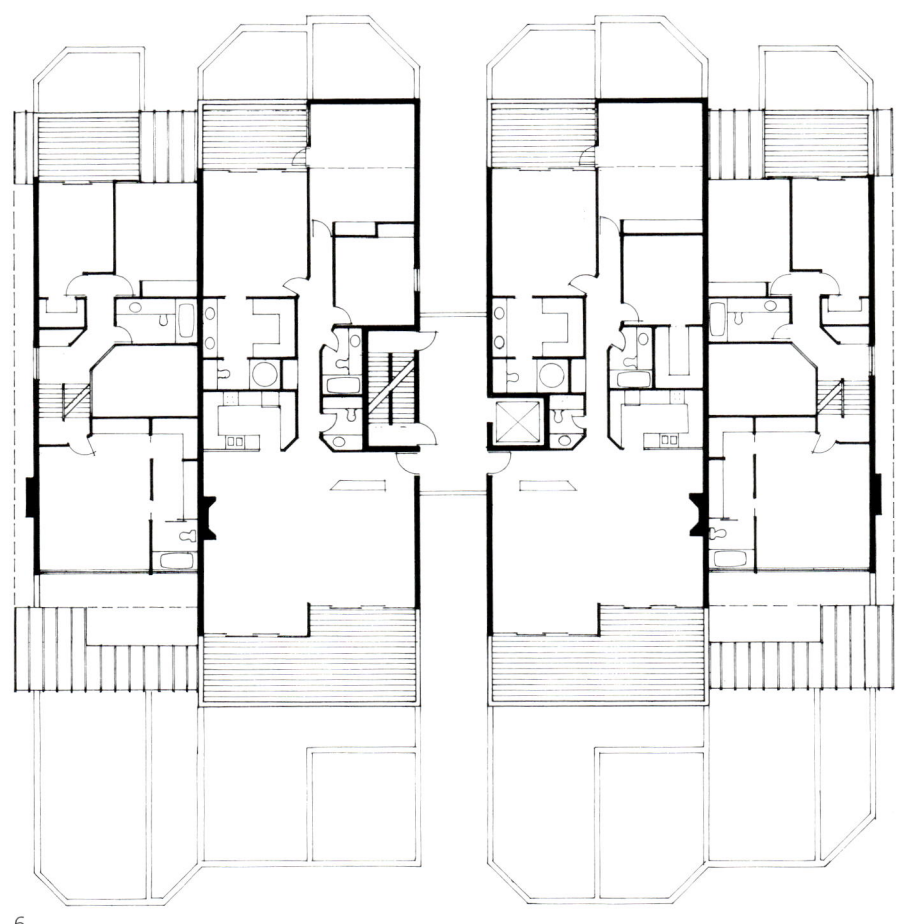

6

7

8

6   Level two floor plan
7   Level three floor plan
8   Interior
9&11   Sections
10   Penthouse level floor plan

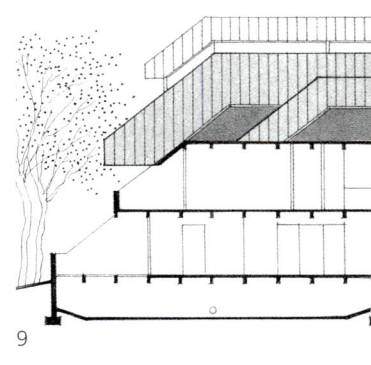

9

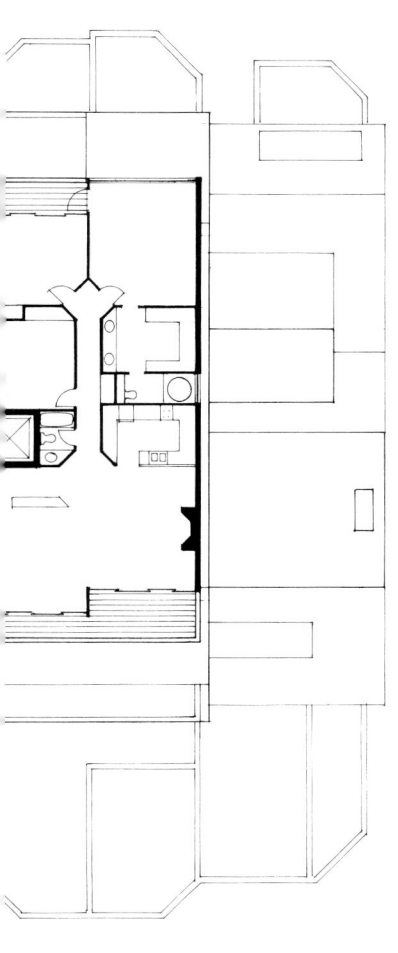

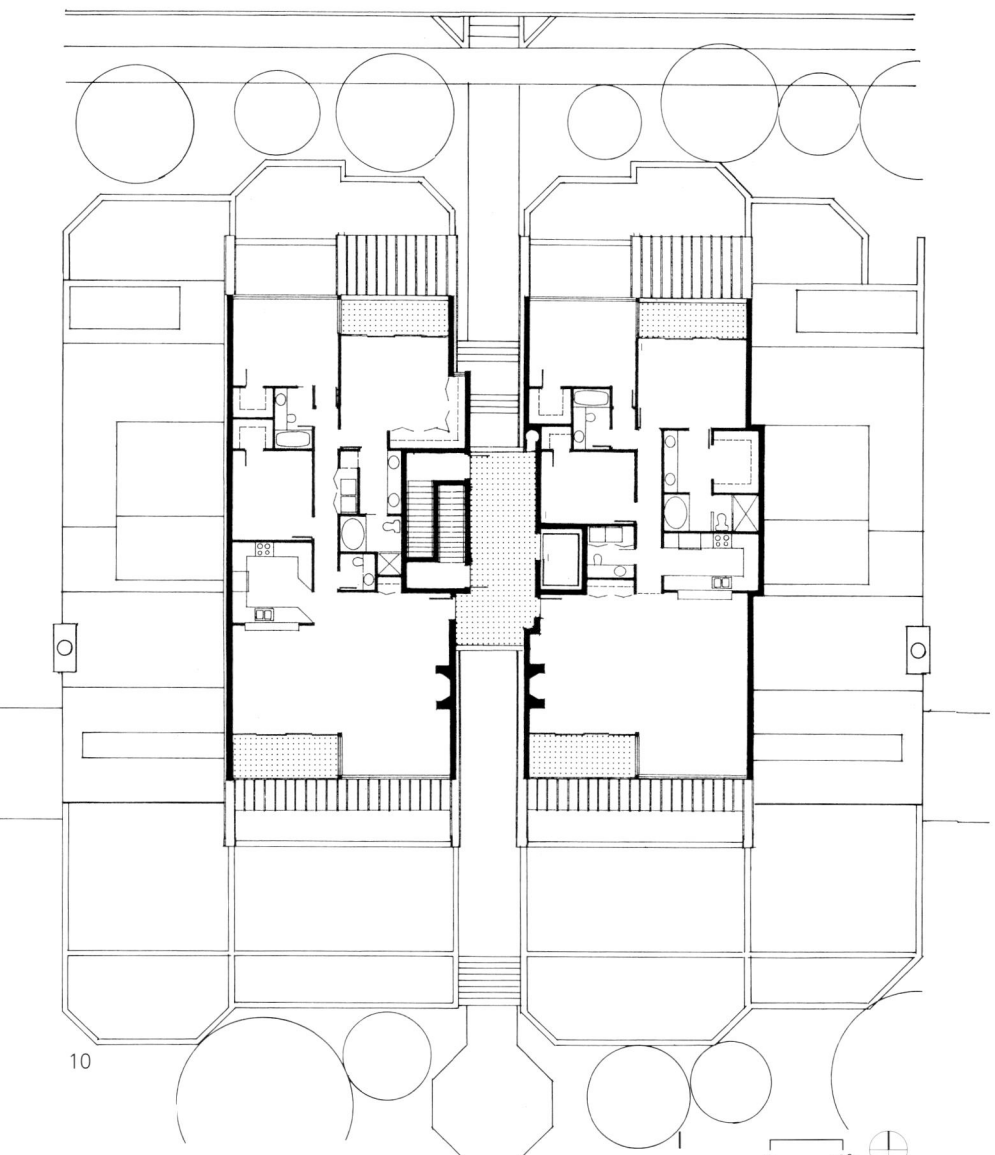

10

0    10ft

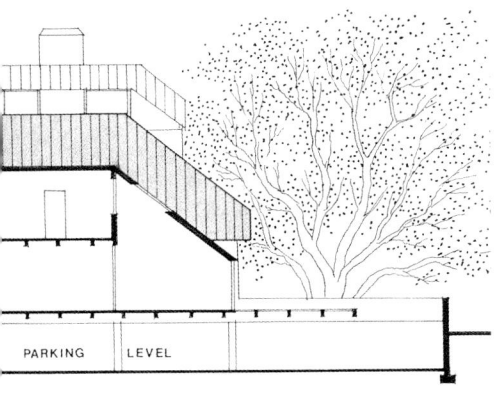

PARKING    LEVEL

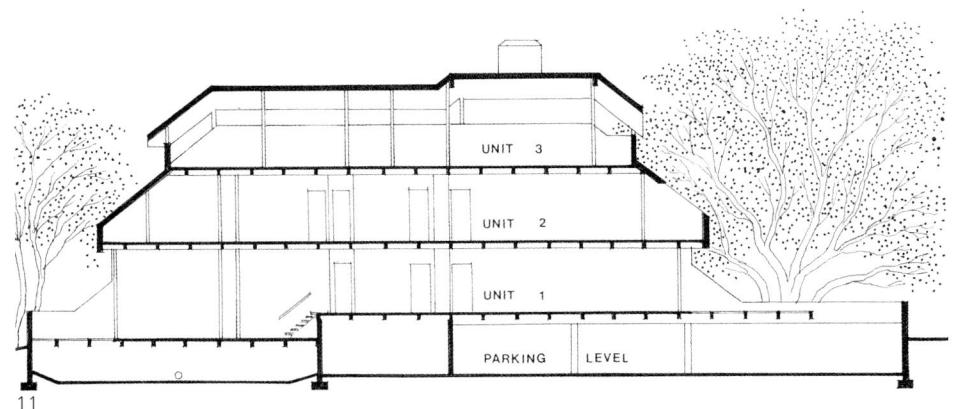

UNIT 3

UNIT 2

UNIT 1

PARKING    LEVEL

11

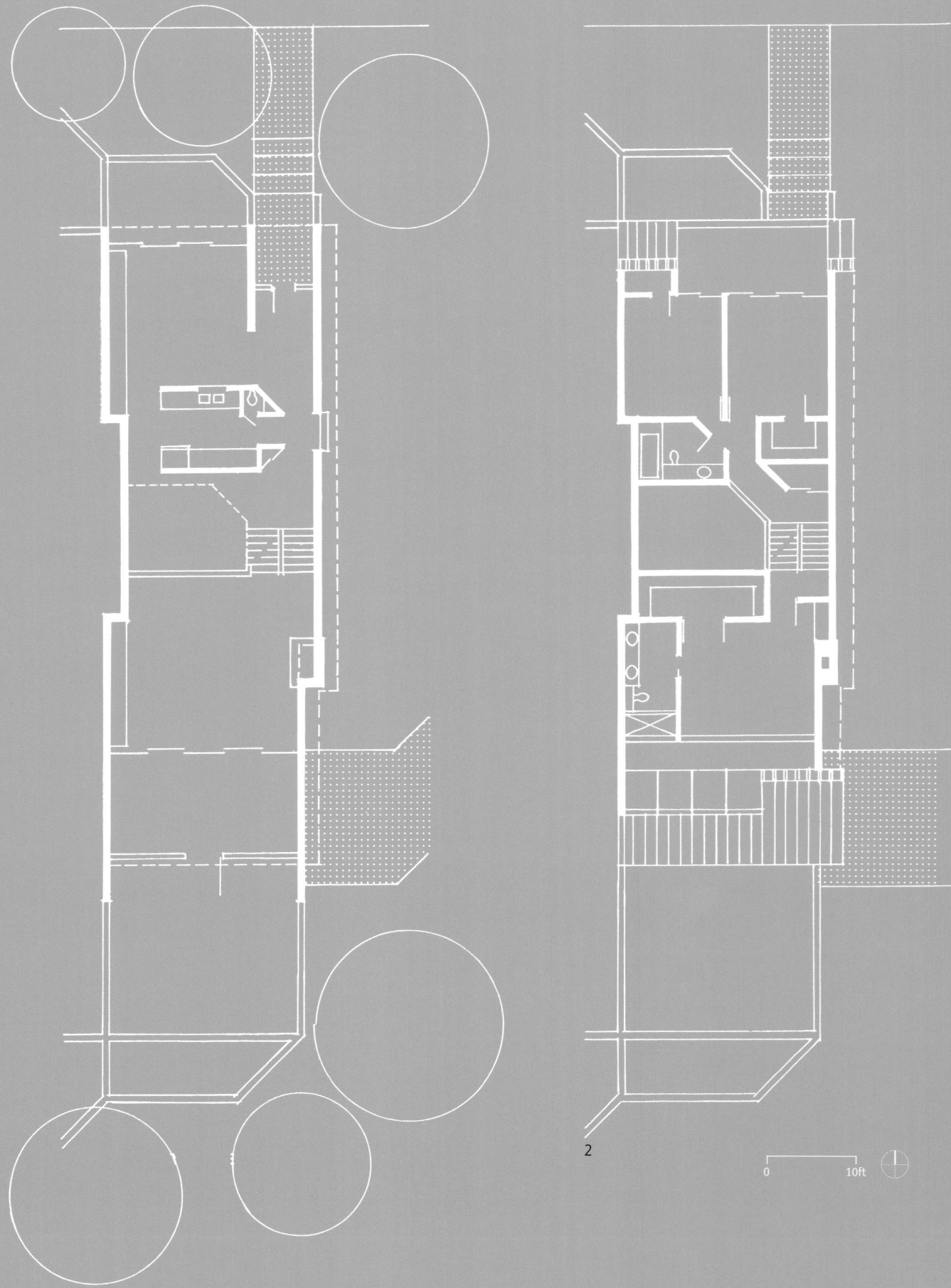

1

2

0          10ft

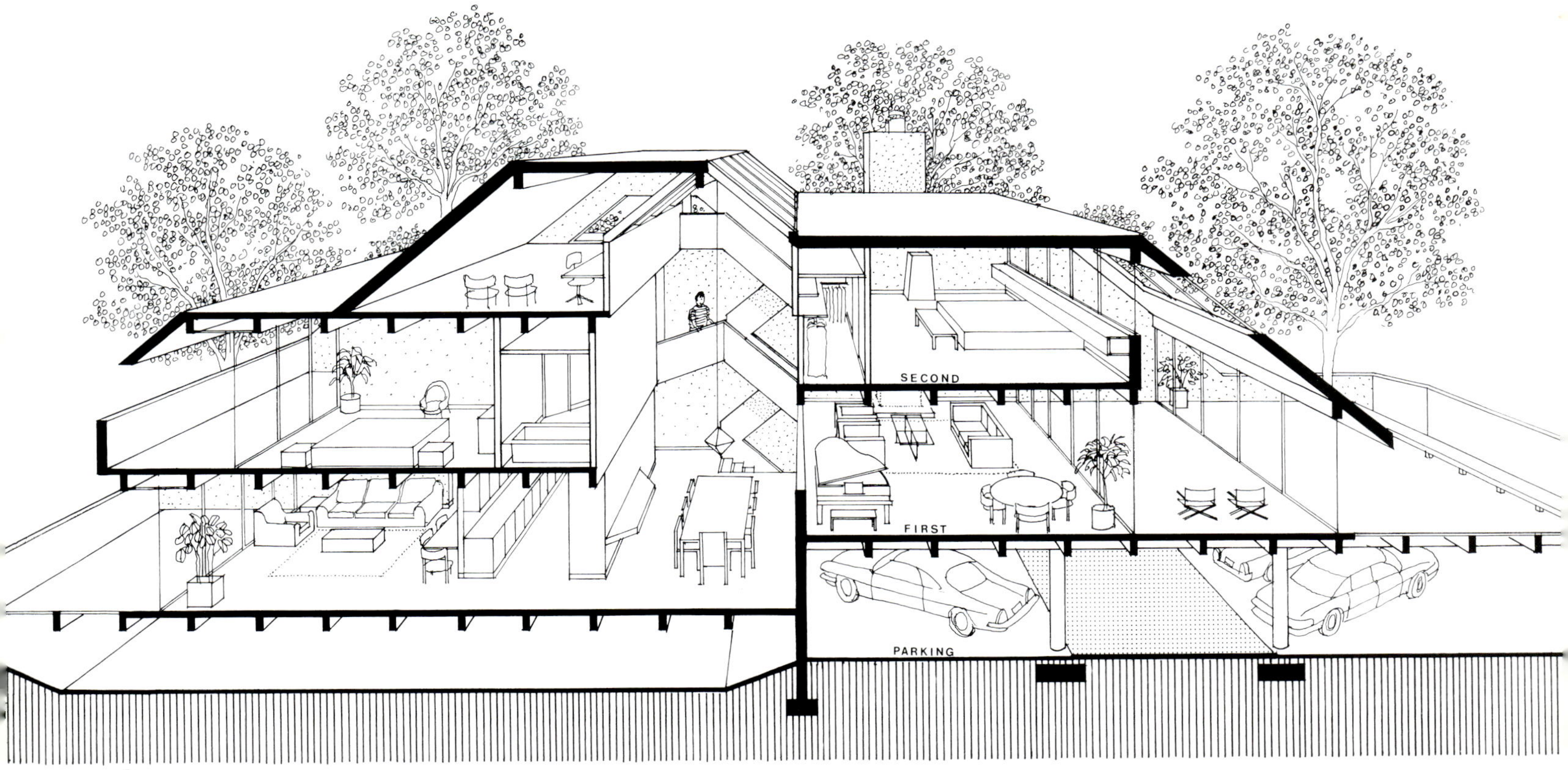

3

**Design/Construction
1989/1990**

Tampa, Florida
Mr and Mrs John Howey
2,840 square feet
Metal studs, drywall, seashell
stucco, carpet, wood, marble
and ceramic tile flooring,
copper, glass, and aluminum

1 Lower level floor plan
2 Upper level floor plan
3 Section perspective

# 25

## 2538 Bay Park Place

Stretched out from street to park, this three-story town-home has private front and rear entries. A full-height dining room with skylights and side stair is the transition space connecting six split levels. On the park side, a large open deck and screened porch with views to the park flank the formal living room and master bedroom suite. On the street side, the main entry connects to the kitchen, dining, and family room. Above this level are the living room and children's and master bedrooms. Finally, a top-level, skylit, studio-bedroom overlooks the dining room three levels below. The unit's concrete ceiling joists and decks are exposed to create a linear ceiling pattern in the major spaces.

1

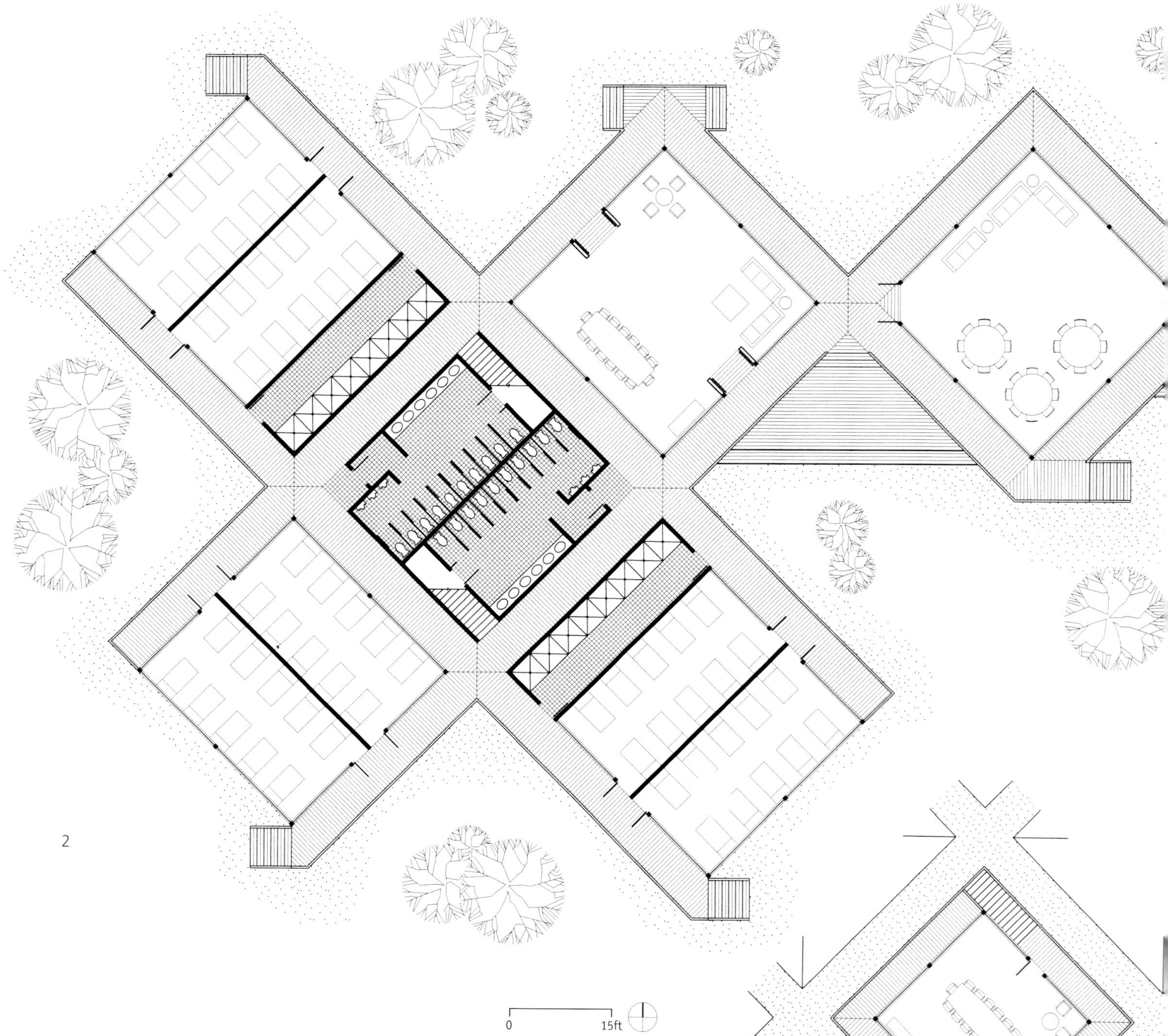

2

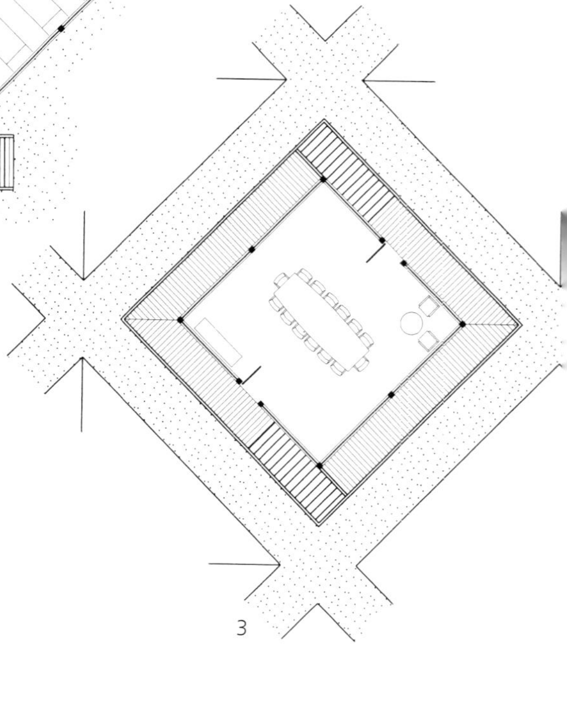

0        15ft

3

1   Elevation
2   Main level floor plan
3   Conference level floor plan
4   Site plan

Dayspring is one of the nation's foremost camp and conference centers. Located on the edge of the Manatee River near the Gulf of Mexico, its 92-acre site offers guests the opportunity to experience Florida's natural beauty with peace and tranquility in a religious setting. Designed to provide facilities for camping, conferences and retreats, the Center had outgrown its original multi-use building.

Howey's brief was to add a cluster of four youth cabins that could accommodate 20 residents each, and two seminar units. Six separate family cabins were also required. In order to catch the prevailing breezes and the view to a nearby pond and beyond, Howey raised the youth cabins 3 feet above grade. Elevated wooden walkways connected the private cabins with the public conference units and the main building and dining facility. The youth cabins were set at 45-degree angles to allow views to the pond from all units. Hipped roofs with exposed wood trusses and wall framing were the interior cabin finishes. The individual family cabins were completed with drywall, tile, and carpet. A loop driveway was designed to connect the main building with the youth and family cabins.

**26**

## Dayspring Conference Center

### Design 1987

Ellenton, Florida
Southwest Florida Episcopal Diocese
14,000 square feet
Concrete footings, post and beam framing, native stone, cedar roofs, glass, aluminum, cypress siding and decks

4

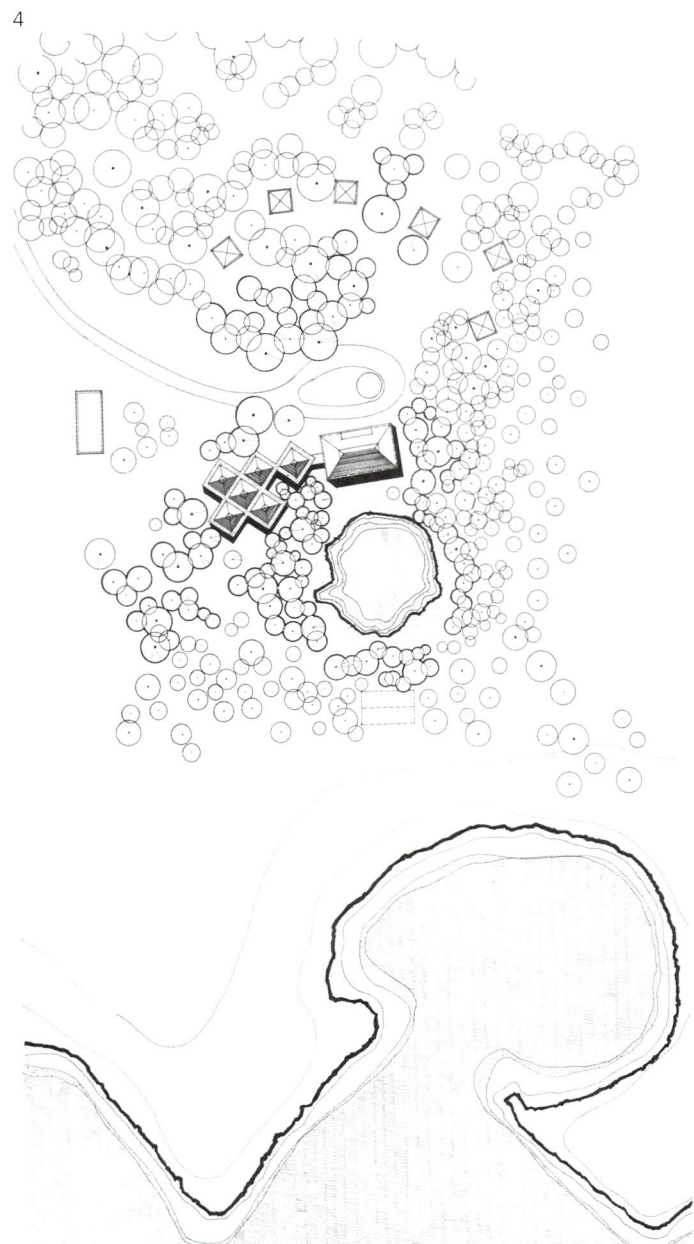

1

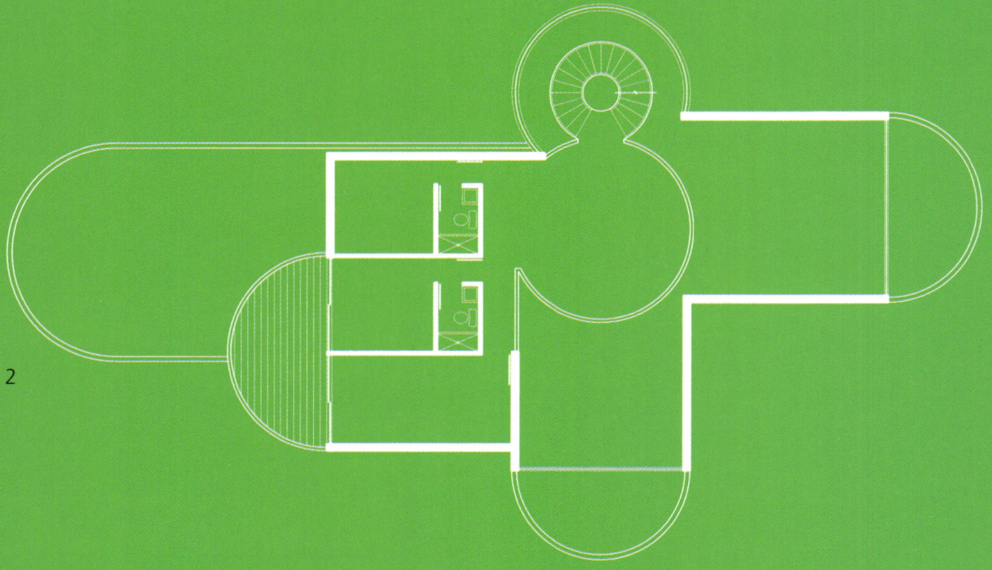

2

3

4

0    10ft

Port Richey, Florida
Mr and Mrs Peter Gilio
40 acres
Concrete piles, grade beams,
slab on grade, stucco, wood
frame, vertical cypress siding,
and built-up roof

This large tract of land contains two ecosystems: a bog fed by three interconnecting ponds, and a canopy of trees over the higher dry ground. The owners retained Howey to create a private estate for themselves, as well as future sites for individual residences on their land. In the final scheme, Howey placed the client's home near the central high elevation, with future lots dispersed along the property perimeters. A circular retaining wall defines their estate grounds and anchors the house to the land. Arrival is by entry-drive just below the home's main living level. The raised foyer to living, kitchen, and dining is accessed by a series of steps. Circular stairs connect children's bedrooms with the master bedroom suite perched at the top.

# 27

## Gilio Residence

1 Level three/master suite floor plan
2 Level two/children's floor plan
3 Level one/main living floor plan
4 View looking north
5 Section

5

1

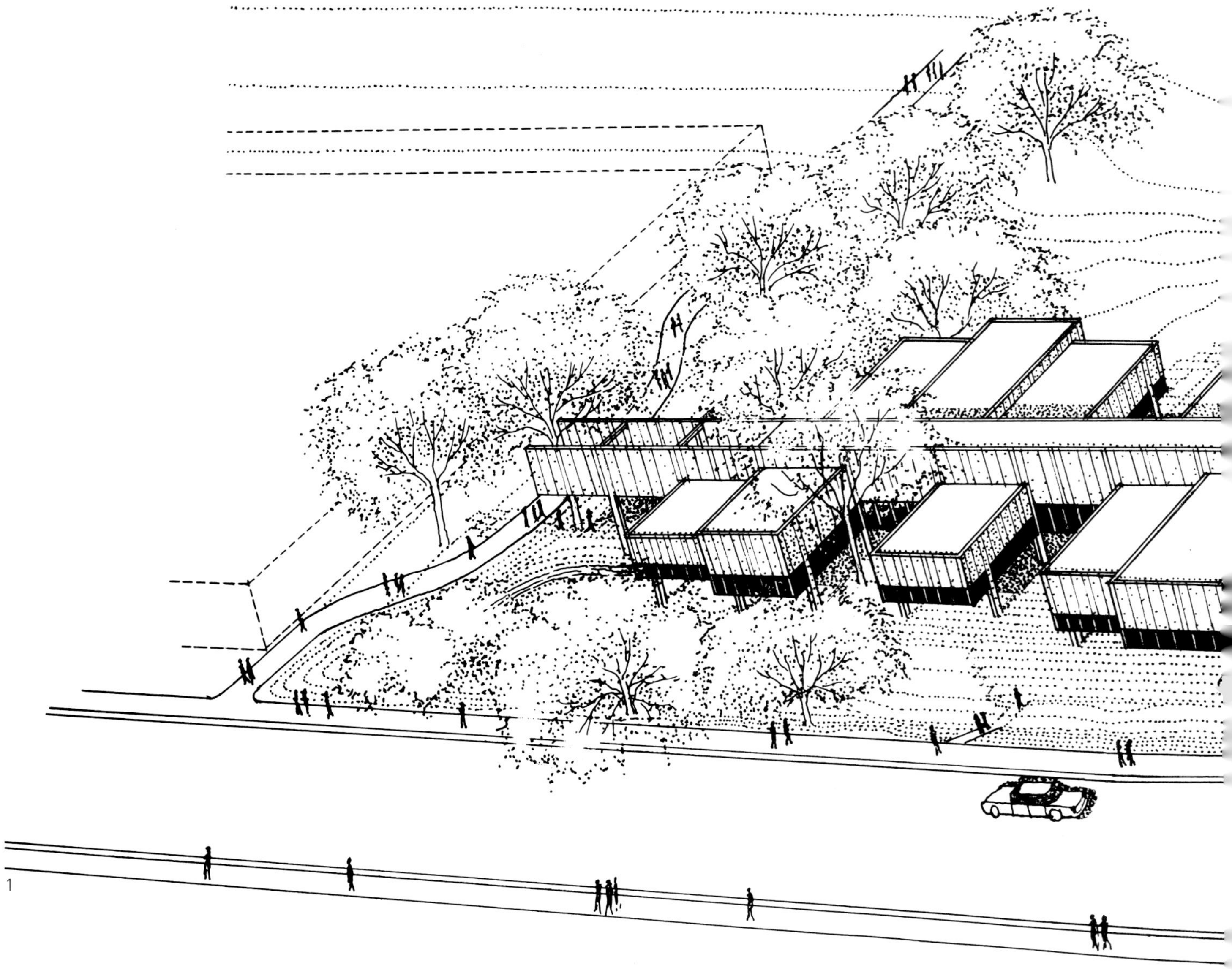

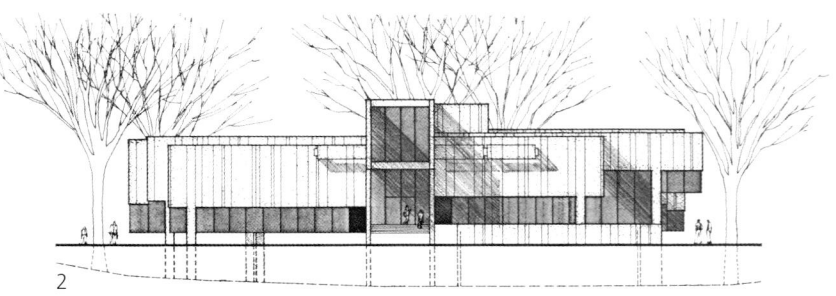

1 Perspective
2 East elevation
3 Longitudinal section

2

3

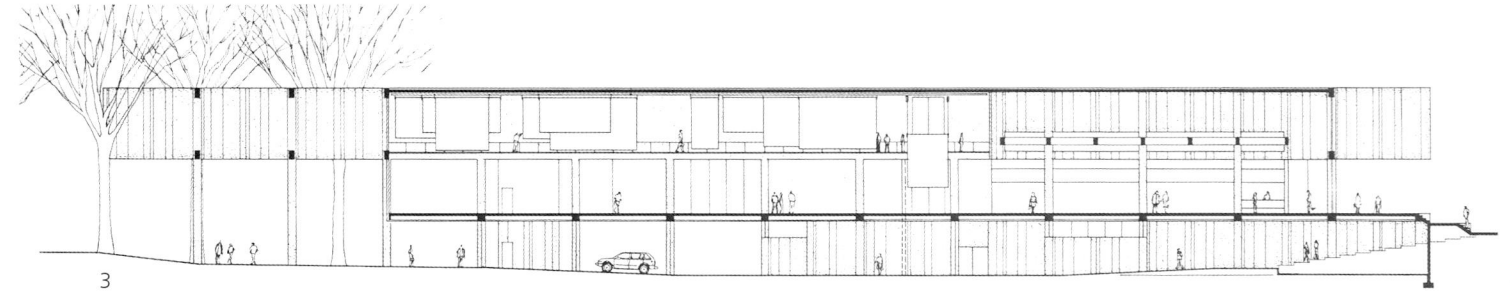

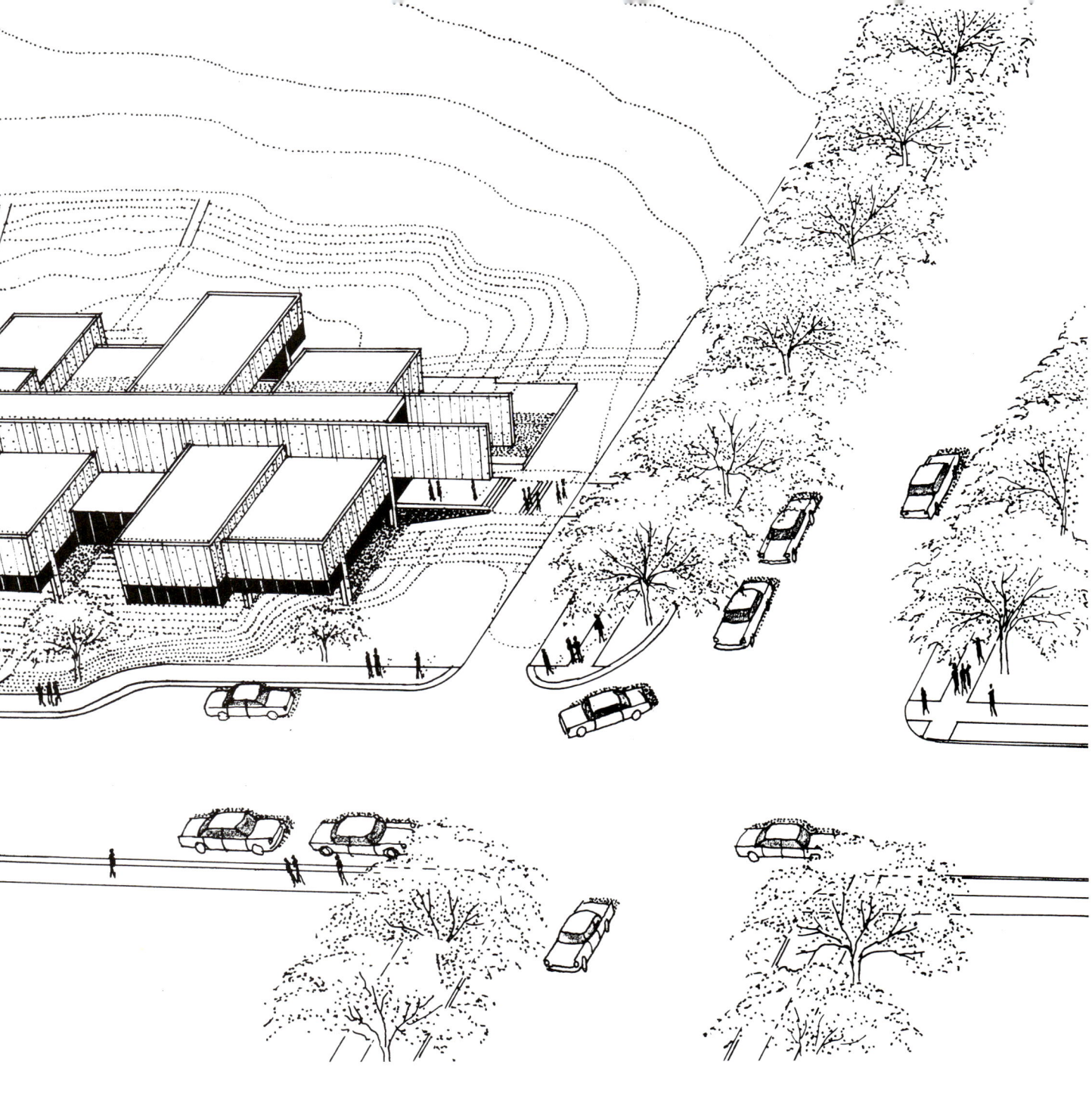

This entry was one of six finalists in a national competition for a new museum of art at the University of Florida. The uniqueness of the site, with its elongated bowl shape, large oak trees, and the possibility of water features, led Howey to bridge this existing dip with the main museum structure, affording parking, service, staff areas and storage underneath its lowest level. Inside, visitor services and all major galleries are situated on the main level, accessible from the central gallery corridor. Centered above the main galleries is a continuous attic utility space with tracks where temporary museum partitions and paintings up to 14 feet high may be stored. Administrative and curatorial offices are located on a mezzanine level next to the lower lobby. A double-glazed, indirect, natural lighting system was proposed to provide museum-quality, natural illumination in the galleries.

## 28

### Museum Competition

### Design 1985

Gainesville, Florida
University of Florida
45,000 square feet
Cast-in-place, precast concrete
floor and roof structure, and
wall panels

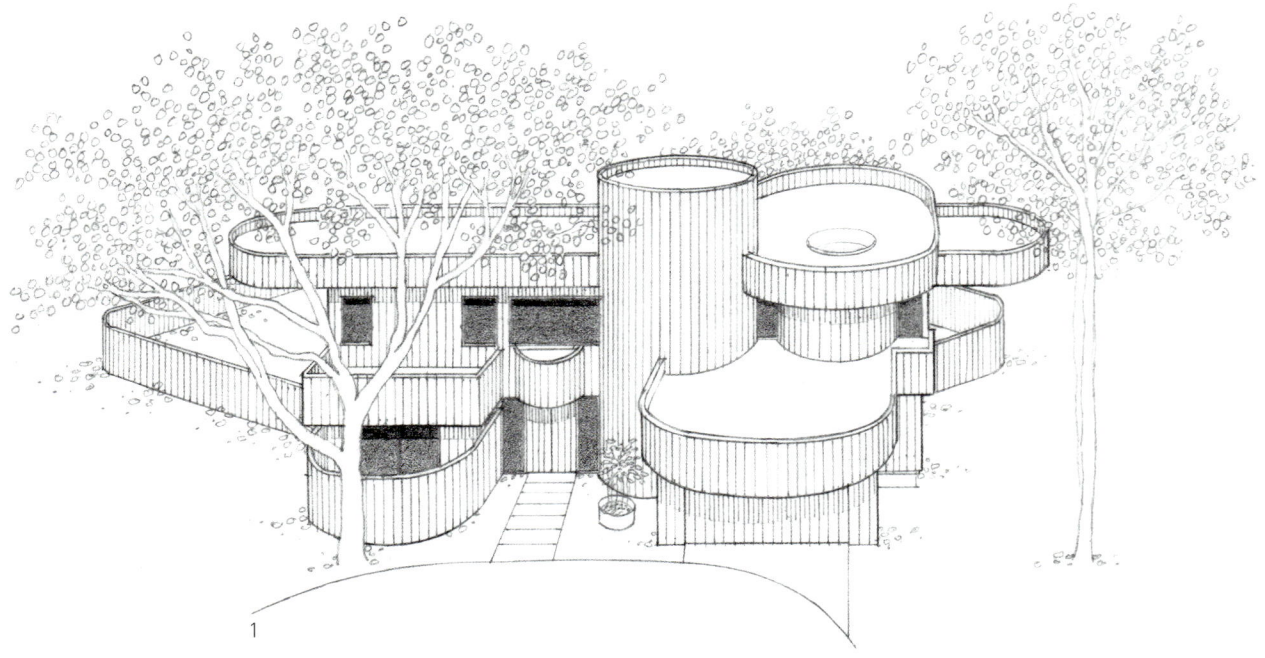

1

3

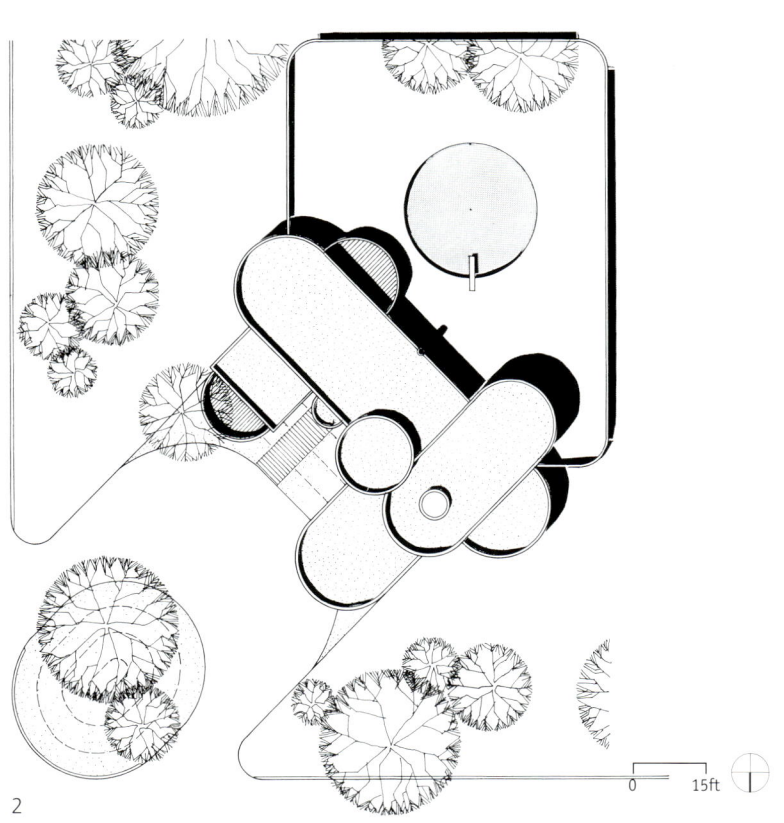

2

0        15ft

**Design/Completion
1979/1980**

Tampa, Florida
A Richard Williers
3,000 square feet
Slab on grade, wood and steel
framing, vertical lapped
or ship-lapped 1 x 6 cedar,
copper, bronze, cypress
decks, tinted glass, acrylic
skylight, drywall, carpet,
and ceramic tile

Situated on an in-town wooded lot for a bachelor whose place of business is nearby, this residence was designed by Howey with two zones in mind. The first zone is entered from beneath a bridge that leads to a two-story living area. At one side is the formal dining room, kitchen, bar, and garage. At the other side is a guest bedroom wing. The second zone above is the personal sleeping and recreation area. The sleeping area has a dressing room and bath with a nautilus-inspired shower for two. The bedroom is connected by bridge to a large recreation space at the other end of the house, where hot tub and exercise equipment are located. Because the residence is situated on a corner lot, and to save a large oak tree, the structure was turned 45 degrees to its site boundaries. All zoned spaces focus out, with large glass areas, balconies and decks open to a rear, wall-enclosed, landscaped swimming pool area. Formal entry is to the gallery bordering the living space, with a circular stair from the gallery to the second-level balcony. All spaces have high bands of continuous glass to provide uninterrupted, private views of the many oak trees and natural landscaping.

4

1   Perspective
2   Site plan
3&4  Exterior views

# 29
## Williers House

5

6

0    10ft

7

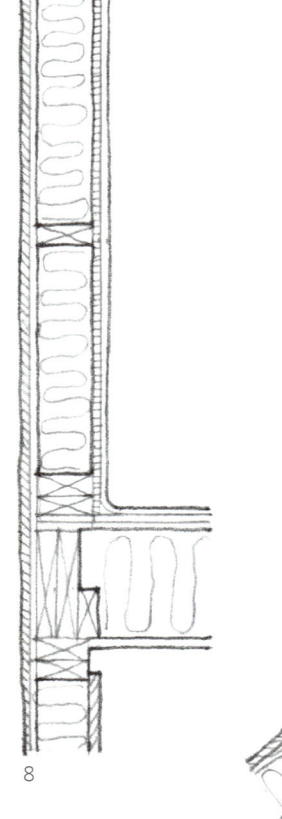

8

9

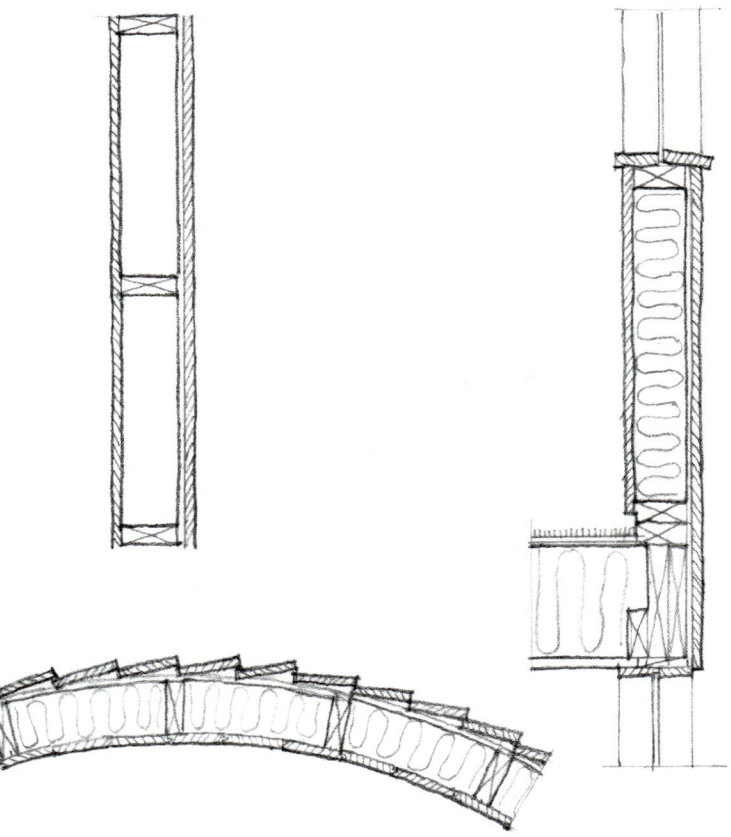

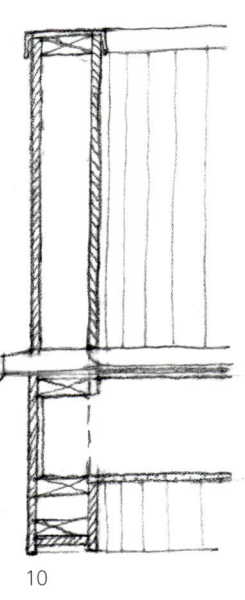

10

5    Upper floor plan
6    Lower floor plan
7&9  Interior views
8&10 Detail sketches

12

11　Master bedroom view over living space
12　View to master bathroom

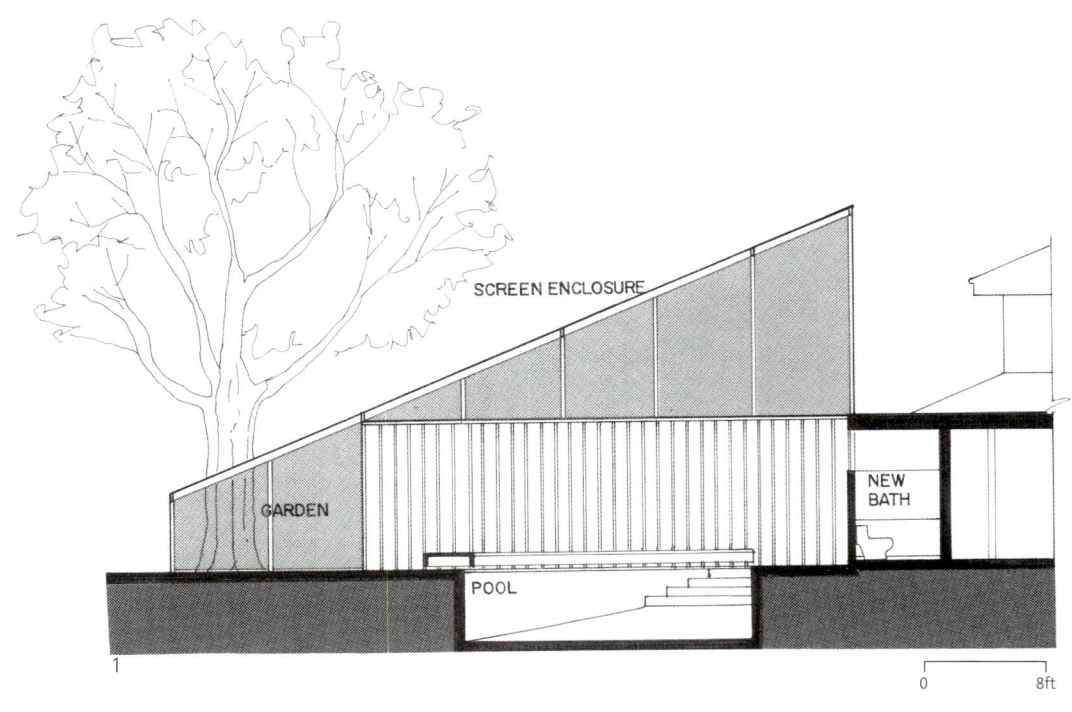

SCREEN ENCLOSURE

GARDEN

NEW BATH

POOL

1

0          8ft

2

3

1 Section
2–4 Interior and exterior
    views of addition

# 30

## Residence Additions

**Design/Completion**
**1975/1976**

Tampa, Florida
Mr and Mrs Robert Blanchard
3,500 square feet
Poured-in-place concrete,
wood framing, gypsum,
cypress board and batten,
cedar decking, fiberglass
screen and aluminum frame

The owners had outgrown their current residence and wished to take advantage of expansion into their large back yard with a new screen-enclosed pool and deck complex. A new kitchen, informal dining room, bathroom, expanded family room, and a three-car garage would border this new outdoor area. The site lay in an oak hammock with lush subtropical undergrowth. A matching front entry walk, with attendant landscaping, was also requested. Examination of the property revealed that it was possible to locate the pool with a 42-inch grand oak tree remaining at the edge of the enclosure, and with the new garage forming one wall of the complex. An elevated sunbathing platform along one perimeter of the pool becomes a waterfall at its lower edge. The enlarged garden was planned to grow on both sides of the screen enclosure to give the feeling of spaciousness and create a natural background for the pool when viewed from the house.

4

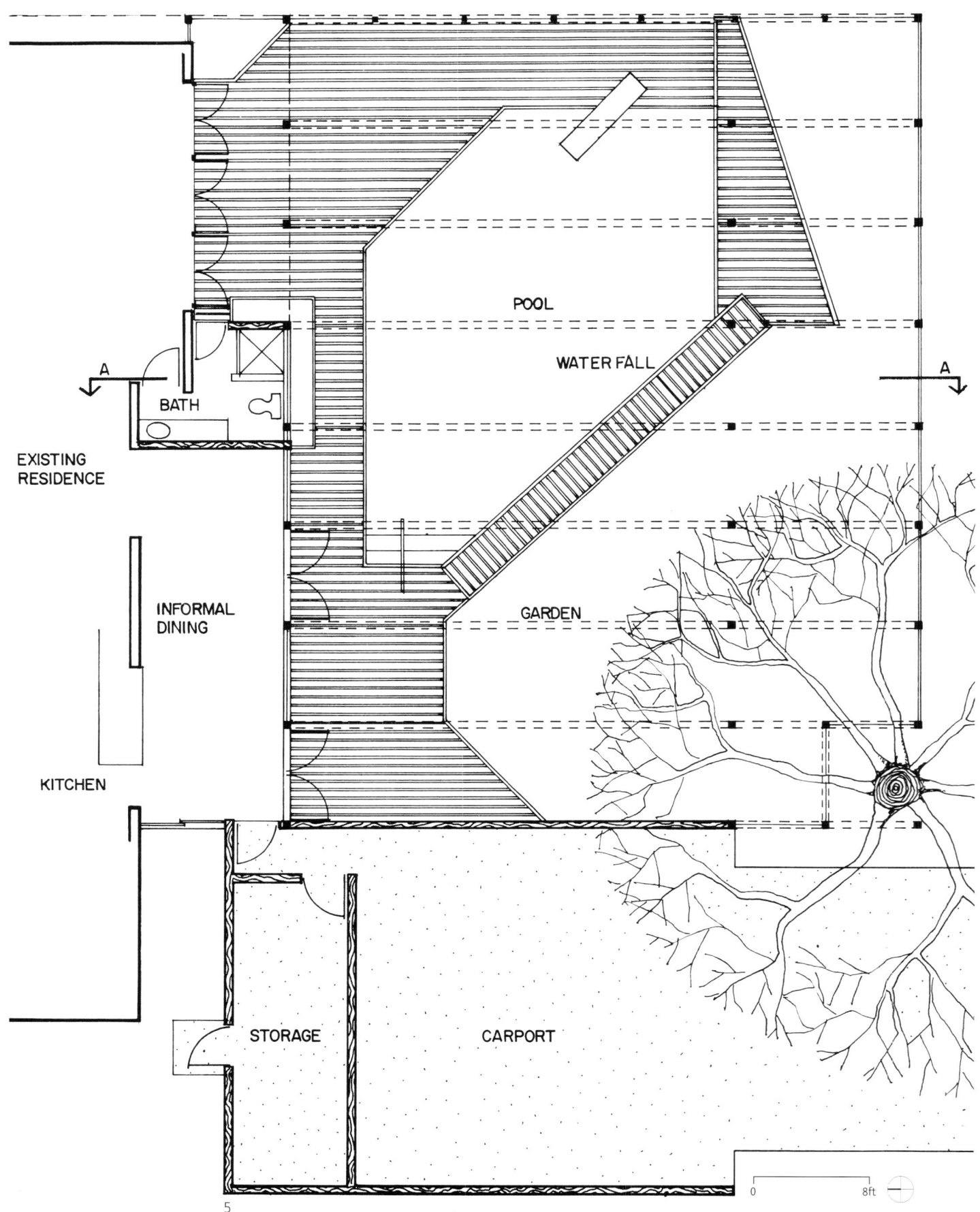

POOL

WATER FALL

A

EXISTING
RESIDENCE

BATH

INFORMAL
DINING

GARDEN

KITCHEN

STORAGE

CARPORT

A

0          8ft

5

6

7

8

5   Site plan
6–8   Views of addition

1

2

3

4

5

6

This six-unit town-home infill project in an established Tampa neighborhood included the first residence designed by Howey for his family. Of 21 existing oak trees on the site, 20 were saved. The interior of each unit has three stories, each divided into six half-levels accessed by a central stair. The lower three levels are garage and living spaces, while the upper three levels are bedrooms. The entry, kitchen, dining and living rooms are raised 4 feet 6 inches above grade for views over a deck enclosed by a low wall. The complex is earth-bermed at the street to achieve a lower residential look. The town-home roofs are sloped to match the adjacent neighboring two-story residential roofs. The building angularity continues inside where ceilings fold into the stair space. Three front-facing units have driveway access directly from the street, while a brick driveway from the street wraps around to access three rear-facing units. By rotating every other unit 180 degrees, a pattern of undulating windows and roofs is created. In 1976, the unit costs were $55,000 each.

# 31
## Bay Villa Townhomes

### Design/Completion
### 1974/1976

Tampa, Florida
Bay Villa, Inc.
12,000 square feet
Spread concrete footings,
concrete block party walls,
frame floors and roof,
battened seam galvalume,
brick, stucco, glass,
aluminum, and cedar

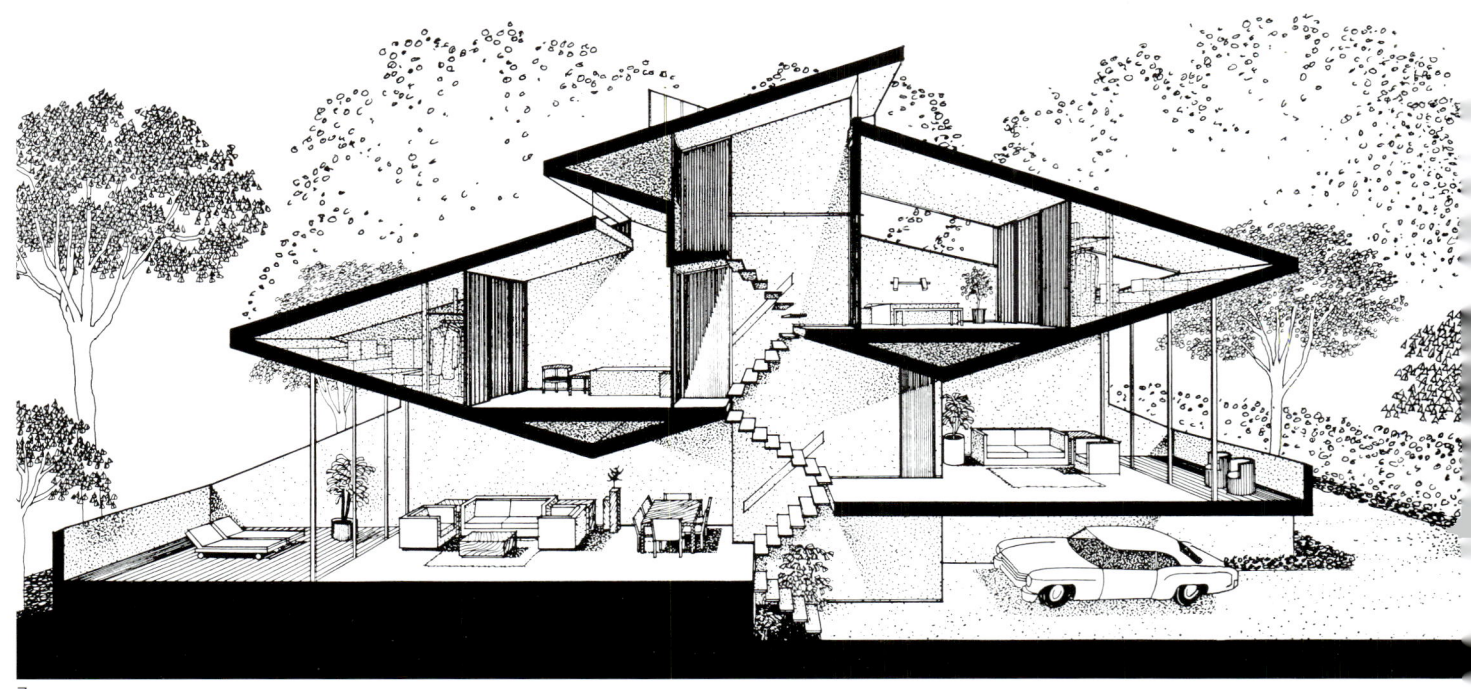

7

8

9

7   Section perspective
8&9  Interior views
10   Level 2 and 2.5 floor plan
11   Level 1 and 1.5 floor plan
12   Level 0 and 0.5 floor plan

10

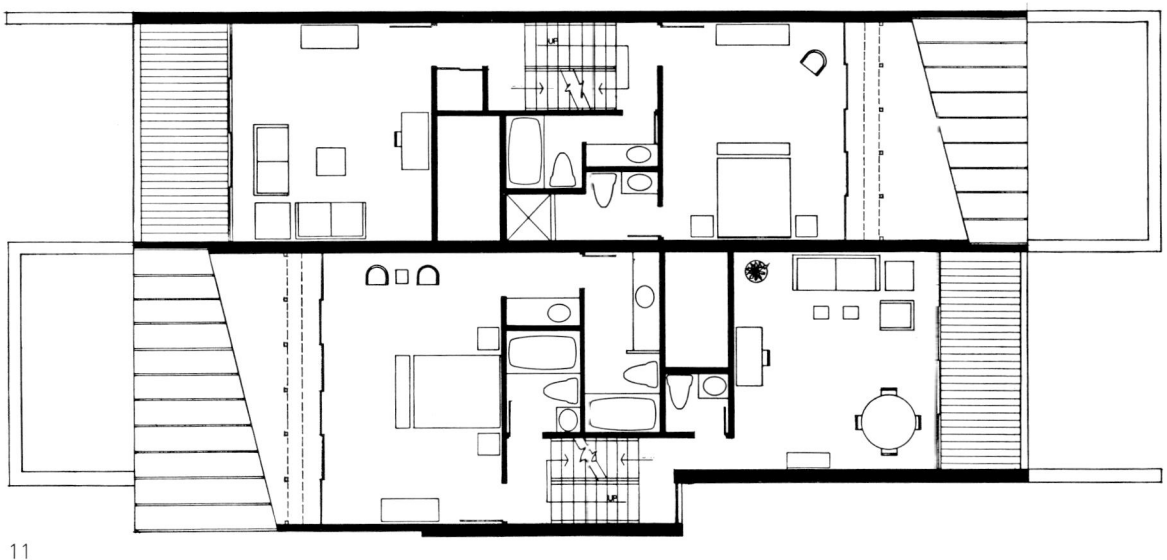

11

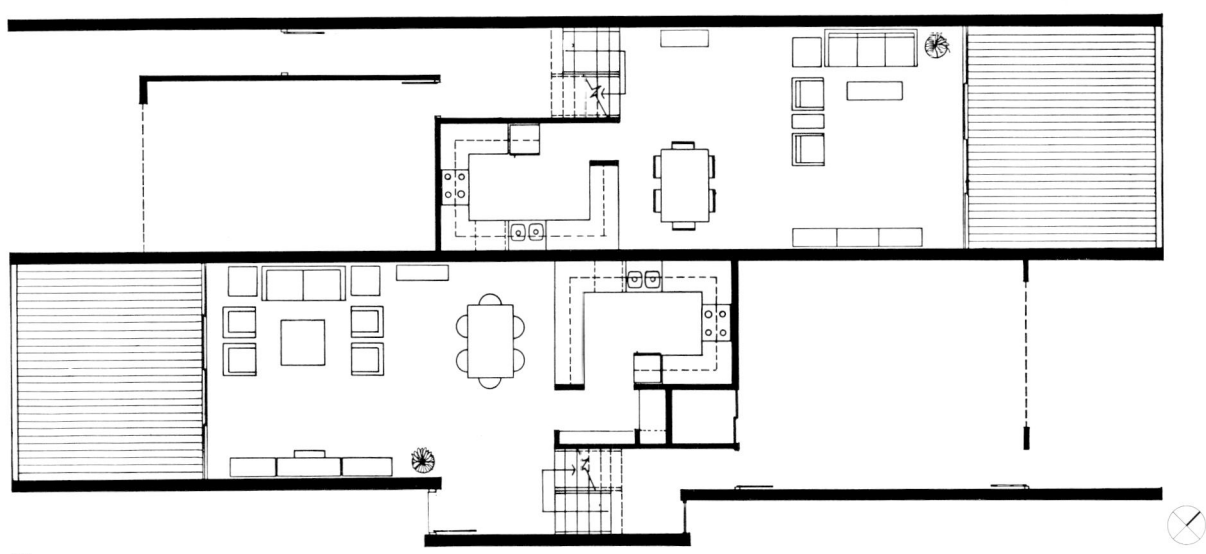

12

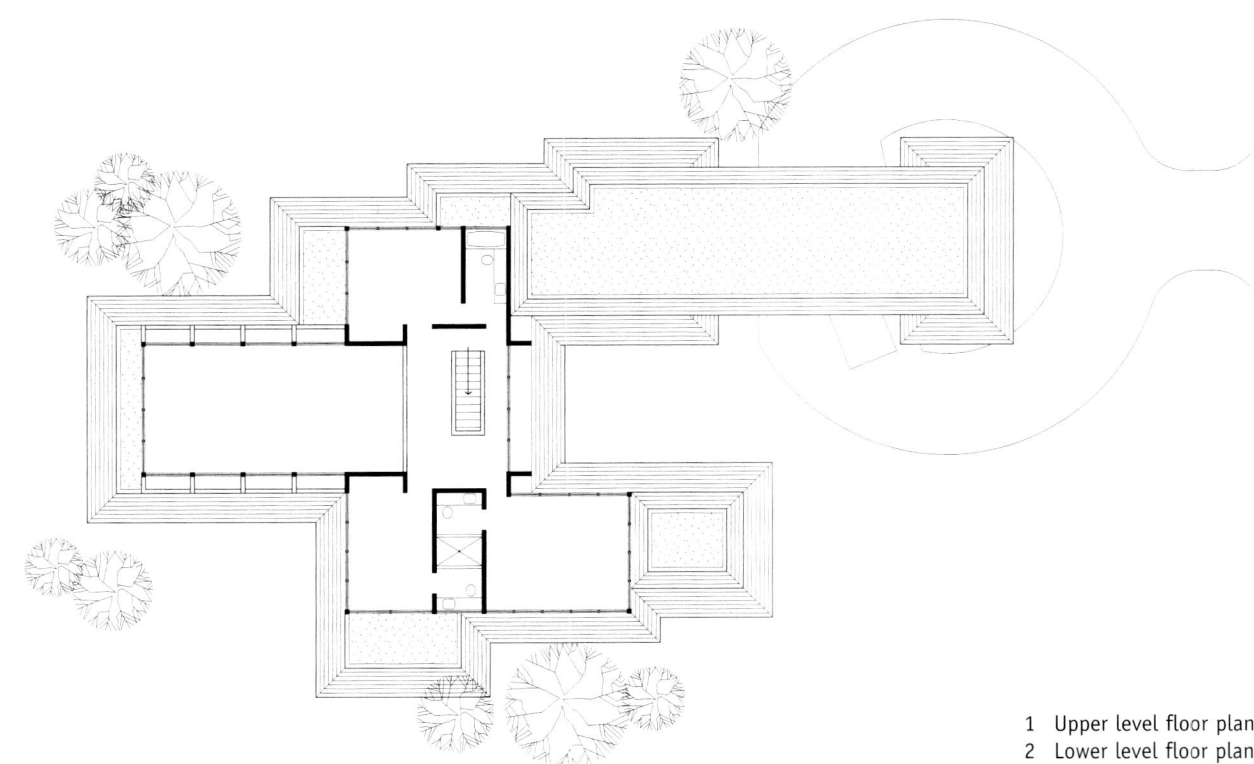

1

1  Upper level floor plan
2  Lower level floor plan
3  Section
4  Rendering

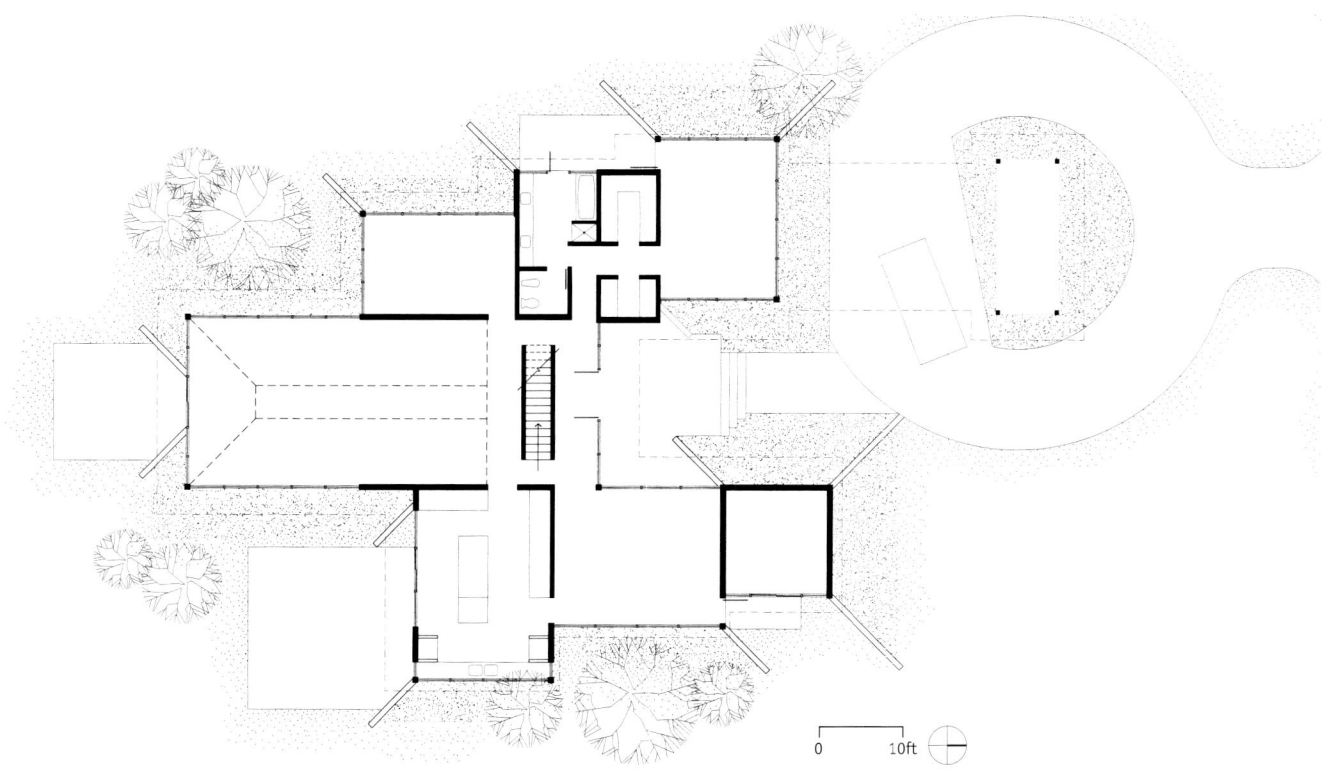

2

0        10ft

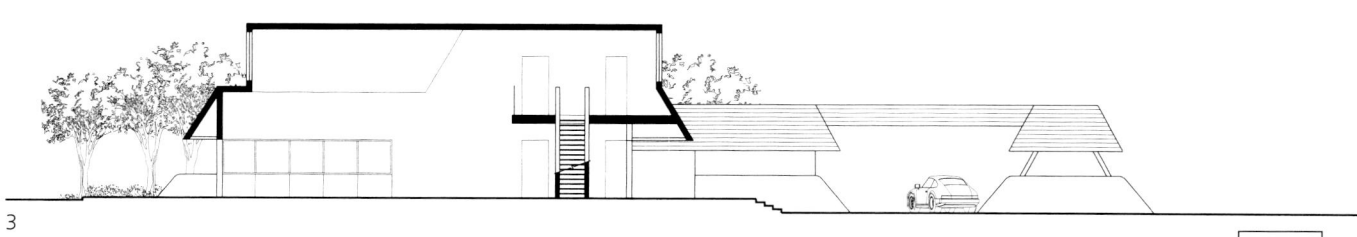

3

0        10ft

## Design 1973/1974

Davis Island, Tampa
Mr and Mrs Vance Smith
4,000 square feet
Concrete foundations, wood
and steel framing, masonry,
stucco, and wood siding

This in-town island site, with its concrete seawall and boat slip, fronts a canal that leads to Hillsborough Bay. Its land, dredged up from the bay in the 1920s, forms a narrow parallelogram with neighbors close on either long side. The major view is to the water. By stepping individual rooms, such as the library and master bedroom, along the lot-lines, each receives a private view to the canal. The building sidewalls were earth-bermed to further insulate these spaces from the neighbors.

Inside, movement is linear, from the two-story central foyer, to the living area, and then to the outside patio and the water. Tucked into this horizontal layering at the second level are three bedrooms that are grouped around the central space. A first-level porte-cochere extends the structure's horizontality to the street. After preparing three schemes, Howey's stepped-roof design was approved. At that point, the mid-1970s recession intervened, terminating the project.

4

# 32

## Smith Residence

1 Upper level floor plan
2 Lower level floor plan
3 Sections
4 Perspective looking north

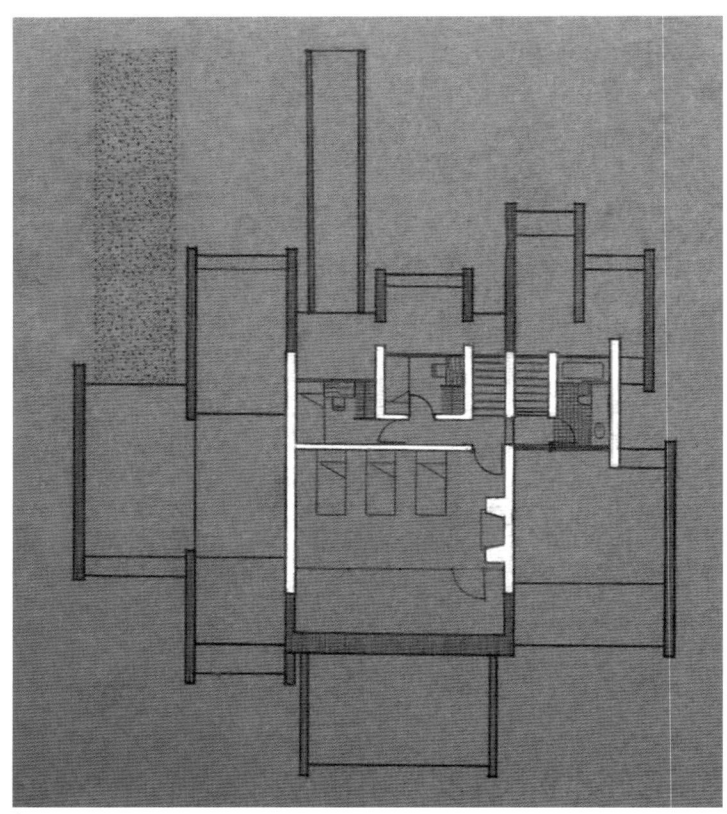

1

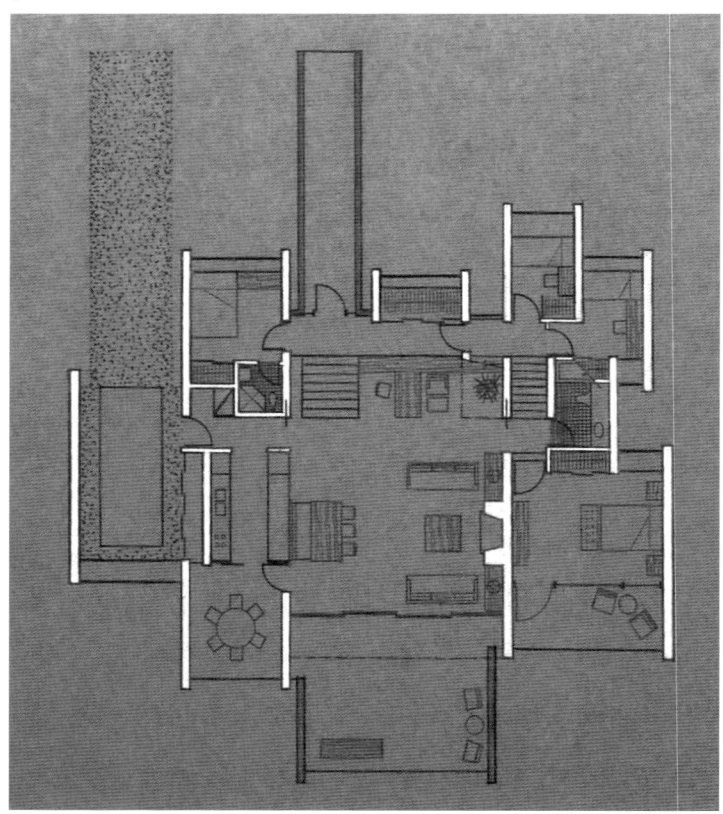

2

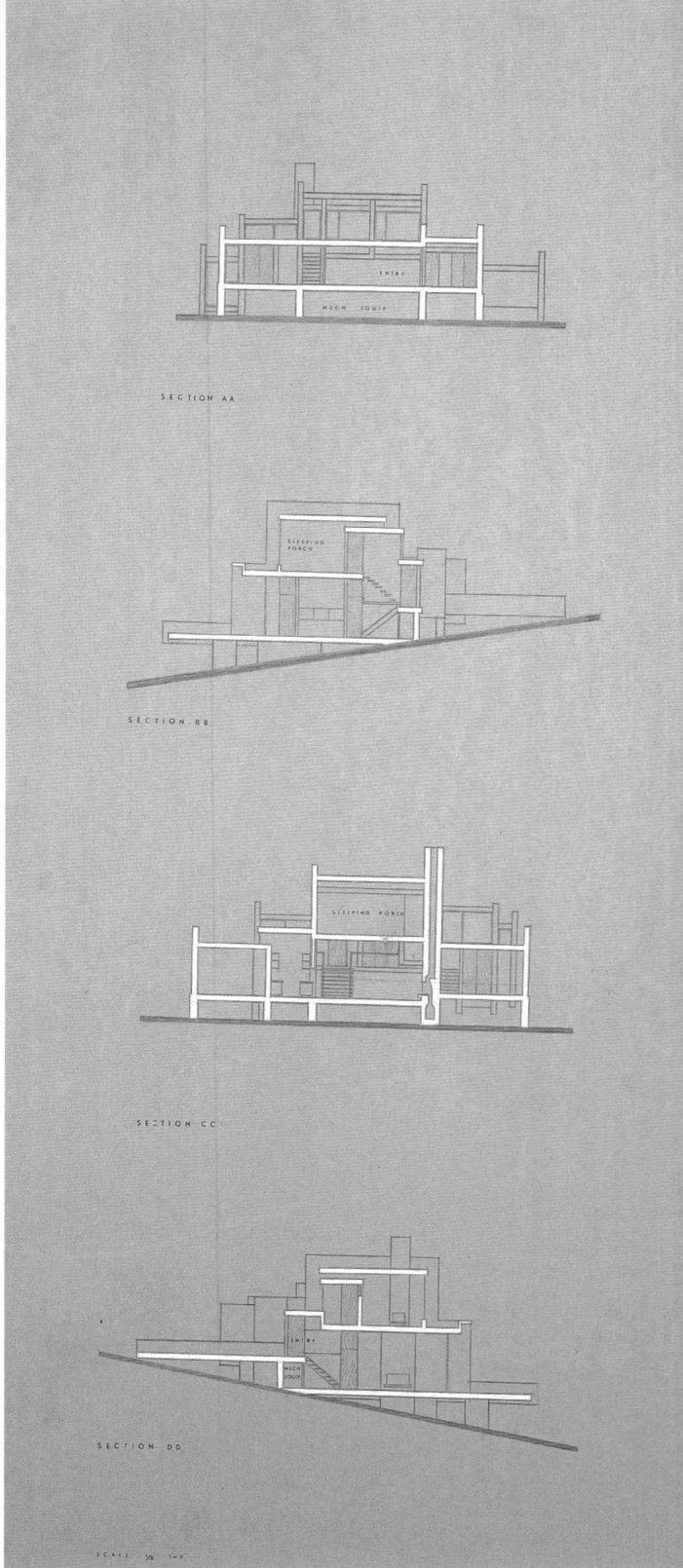

3

4

This multi-level residence was the first of two residences Howey designed for the same client over a 20-year period. The residence was to be located on a 2-acre wooded site on a bluff overlooking the Chattahoochee River in northern Atlanta. The client's desires were unusual in several respects. To meet the $25,000 budget and accommodate a family of six, four cell-like children's bedrooms with built-in furniture were required, along with the master bedroom and a guest room. These bedrooms were to be accessible to an upper-level, screened, sleeping porch that would be used during the summer months. The combined living–dining–recreation space with a massive stone fireplace was located on the main level. A galley kitchen, carport, and small workshop completed the requirements. Since layers of granite rock crossed much of the site, building on and above the existing site grade was chosen rather than leveling or excavating the land. Work stopped when the clients moved from Atlanta to North Carolina.

### Design 1965

Atlanta, Georgia
Mr and Mrs Payson Kennedy
2,500 square feet
Poured concrete piers support
a raised wood framing system,
wood siding, native stone,
drywall, aluminum, and glass

# 33

## Kennedy Residence One

EARTH

# 34
## Summer Residence

Howey designed this French vacation house for a well-known twentieth-century architectural photographer and his wife. Situated in a hilly agricultural area with rock walls and gabled farmhouses, the sloping site was edged with hedgerows and surrounded by vineyards. Requirements were minimal: living, dining, and kitchen areas would be in one undivided space; there would be a single bedroom, a dressing area, and one bathroom. On the exterior there was to be a stone terrace at the main entry and an attached garage. The design, while contemporary, was compatible with the stone farmhouses in the area. The construction was not realized due to bureaucratic red tape.

**Design 1993**
Loire River Valley, France
Mr and Mrs Alexandre Georges
1,500 square feet
Concrete, native stone, wood frame with trusses, stucco, and glass

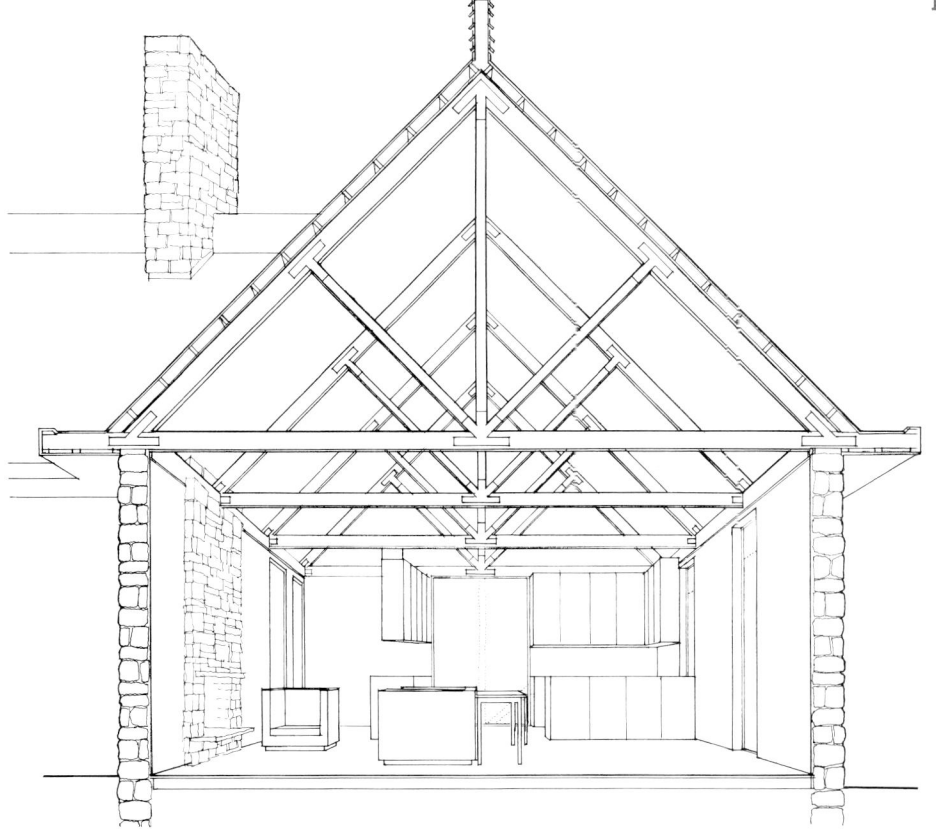

Opposite  Perspective
2  Section perspective

2

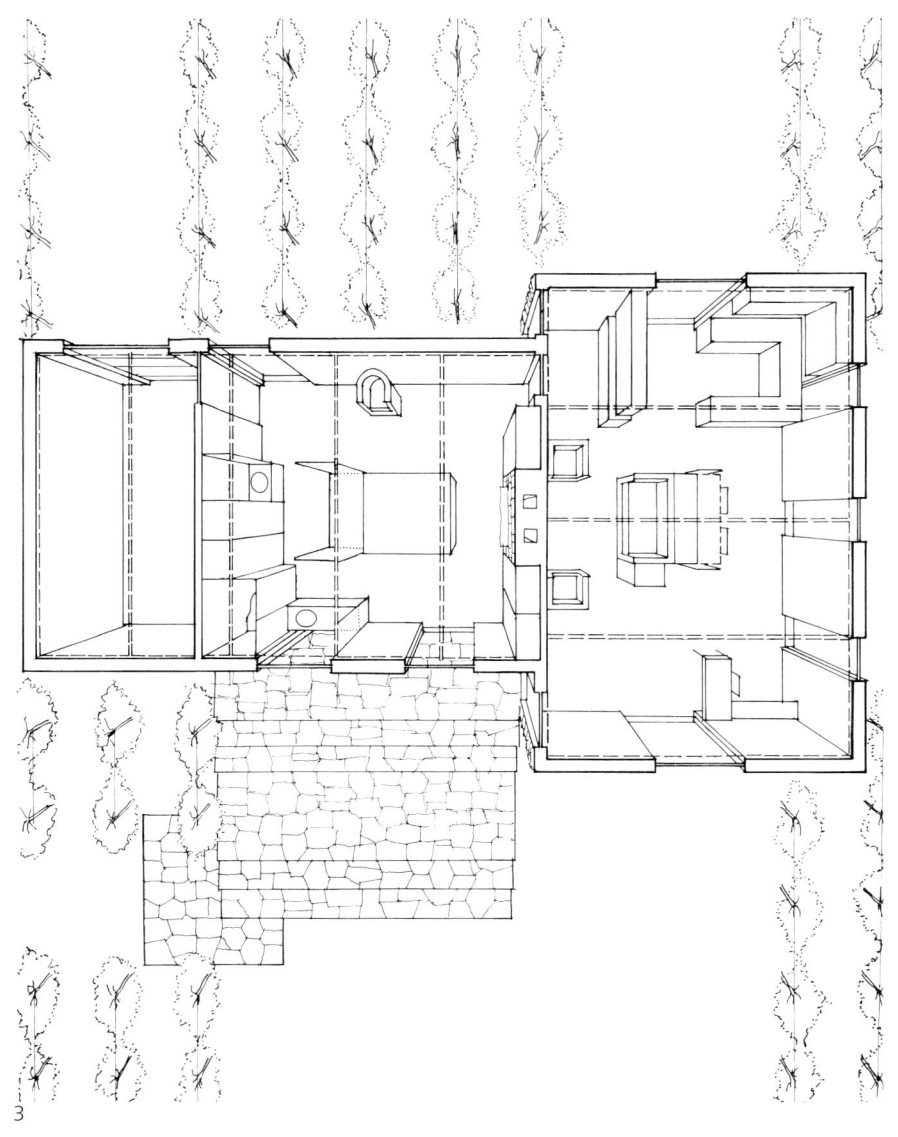

3

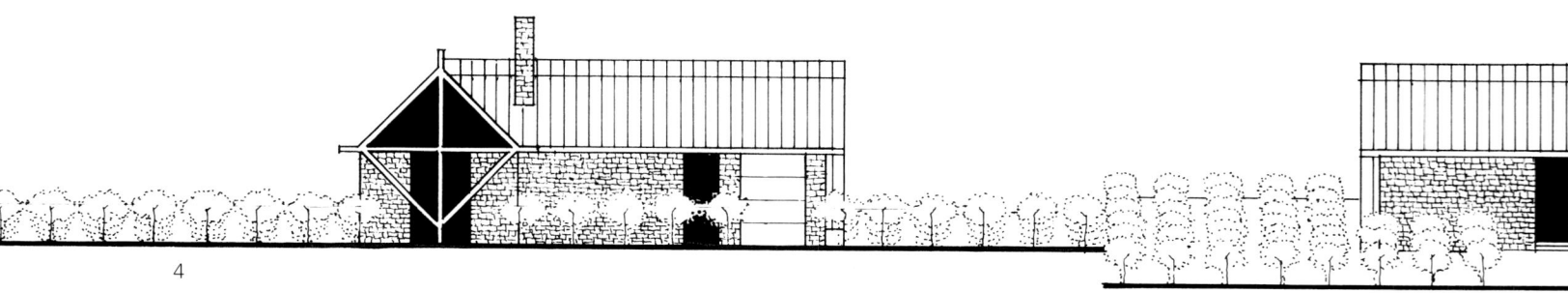

4

5

**PLAN, FACADES**

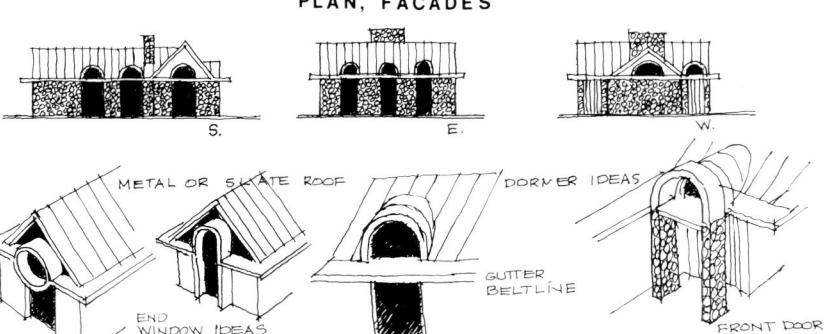

S.        E.        W.

METAL OR SLATE ROOF

DORMER IDEAS

GUTTER
BELTLINE

END
WINDOW IDEAS

FRONT DOOR

**1. ARCHES**

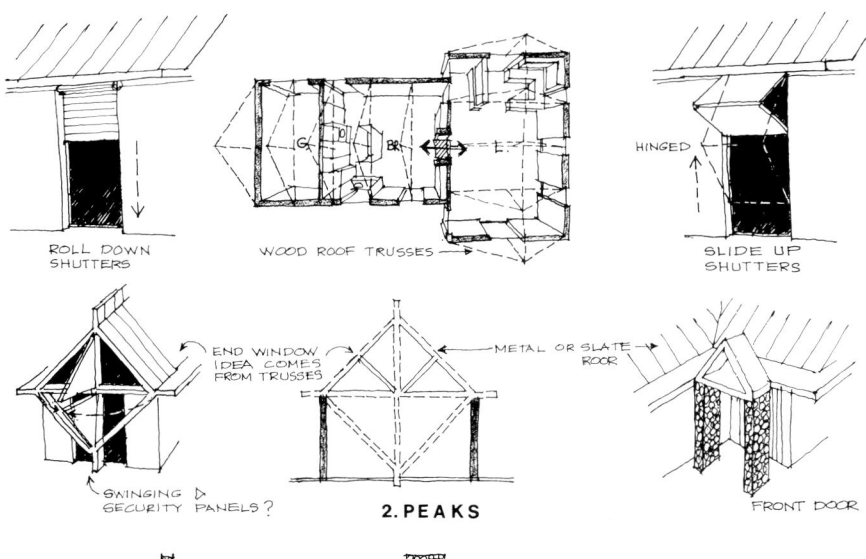

ROLL DOWN
SHUTTERS

WOOD ROOF TRUSSES

HINGED

SLIDE UP
SHUTTERS

END WINDOW
IDEA COMES
FROM TRUSSES

METAL OR SLATE
ROOF

SWINGING
SECURITY PANELS?

**2. PEAKS**

FRONT DOOR

S.        E.

6

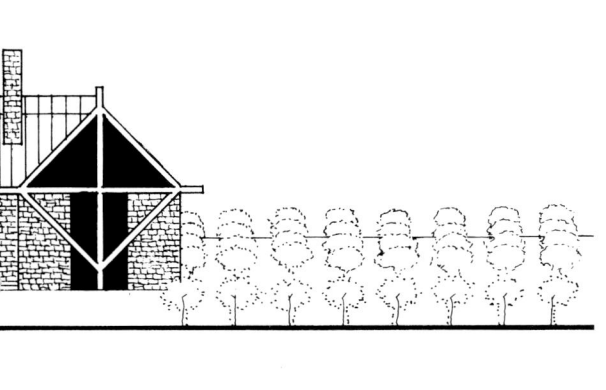

7

**INTERIORS**

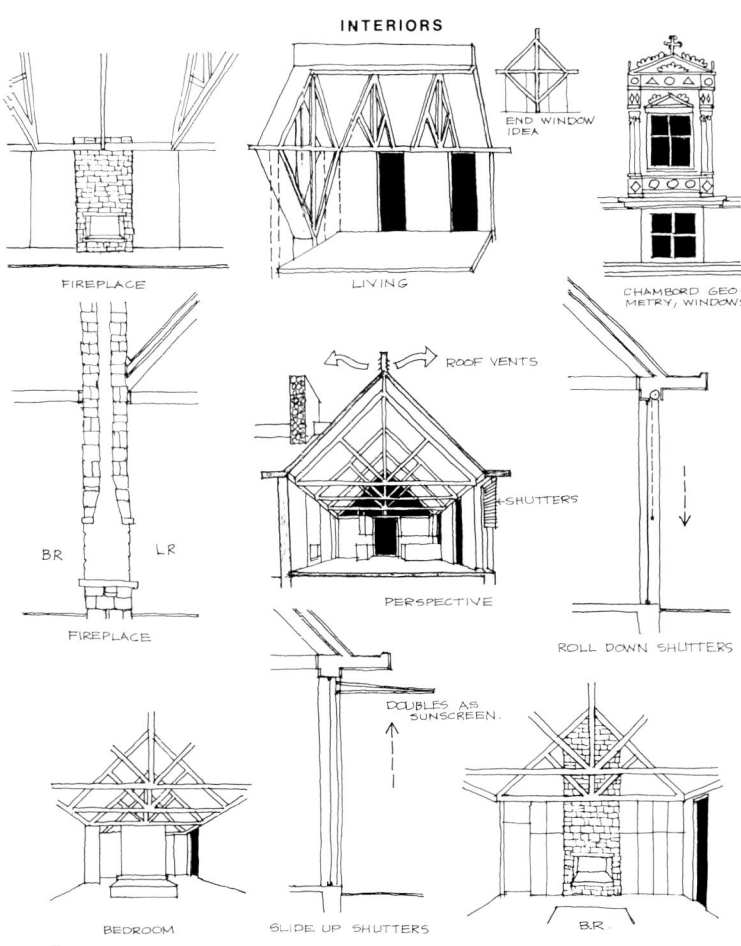

FIREPLACE

LIVING

END WINDOW
IDEA

CHAMBORD GEO-
METRY, WINDOWS

BR        LR

FIREPLACE

ROOF VENTS

SHUTTERS

PERSPECTIVE

ROLL DOWN SHUTTERS

BEDROOM

DOUBLES AS
SUNSCREEN.

SLIDE UP SHUTTERS

B.R.

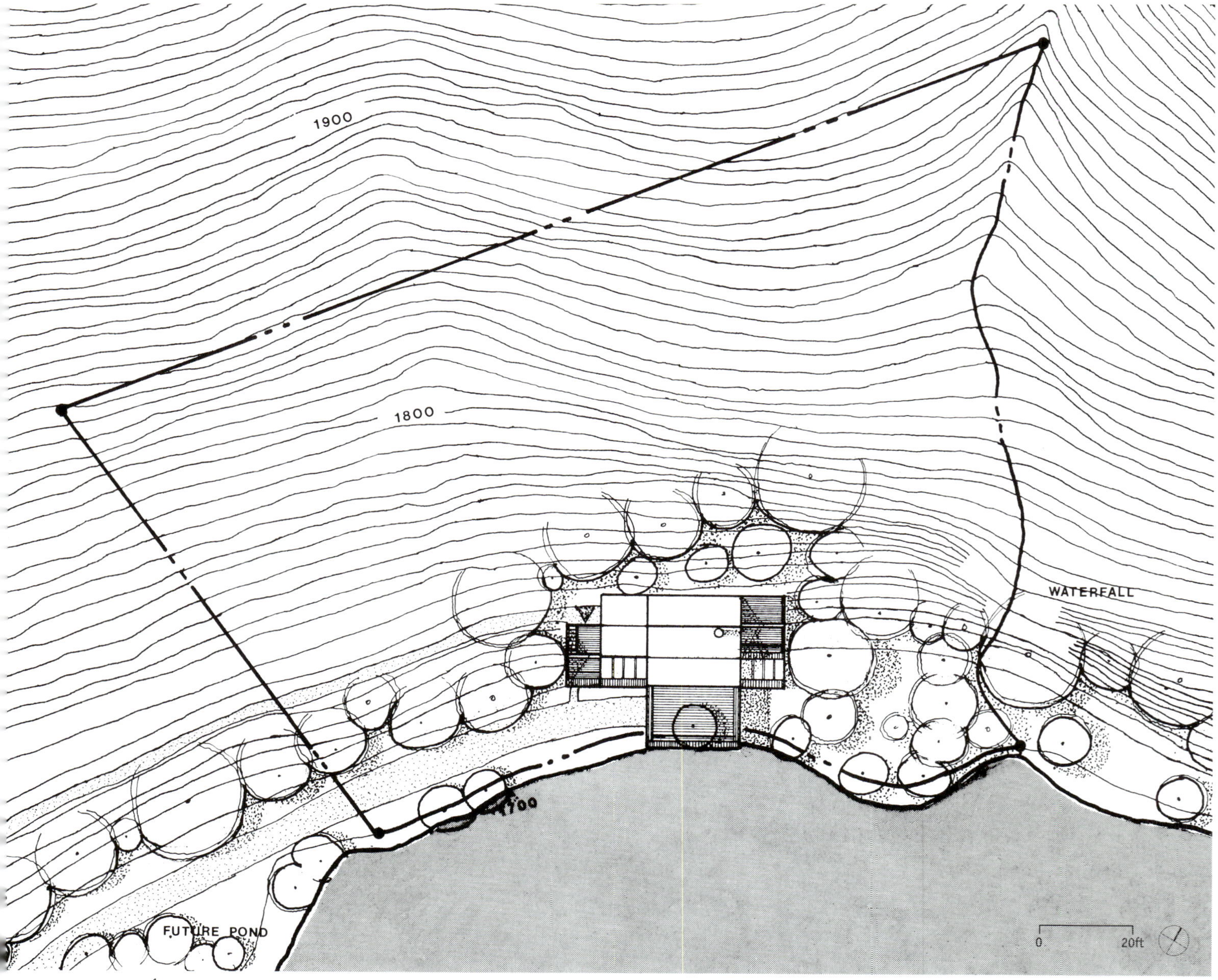

1900

1800

WATERFALL

1700

FUTURE POND

0    20ft

1

3

2

## Design/Completion
## 1982/1984

Wesser, North Carolina
Mr and Mrs Payson Kennedy
2,900 square feet
Wood trusses on reinforced
concrete piers set on rock;
tongue and groove wood
decking between trusses for
floors, ceilings and roofs;
wood siding, native stone,
drywall, and glass

This residence was designed for two adventurers, a husband and wife, who founded a successful outdoor recreation center in North Carolina in the 1970s.

Because of their background in trekking and whitewater trips around the world, the clients selected an unusually rocky site with a 45-degree slope to the old bed of the Nantahala River. The site provides a 180-degree southerly view; a small waterfall borders the eastern side of the property. Large glass areas to the south were desired, to take advantage of passive solar gain in the winter, and the views of a pond, which the owners created on the abandoned riverbed.

Client requirements were minimal. Entry is from a private approach trail to the kitchen, dining, and living area that has a large stone fireplace. A separate guest bedroom with private shower on the main level was necessary for frequent overnight guests. Above the living area is a large loft with the master bedroom, a bedroom/work area, and storage with deck access to the outside shower below. The clients desired an open atmosphere that had a strong relationship to the outdoors. This connection to the natural surroundings is expressed with large open wood trusses, and the interior admittance of several rock outcroppings that function as walls and floors.

# 35
## Kennedy Residence Two

4

5

1 Site plan
2&3 Landscape views
4 East view during construction
5 Exterior view

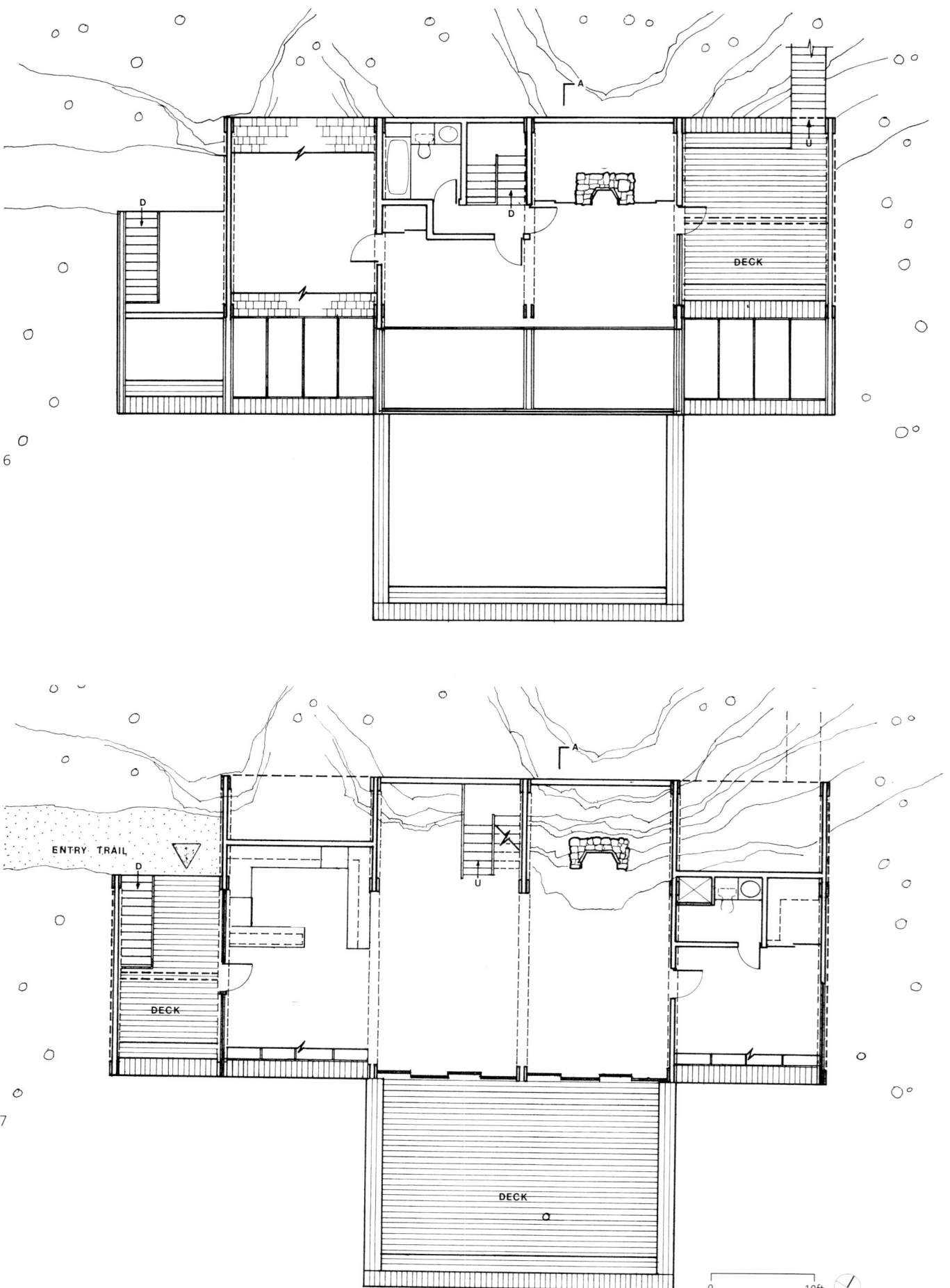

DECK

ENTRY TRAIL

DECK

DECK

0    10ft

6  Upper level floor plan
7  Lower level floor plan
8  Interior view

1

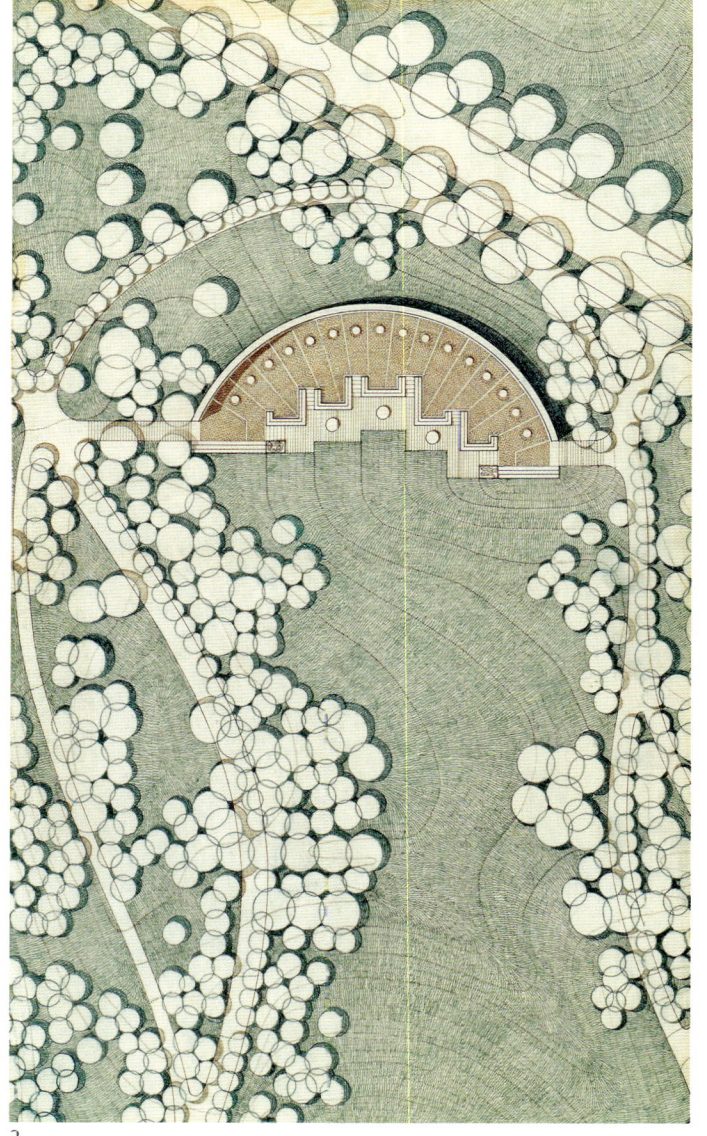

2

3

4

The most notable of the 1980s American architectural competitions was the Vietnam War Memorial, which attracted more than 1,100 entries, establishing a record for that decade. Because of the controversial nature of the war in which more than 58,000 Americans died, it was particularly important to create a design that would bring serenity and closure to this time in history.

Howey's entry idea was a single, 17-foot high wall forming the arc of a circle, which acted as a terminus for the west end of Constitution Gardens, where the site was located. The curved wall embraces a small plaza with round stone perimeter seating. At the plaza's edge, away from the wall, is additional seating with places for symbolic bronze sculptures to be located. The change in view, as one walks along the wall's curved surface, creates a progression of experience while looking for a specific name or names of the dead and missing carved into the marble wall panels. On looking outward from the wall, the Washington Monument appears on axis in the distance.

*With William Henderson*

**Design 1981**

Washington, DC
1 acre
Poured concrete footing and wall, white marble facing, granite plaza pavers, white marble seating and perimeter walks

# 36

## Vietnam War Memorial Competition

1 West elevation (exterior)
2 Site plan
3 Perspective
4 East elevation (interior)

1

2

3

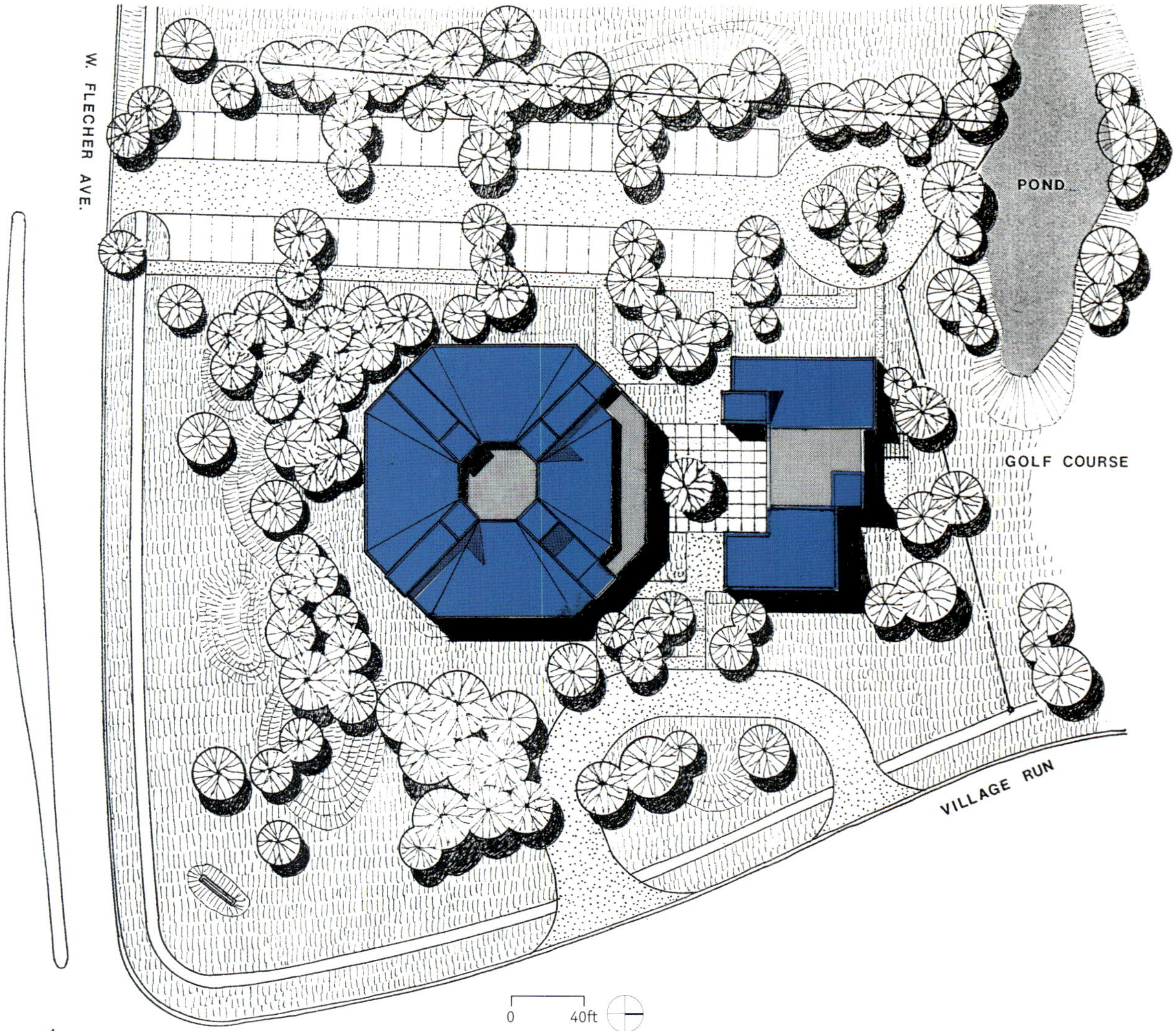

4

W. FLECHER AVE.

POND

GOLF COURSE

VILLAGE RUN

0        40ft

1&2 Exterior view through trees
3 Exterior view of roof
4 Site plan
5 Exterior view from entry

**Design/Completion
1981/1984**

Tampa, Florida
Village Presbyterian Church
20,000 square feet
Continuous steel frame and
trusses support wood ceiling
and roof structure for the
sanctuary; masonry perimeter
walls; vertical cedar siding
on the interior and exterior;
ceramic tile roofs

5

Located on the site of a former sales building for a popular community of residences, town-homes, and apartments, this church was established to serve the immediate neighborhood. Bordered on one side by a golf course and on the other sides by major roads, the perimeter land was earth-bermed to make a visual barrier between the new sanctuary and its streets.

# 37

## Presbyterian Church

The brief called for a sanctuary with seating for 750, classrooms, and administrative offices. The old church, created from the original sales building, was retained as the Fellowship Hall. The new octagonal sanctuary, with four tower-light monitors providing indirect daylight to the interior, is the focal design element. At night, the monitor illumination provides identification outward to the community. One enters under a balcony that wraps around three sides of the main sanctuary space. Paired steel trusses frame the chancel, which is identified by a simple wooden cross. On the exterior of both buildings, the cedar siding and blue ceramic roof tiles tie the new and original structures together.

6   Interior view
7   Section
8   Level one floor plan
9   Level two floor plan

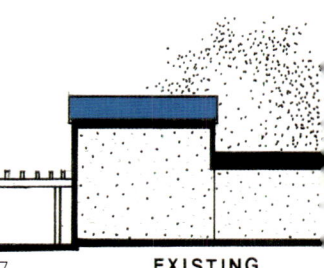

7        EXISTING

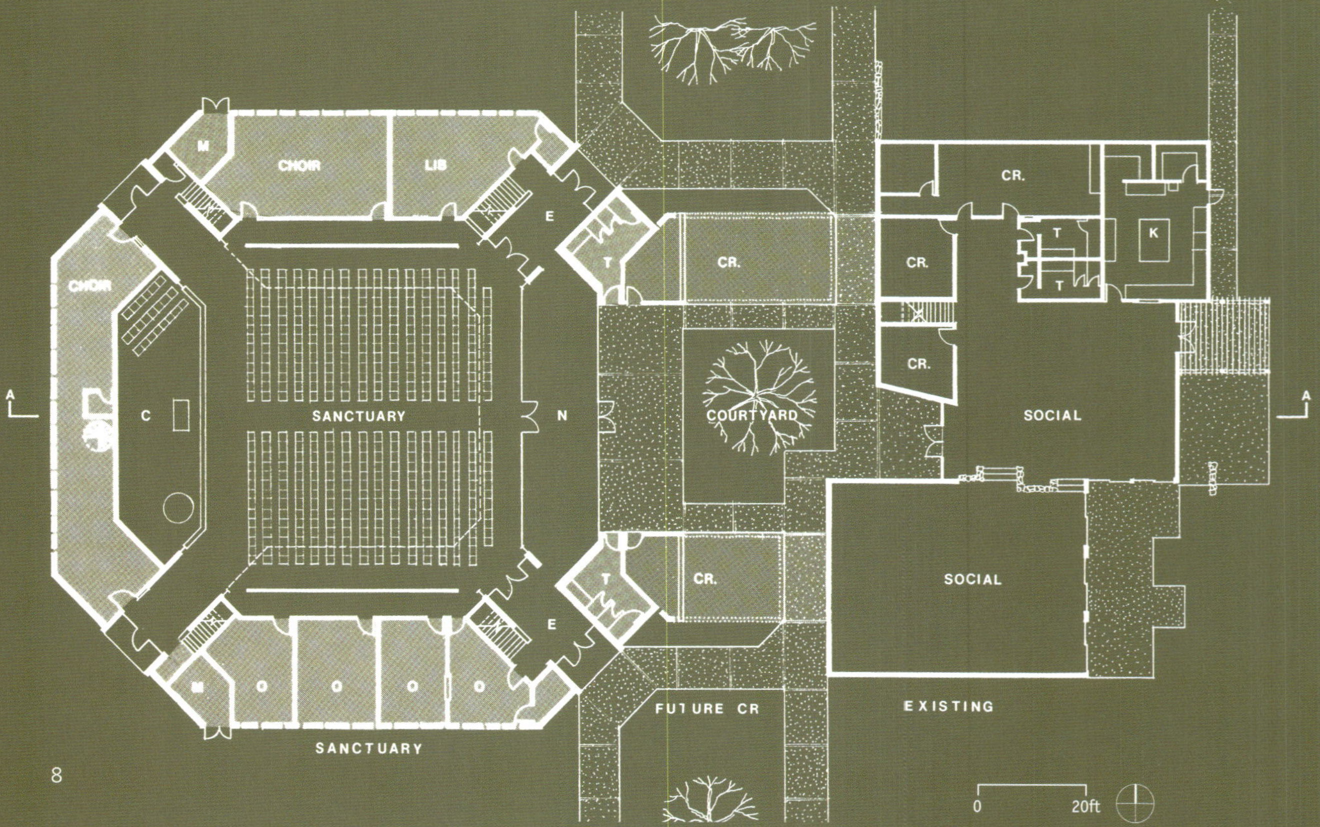

8

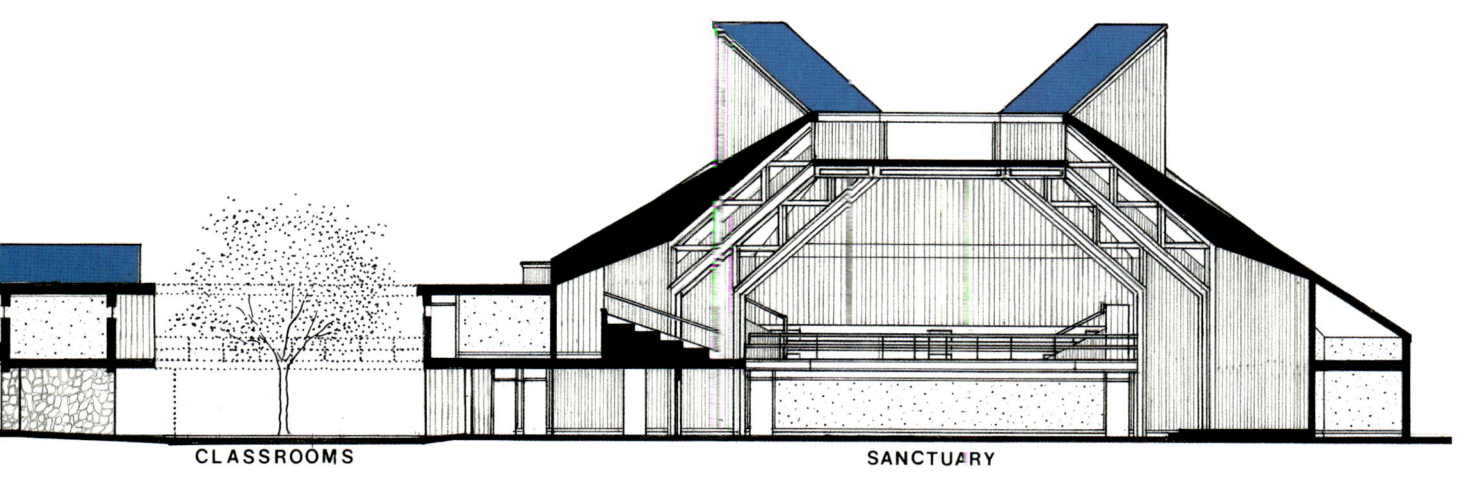

CLASSROOMS                                                              SANCTUARY

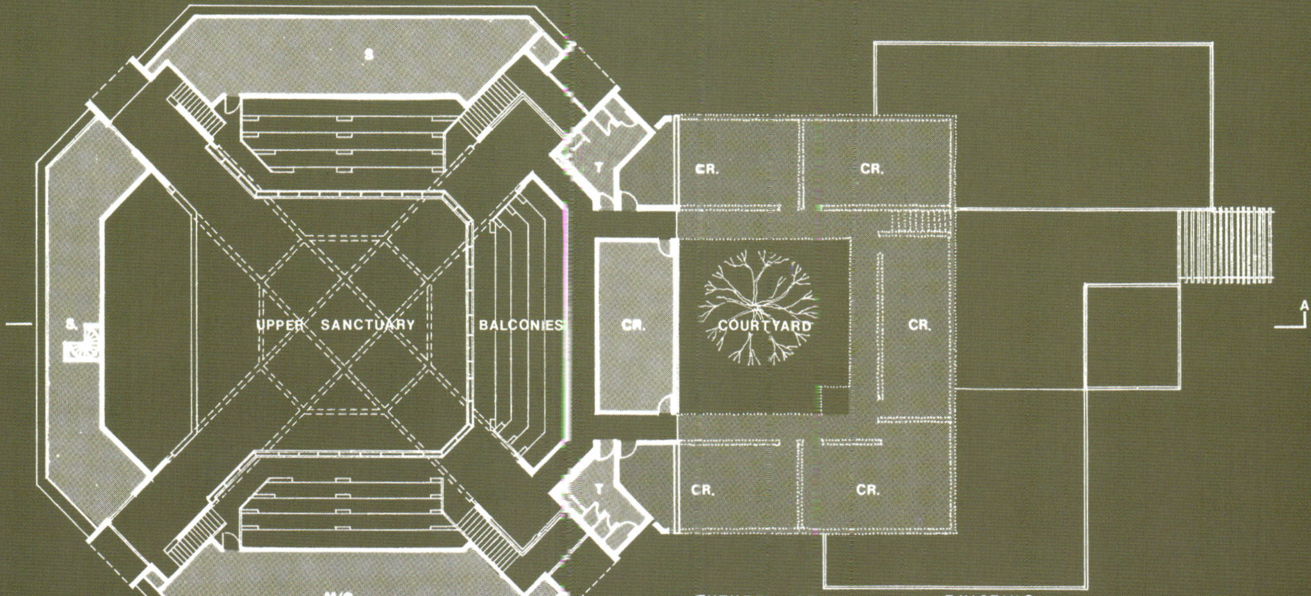

UPPER SANCTUARY    BALCONIES    CR.          COURTYARD    CR.

CR.                    CR.

CR.                                      CR.

M/S                                      CR.          CR.

SANCTUARY

9

FUTURE    CF    EXISTING

0        20ft

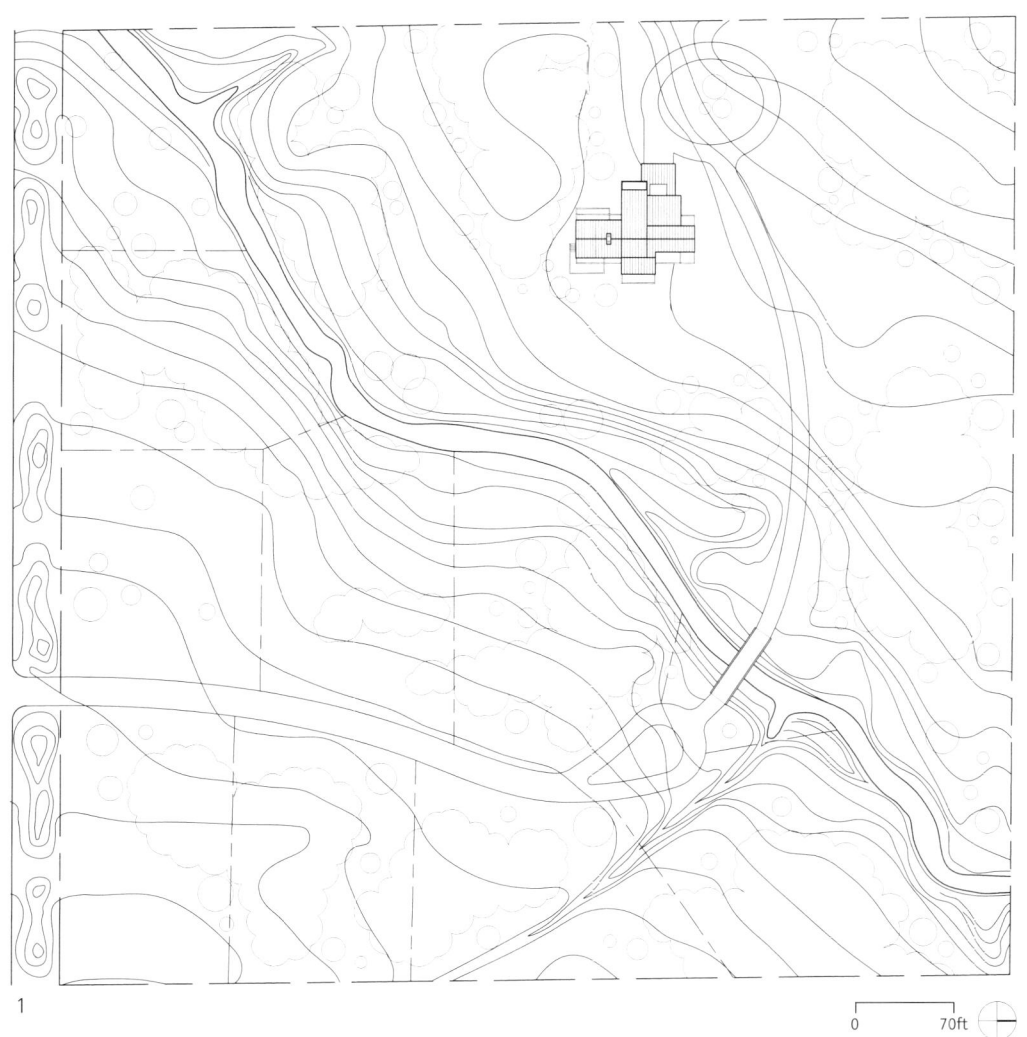

1

0        70ft

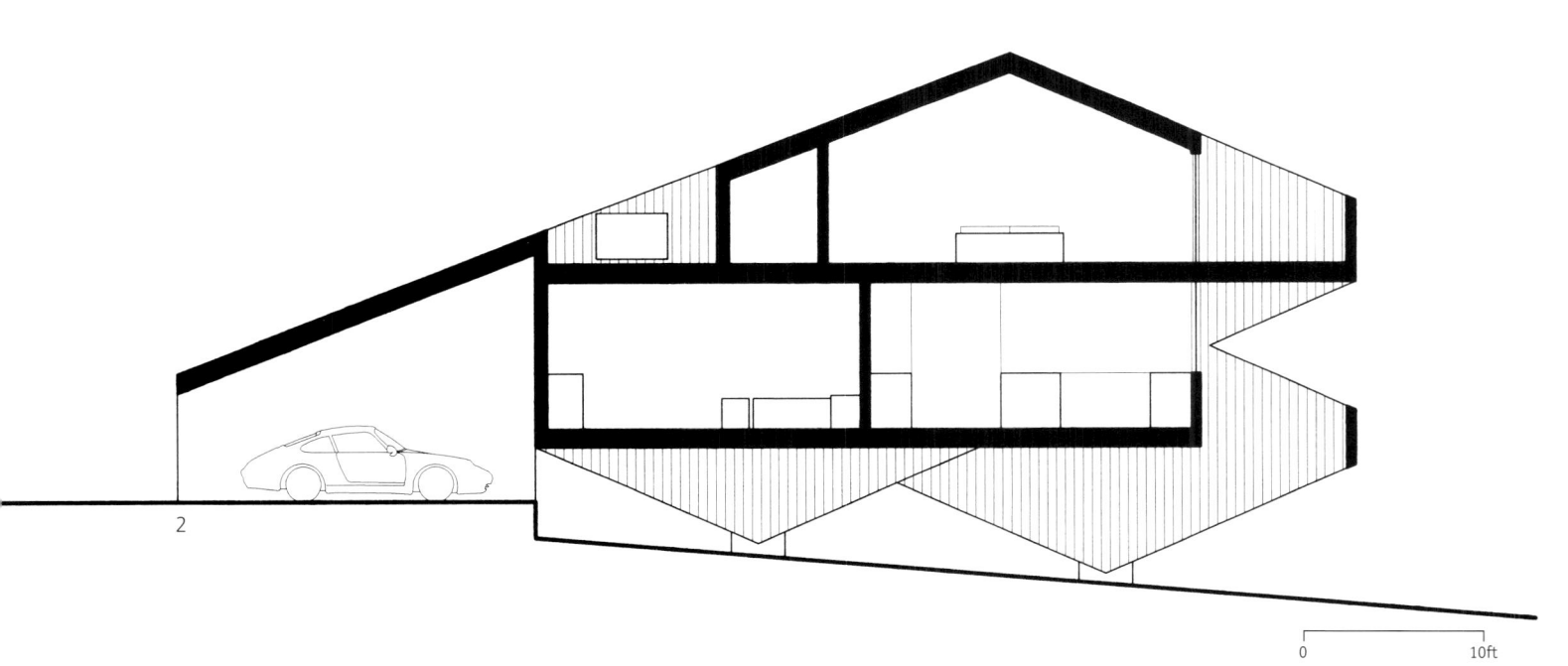

2

0        10ft

This prize tract of land, rising on both sides of Curlew Creek, was purchased by a couple who commissioned Howey to develop a buffered landscaped entry for eight luxury homes, including their own residence. Configured for privacy, the lots are situated among a thick stand of oaks, palms, and lush growth along the creek, which in turn becomes the backyard for five of the houses. Located at the rear of the property is a bridge over the creek to the owners' private property and residence.

By placing the owners' residence at the highest corner of the site, Howey provided a panoramic view of the creek and treetops that conceal the entry road and other residences from sight. The structure itself is multilevel with the entrance at the top side. Living and private spaces radiate from the central stair entry, with treads and railings suspended from vertical tension rods hung from the roof to the entry floor.

## Design 1980

Clearwater, Florida
Mr and Mrs John Shuman
10.5 acres
Concrete footings, wood
frame, cypress siding, stucco,
metal battened-seam roof

# 38
## Countresquire

1  Site plan
2  Section
3  Perspective sketch

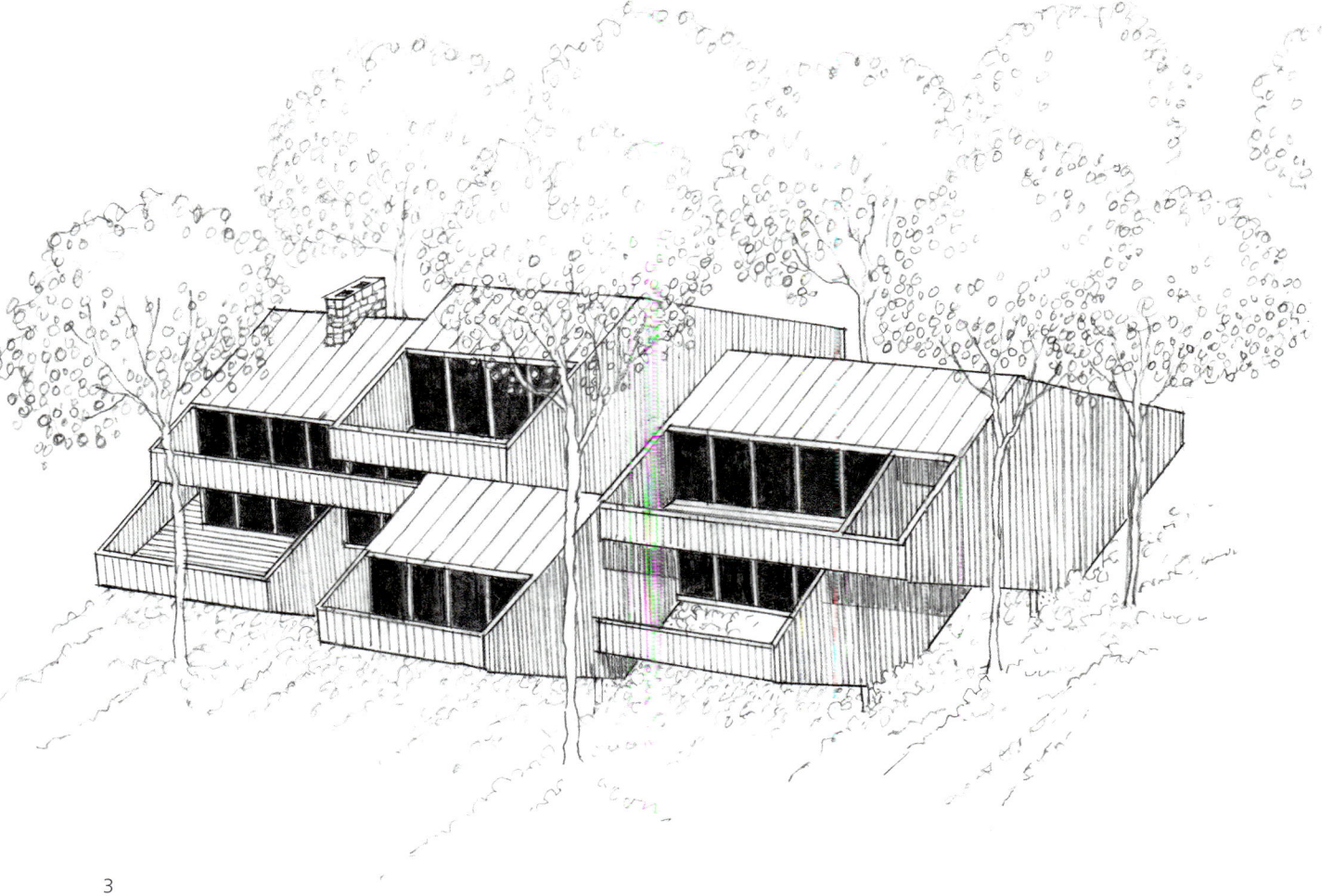

3

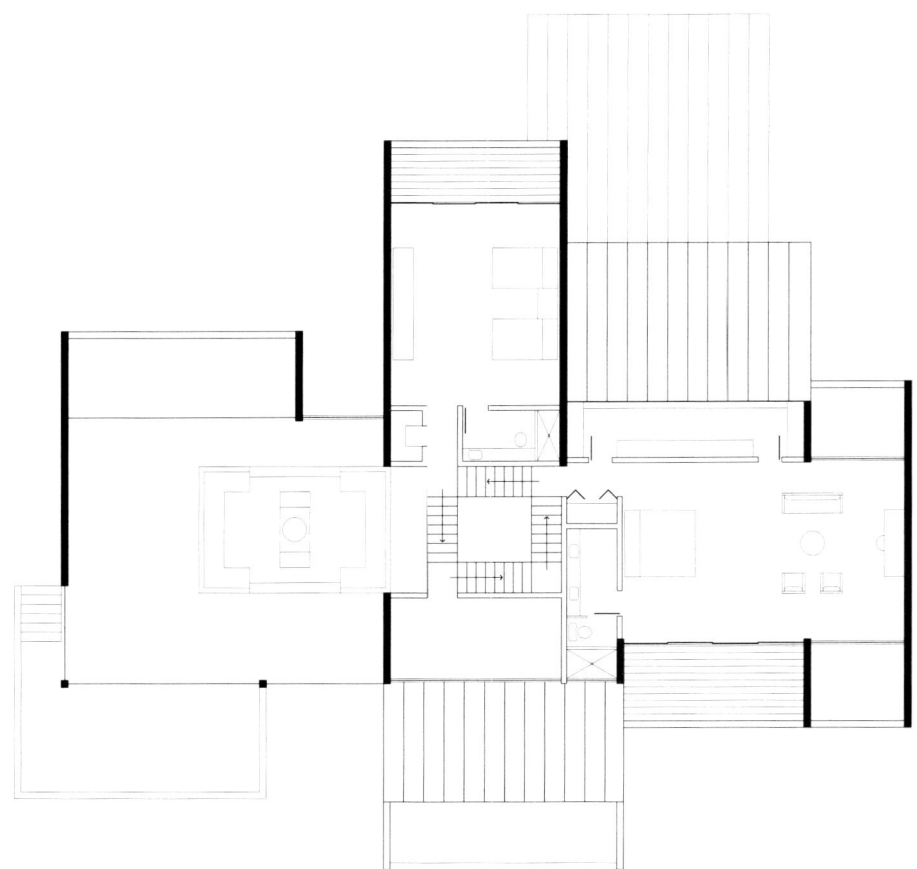

4

5

0   10ft

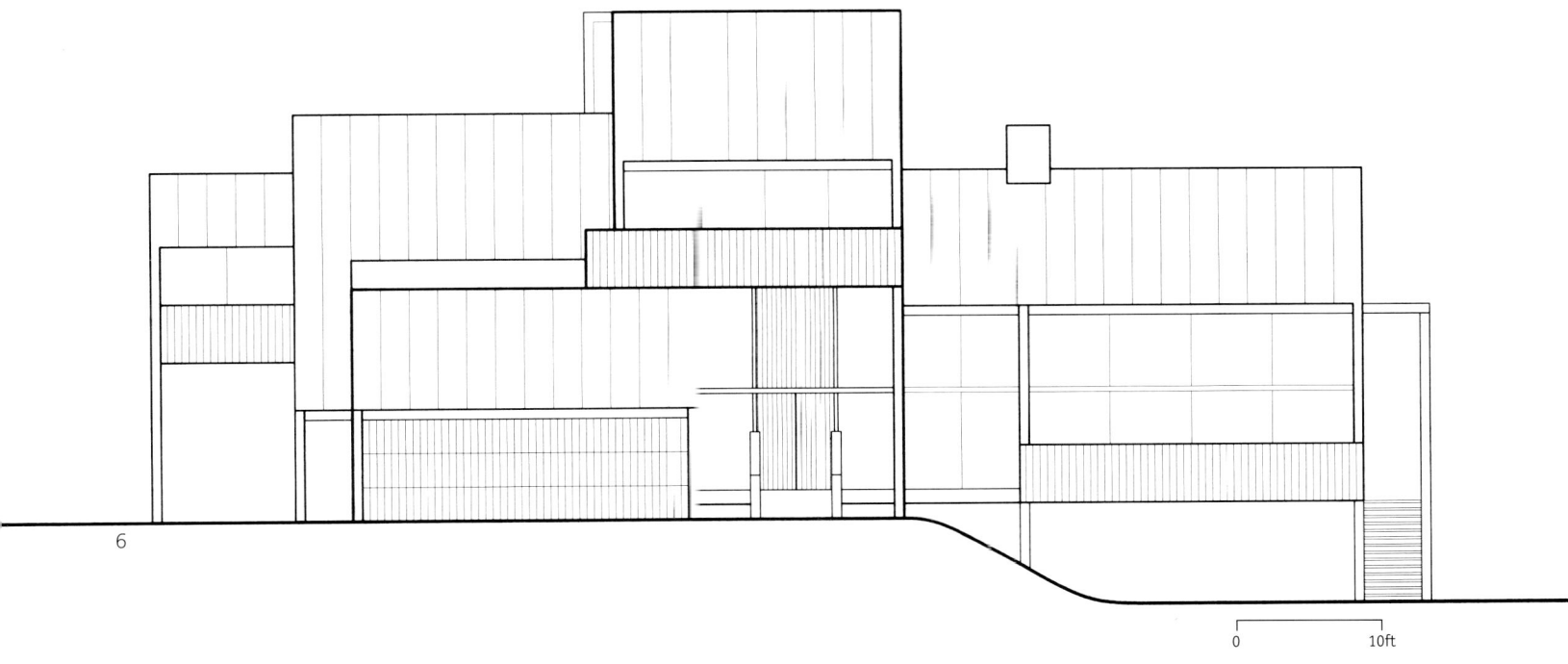

6

0    10ft

4    Upper floor plan
5    Lower floor plan
6    South elevation
7    Entry sketch

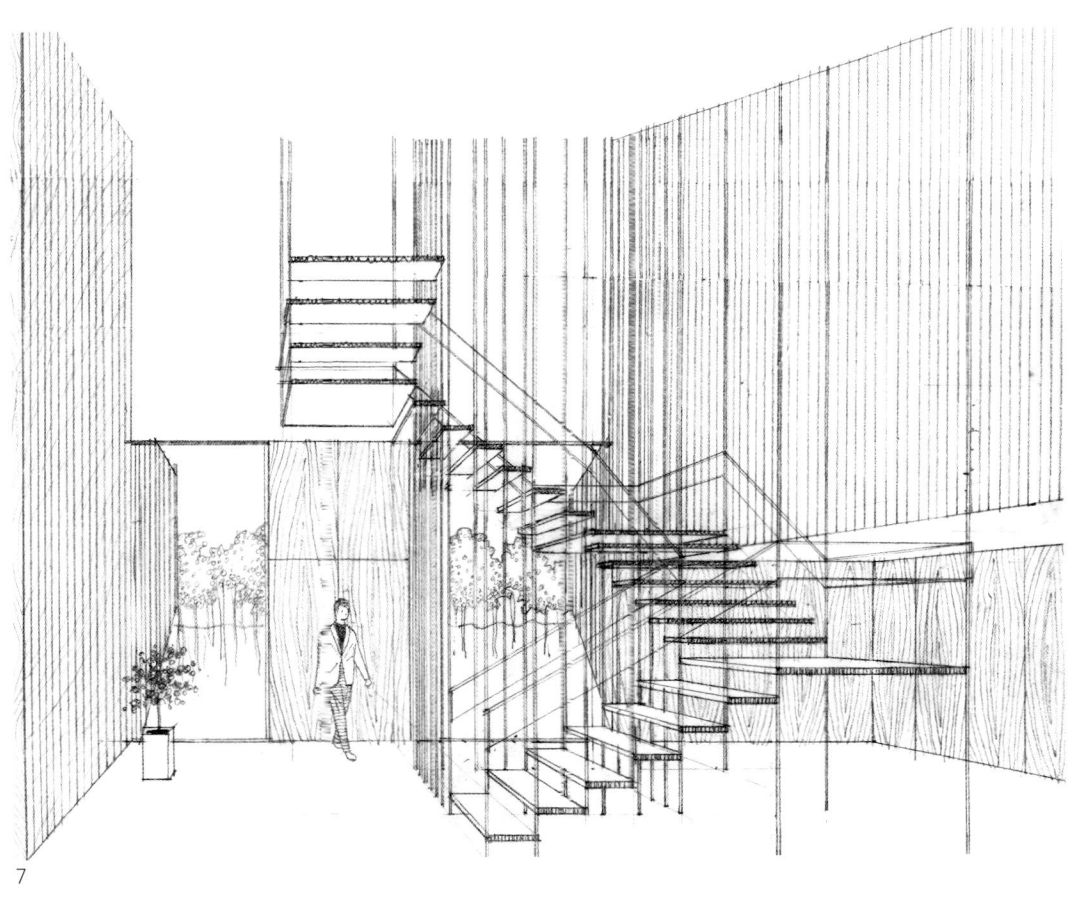

7

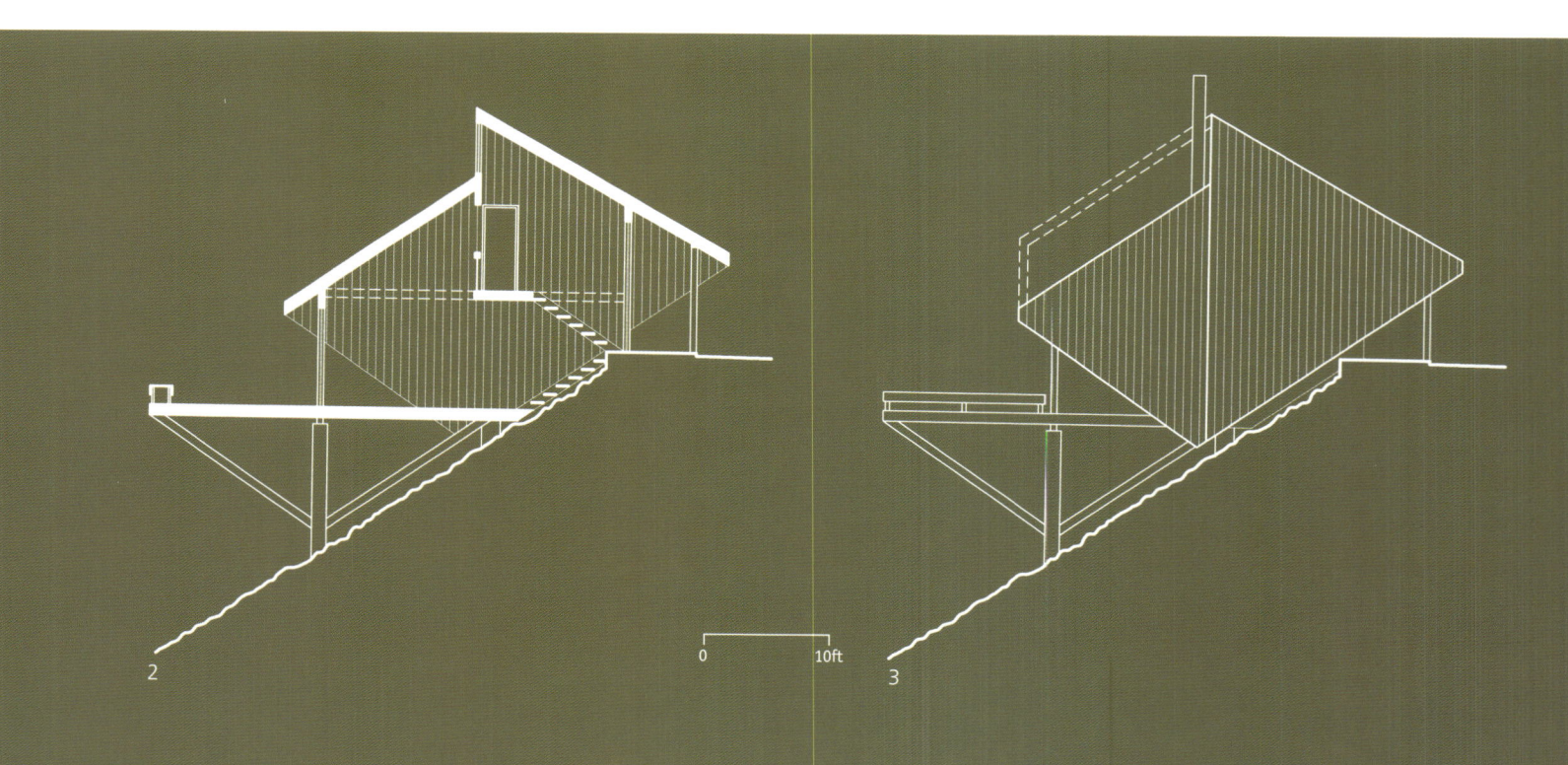

1 Site plan
2 Section
3 Elevation
4 45-degree guide cabin
side elevation
5 Primitive 30-degree
camping elevation

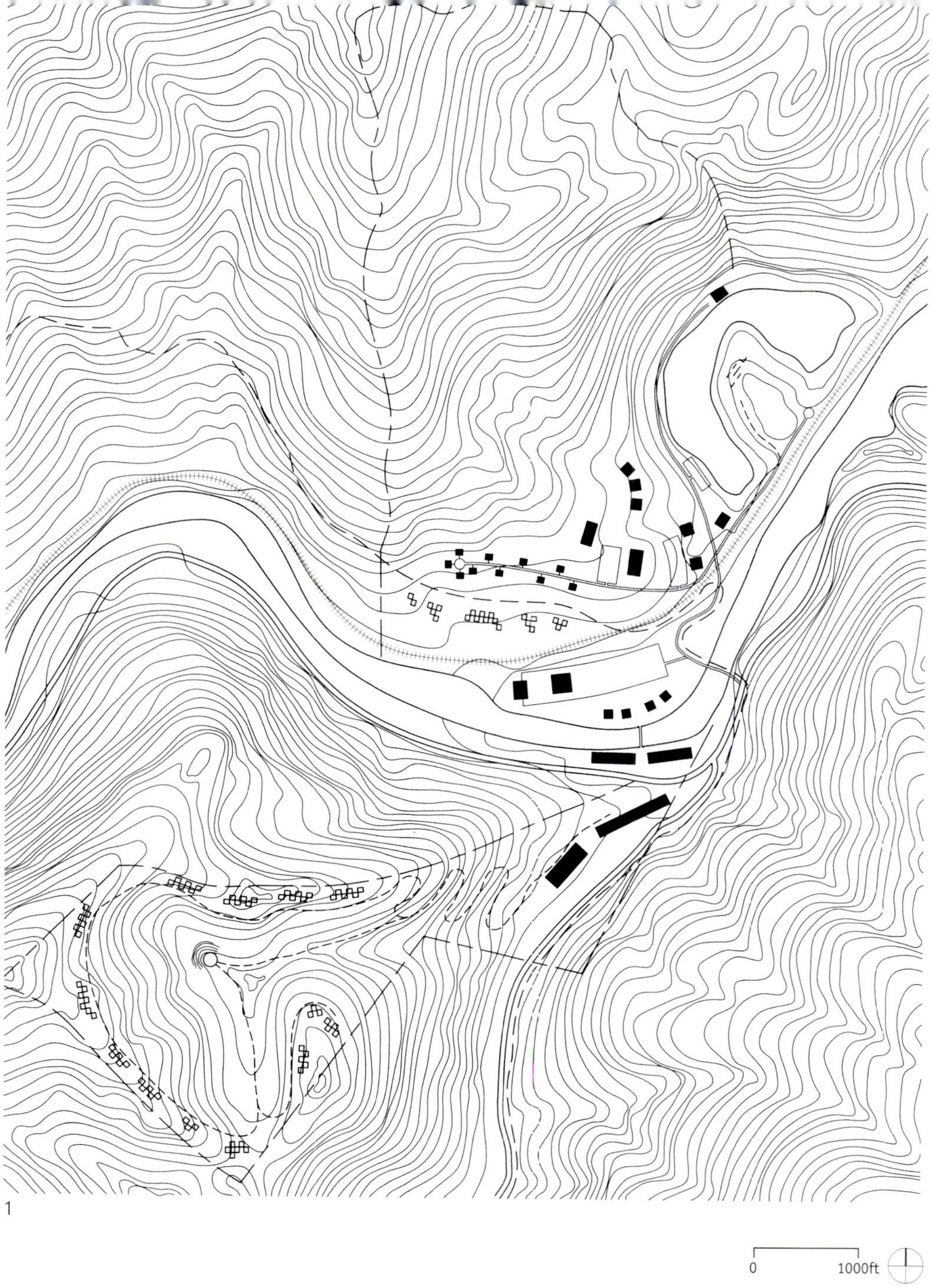

1

0                    1000ft

2

0        10ft

3

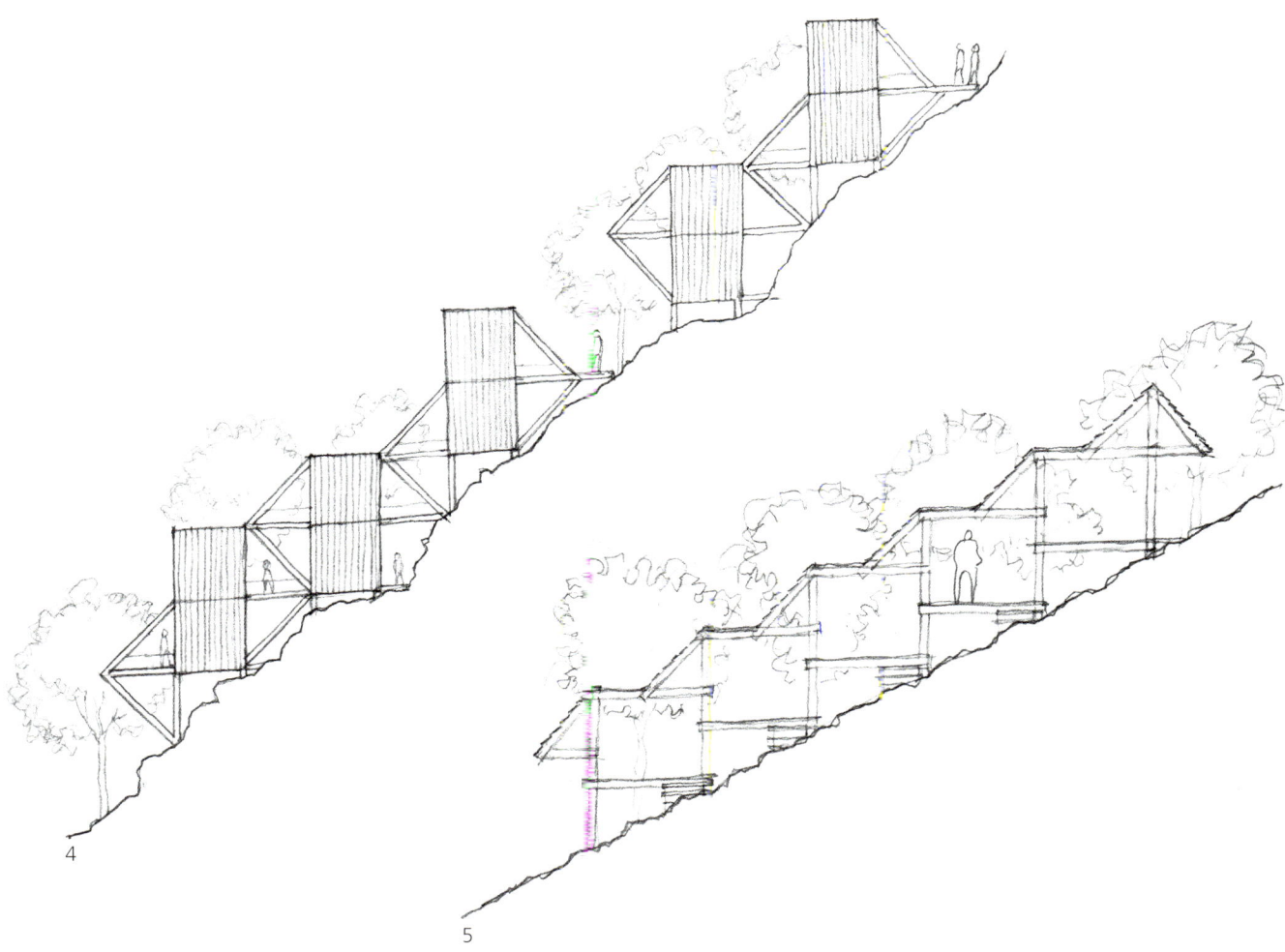

4

5

The center, located at the junction of the Nantahala River and the Appalachian Trail, was created to offer camping, hiking, rock climbing, white-water rafting, canoeing, and kayaking to the public. A railroad used for sightseeing trips runs along the river next to the Recreation Center.

The site plan includes the raft rental facility, train station, snack bar, rest stations, and public parking on the north edge of the river. Above this complex are the main restaurant, rental cottages, and conference facilities. Along the edge of the parking area is the Appalachian Trail and hikers' shelters. Across the river are the Center's main offices, a separate hiker's motel, and maintenance facilities. An informal restaurant, service station, and outfitter's store overlook the river. Further south along the trail are additional campsites, hikers' shelters, and a small amphitheater set in a natural bowl.

The site-development challenge was to place the building sites, roads, parking area, and a sewage treatment and water system onsite without disturbing the land's ecology, natural beauty, or views of the surrounding mountains or river. To achieve this, Howey proposed lifting structures above the often rocky, sloping land with, in many cases, entry from the high side and view-balconies on the lower side. The use of native stone, wood, glass, and unpaved paths further minimizes intrusion into the site environment.

## Design/Construction
## 1980/1984

Wesser, North Carolina
Nantahala Outdoor Center
20.5 acres
Concrete pier footings, wood floor and roof framing, vertical siding, cedar shingle roofs, wood decks and flooring, glass, and native stone

# 39

**Outdoor Recreation Center**

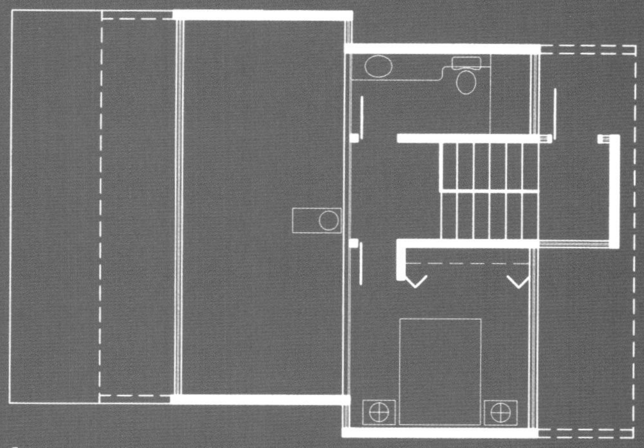

6

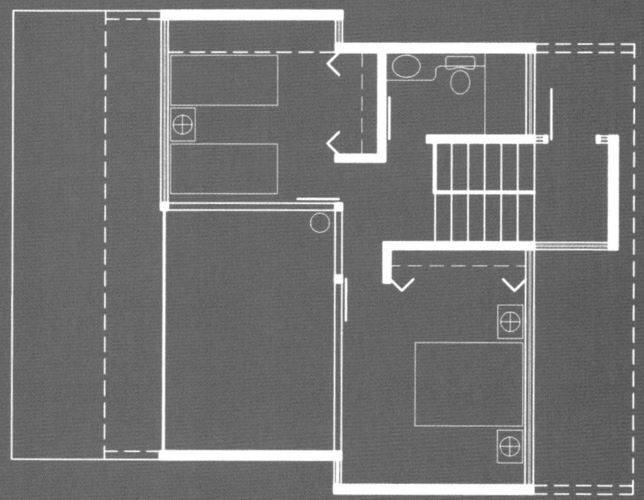

7

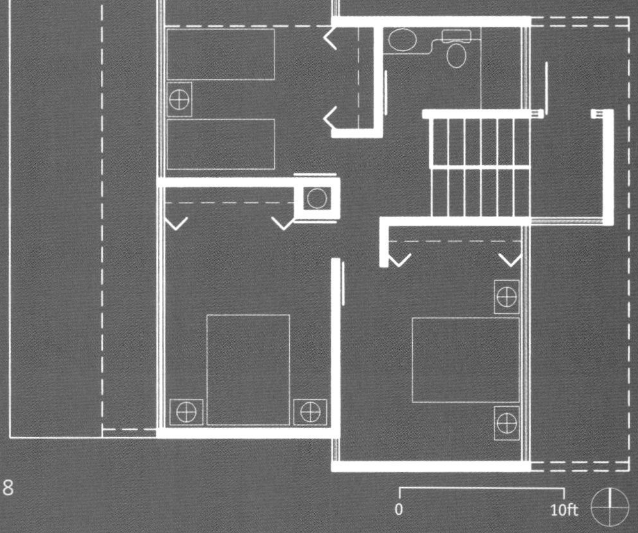

8

0        10ft

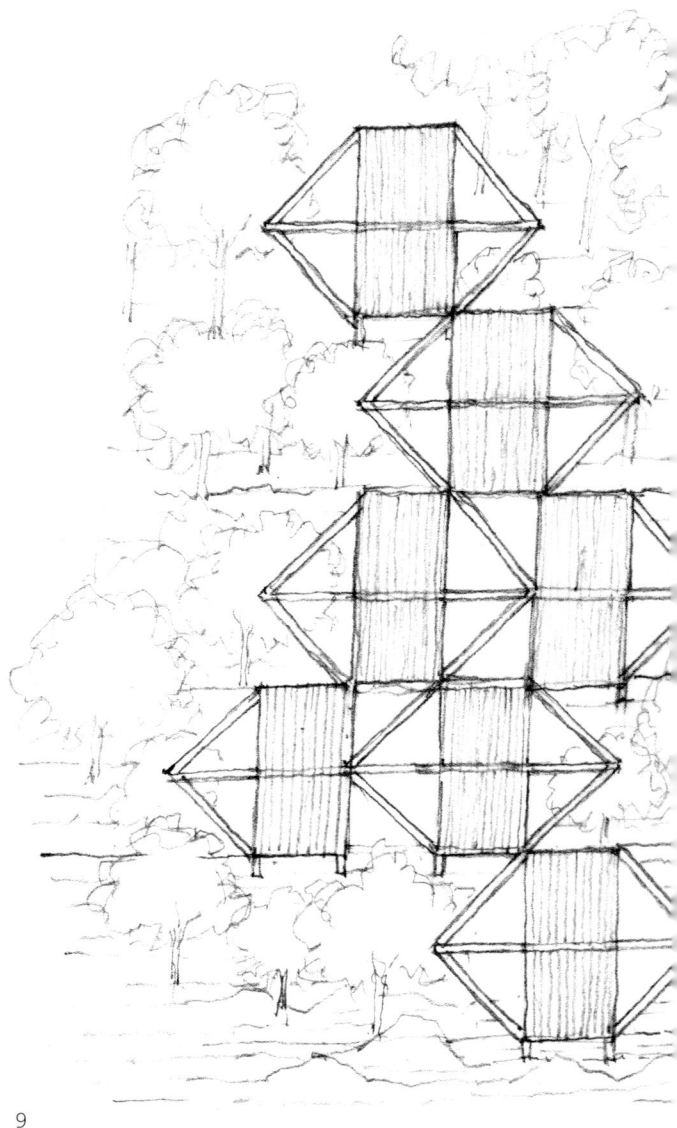

9

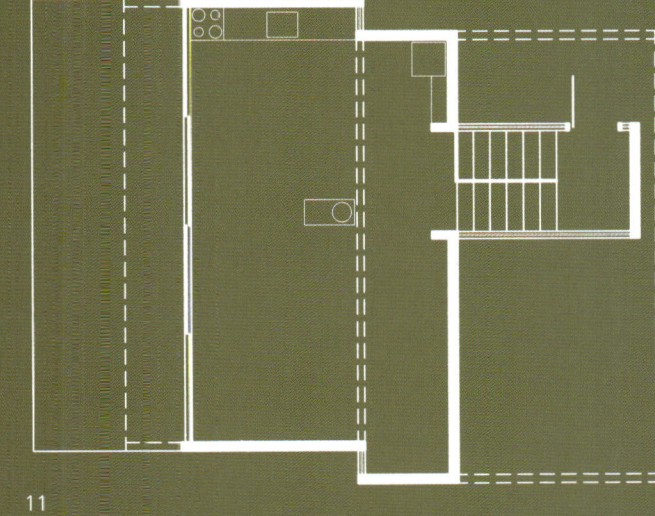

11

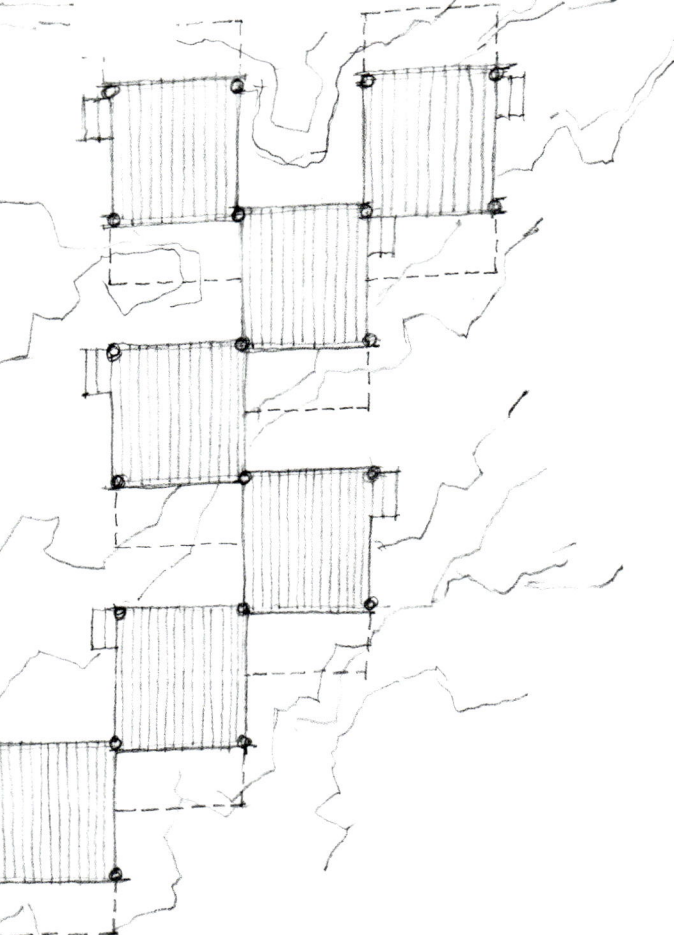

10

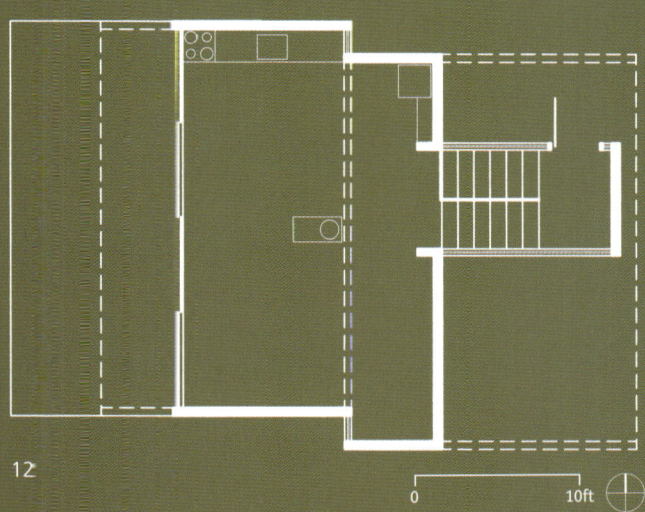

12

0          10ft

1  Model: aerial view of front drive
2  Model: aerial view of side and
   pool enclosure
3  Section
4  Model: pool side view

1

2

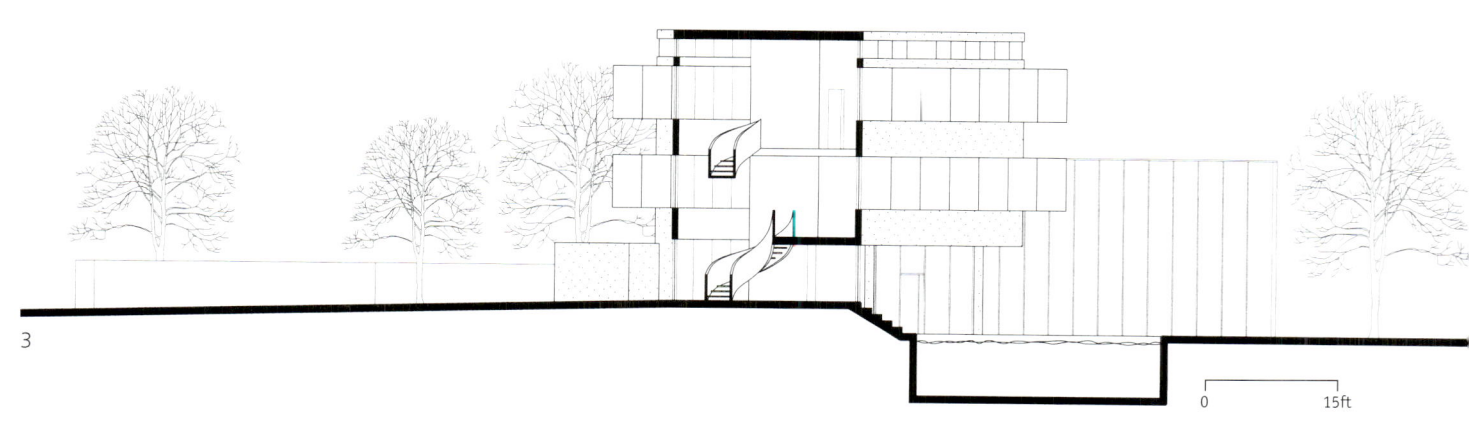

3

0       15ft

# 40

## Menendez Residence

This sparse lot facing a typical Florida canal was the client's compromise choice. Howey's first advice to the clients was to agree on the building location, immediately plant trees, and think about the design of their home from the inside out. In this design, access is into a walled court on a circular drive, with an earthen ramp up to the main entrance. Upon entry, one gains views to the canal over a screen-enclosed swimming pool. Major living spaces and bedrooms are grouped in separate wings on each side of the pool. Veiled layers of light filter through the various textures of screen to create translucency with an inward focus. Exterior windows are grouped in bands, with screens boxed out to allow for pivoting windows. The cool, sheer planes of screen interlock and float through space to reveal the inside and outside of this structure of concrete columns and stuccoed masonry walls.

4

### Design 1980

Tampa, Florida
Dr and Mrs Luis Menendez
6,200 square feet
Concrete footings, columns,
and slabs, wood and steel
framing, masonry, stucco,
and screen

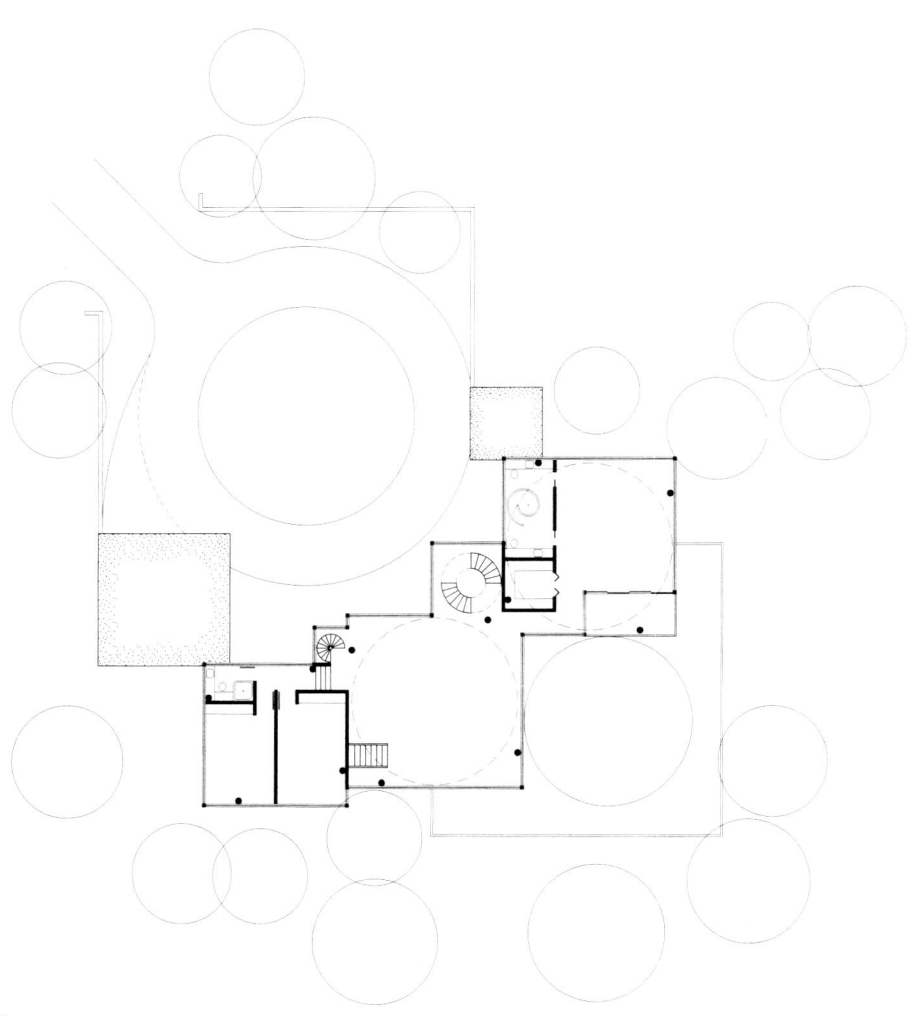

5

6

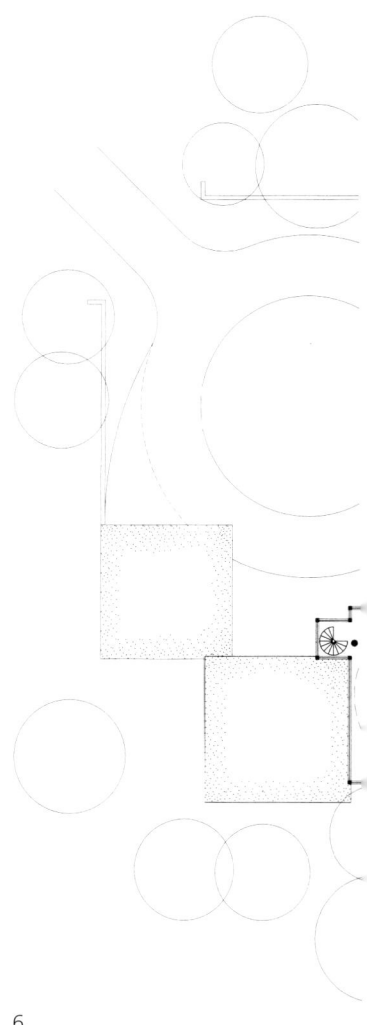

7

0       15ft

5 Level two floor plan
6 Level three floor plan
7 Level one floor plan
8 Interior concept sketch
9 South elevation

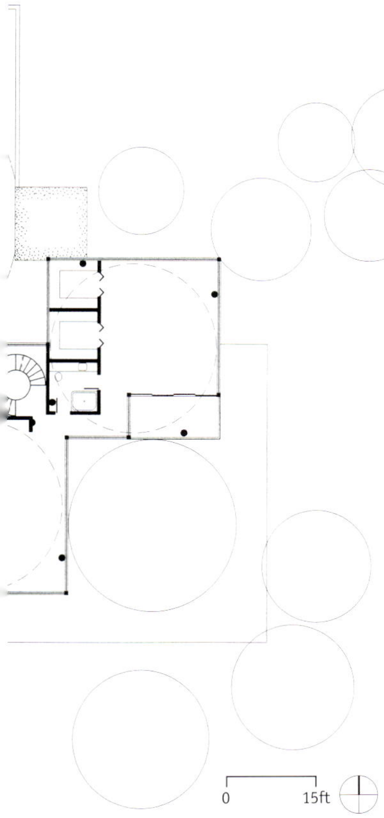


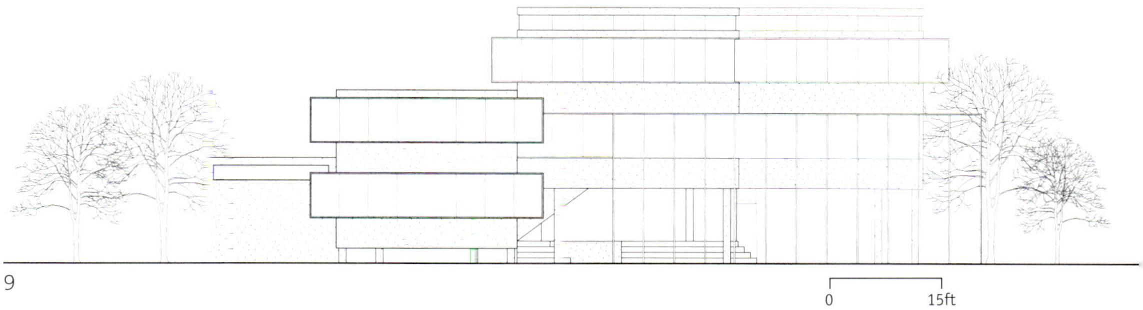


9

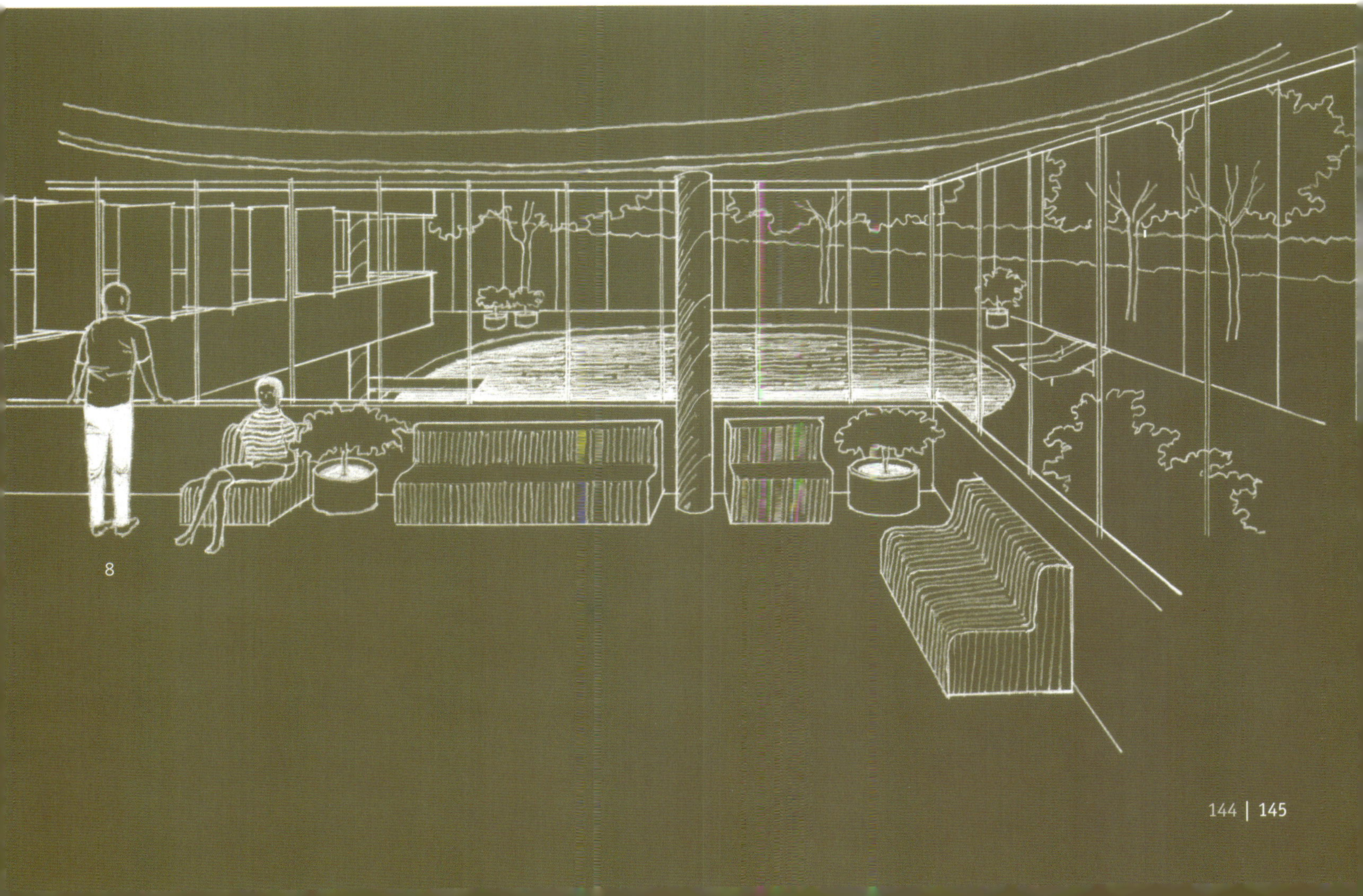

8

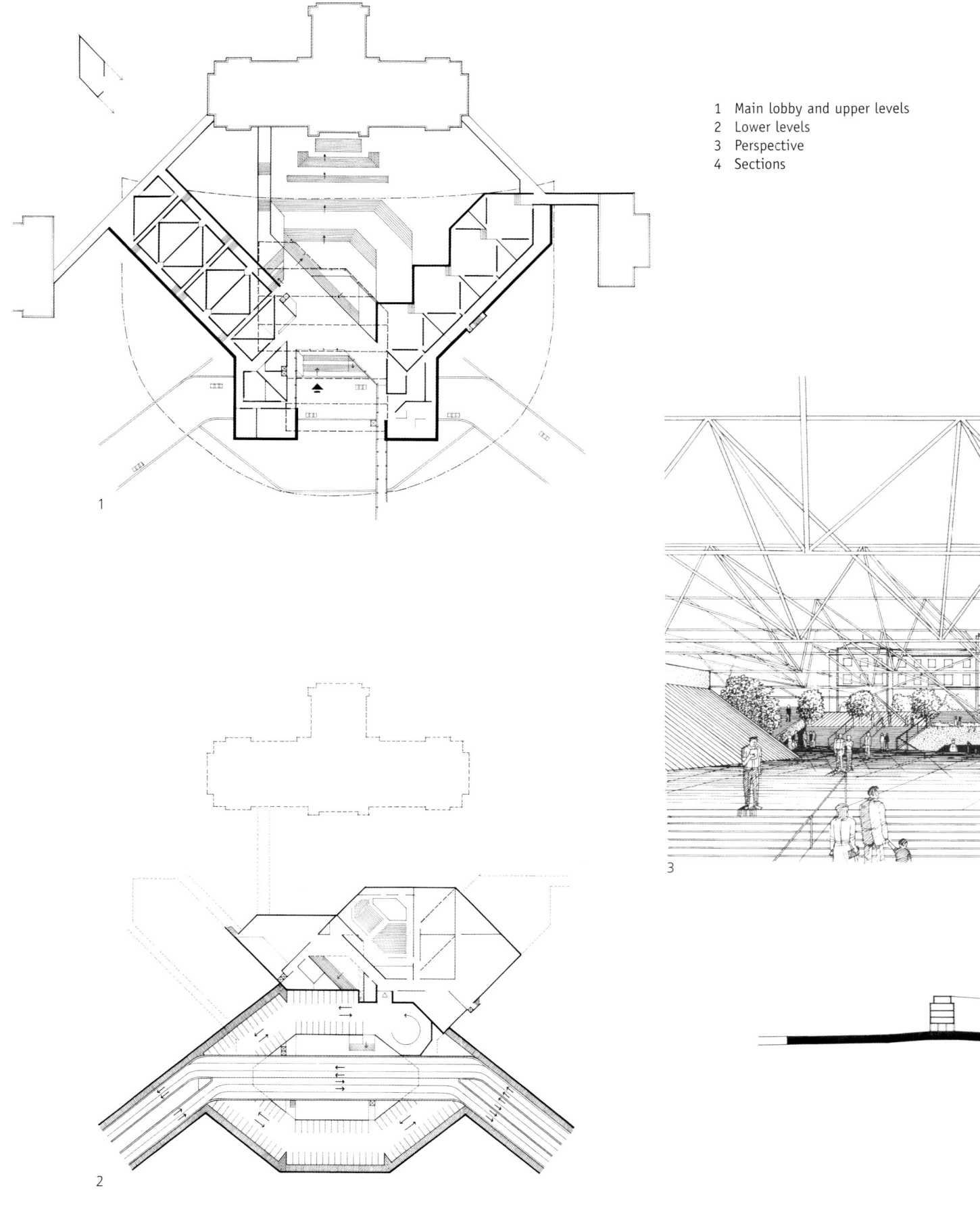

1 Main lobby and upper levels
2 Lower levels
3 Perspective
4 Sections

1

3

2

4

This national terratectural competition consisted of legislative and museum additions to be placed underground at the foot of the Minnesota State Capitol. The original structure, designed in 1895 by Cass Gilbert, was expanded over the years with two additional state buildings on either side of the Capitol. Howey's subterranean solution seeks to ease the transition between the Capitol lawn and the new annex by building a series of descending terraces that continue the Capitol's monumental stairs into the new addition. A roof of glazed, long-span trusses extends over the new annex lobby. The roof's central location serves notice of the invisible building's presence and relationship to the three existing surface buildings. Parking for 600 cars is underground; the lawn above is landscaped with semicircular rows of ginko trees.

*With Carl Abbott, FAIA*

## Design 1976

St. Paul, Minnesota
Additions to Minnesota State Capitol
275,000 square feet
Concrete foundations, architectural concrete, limestone, steel trusses, and laminated glass skylights

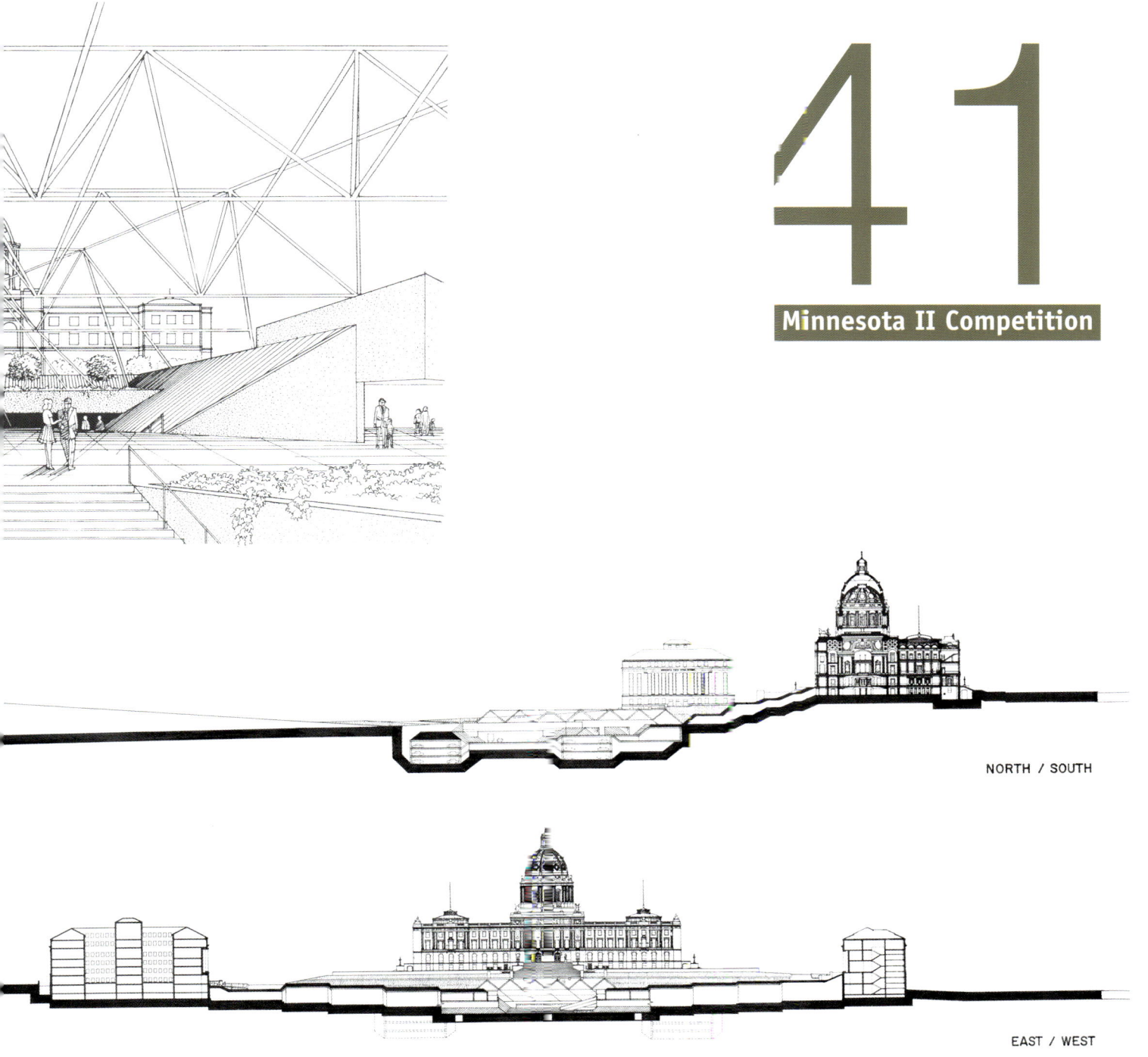

# 41
**Minnesota II Competition**

NORTH / SOUTH

EAST / WEST

1

2

4

1–5   Exterior views

3

# 42

5

**Design/Completion**
**1974/1977**

Plant City and Ruskin, Florida
Hillsborough County
7,400 square feet
Cast concrete footings; precast
and pre-stressed concrete
columns, beams and roof
units; exposed concrete block;
concrete floors

This utilitarian structure was designed by Howey to provide work bays for the repair of heavy road equipment, trucks, and buses used by the county. Outside covered storage for equipment and a separate smaller office building completed the complex. Low-maintenance, durable materials were integral to the total concept. Because of the long work bays raised-roof monitors were created above the bays to allow natural light into the building. A kit of building parts consisting of precast concrete columns, beams, and double-tee roof units was trucked to the site where the total shell was erected in one day. Subsequently, the concrete floors, block walls, mechanical, electrical, and office interior surfaces were completed. A duplicate facility was later constructed in Ruskin.

6&7  Interior views
  8  Floor plan
  9  Section

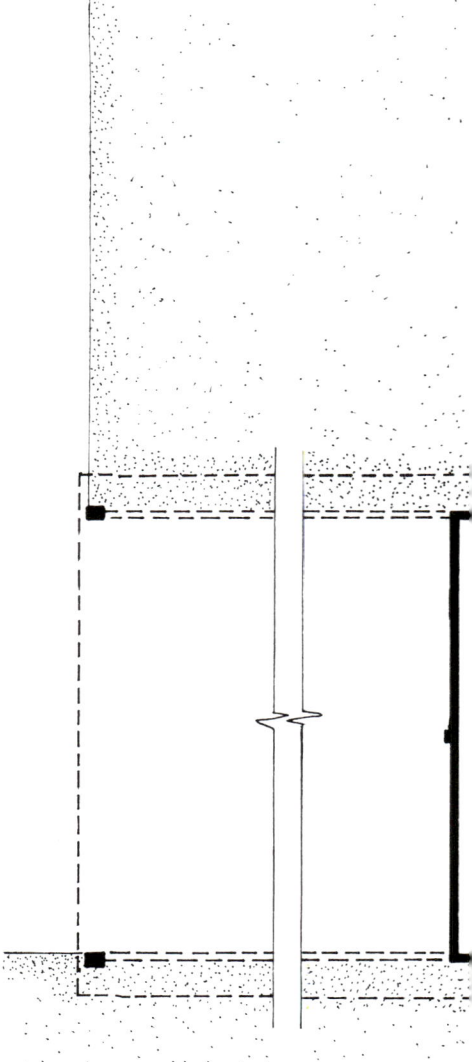

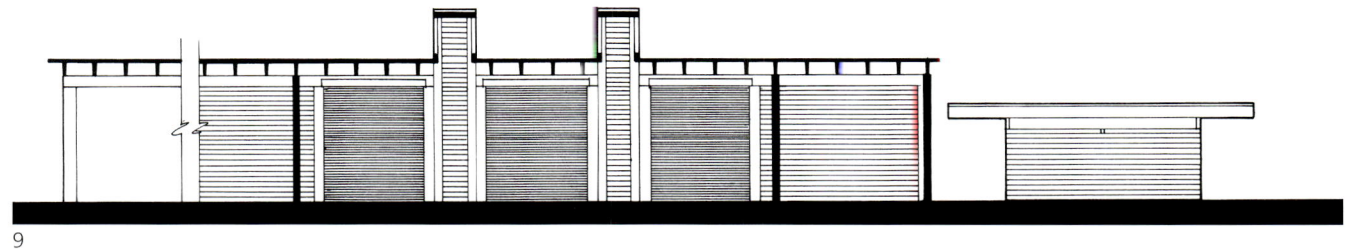

9

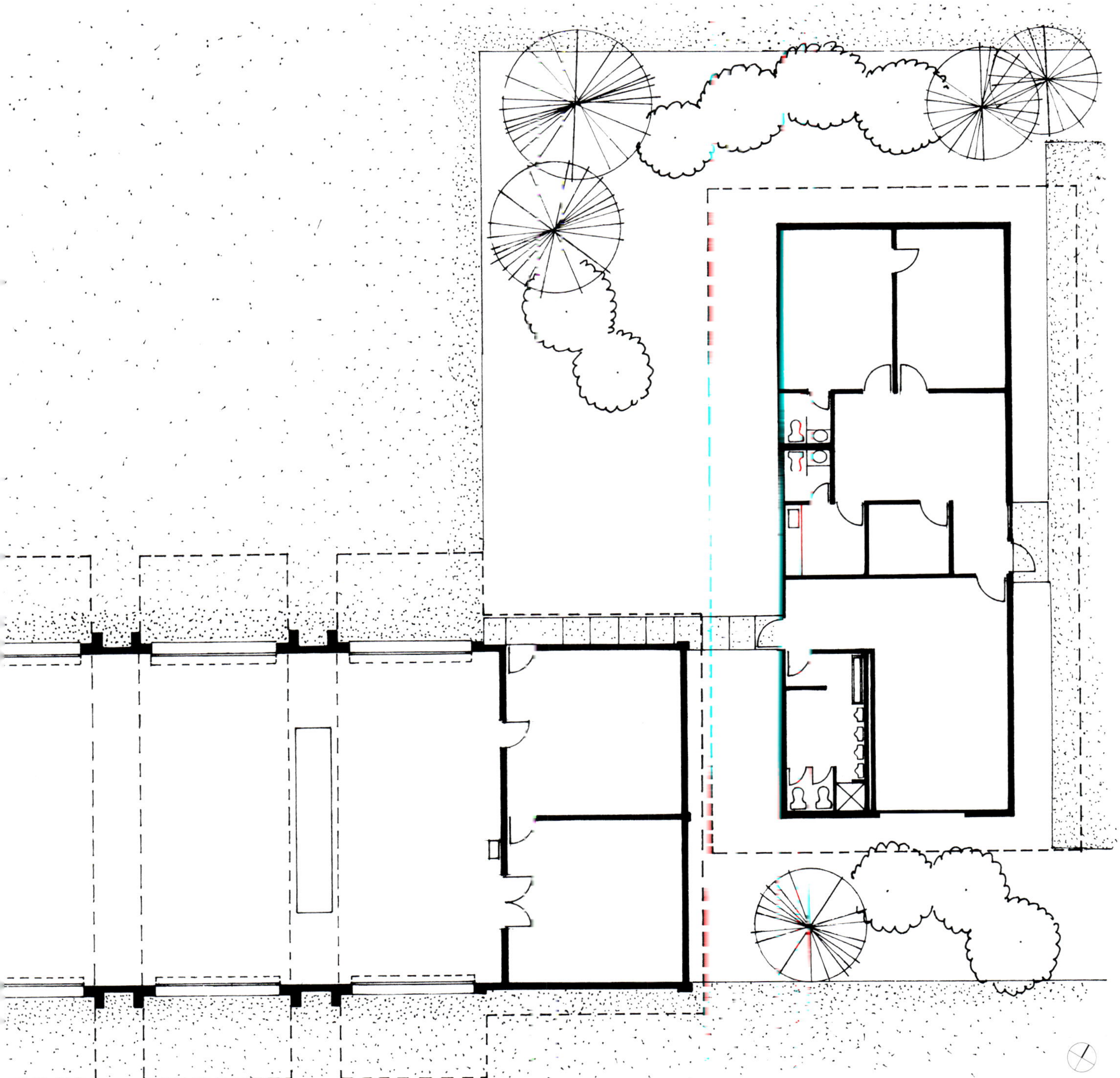

1

2

## Design/Completion
## 1972/1974

Orlando, Florida
Mr and Mrs John McPherson
5,000 square feet
Concrete foundation, slab above grade, masonry walls, wood roof structure, cedar shakes, re-sawn cedar siding, copper, bronze, ceramic tile, carpet, and brick pavers

The small, quarter-acre suburban site mandated an enclosed courtyard scheme to meet the privacy requirements of the clients. By using large glass areas in the living and private spaces that focus outward to a main landscaped courtyard and several smaller patios, Howey was able to create an intimate indoor–outdoor relationship within the perimeter privacy walls. The main entrance leads to an art gallery that also becomes the hall connecting living, personal, and service spaces. The rooms on each side of the gallery have individual shed roofs with light monitors at their high points over the central, lower, flat gallery roof. To provide accurate climate control, a double air-conditioning system was designed with the supply ducts located in the gallery ceiling and return ducts installed under the floor. The 2-foot, 6-inch above-grade elevation of the house allows the installation of a completely sealed, under-floor ducted return system for air conditioning and heating.

1–4 Exterior views

# 43
## McPherson Residence

3

4

5

6

5&6 Exterior views
7–9 Interior views
10 Floor plan
11&12 Section perspectives

7

8

11

0                    10ft

9

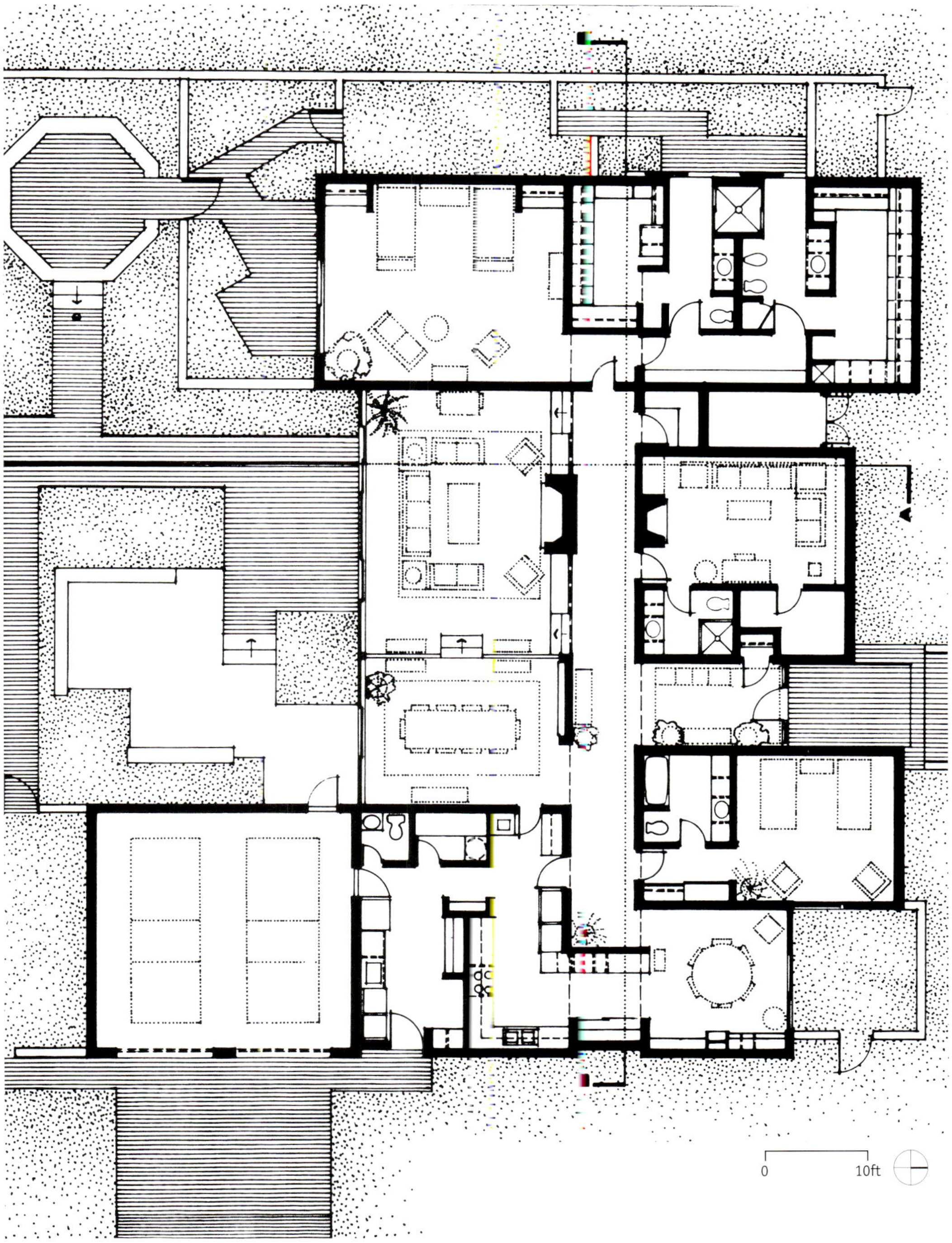

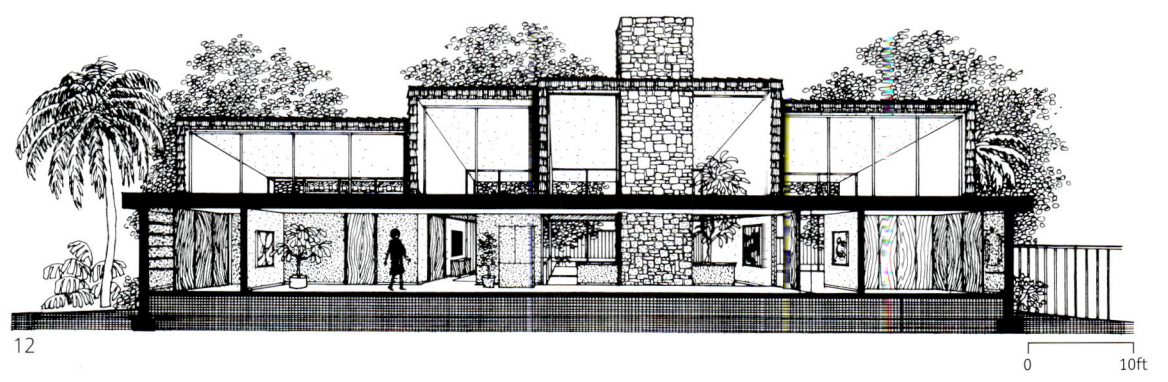

10

12

0          10ft

0          10ft

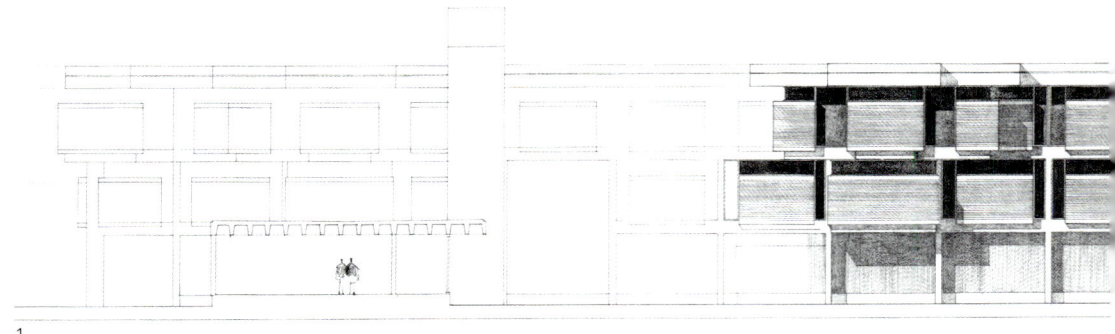

1

1 Elevation and
  section sketch
2,4&5 Exterior views
3 Site plan

2

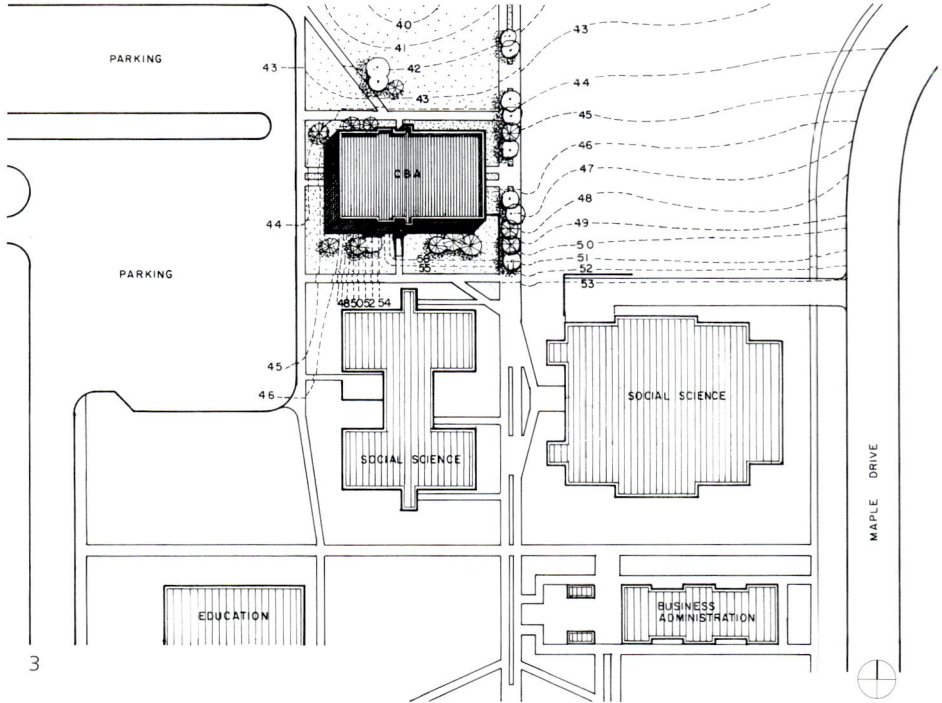

3

4

# 44

## CBA Building

Requirements for this multi-use college building were to house both student classrooms and faculty offices, which would be together, yet separate, in the same structure.

**Design/Completion**
**1969/1975**
Tampa, Florida
University of South Florida
34,000 square feet
Concrete footings, columns and beams; pan construction, brick, architecturally exposed concrete, masonry partitions, bronze, glass, and copper

Howey discovered a natural drop of 11 feet on the site, forming an east–west bank against which he set the structure. This allowed the major building and faculty entrance to be at the top of this ridge and student classrooms and entrances below the two faculty levels. Stairs and an elevator connect all levels. Two double-loaded faculty corridors loop to provide access to both perimeter-view offices and to interior offices. Outside office walls cantilever to provide additional nooks for furnishings, as well as overhangs for sun protection at each level. The resultant design provides 100 offices, 10 seminar-reception spaces, and classrooms for 700 students.

5

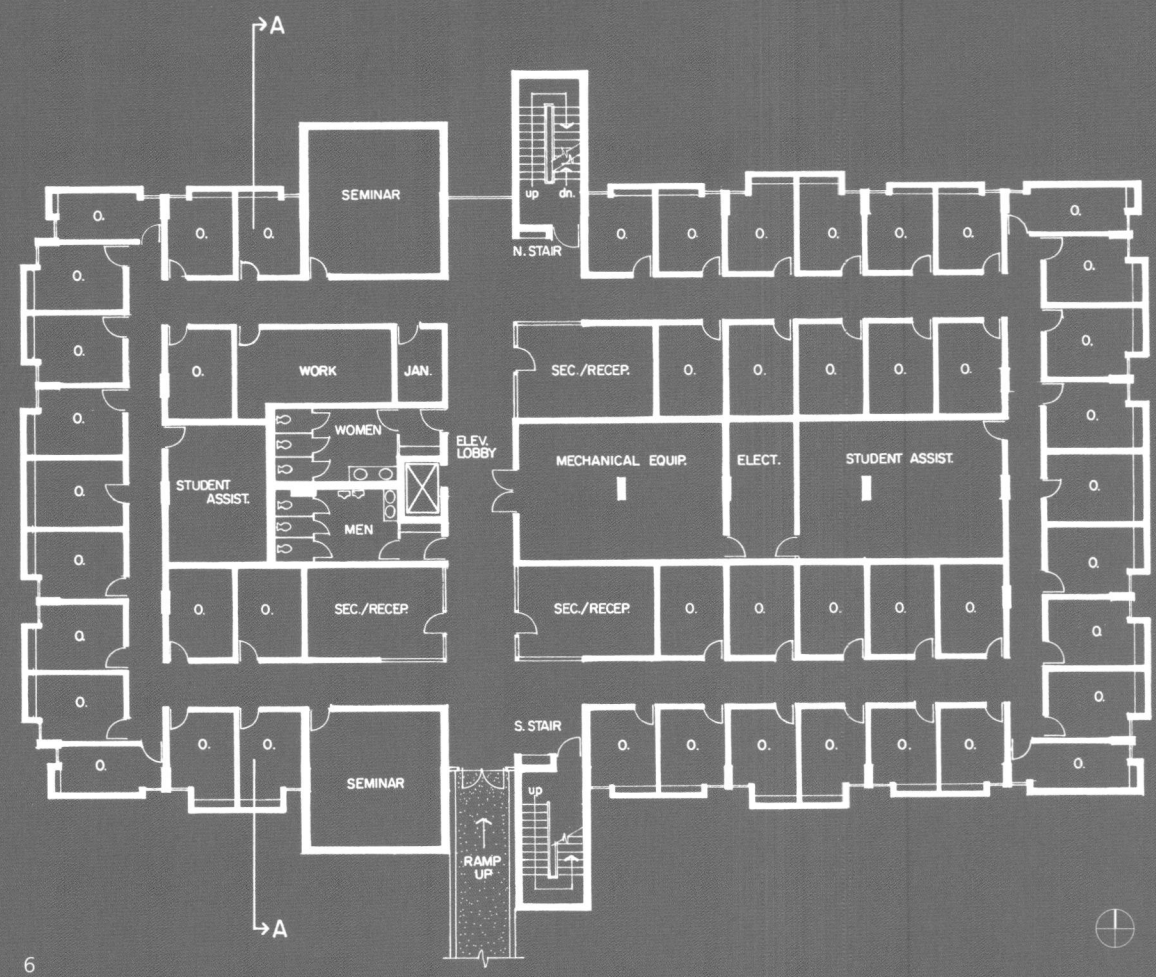

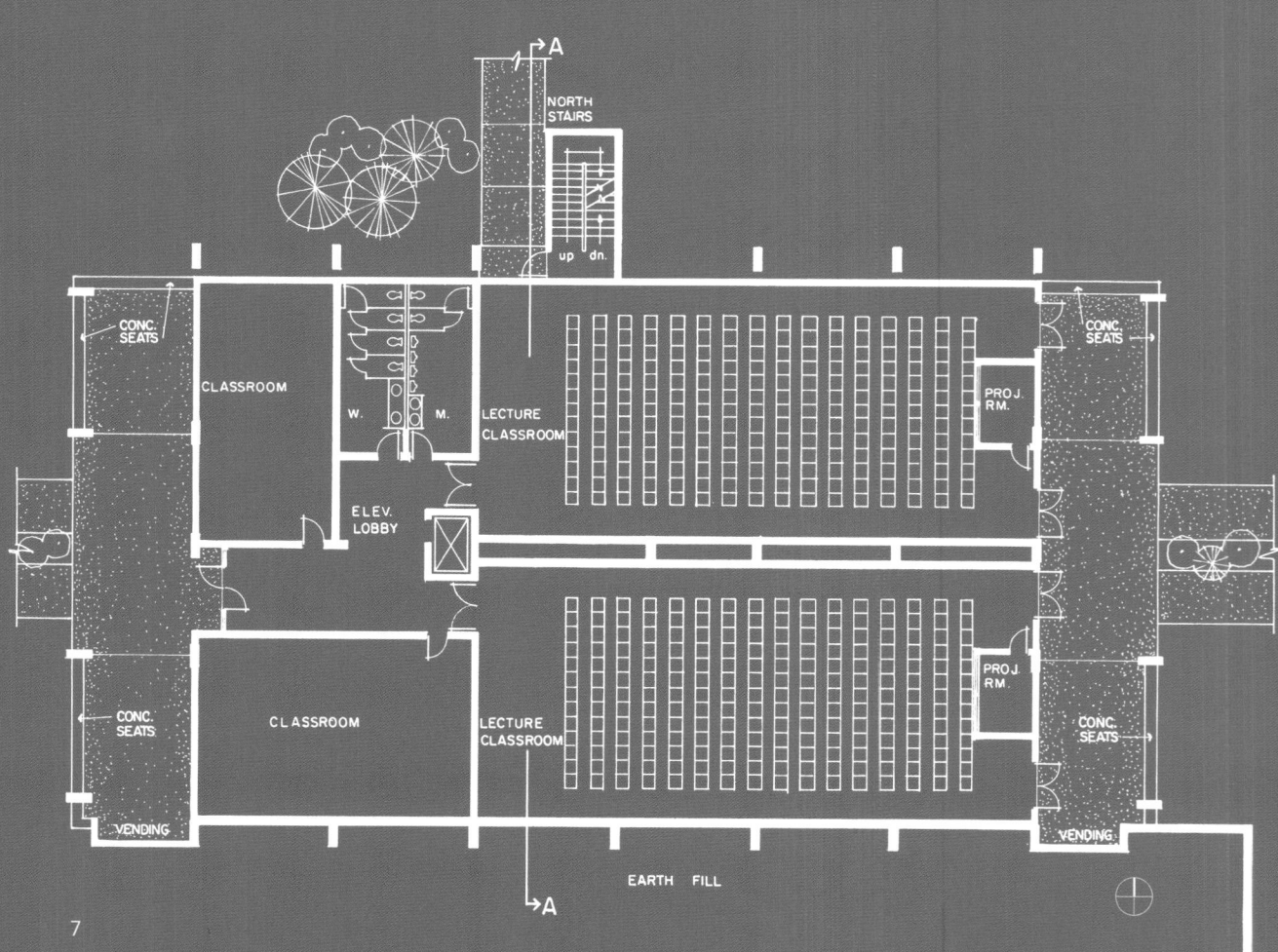

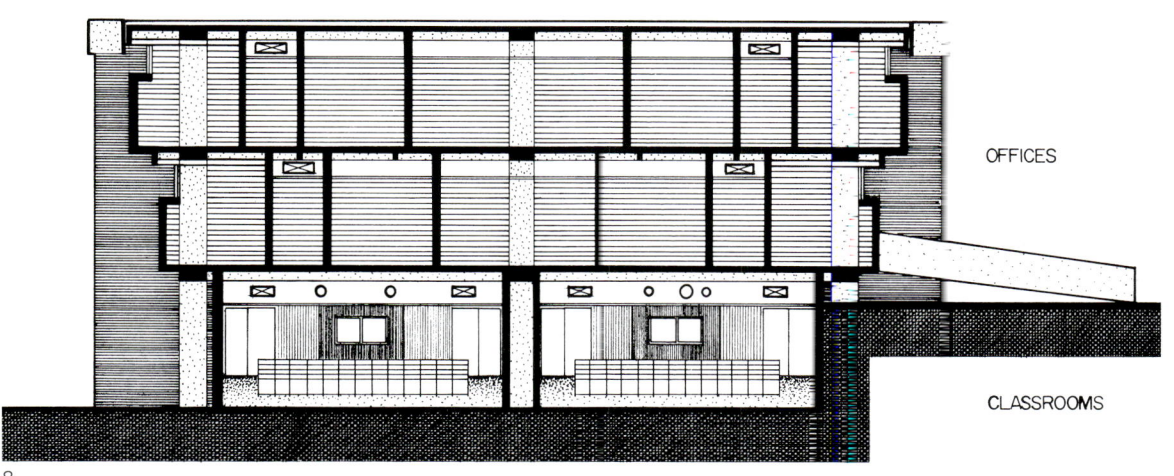

8

OFFICES

CLASSROOMS

9

6   First floor plan
7   Basement floor plan
8   Section
9   Classroom

1 Entry level floor plan
2 Section
3 Perspective

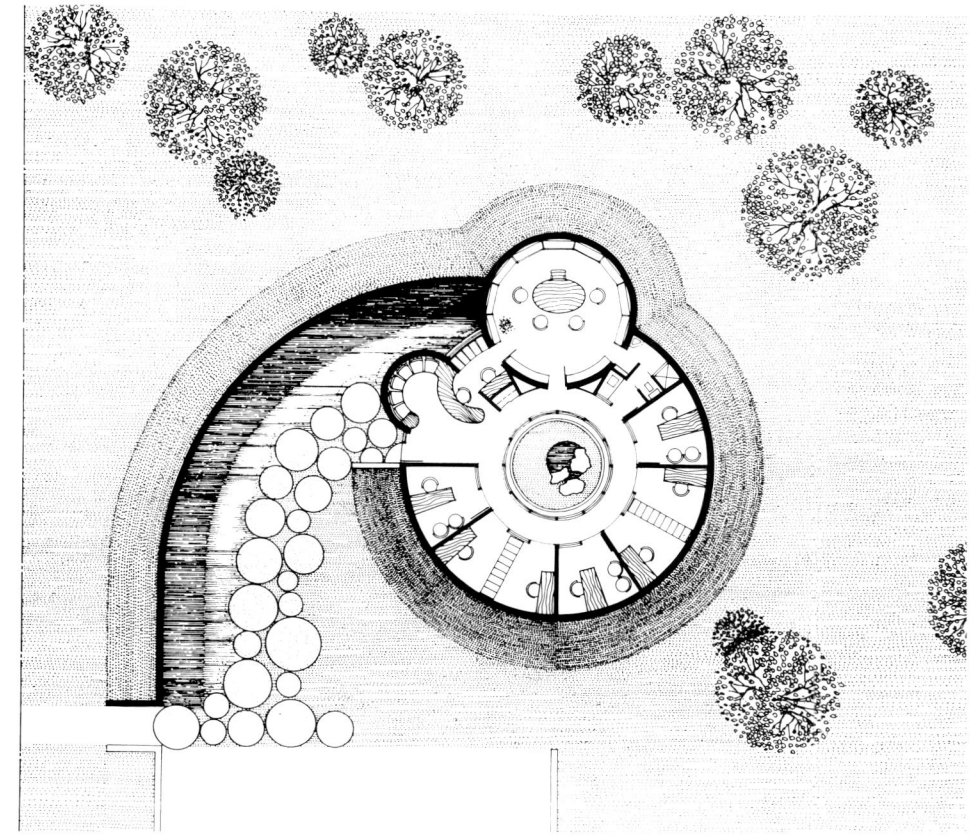

1

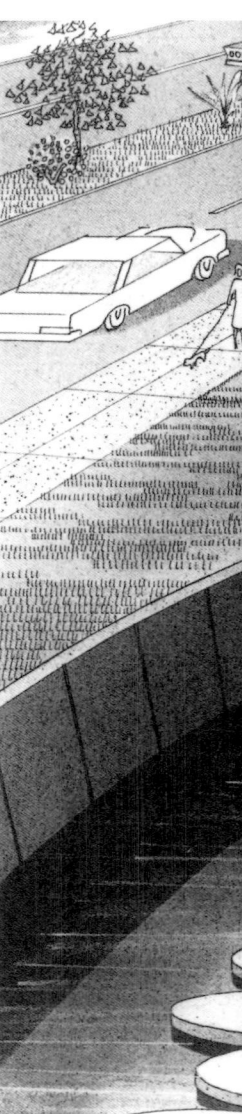

3

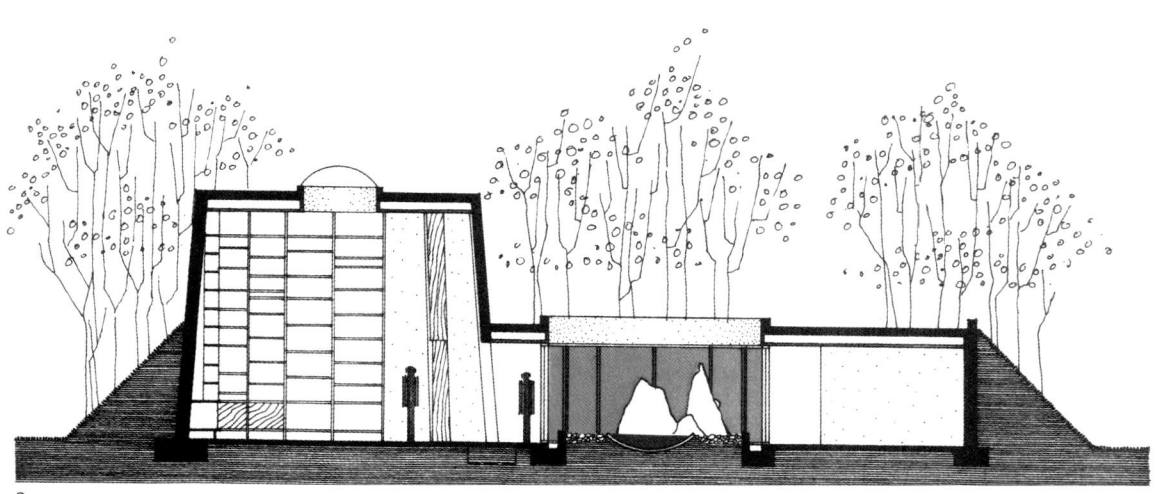

2

This project was the first of three designed by Howey for the same owner. The site borders a busy street with nondescript neighbors. To provide visual and acoustic privacy, a continuous masonry wall was devised, beginning at the parking area and then wrapping around the circular building design. As one enters the building, its curved masonry walls open into a reception and waiting area, and then into a ring corridor with offices radiating from it. Next to the reception area is a large circular conference room with skylight. At the center is a circular, open, glass-walled courtyard. The main entry wall is glass with a smaller skylight over the reception area. The office exterior wall is earth-bermed at 45 degrees, with a ground cover of Confederate jasmine.

# 45

**Attorney's Office**

**Design 1966**

Tampa, Florida
Charles F Wishart
3,230 square feet
Concrete, concrete block, steel
bar joists, metal deck, glass,
aluminum, textured stucco,
clay pavers, and carpet

URBAN

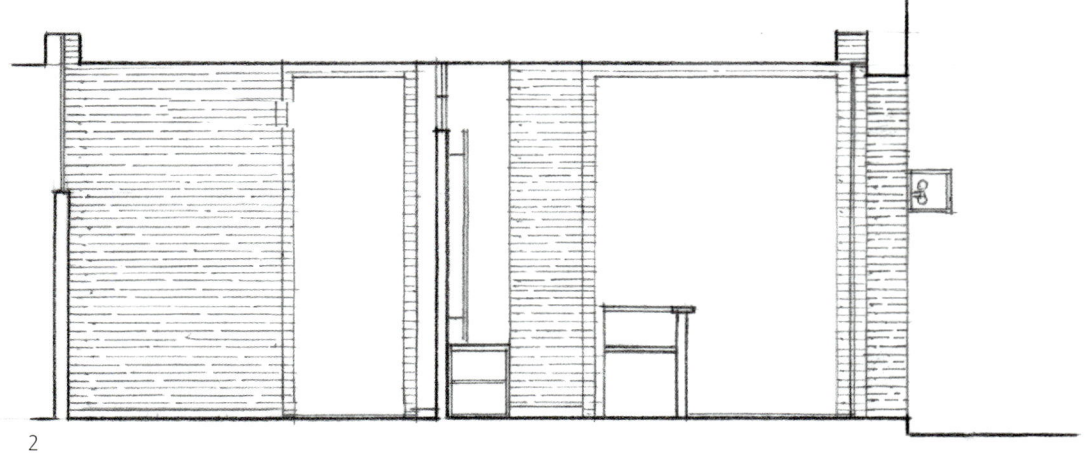

1

2

## Gravity Court Reporting

Streetfront exposure was of prime importance to this court reporting group that needed identification for and ease of access to its offices for its numerous clients. The reception area occupies the corner first floor space with conference rooms behind.

Here, depositions are taken and transcribed by the reporters. Transcripts are then available for collection by clients at the reception counter. Illumination of the entry wall and logo provides additional visibility at night.

**Design/Completion
2003/2004**
Tampa, Florida
1,000 square feet

1 Night view of entrance
2 Cross section at
  reception/conference
3 Plan

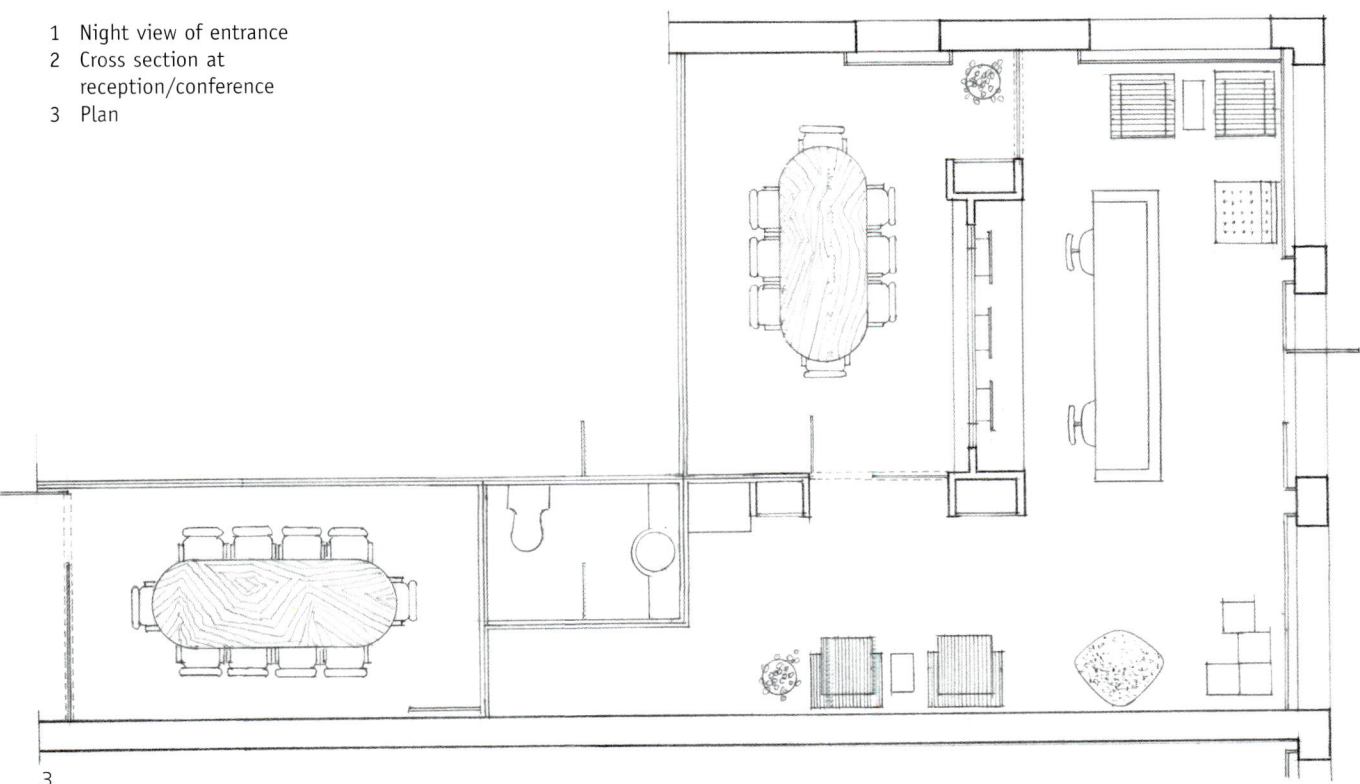

3

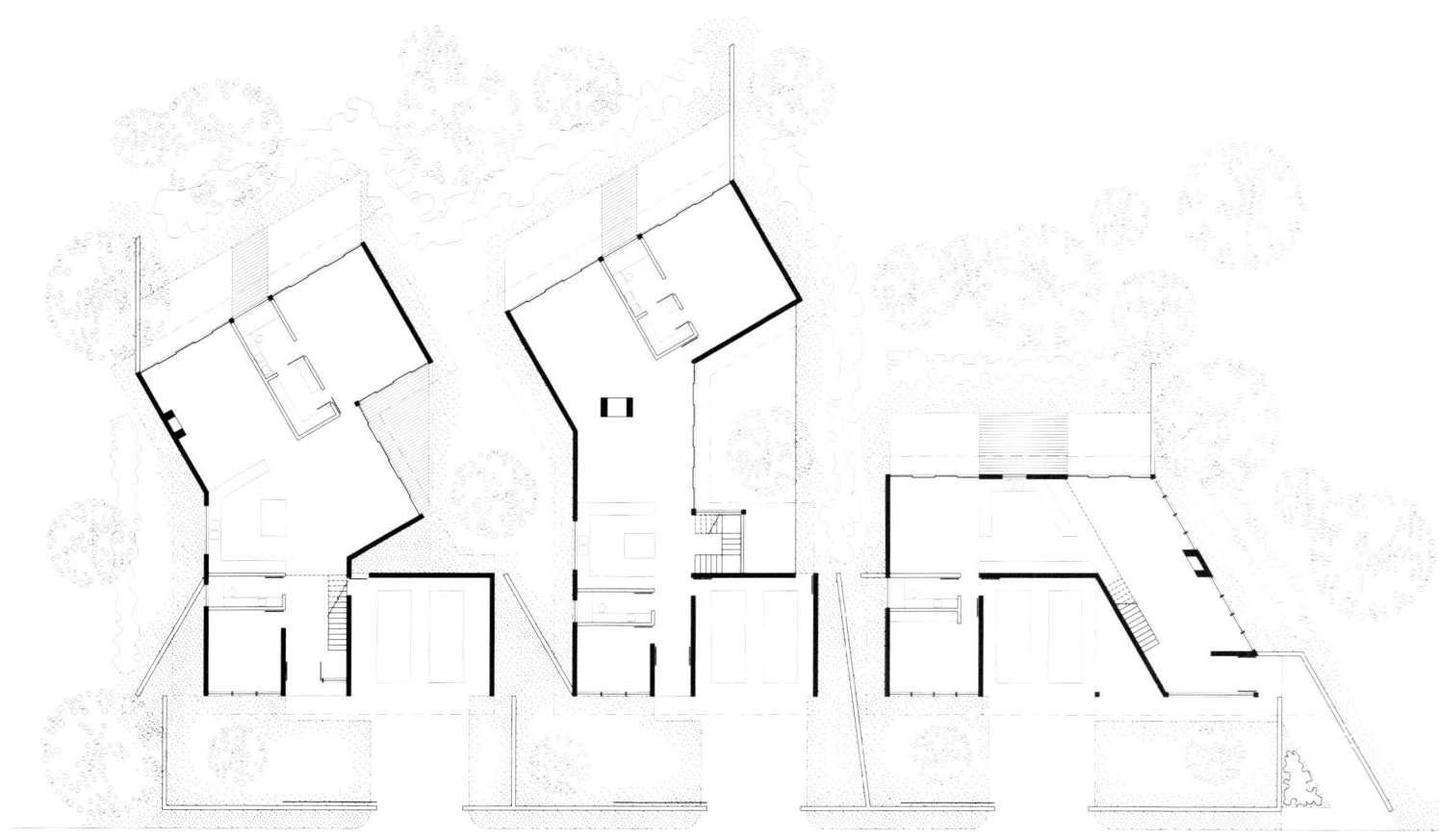

1

0        15ft

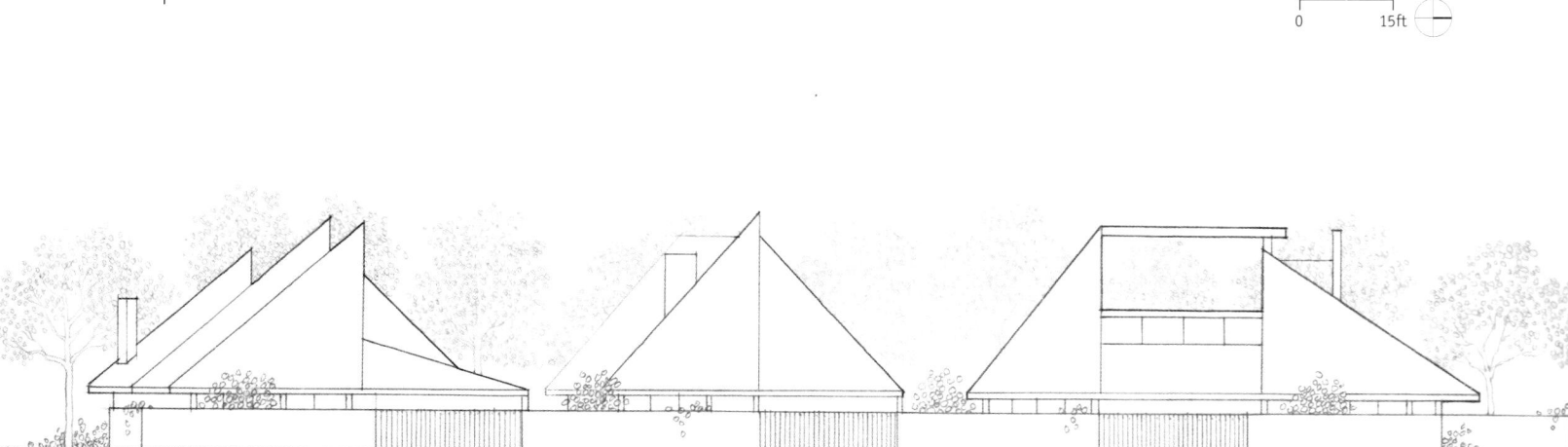

2

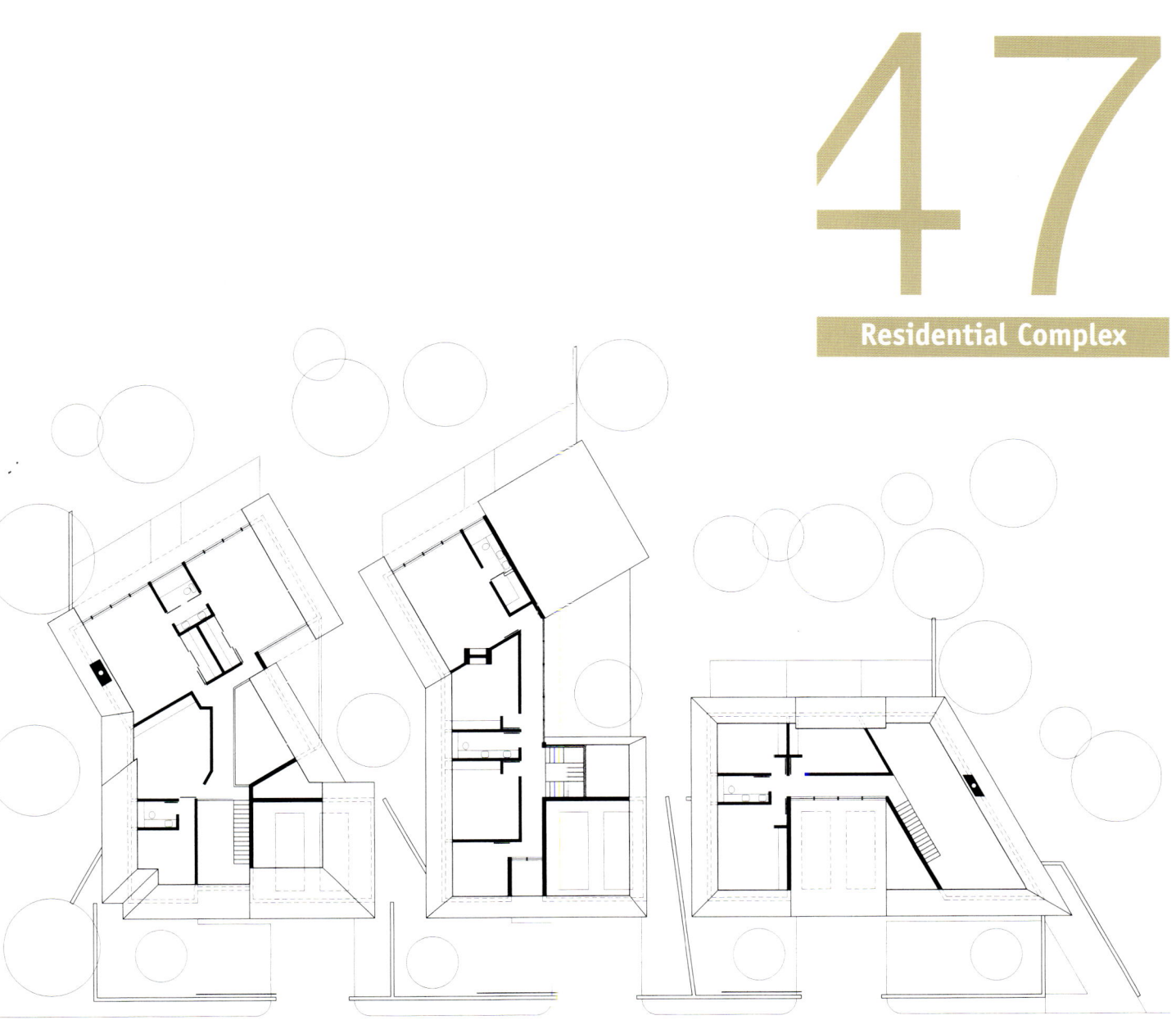

3

0        15ft

## Design 2002

Tampa, Florida
Donald Blair
11,500 square feet
Spread footings, masonry
walls, wood framing above
second levels, stucco, tile,
carpet, gypsum walls
and ceilings

Inspired by the outdoor walled courtyards in the historic Plaka district of Athens, Greece, Horvey devised a system of interlocking privacy walls for three side-by-side residences to be developed in an emerging residential district. Entry is from the street by auto into each courtyard, or through gates into the foyers. Living, dining, service spaces, and an optional bedroom suite or den are at grade. Bedrooms occupy the second level. Because the site is irregular with many oak trees, it was necessary in some cases to "borrow" space from one adjacent property to visually expand views for the living spaces of its next-door neighbor. The idea of a village—separate, yet together—prevails through the connection of the 6-foot-high common walls. Each design is unique but tied together with the common use of the same stuccoed walls and tile roofs. Pools, decks, and landscaping features are located within the walled perimeters.

1

2

3

City of Tampa
800 square feet
Concrete slab footings, jumbo
brick, steel gates and bollards

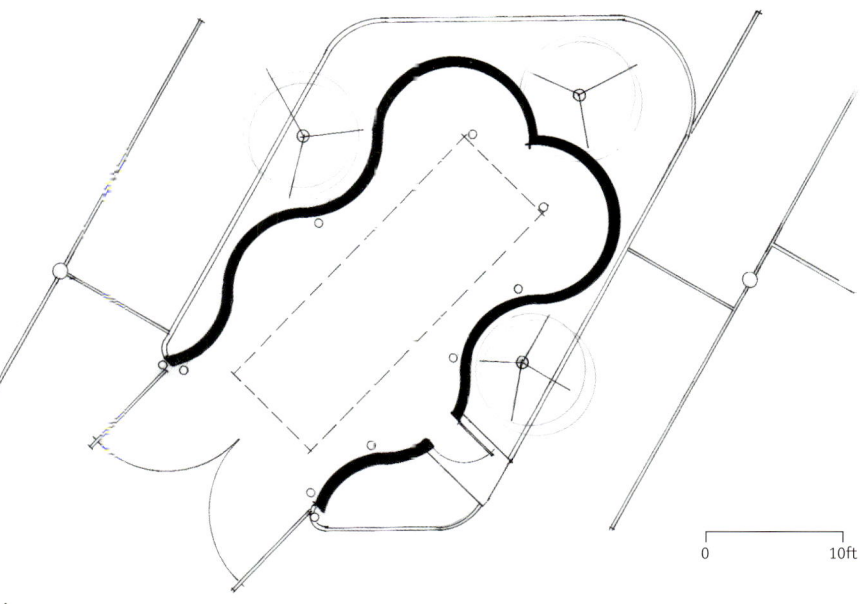

4

The rapid growth of a popular Tampa historic district, called Ybor City, created the need for oversized, automatic trash compactors in public areas. Because of the location near active, ground-level parking entrances to numerous brick entertainment establishments, the design required visual screening for concealment as well as security. It was determined that brick was the most compatible material to fit in with the district's appearance. A serpentine brick wall, based on Thomas Jefferson's concept at the University of Virginia, was adapted to meet Tampa's aesthetic requirements. By converting four parking spaces to a planter area for each enclosure, the historic district is able to satisfy this service need. New curbs, landscaping, and night lighting complete the design.

# 48
## Service Screen Enclosures

5

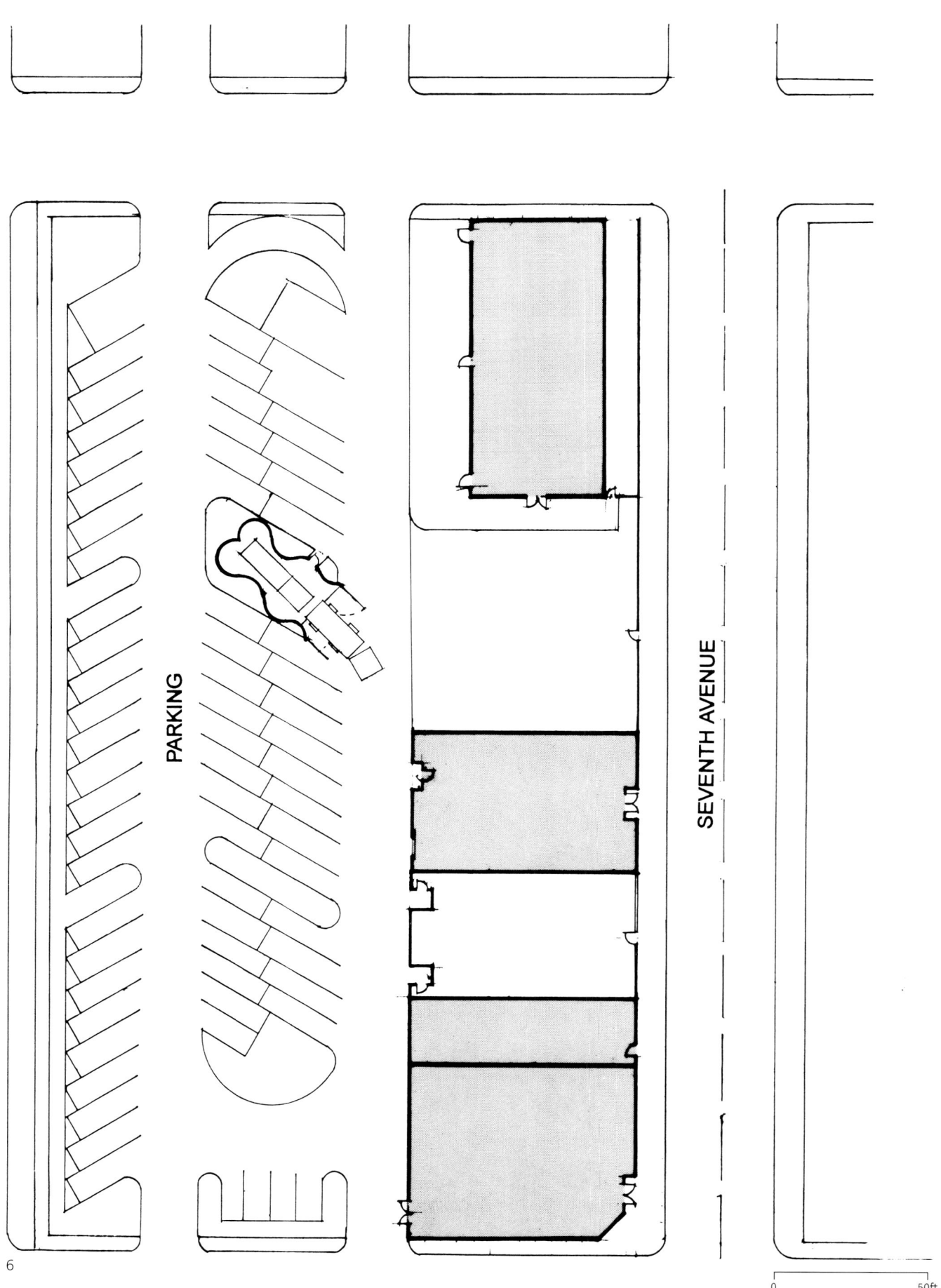

PARKING

CHURCH

SEVENTH AVENUE

6

0                50ft

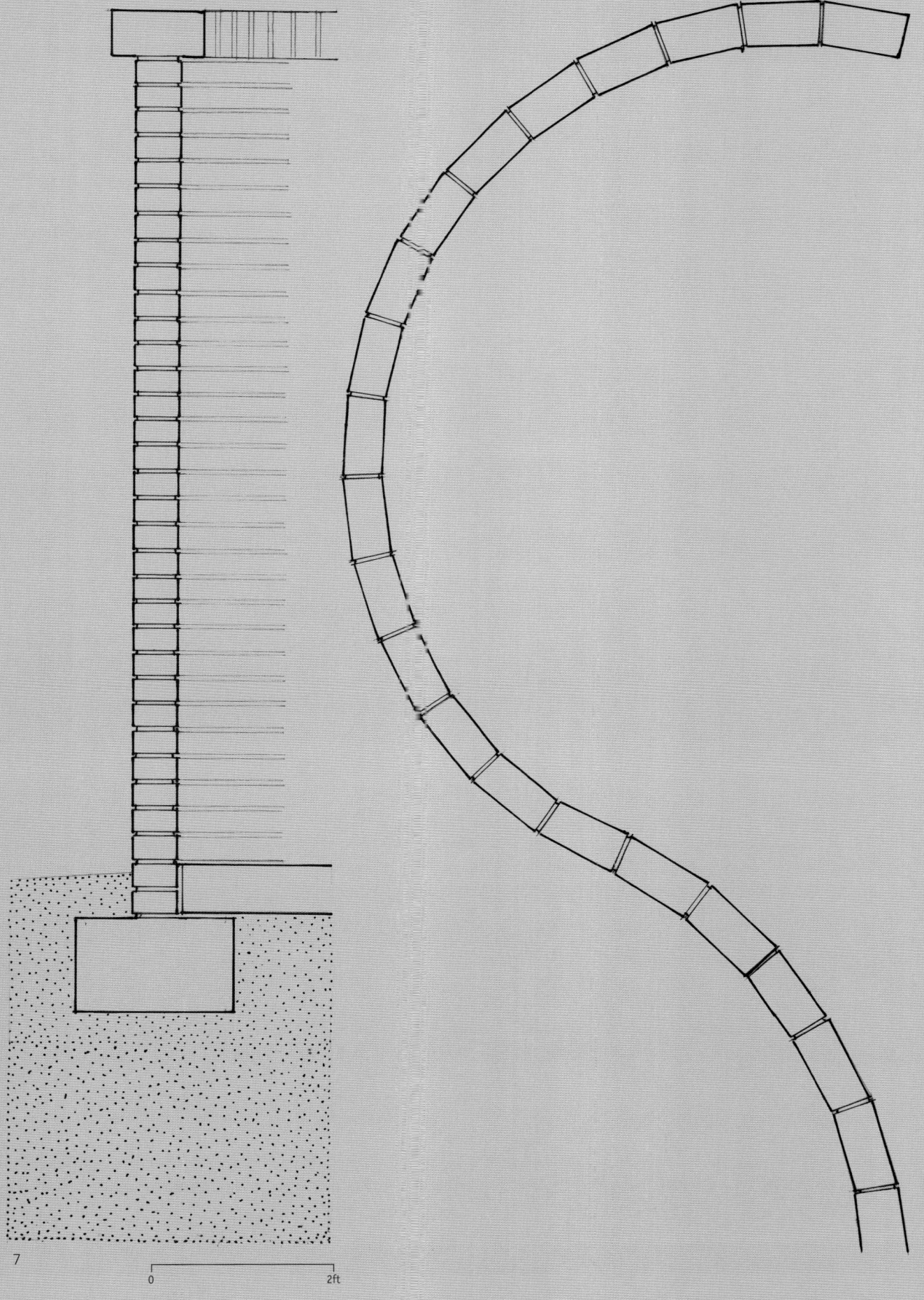

7

0                  2ft

6  Site plan
7  Section and partial plan

This international competition was held for the design of a new Times Square ticket facility to be assembled from a kit of parts on the existing TKTS site. The intention of Howey's TKTS proposal was to create a quiet presence in the Broadway cacophony of kinetic signs, people, and traffic surrounding the site day and night. The proposed translucent wall panels undulate like a glowing stage curtain, opening in larger scale at the ticket booth counters, and then slowly closing together at the rear. Inside, a pre-assembled roof core supports the interior roof trusses that radiate out to their perimeter supports and wall panels. Some panels will become media and information signs, while others become enclosing walls, exit doors, and clear glass ticket windows within their translucent panels. Continuous bands of fiber optic lights are embedded in the sidewalks around the facility to guide ticket patrons to and from the booths. Strands of fiber optics emerge from the sidewalks to run up the supports and along the roof trusses for night illumination. There is an energetic edginess to Manhattan people on the go, pointed tower tops, and Broadway slashing through Times Square to create street situations, such as TKTS, with triangular islands. The design is meant to be a reflection of this New York energy.

Design 2000

New York, New York
11,125 square feet
Prefab steel trusses, roof deck, columns, supports, lexan and glass wall panels, stainless steel cables, and continuous fiber optic strands

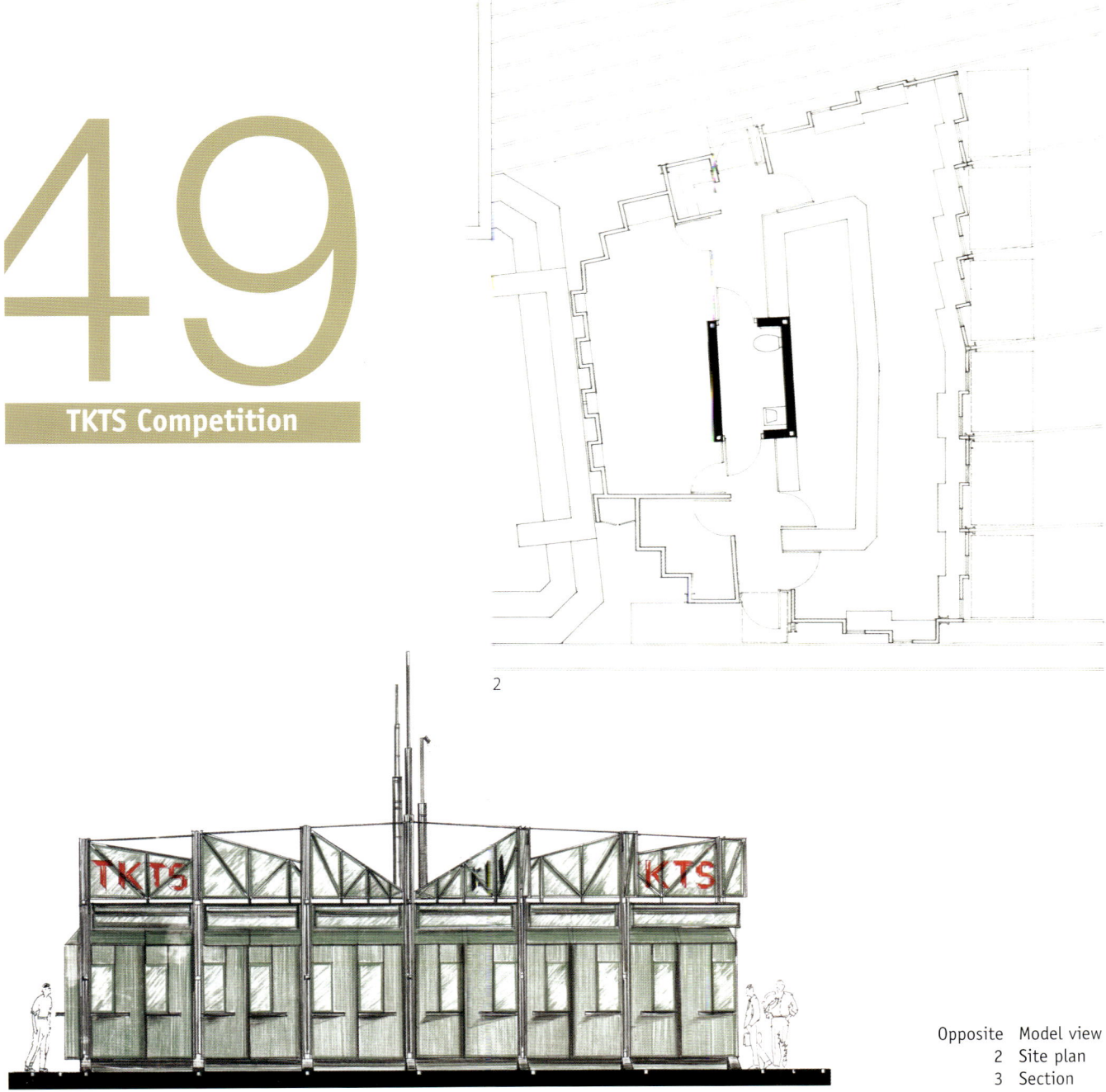

# 49

## TKTS Competition

2

3

Opposite  Model view
2  Site plan
3  Section

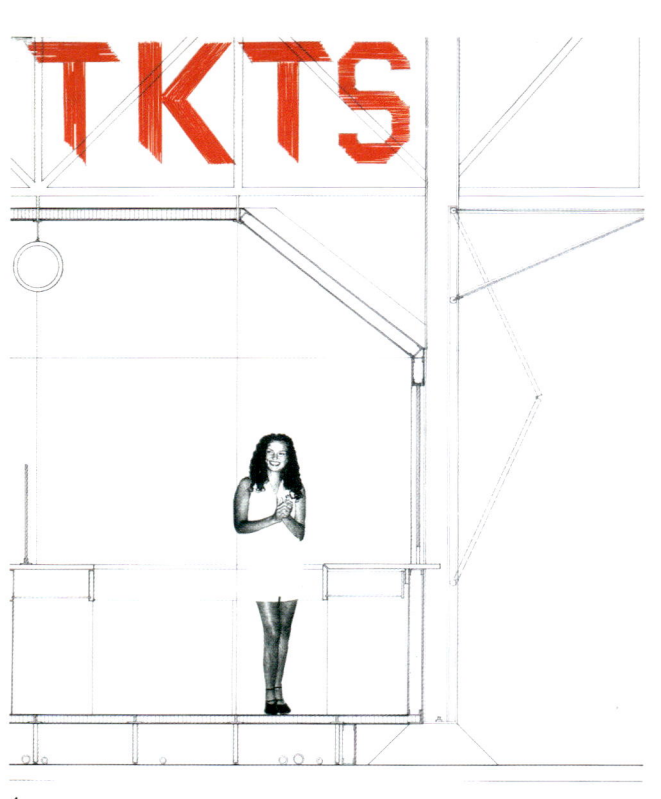

4

5

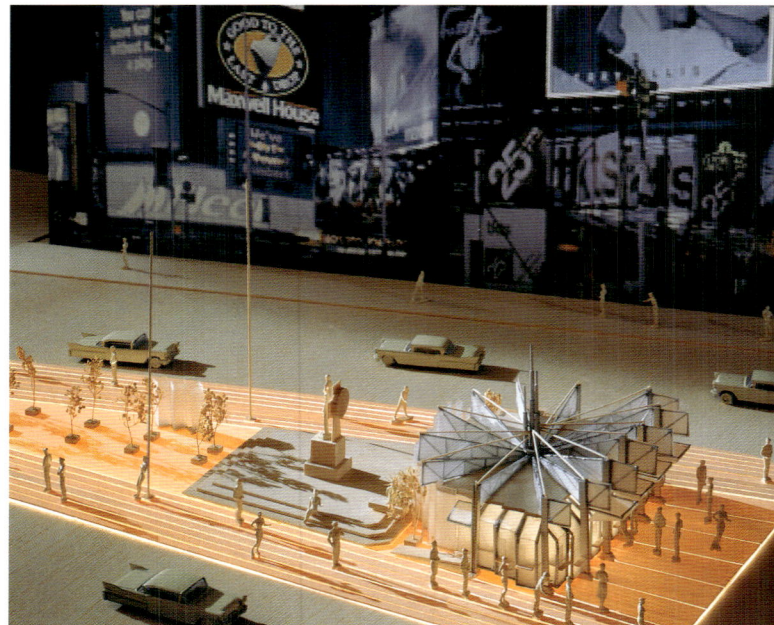

6

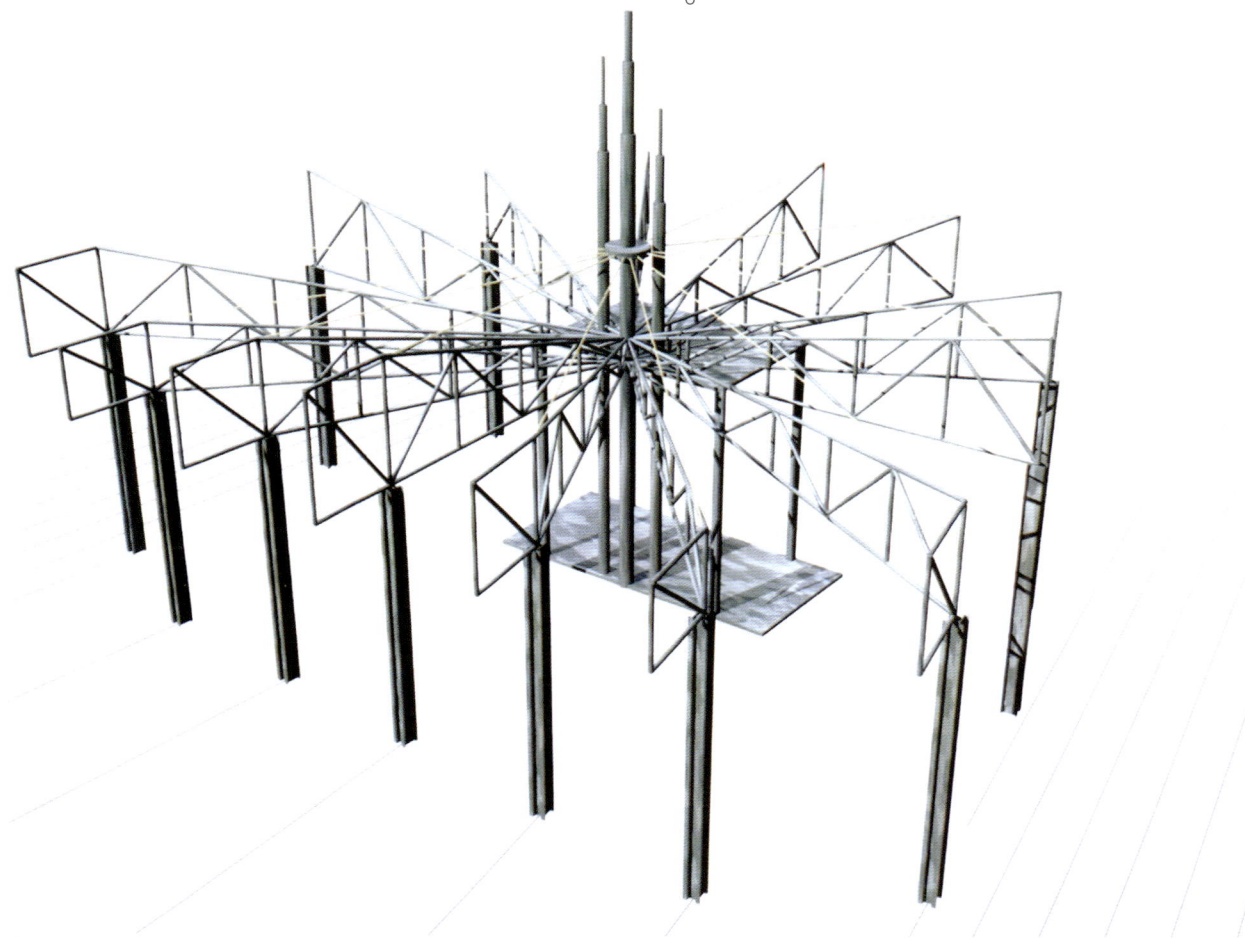

7

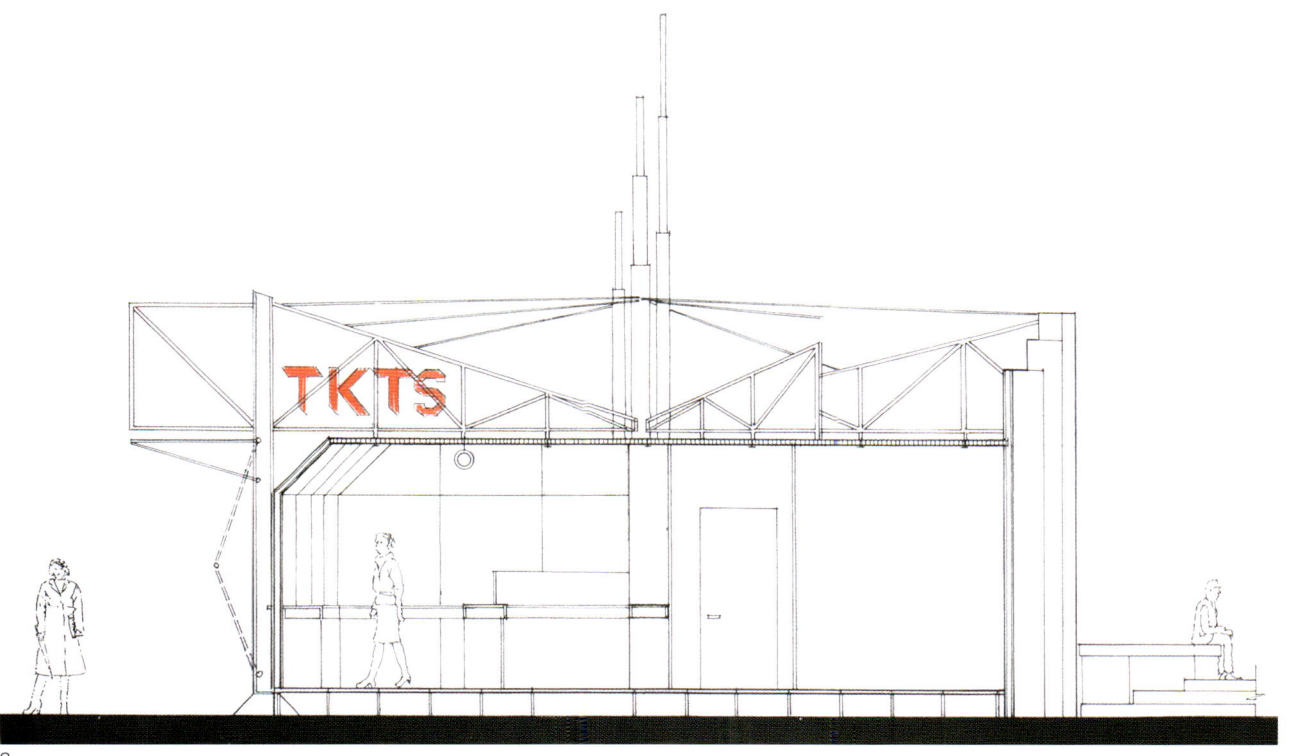

8

9

4&8 Sections
5 Model photograph
6&9 Model views
7 Structure

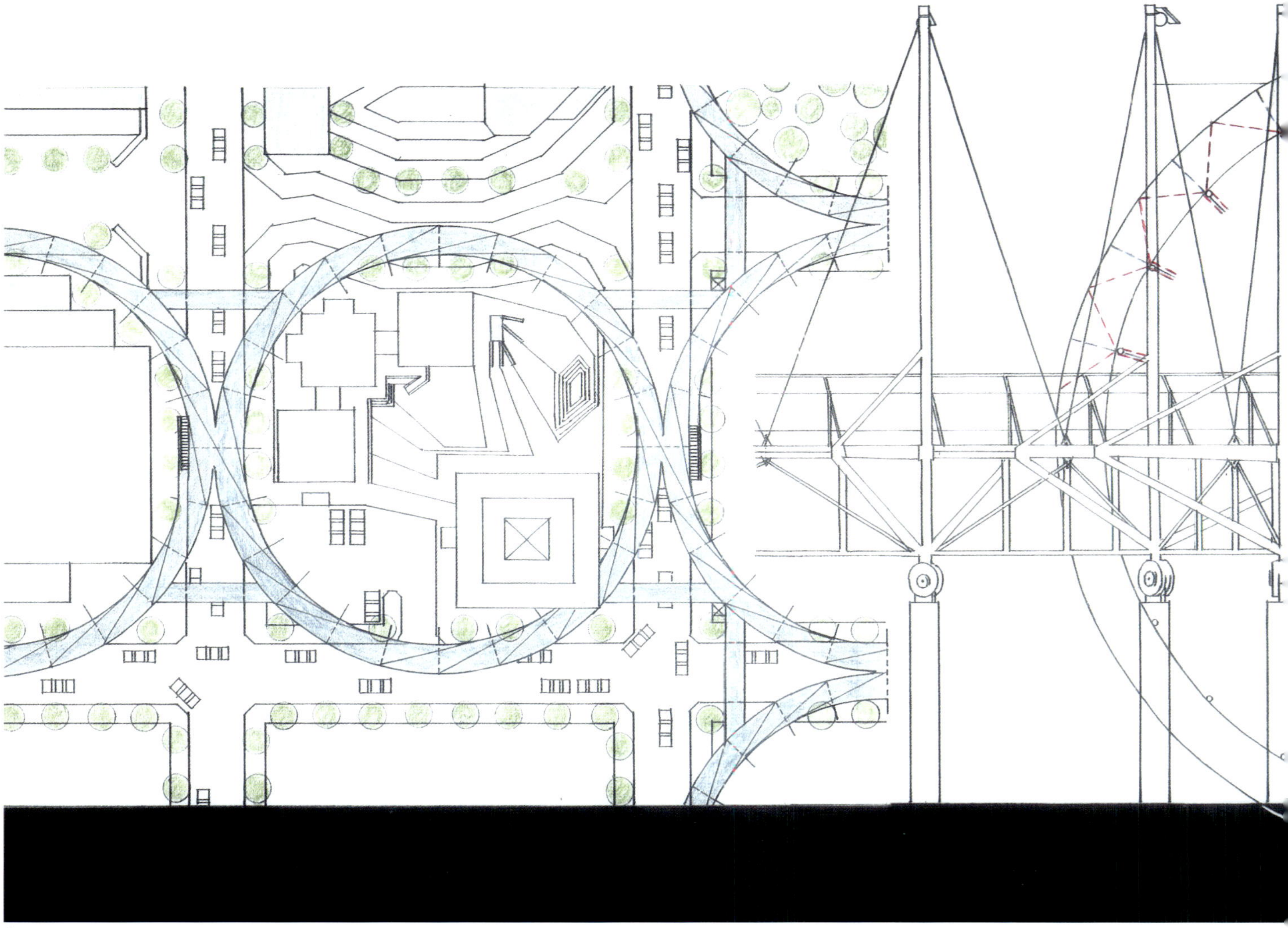

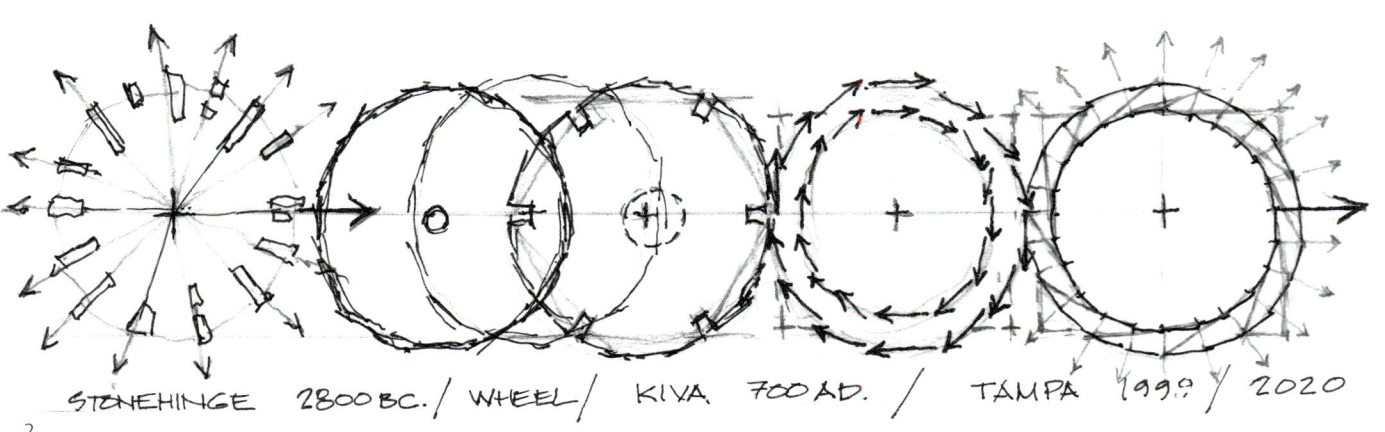

1

2  STONEHINGE  2800 BC. / WHEEL / KIVA. 700 A.D. /  TAMPA  1999 / 2020

1  Plan/section
2  Timeline concept sketch
3  Model aerial view

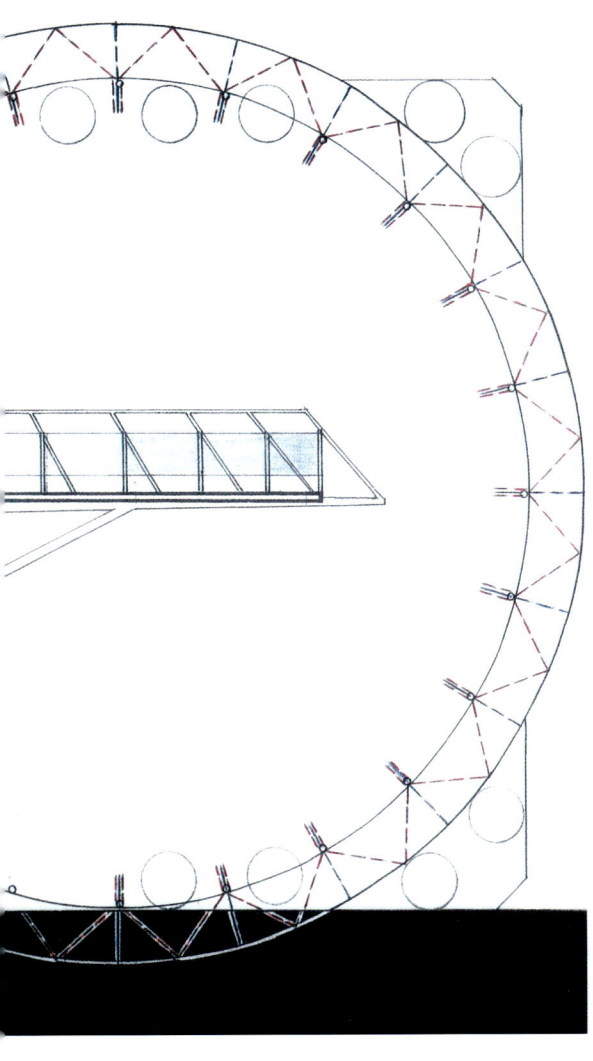

3

## Design 1999

Tampa, Florida
City of Tampa
210 acres
Concrete footings and
columns, raised pedestrian
rings of concrete, steel and
glass set in existing downtown
Tampa street grid

This urban proposal was submitted to the city of Tampa in response to an expressed interest in downtown revitalization. The proposal included a large-scale model of the existing core area. The model shown in the photos is a small-scale example of what the final, larger city model would look like. Also shown is a new elevated layer of circular, pedestrian sidewalks linking the major downtown venues of City Hall, County Courthouse, Tampa Art Museum, Convention Center, hotels, parking and sports arena. The second level pedestrian-ways also link the square city blocks at street level where potential parks, amphitheaters, commercial, and residential structures would be constructed. The ring design affords new elevated corner entrances to existing buildings, while creating shade cover below for pedestrians walking or waiting at transit stops. This system serves as both unifier and generator for present and future waves of downtown development. The proposal ultimately was not built.

**50**

**City Center Renewal Project**

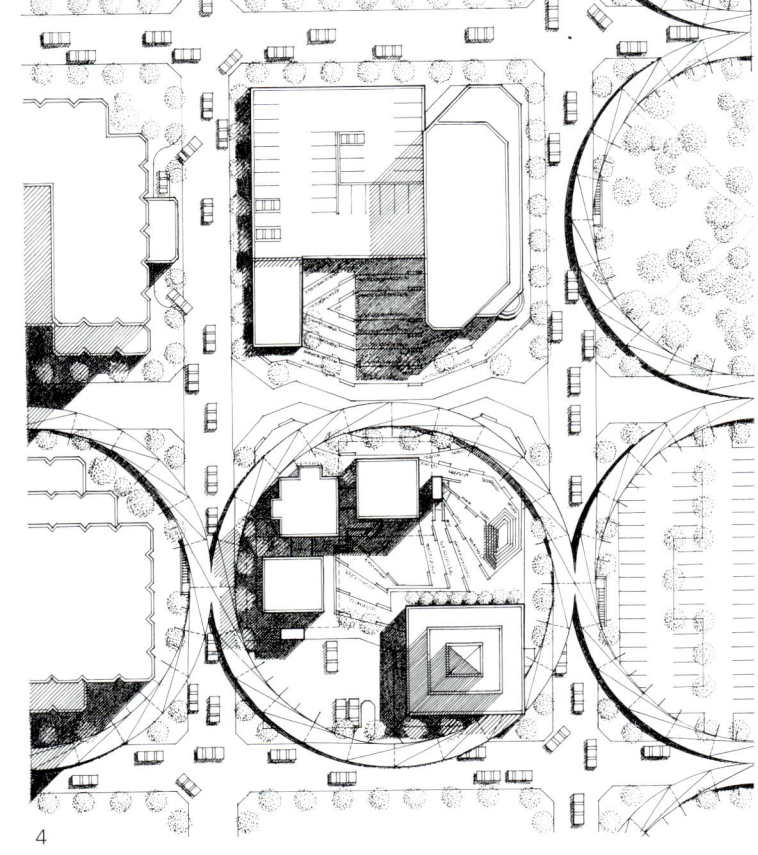

4

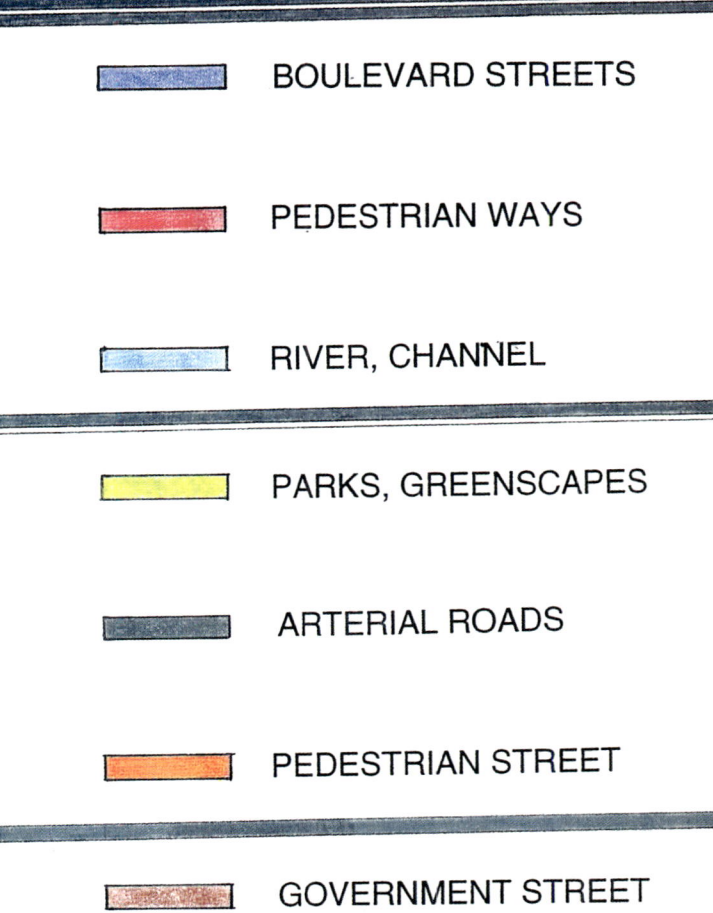

BOULEVARD STREETS

PEDESTRIAN WAYS

RIVER, CHANNEL

PARKS, GREENSCAPES

ARTERIAL ROADS

PEDESTRIAN STREET

GOVERNMENT STREET

TRANSIT WAY STREET

5

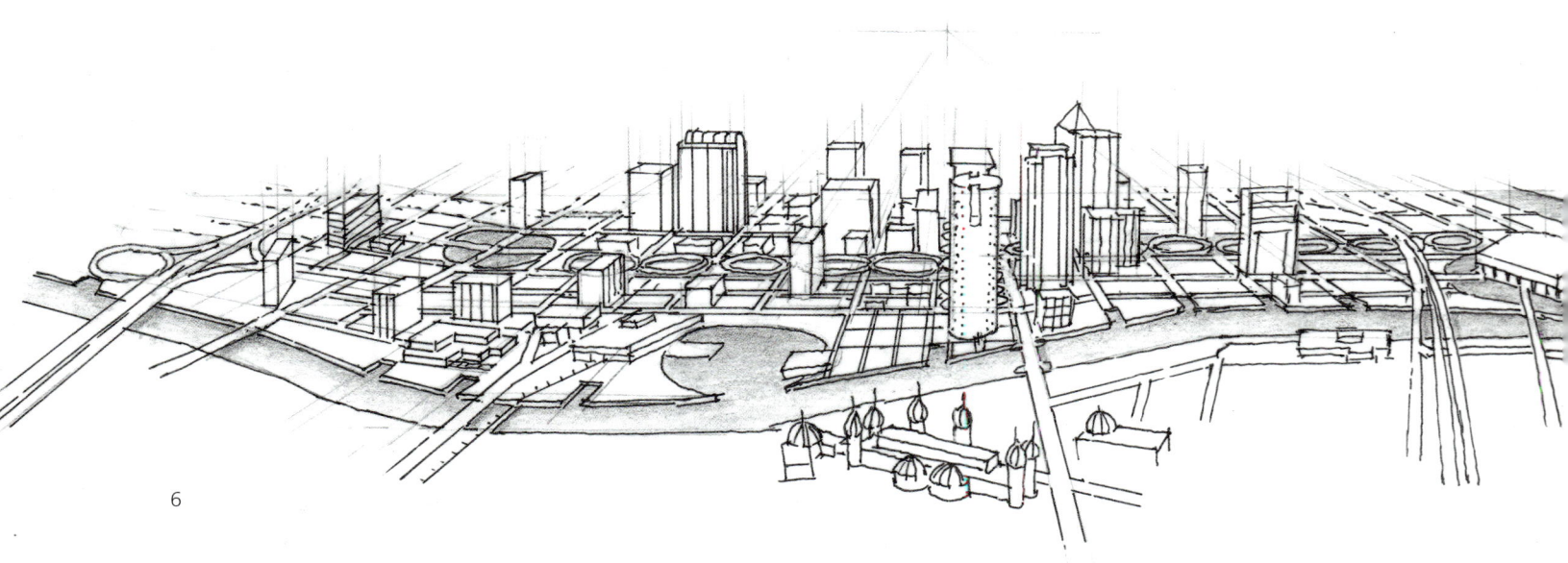

6

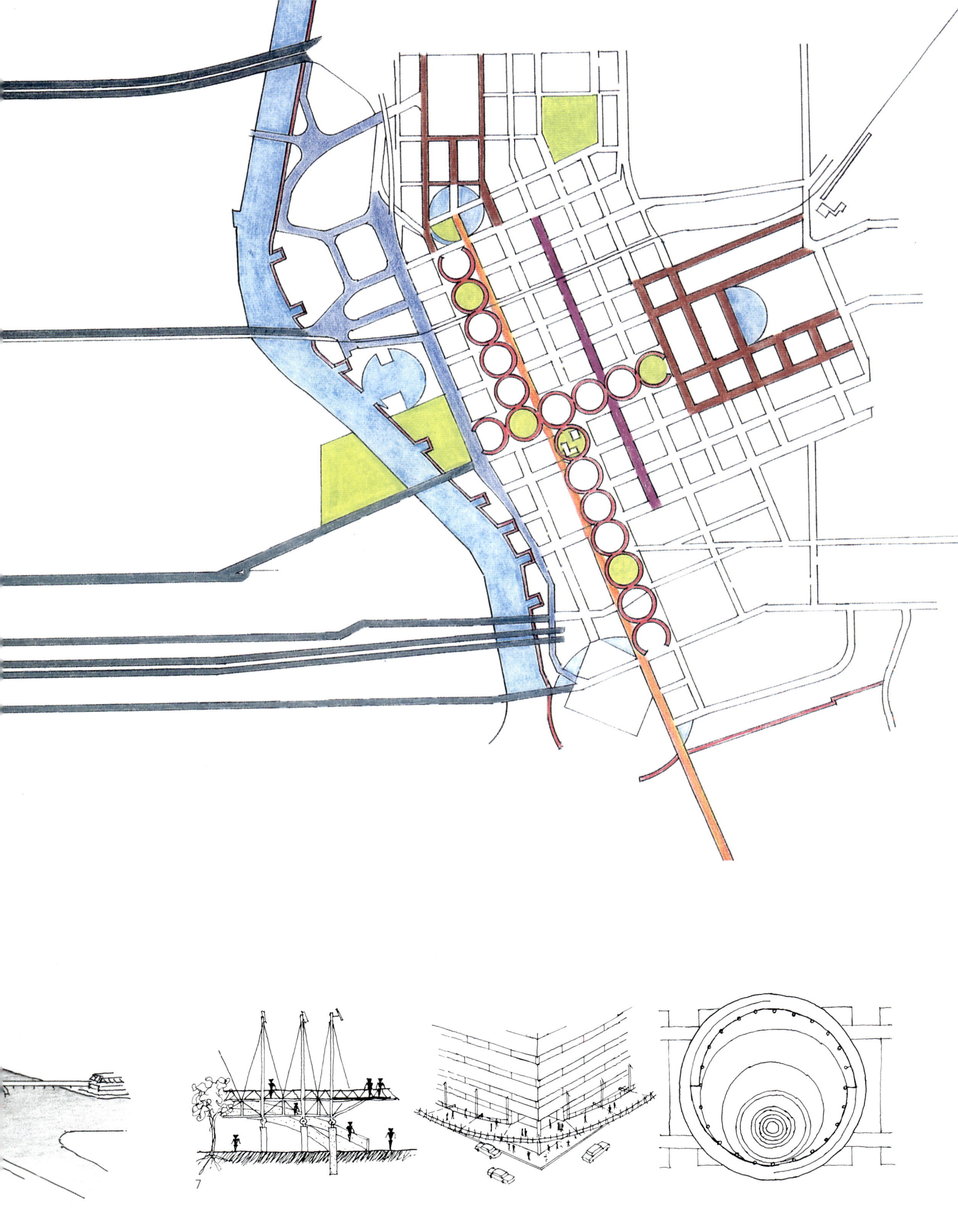

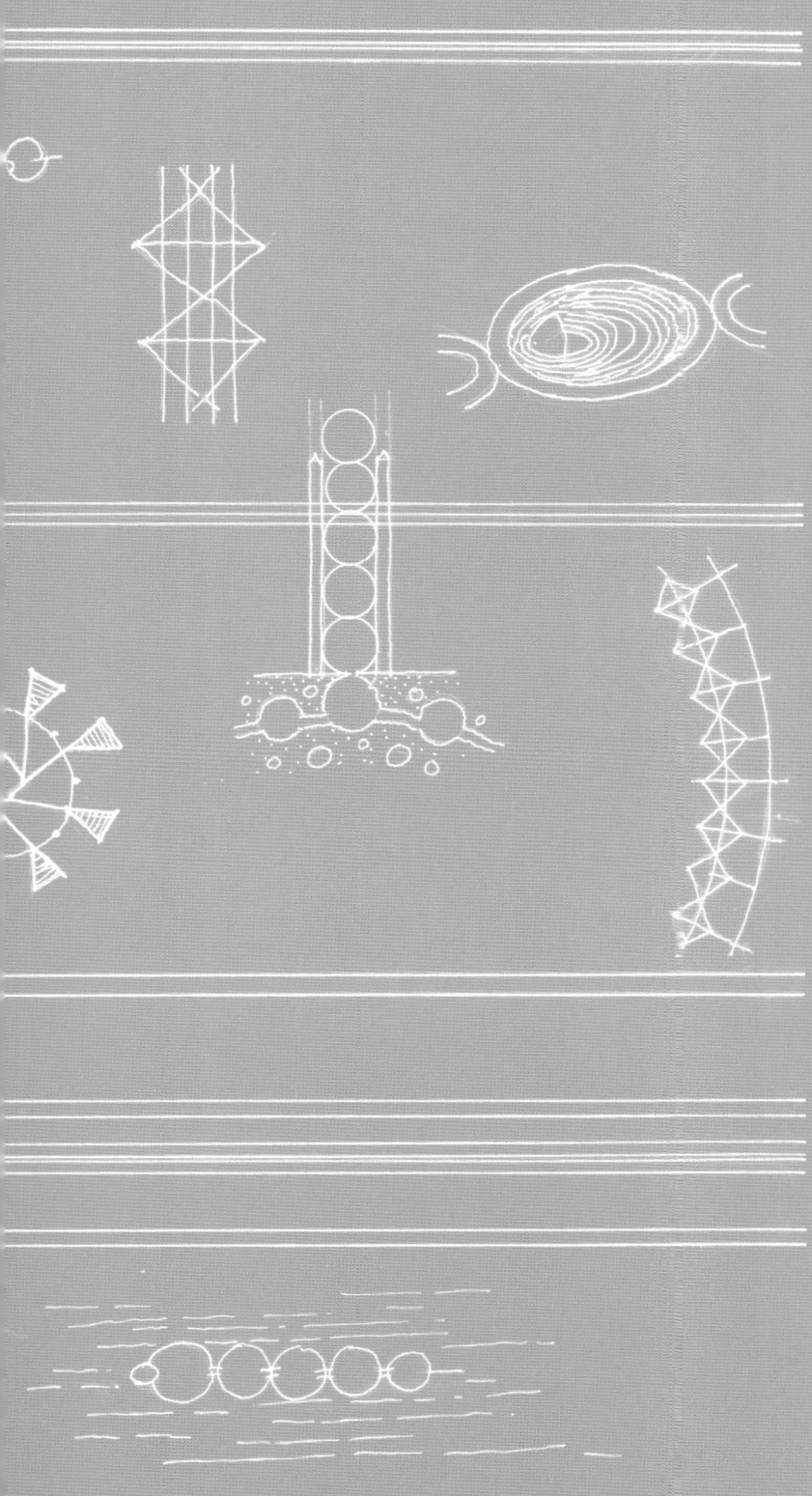

9

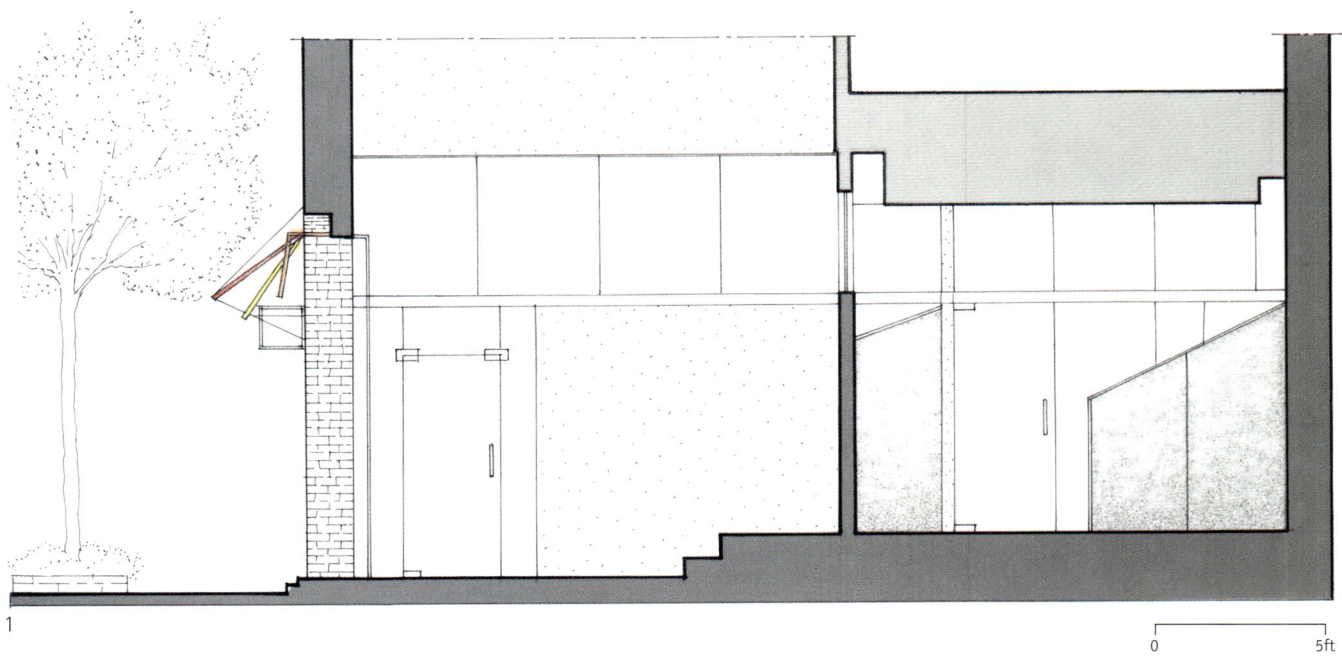

1

0        5ft

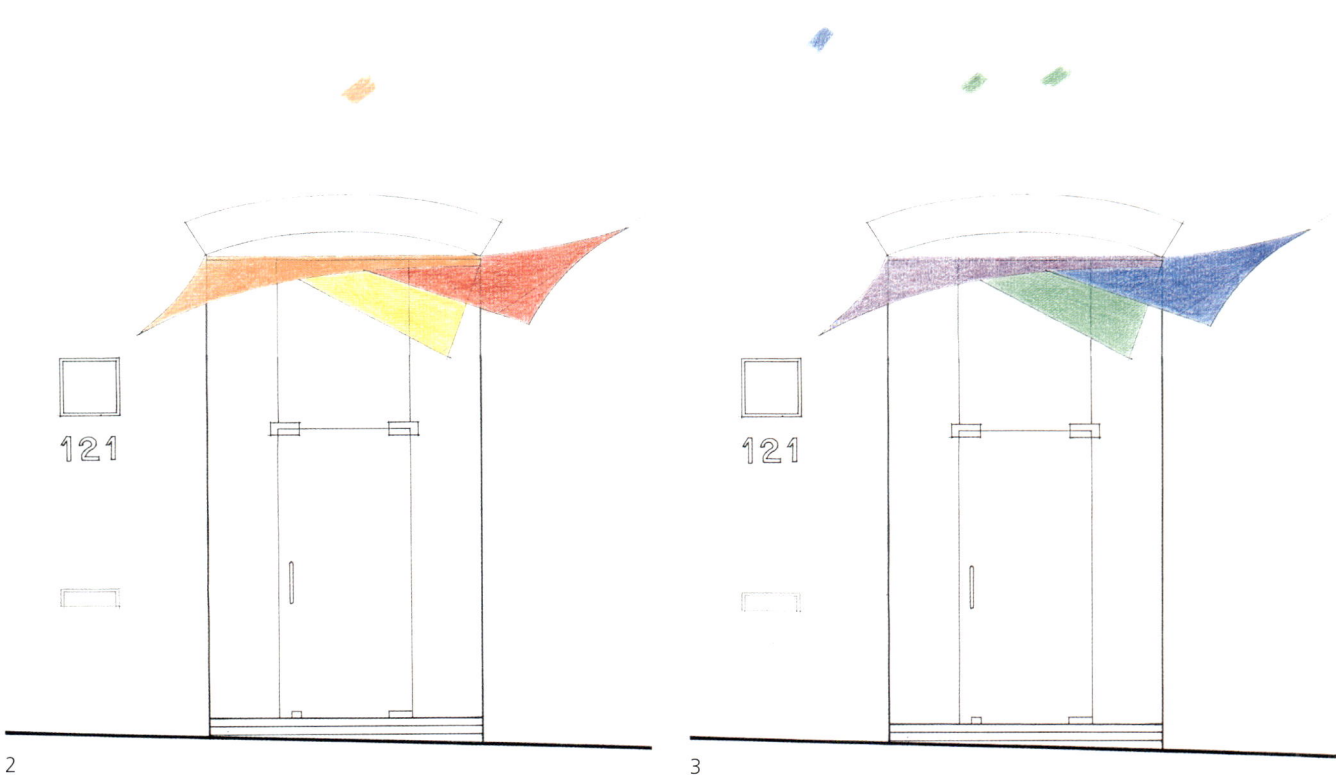

121

121

2                                        3

The challenge here was to create a side entrance presence with night time illumination for an office whose entrance door is located under exit stairs. City code allows marquees of certain dimensions above entries. A series of stretched fabric shapes on aluminum spars and cables were designed. Fabric units were made to be interchangeable, with warm red, orange, and yellow fabrics for summer/fall and cool blues, greens, and lavender for winter/spring.

# 51

## Entry Canopy Studies

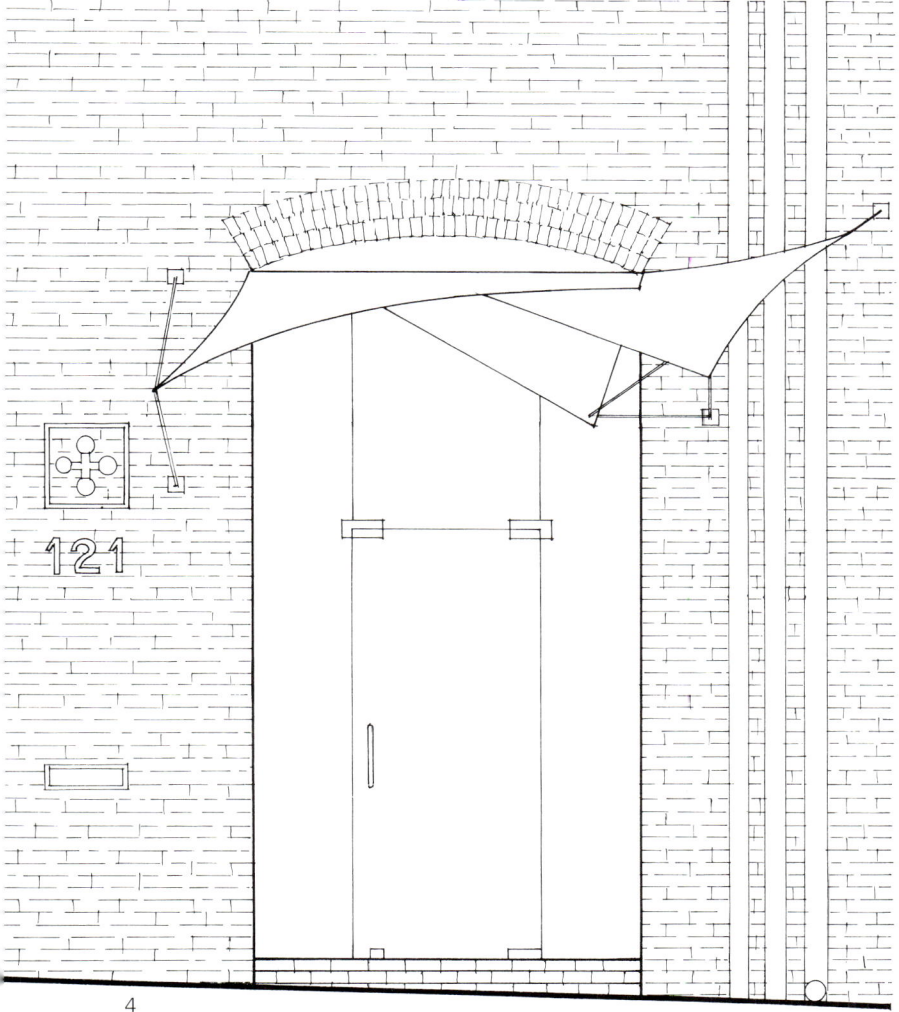

4

1 Section at entry
2 Summer/Fall canopy
3 Winter/Spring canopy
4 Exterior entrance elevation

1 Bird's eye view
of transit system
2 Aerial view of island
from Manhattan

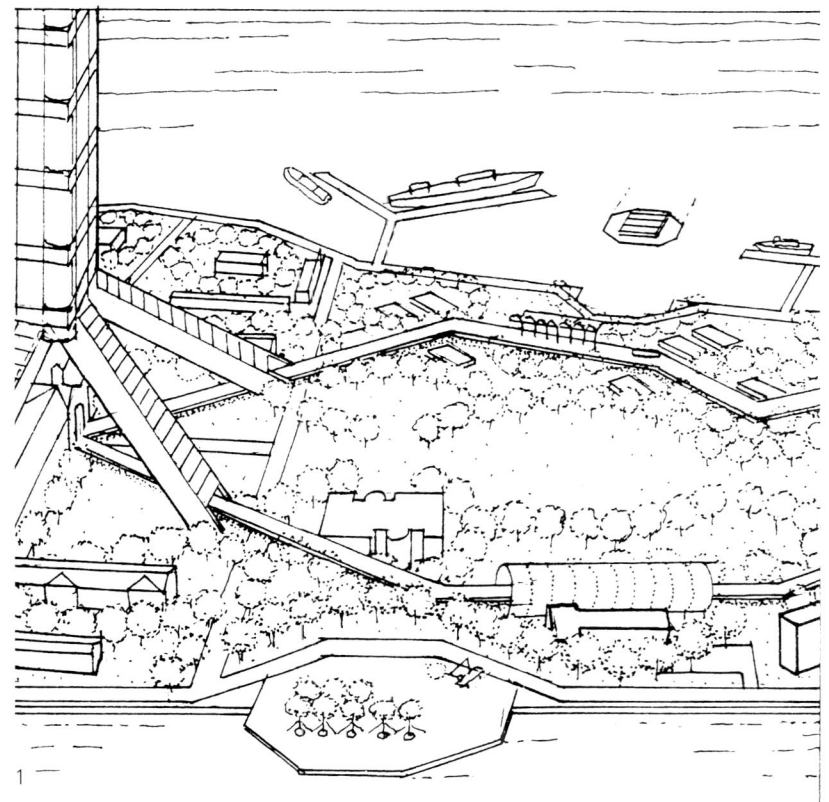

1

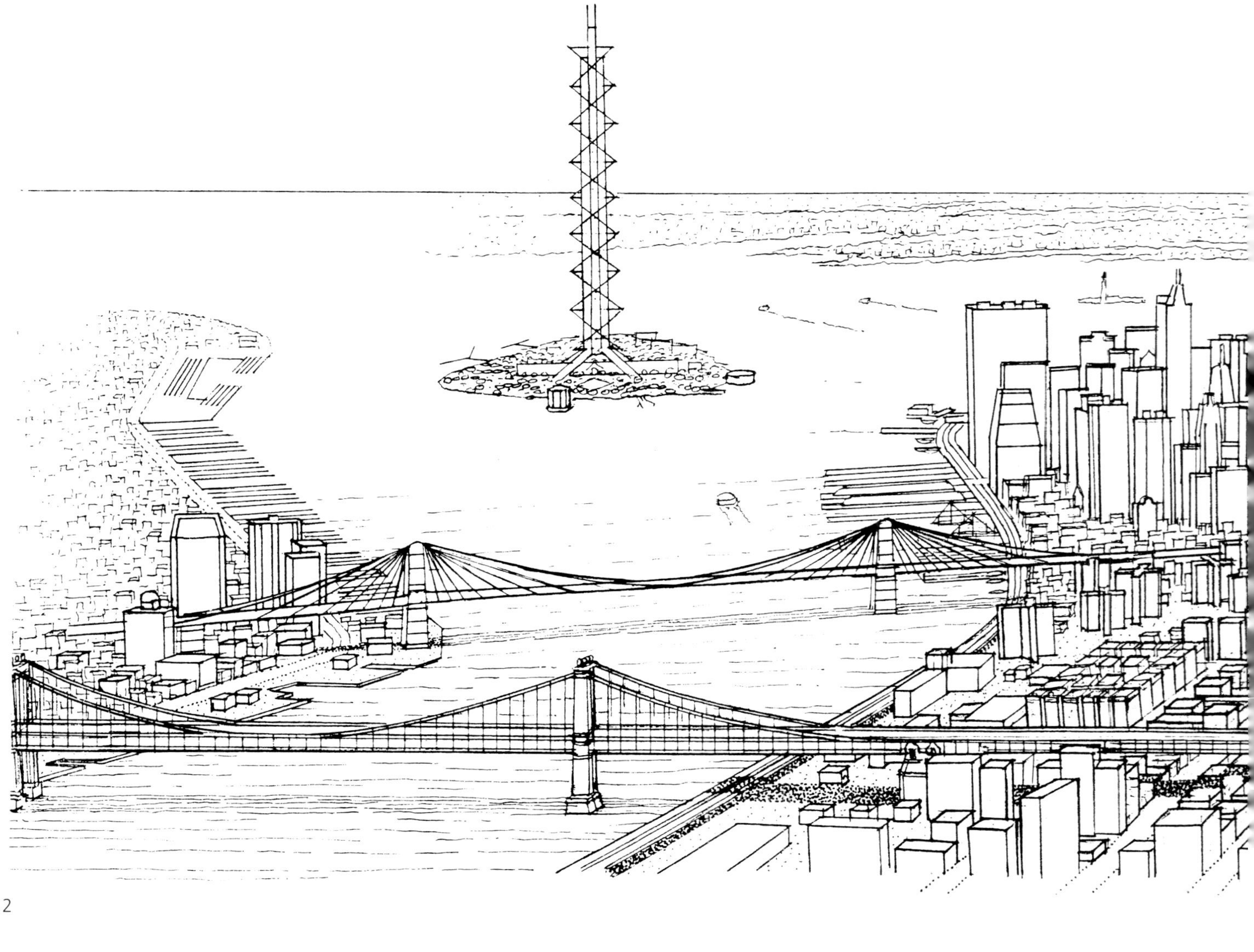

2

# 52

## Governor's Island Competition

**Design 1992**

New York, New York
Van Alen Institute
110 acres

This national competition sought proposals for new uses for Governor's Island, the last remaining piece of open land close to Manhattan. Managed by the U.S. Coast Guard and connected to Manhattan by ferry, this island, with its historic structures of Castle William and Fort Jay, has the potential to be a 21st-century community.

Howey's entry solution envisions a 100-story skyscraper on four legs of garden apartments with retail and an elevated transit system crossing at its base. The overhead tram travels along the island edges to connect low-rise apartments, residences and a community center to both the tower and ferry station. Upper floors of the high-rise would house offices, hotel, and condominium apartments with communications at its top.

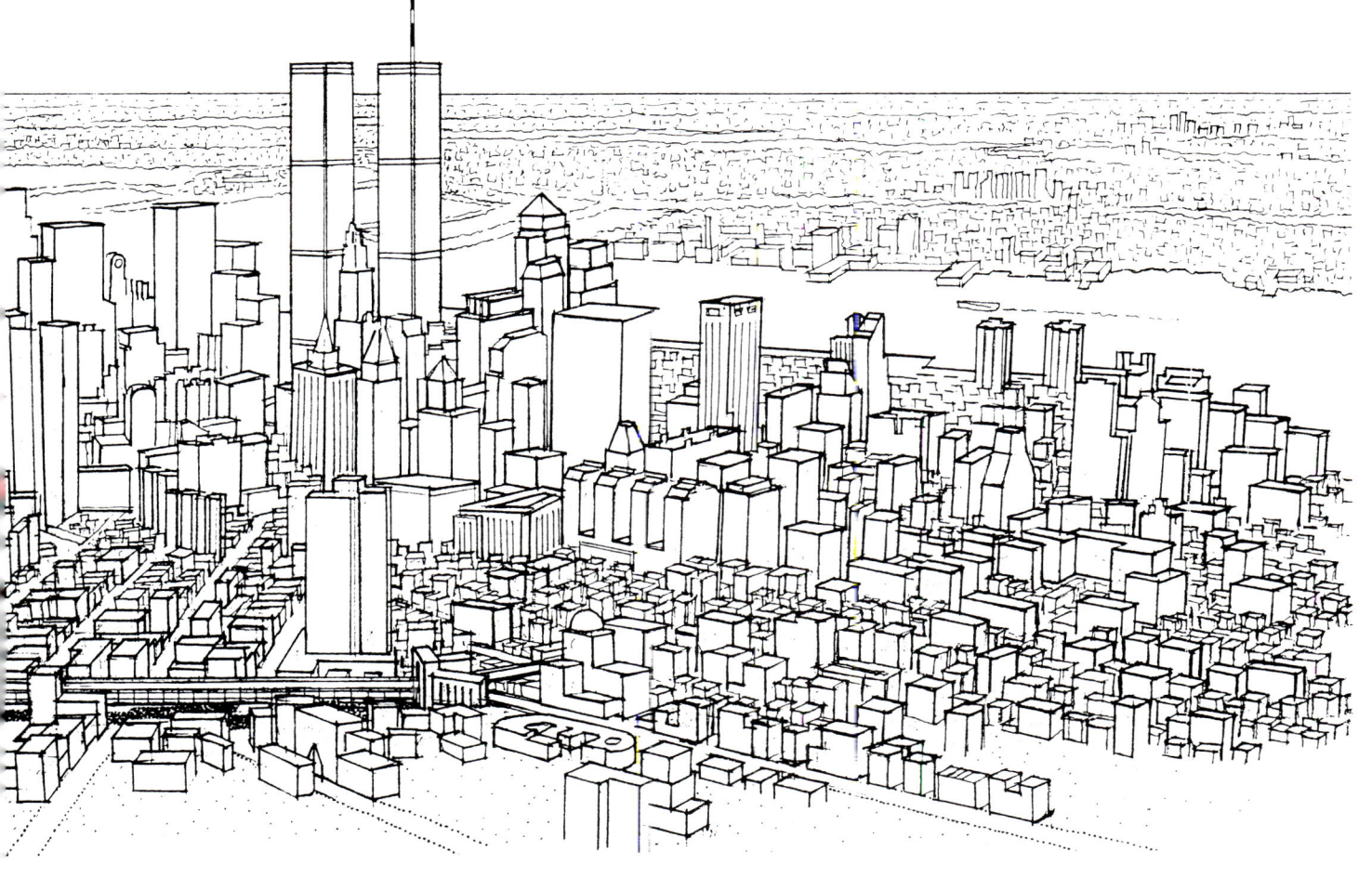

3

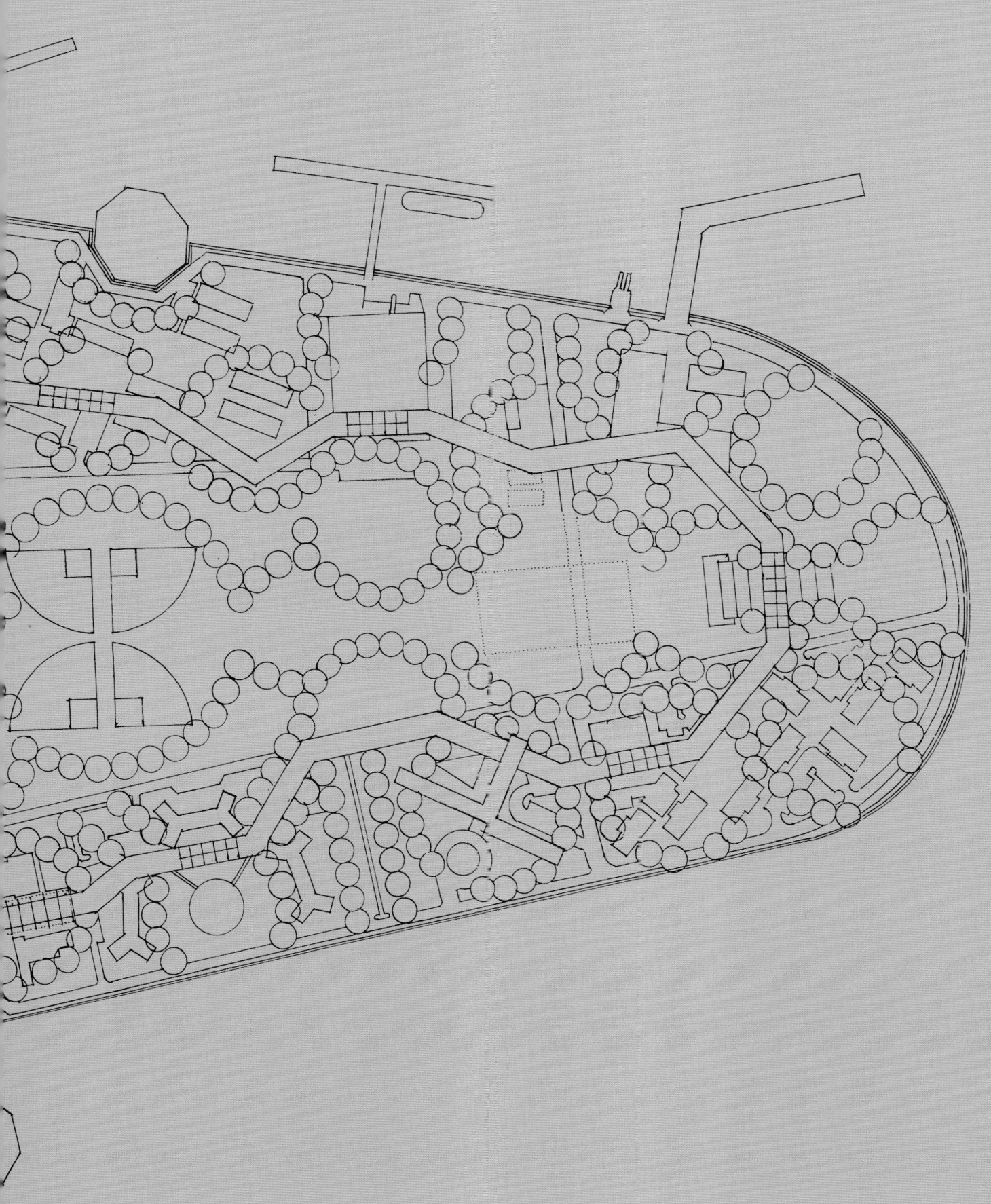

3   Island plan

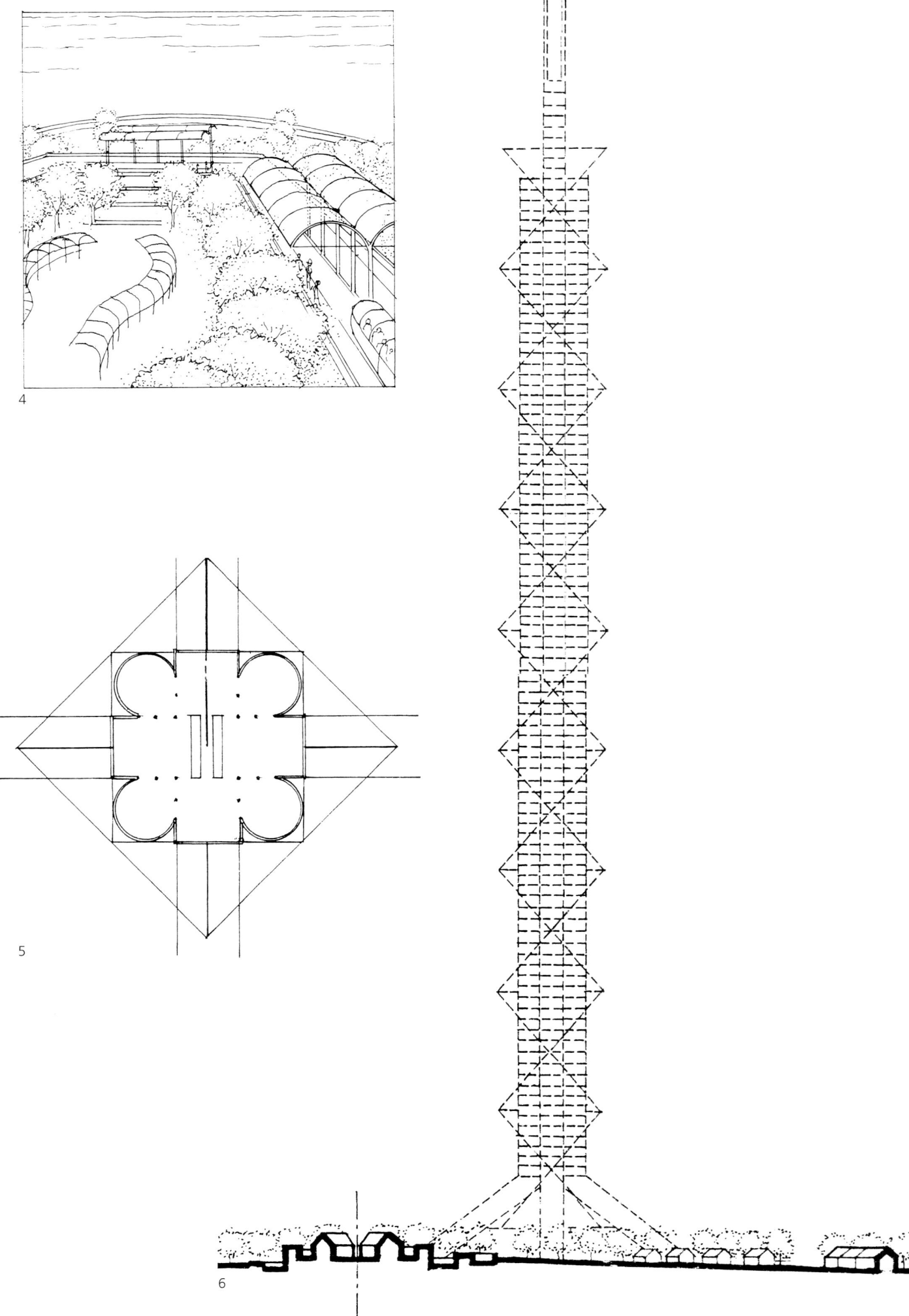

4

5

6

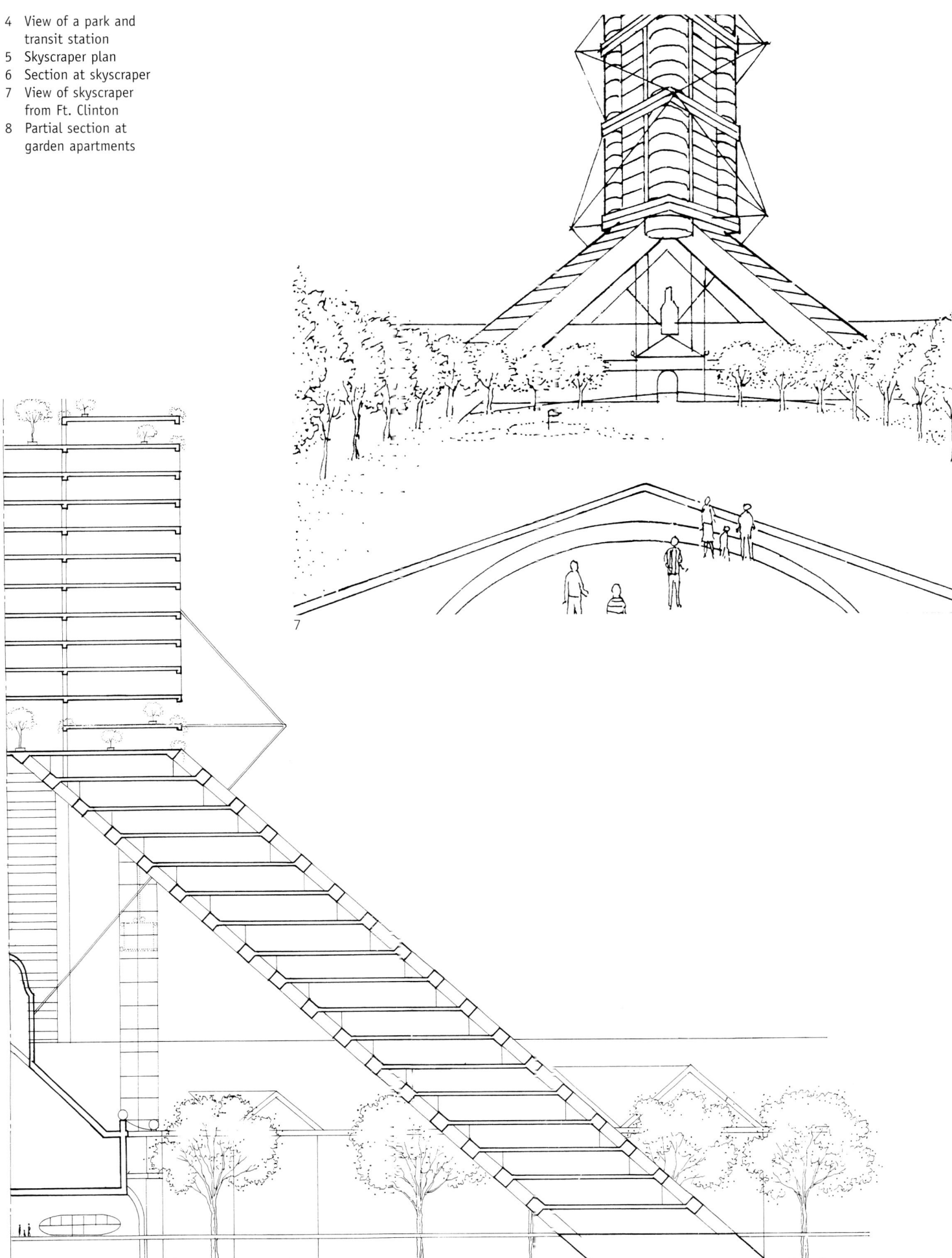

4 View of a park and
  transit station
5 Skyscraper plan
6 Section at skyscraper
7 View of skyscraper
  from Ft. Clinton
8 Partial section at
  garden apartments

7

8

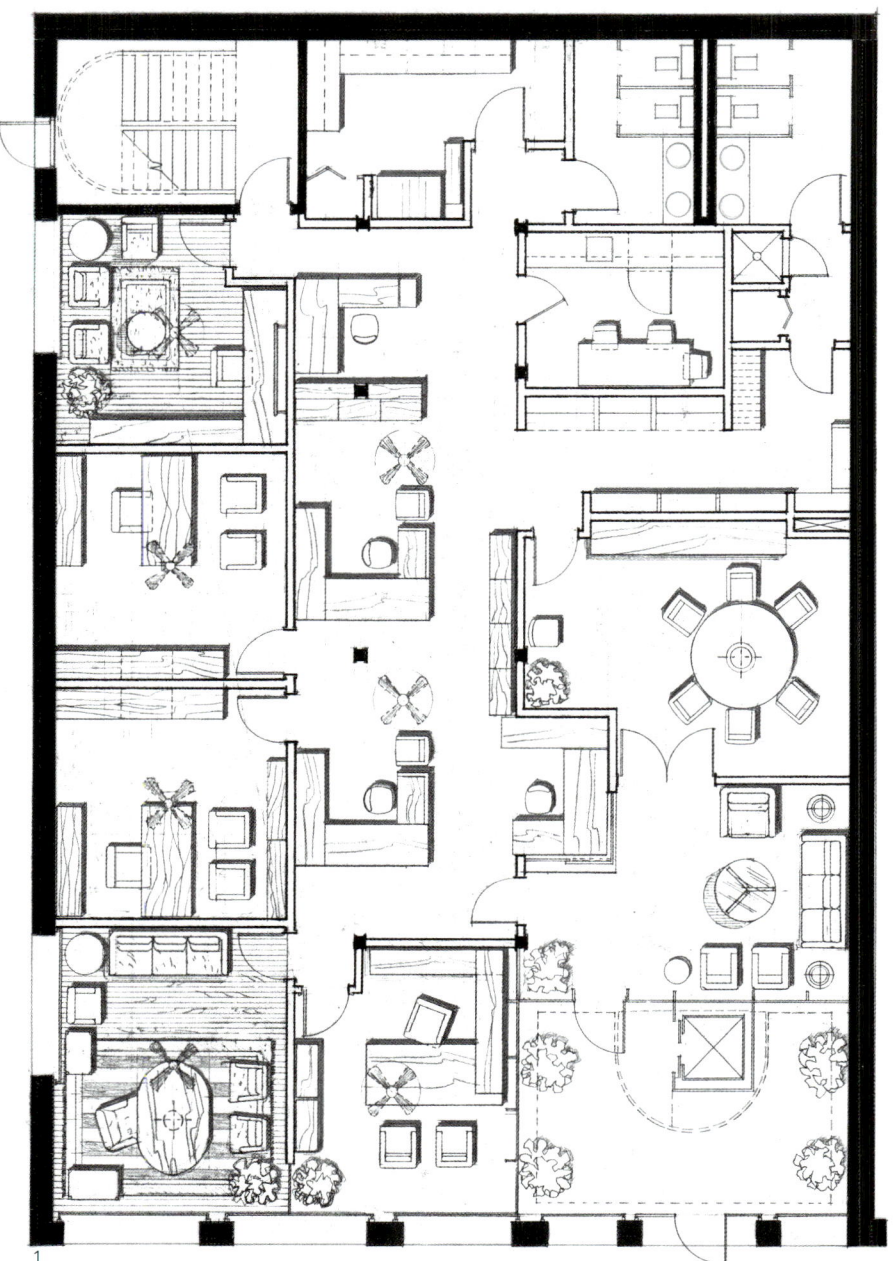

1 Floor plan
2–4 Interior views

0    10ft

2

3

## 53
### Law Offices

A law firm leased first-floor space in a brick warehouse renovated by Howey. The structure is located in a downtown area converted to professional and retail endeavors. The clients particularly liked the high ceilings, brick walls, heart-of-pine strip wood floors, and exposed heavy timber beams and posts. The new, total vision, recessed-glass windows with their frames set inside the brick openings, the new glass-and-steel-framed lobby elevator and interior office partitions with continuous glass strips at their tops allowing natural light into the center of the space, also had appeal. The challenge was to develop an interior space that projected a balance between the architectural elements and the law firm's personality. The brick, steel, glass, and rough sawn wood of the building are offset with the use of carpeting, fabric wall coverings, and lay-in ceiling panels of muted fabric. Chairs are leather or fabric-covered, with metal frames. The lobby/reception walls, shelf and supports are glass, to tie in with the existing glass entry.

*with Dufala von Thaden*

4

### Design/Completion 1985
Tampa, Florida
Beckham, McAliley & Schulz, PA
3 000 square feet
Exposed brick walls, wood
flooring, carpet, drywall, glass,
acoustical ceilings

1

2

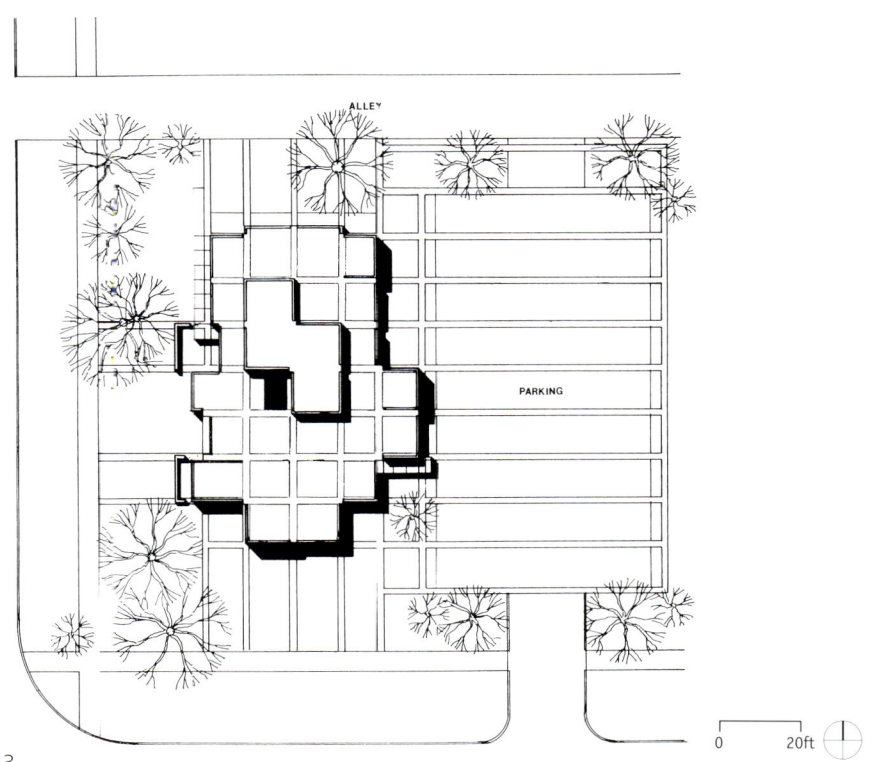

3

## Design/Completion
## 1984/1985

St. Petersburg, Florida
Dr Robert Wharton
3,000 square feet
Slab on grade, masonry non-
load-bearing walls, steel tube
columns, beams, joists and
roof deck system; seashell
stucco, glass, plastic, carpet,
brick and tile pavers

Located at the intersection of two busy suburban streets, the site layout required placing the offices close to one street and near two large oak trees. The solution of irregular perimeter walls within a regular grid plan provided the varying space requirements for the physician and helped to keep out street noise. High horizontal bands of glass window boxes made with silicone joints allowed light to enter. Inside, the windows intersect with the ceiling grid, which becomes continuous ceiling strips of light lenses. Seven-foot-high interior partitions are capped with double-glazed glass between rooms, allowing patients to view the overall ceiling pattern from any examination room.

# 54

## Medical Offices

1,2&4  Exterior views
3  Site plan

4

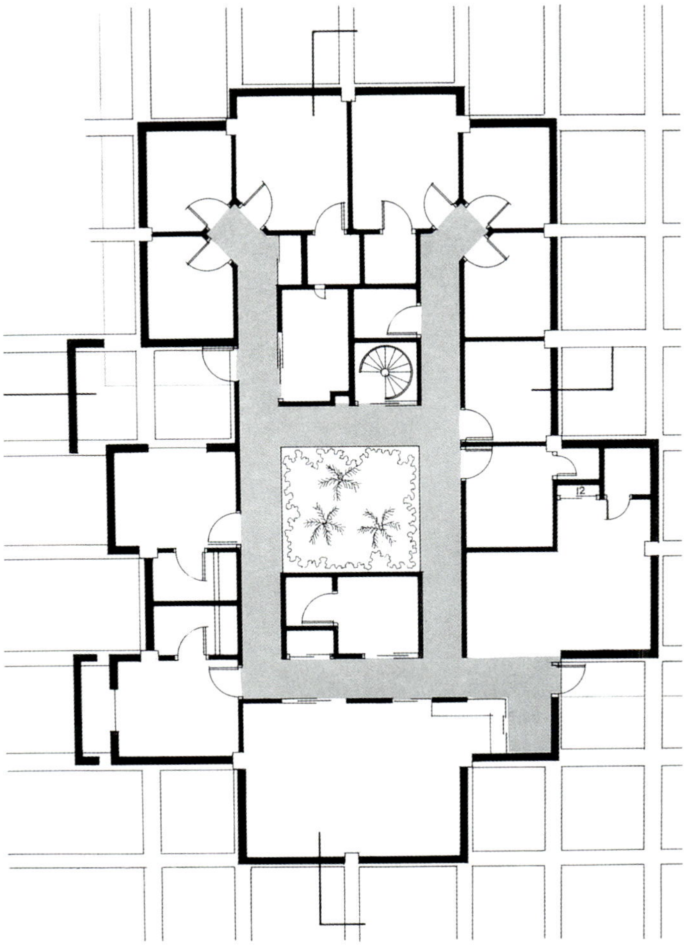

5

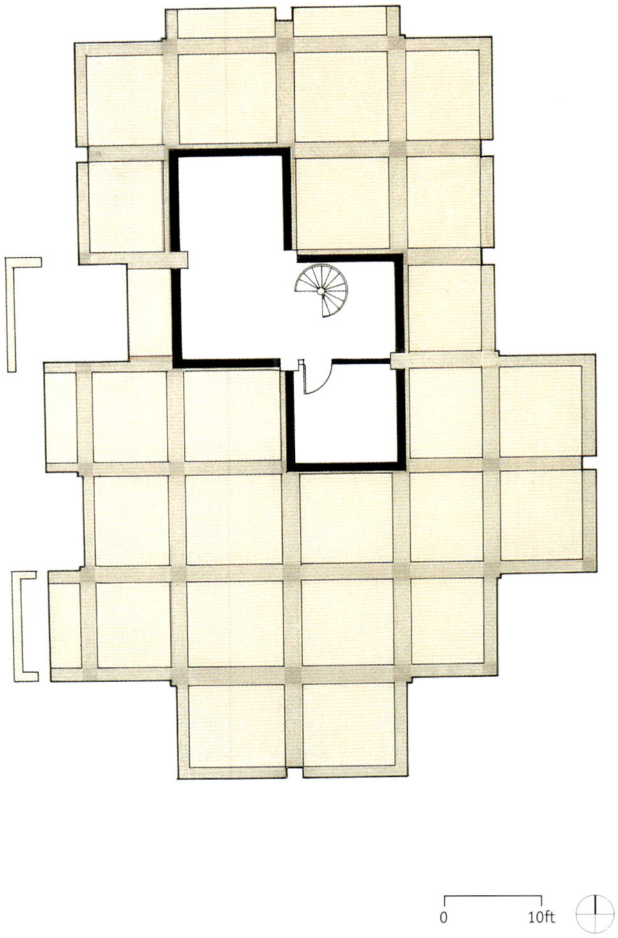

6

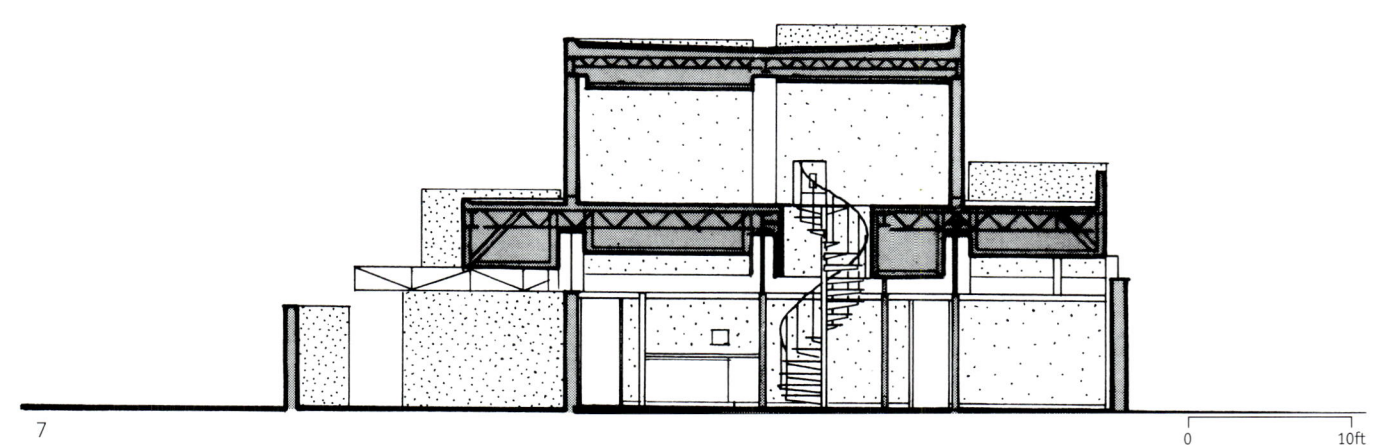

7

0                    10ft

0                    10ft

8

9

5 Main floor plan
6 Library floor plan
7&10 Sections
8 Exterior view
9 Interior view

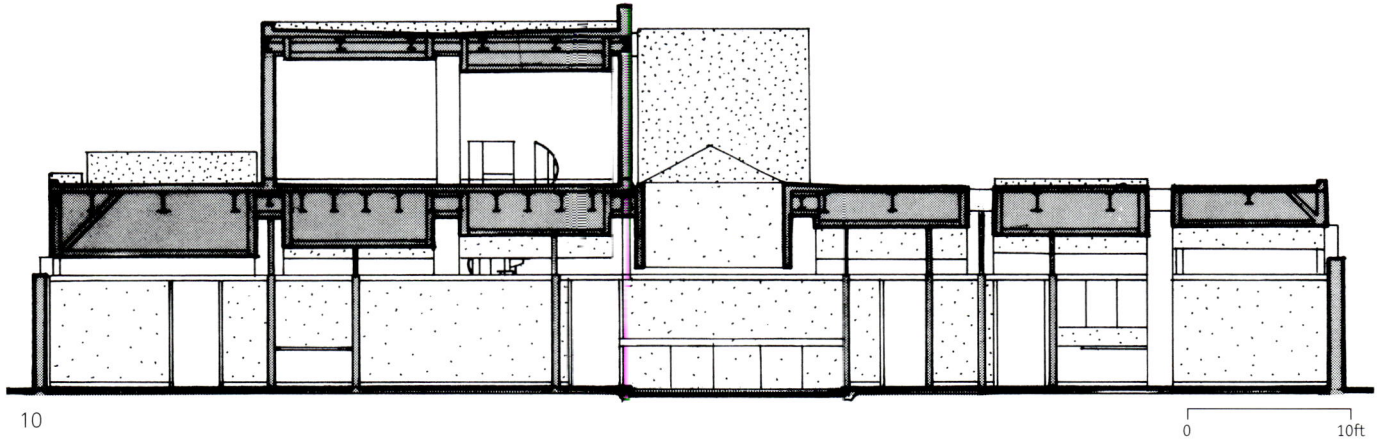

10

0          10ft

1  Isometric view
2  Interior elevation
   of window boxes
3  View of office entry

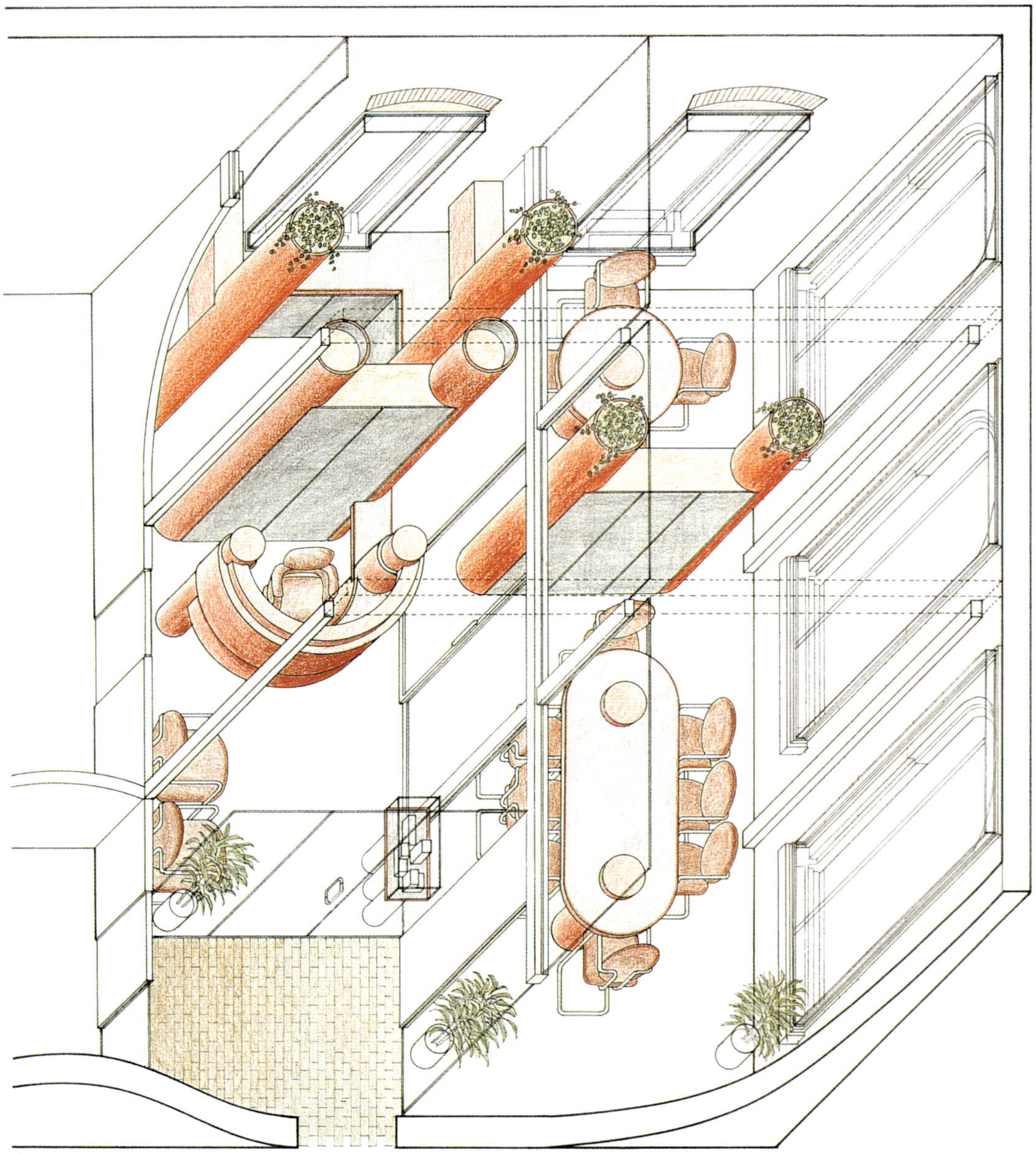

1

2

Design/Completion
1981/1982
Tampa, Florida
2,000 square feet

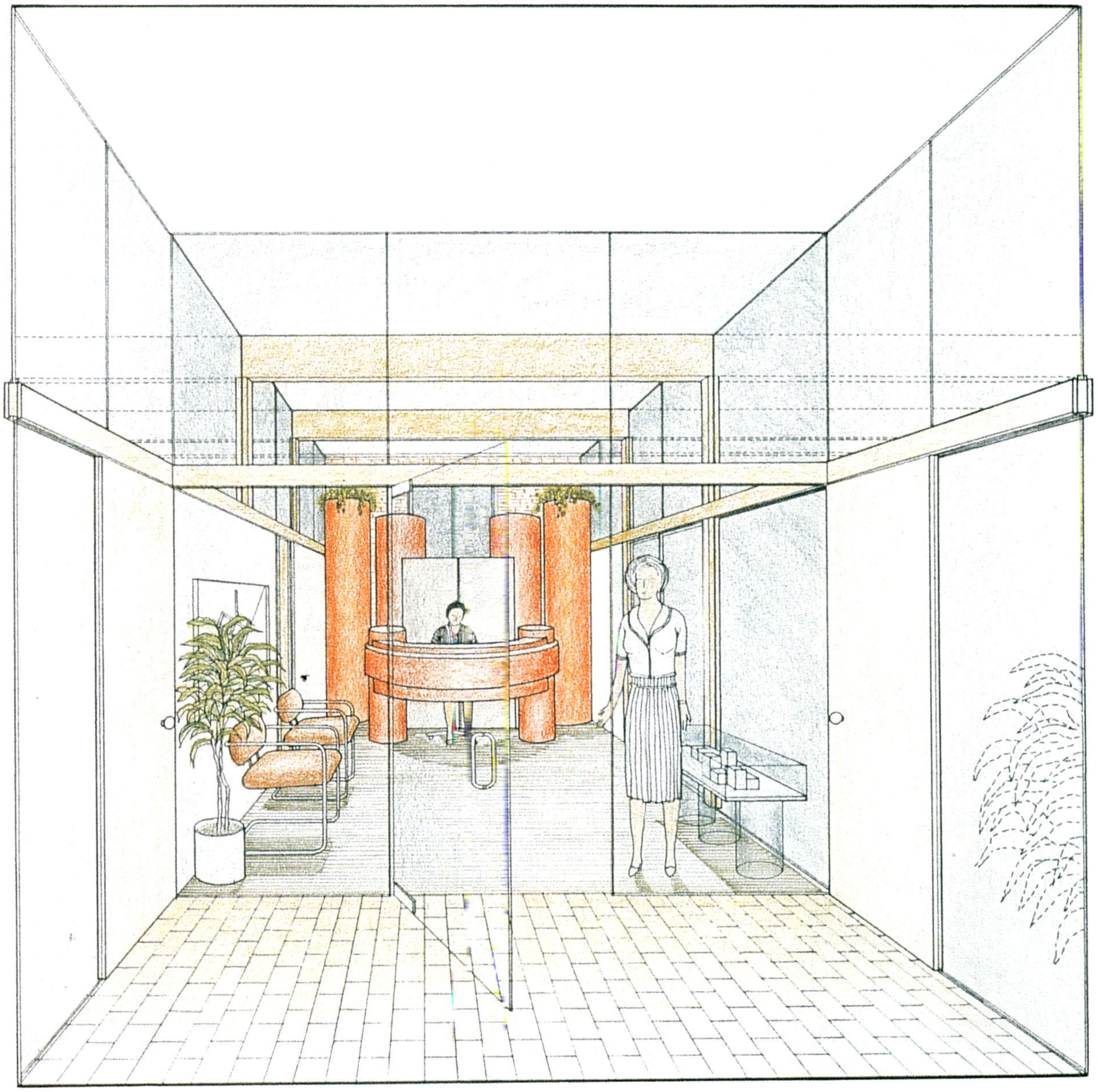

3

John Howey's initial office in the restored 101 South Franklin building was located on the second floor and accessed by a glass-enclosed elevator from the lobby. A design theme of circles and arcs evolved from the historic brick arched front windows. All interior brick surfaces were exposed and window openings were reglazed from the inside with glass boxes containing fiberglass planter units at their sills. Entry to the offices is from a bricked gallery, which leads into the reception area and conference spaces, with private offices and work spaces behind. Drafting service and storage make up the balance of the office.

55

**Architect's Office**

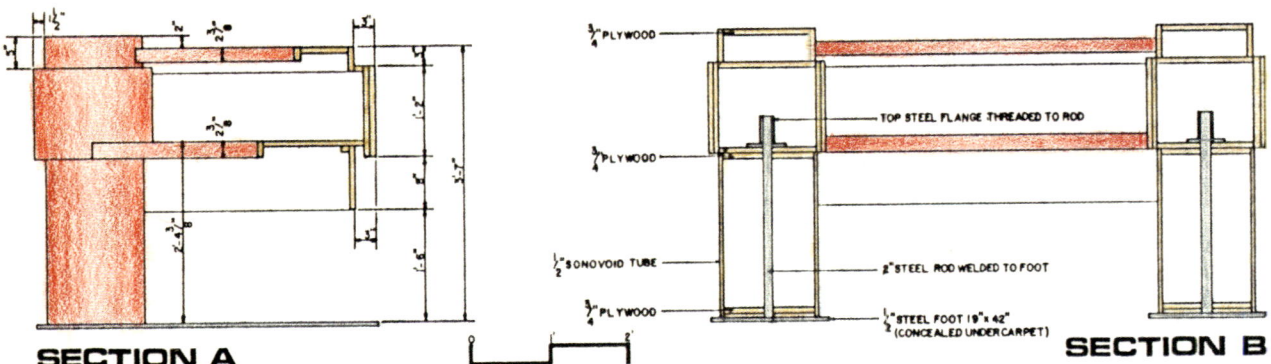

**SECTION A**

1¹⁄₂"
³⁄₄" PLYWOOD
2¹⁄₈"
3"
1¹⁄₂"
5"
2³⁄₈"
3'-2"
1'-2¹⁄₄"
2'-4¹⁄₈"
1'-6"

³⁄₄" PLYWOOD

TOP STEEL FLANGE THREADED TO ROD

³⁄₄" PLYWOOD

½" SONOVOID TUBE

2" STEEL ROD WELDED TO FOOT

³⁄₄" PLYWOOD

½" STEEL FOOT 19" x 42"
(CONCEALED UNDER CARPET)

**SECTION B**

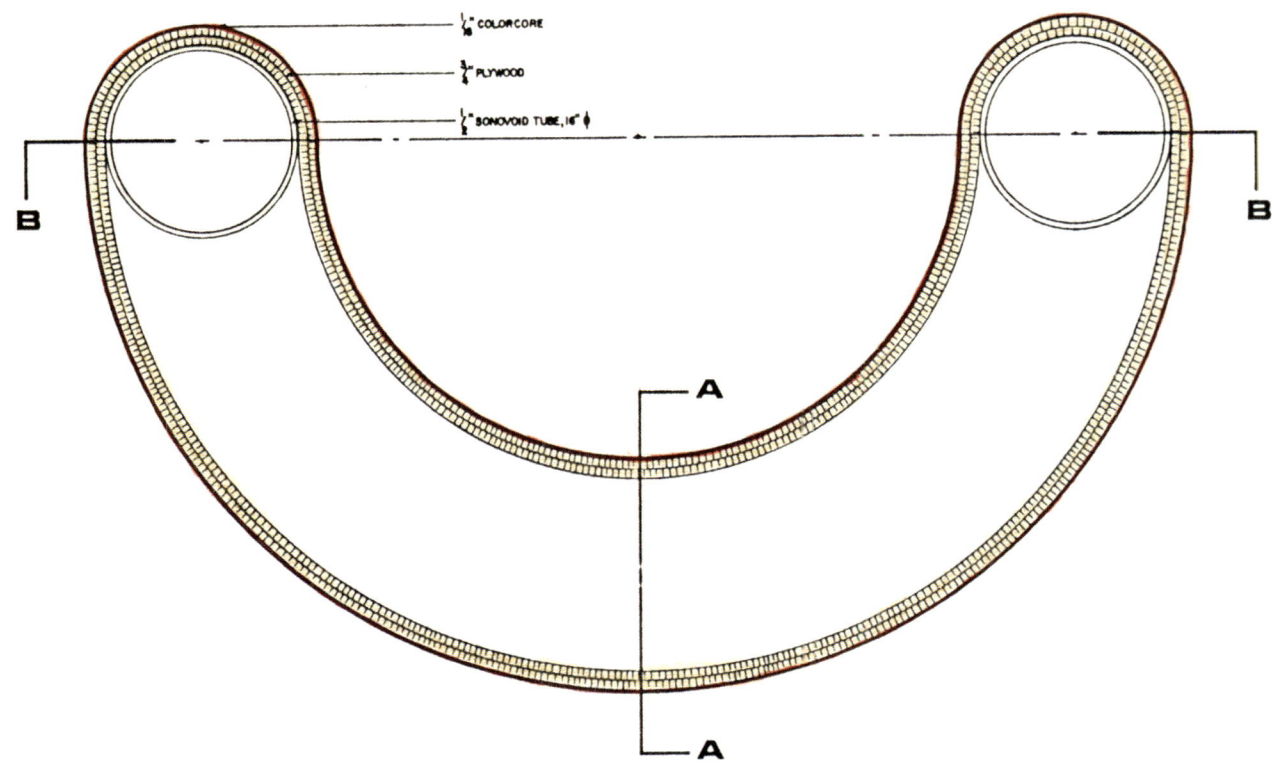

¹⁄₁₆" COLORCORE

³⁄₄" PLYWOOD

½" SONOVOID TUBE, 16" Ø

B — B

A — A

4

4 Reception desk details
5 Reception desk
6 Front reception elevation
7 Side reception/work space elevation
8 Rear reception elevation

6

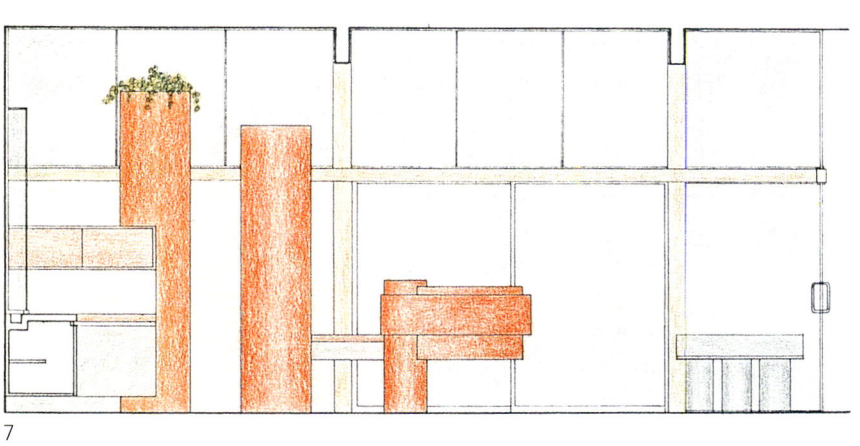

7

8

1

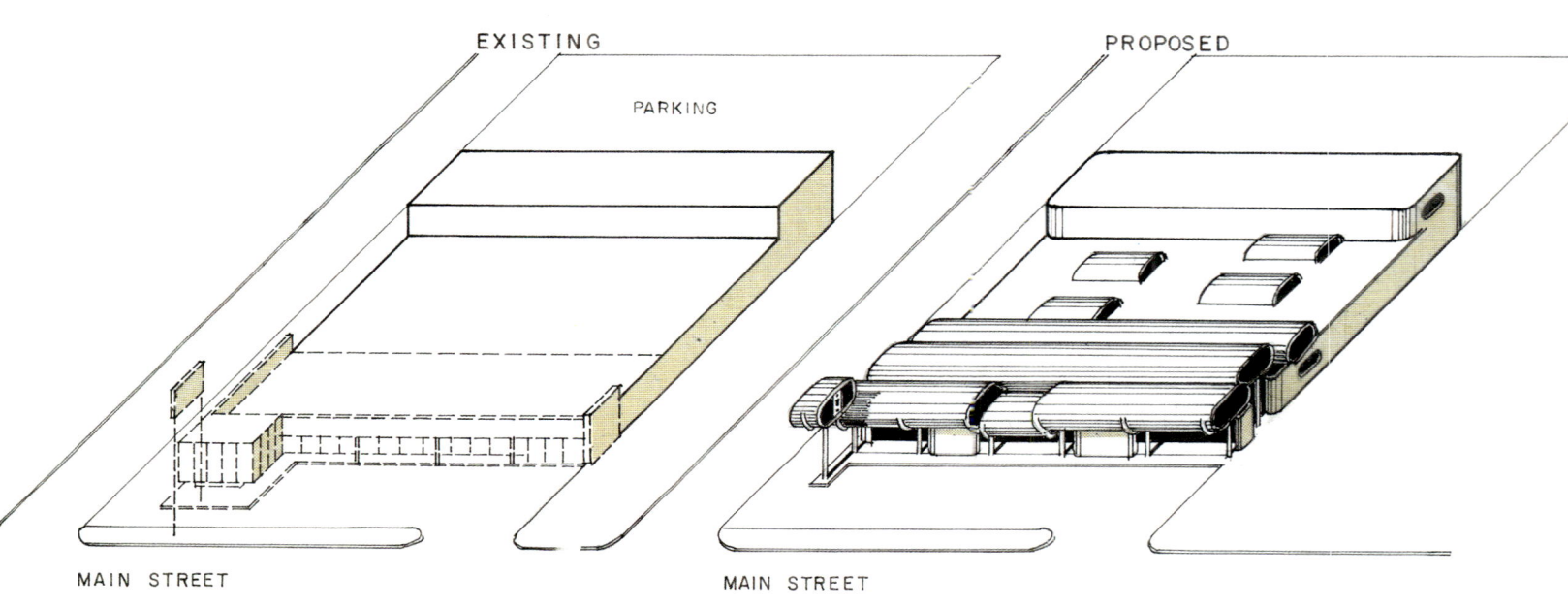

EXISTING

PARKING

MAIN STREET

2

PROPOSED

MAIN STREET

## 56
### Furniture Showroom

1 Perspective
2 Isometric plan
3 Section/elevation

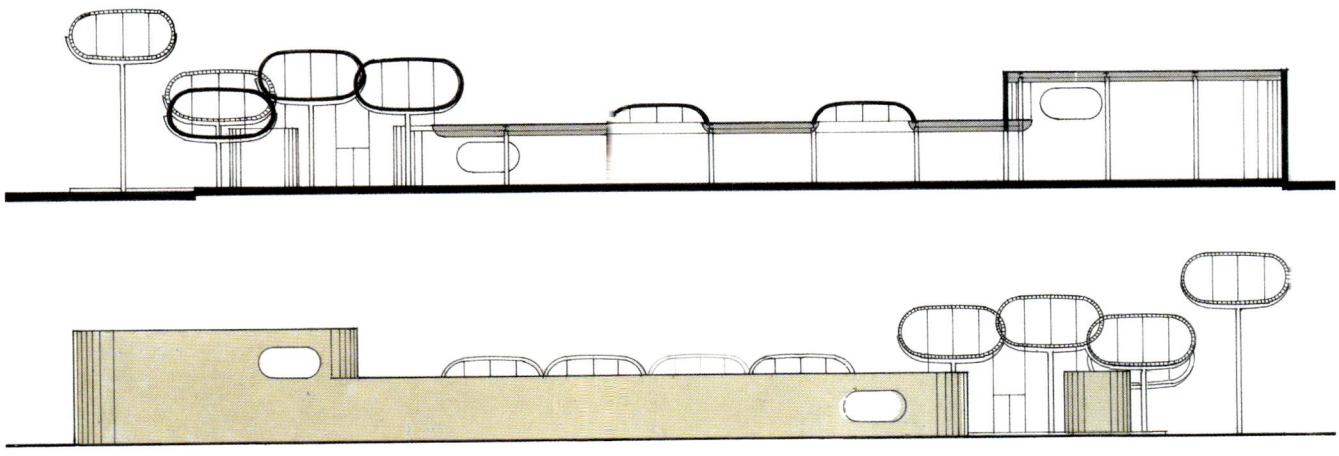

3

The owners asked Howey to design a showroom, separate from their existing furniture company, that would feature classic contemporary design only. Using the letters DG as their new name, they requested a logo that would relate to the design of the new space. Using the rounded edges of the "D" and "G" as inspiration, Howey created a series of rolled-wood tambour second floor units that become a continuous floor, wall, and ceiling. The ends of these units have floor-to-ceiling glass in order to display the company's new furniture and accessory items to the public. The main entrance to the showroom is glass-enclosed at street level. New lower front walls have curved ends to direct views inward to the furniture displays. Side display windows and ceiling skylights for the showroom and existing warehouse behind follow the same circular theme.

### Design 1980

Tampa, Florida
Kane's Furniture
20,000 square feet
Concrete footings, slab, new
steel frames and columns,
shaped 2 x 6 tongue and
groove wood tambour units,
glass, aluminum frames

1

2

3

5

1&4 Renovated Franklin Street façade
2&3 Exterior views prior to
    renovation
  5 Renovated Whiting Street façade
  6 Site plan

4

Located on the southern edge of downtown Tampa in a group of 100-year-old brick warehouses, this two-story corner building housed wholesale establishments and a saloon that serviced the adjacent river port and railroads in 1900. A 1920s stucco finish over the brick walls still existed in 1979 when the present owners purchased the building. Because of their deteriorated condition, the stucco and plaster were removed inside and out to expose the original brick. The main entry was enlarged, recessed, and made two stories high with a new glass-enclosed elevator connecting to a second-level gallery. The renewed interior space contains professional offices and retail shops. Particular attention was given to linking this renovation work with the appearance of its adjacent brick neighbors. Lighting, finishes, texture, color, sidewalks, trees, and planters were installed to treat this existing area as a whole.

**Design/Completion**
**1980/1981**

Tampa, Florida
John Howey Partnership
13,700 square feet
Existing heavy timber floors
and roof supported by brick
load-bearing walls and bell
footings; new wood columns,
beams, steel stairs, elevator,
and gypsum drywall

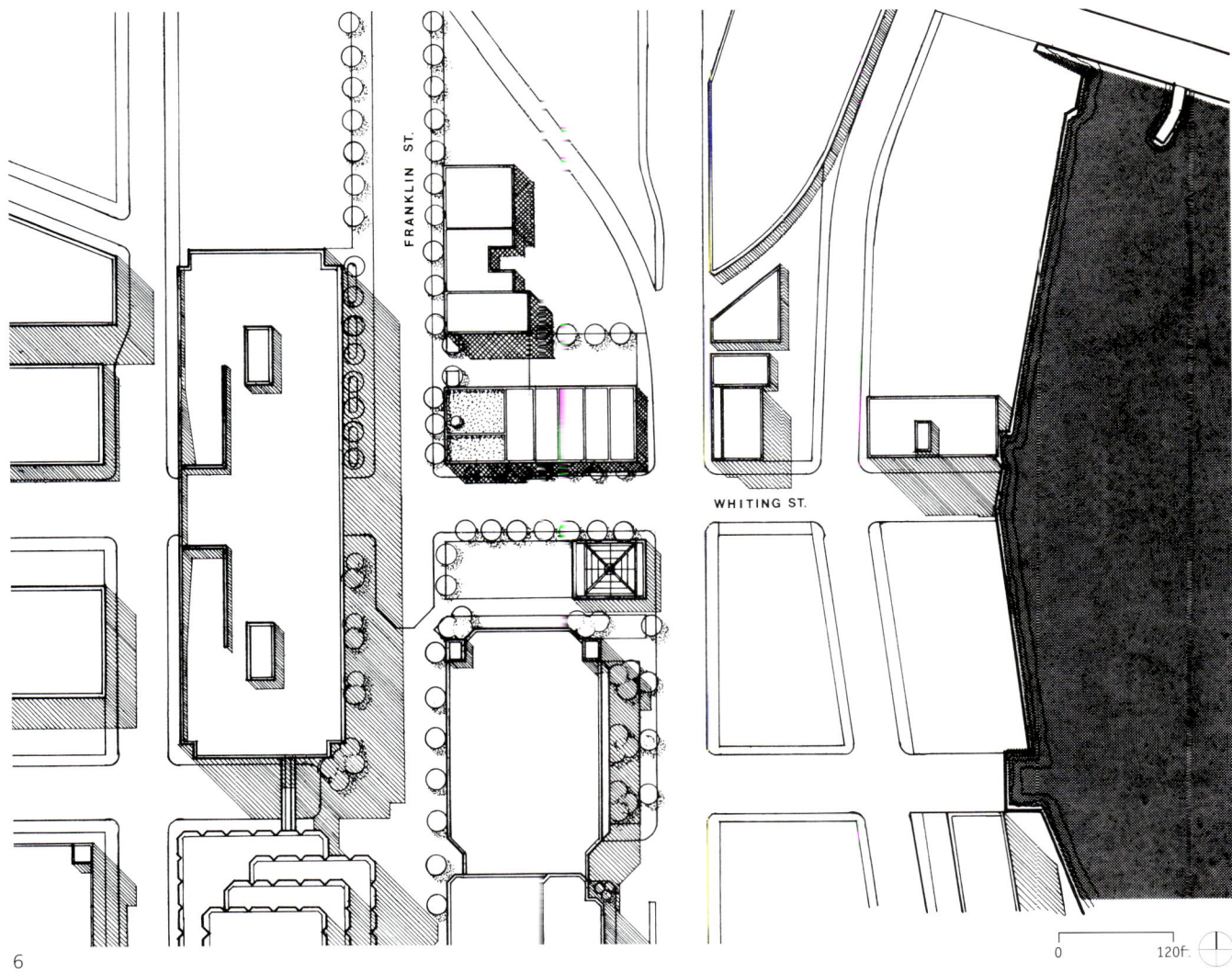

FRANKLIN ST.

WHITING ST.

0    120ft.

6

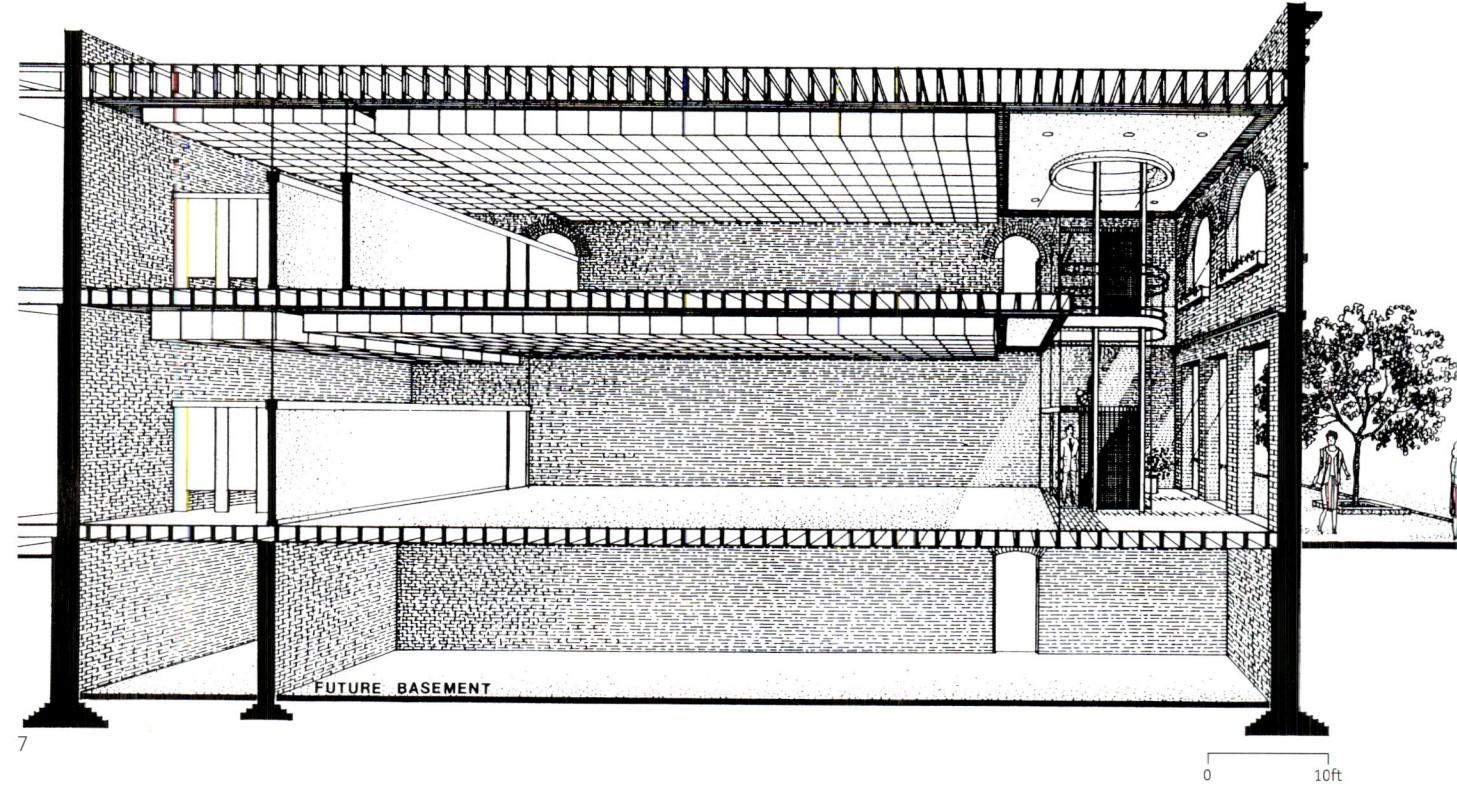

FUTURE BASEMENT

7

0        10ft

8          9

10

7   Section perspective
8–10  Exterior views featuring wall
     plaques and light fittings
11  Detail sketches

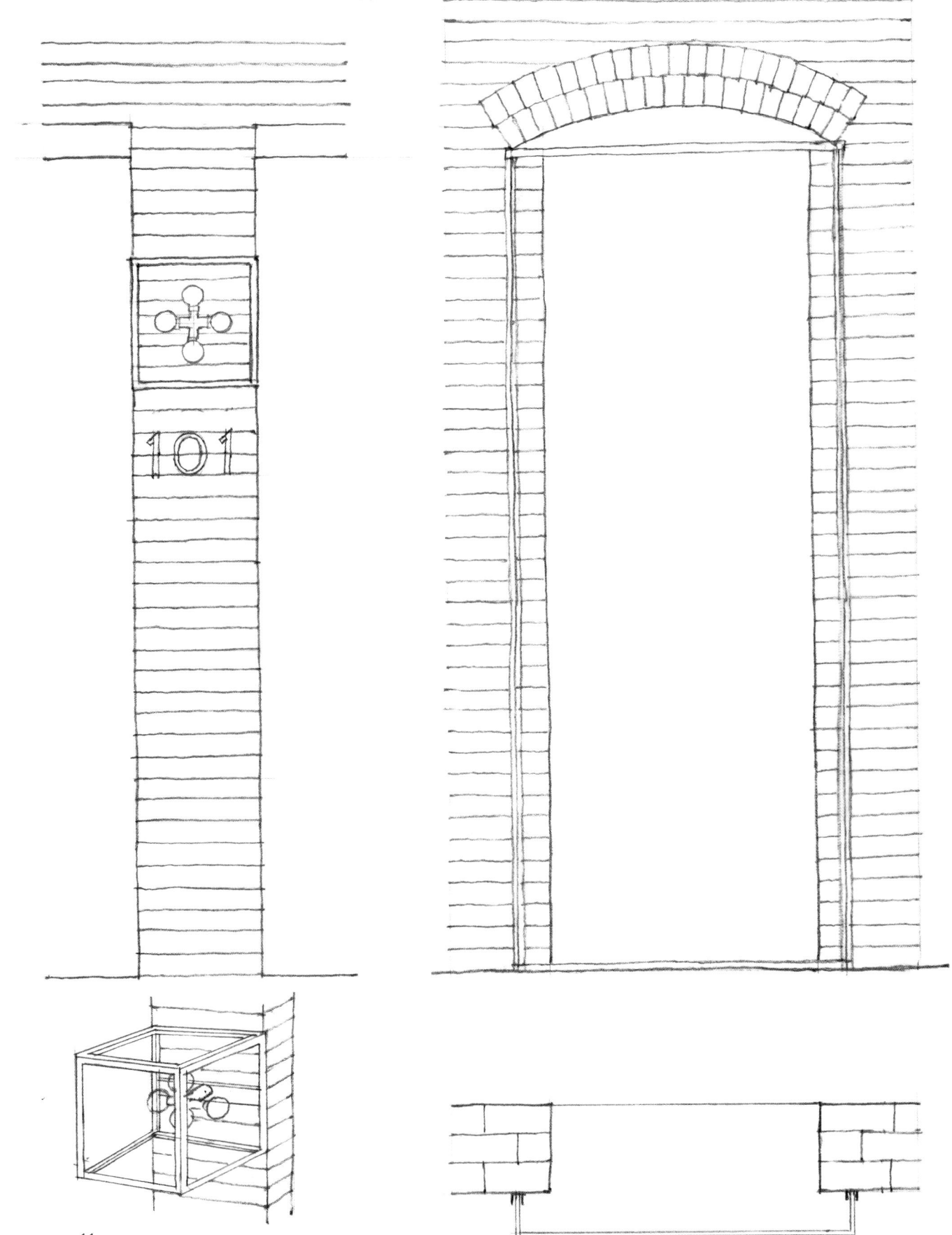

11

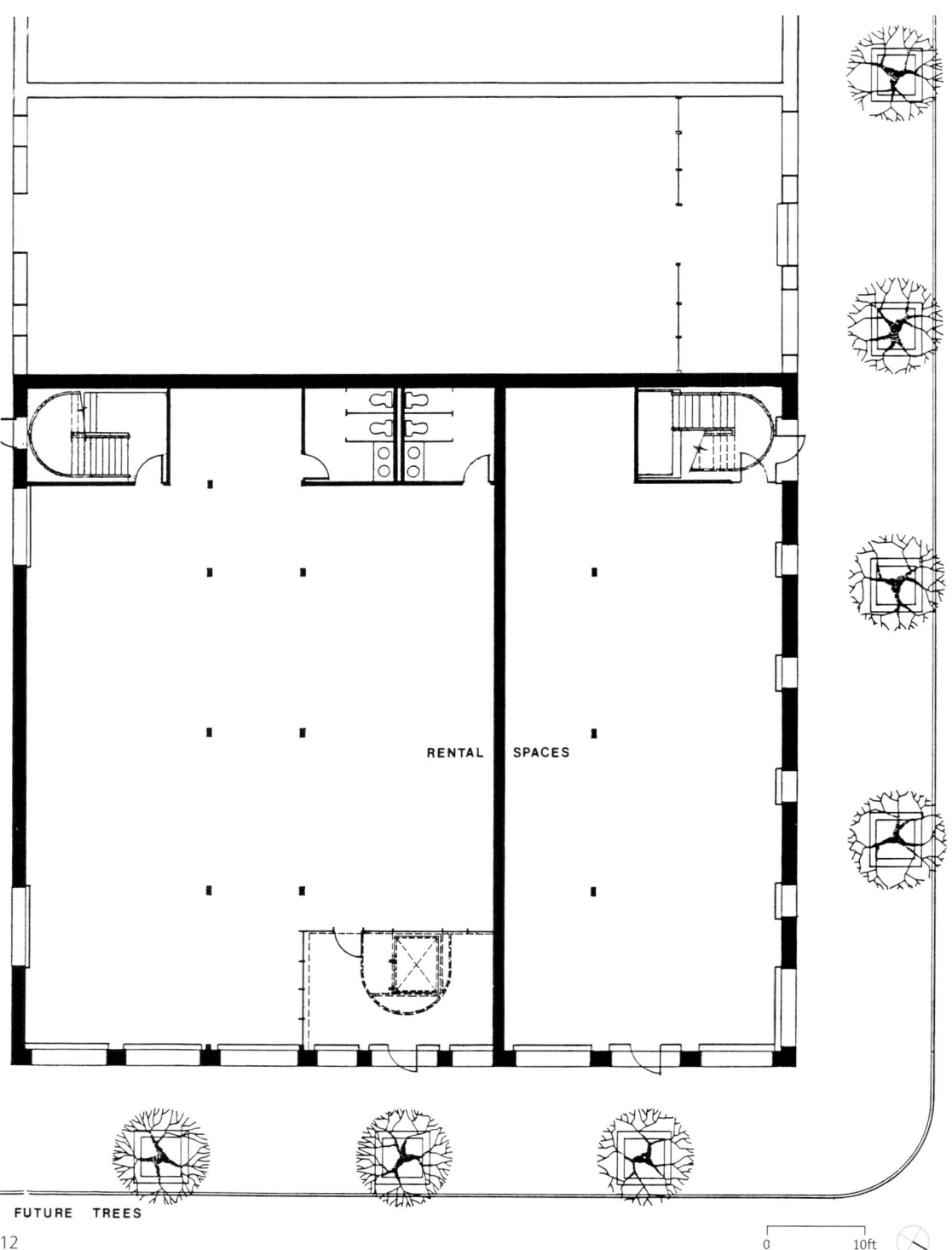

RENTAL   SPACES

FUTURE   TREES

12

0            10ft

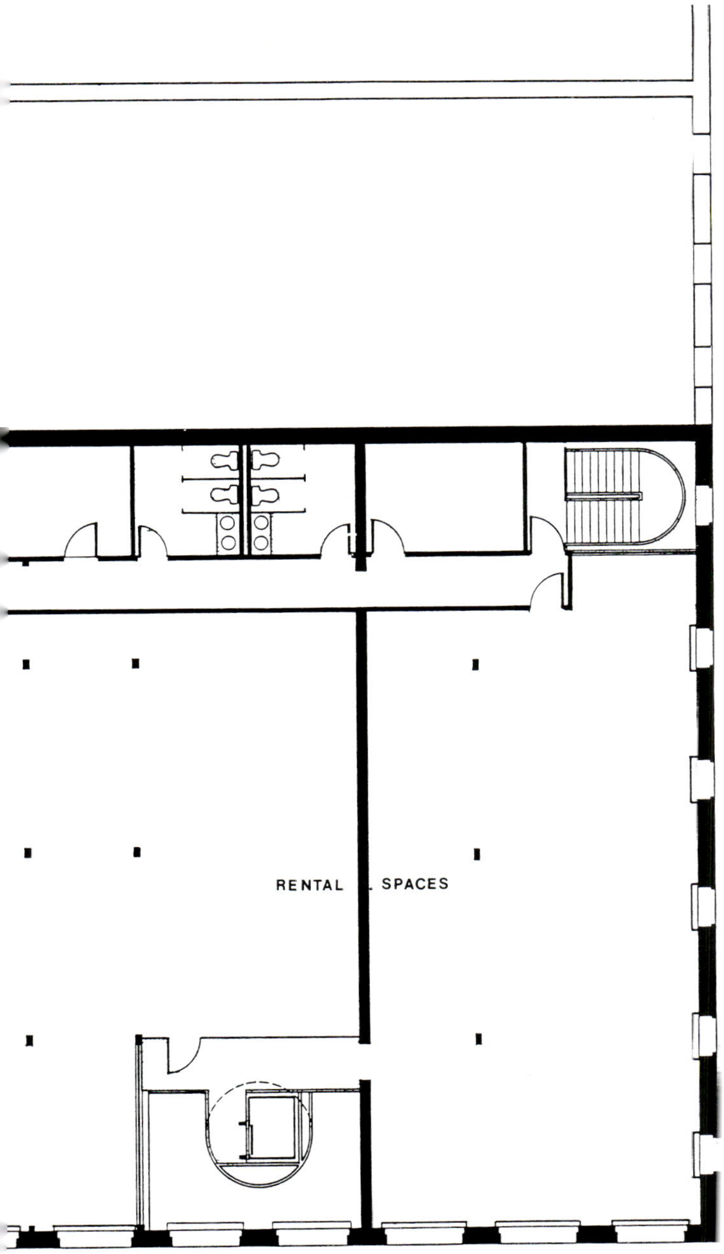

RENTAL SPACES

13

14

15

1

2

3

4

5

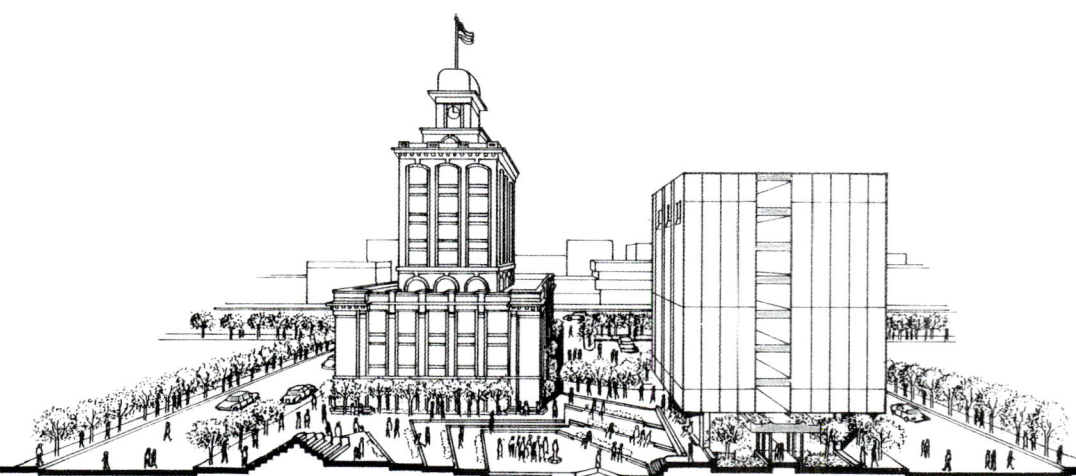

6

1   Aerial view
2   Detail of fountain and steps
3   Signage
4   Detail of steps
5   Fountain detail
6   Section perspective
7   Water cascade
Following pages   Aerial view

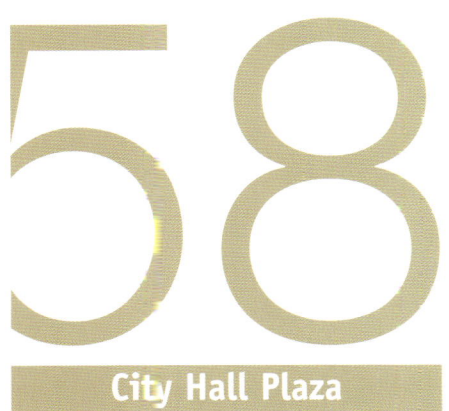

7

# 58

## City Hall Plaza

Design/Completion
1978/1980

City of Tampa, Florida
32,670 square feet
Brick for all surfaces including
walks, steps, seating, stepped
pyramid, and kiosks with
bronze-finish aluminum
panels and handrails

Howey envisioned the plaza as a brick topography, radiating out to its perimeter sidewalks and enclosing city grid. To the passerby, this topography with its water and landscaping was designed to be a welcoming focal and gathering point for the numerous outdoor events sponsored by the city. Examples are celebrations, small ceremonies, public gatherings, fashion shows, art displays, and musical performances. Three levels of the plaza invite visitors to enter the amphitheater area where seven fountains play against a series of brick buttresses interspersed with landscaping at the lowest level. At the upper street level the plaza links the 1915 brick City Hall with the 1980 precast concrete and glass municipal building. The intermediate level consists of seats and walks from which one ascends or descends to the lowest pool level or to the highest sidewalk entry level. Plantings and landscaping were used throughout to steer people through passageways and to keep them from walking off the stepped seats. The plaza perimeters remain active pedestrian sidewalks, while the interior space, reached by wide tiers of steps and ramps, forms the lowest, most private level buffered from street noise.

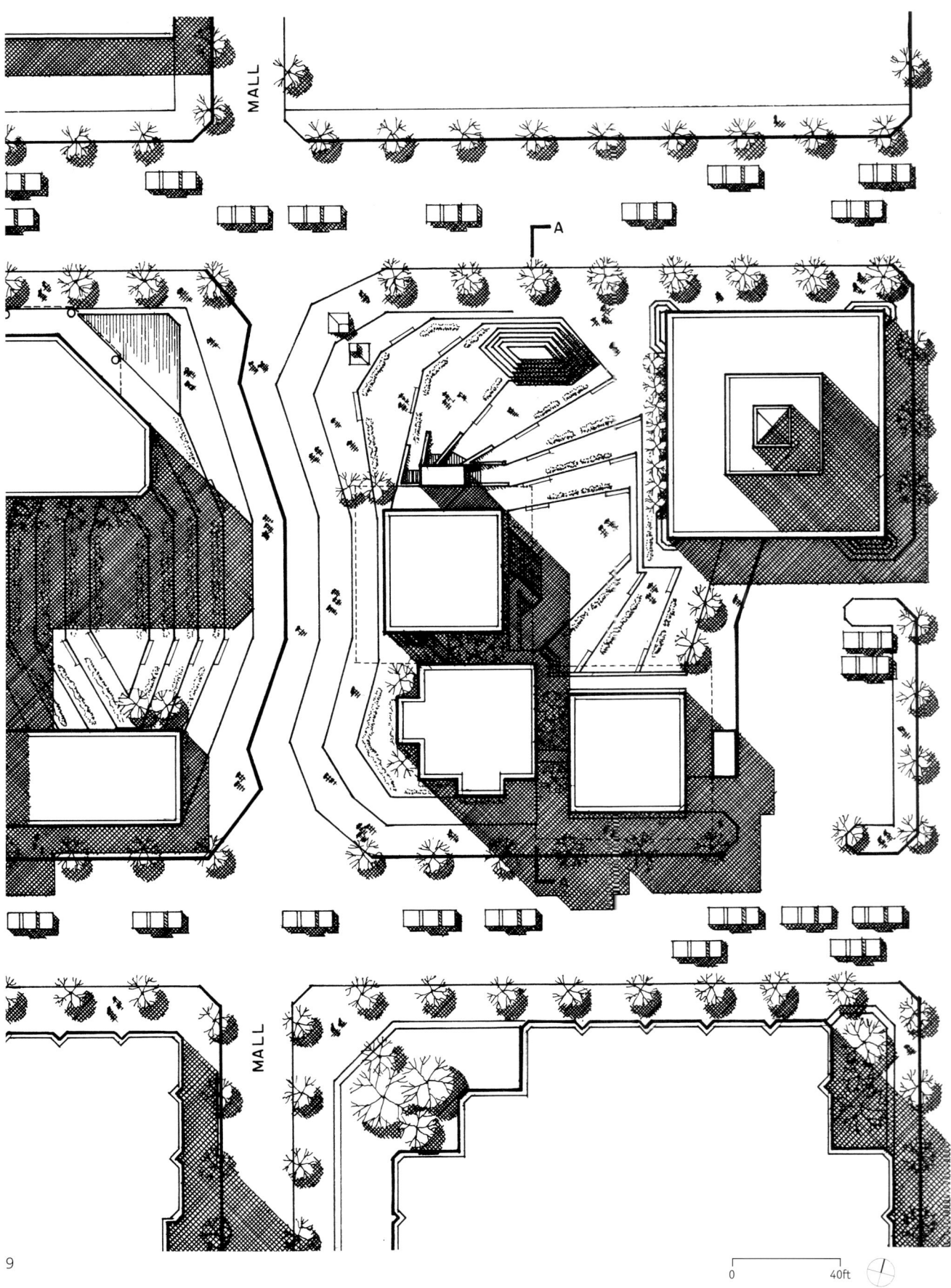

MALL

MALL

A

9

0        40ft

10

11

12

9  Site plan
10 Fountain detail
11 View of old city hall
12 Steps detail

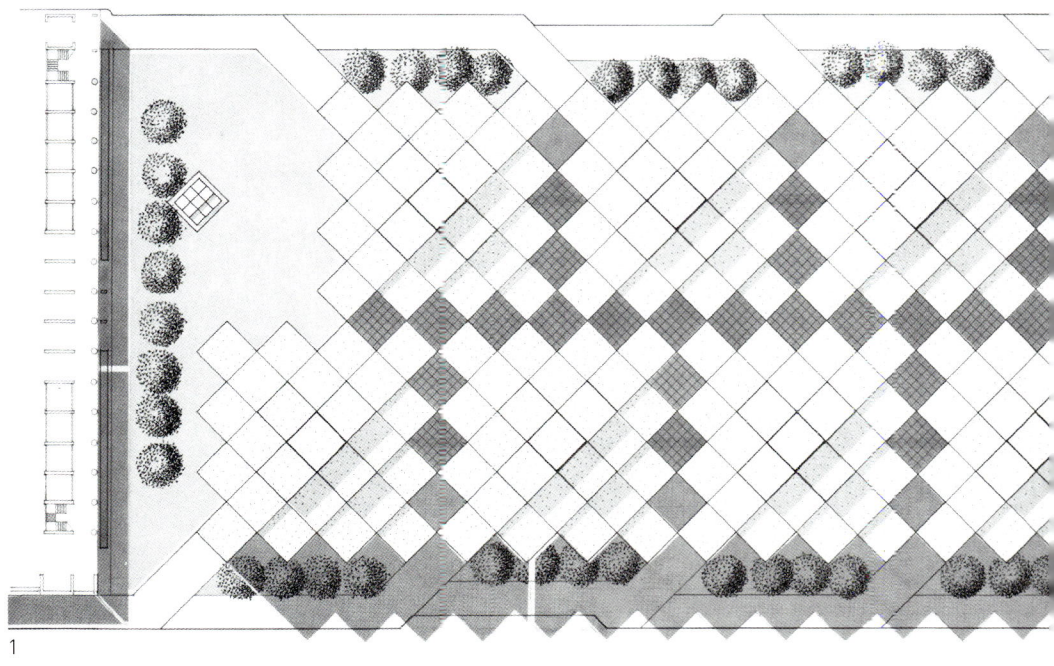

1

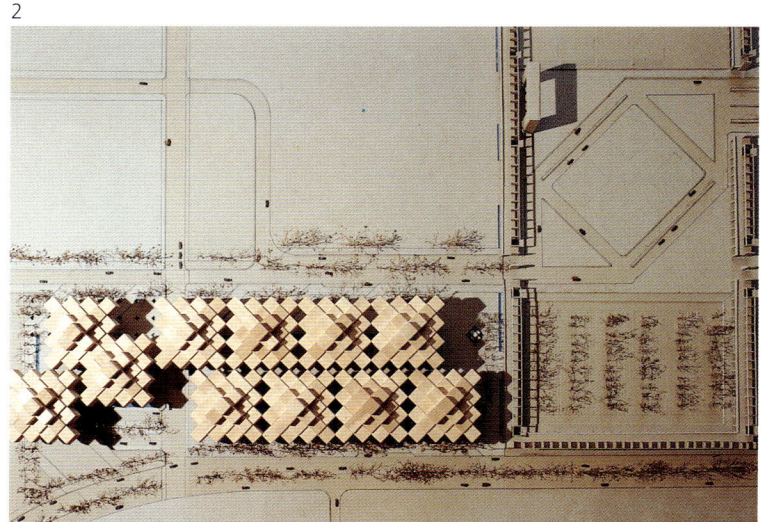

2

3

4

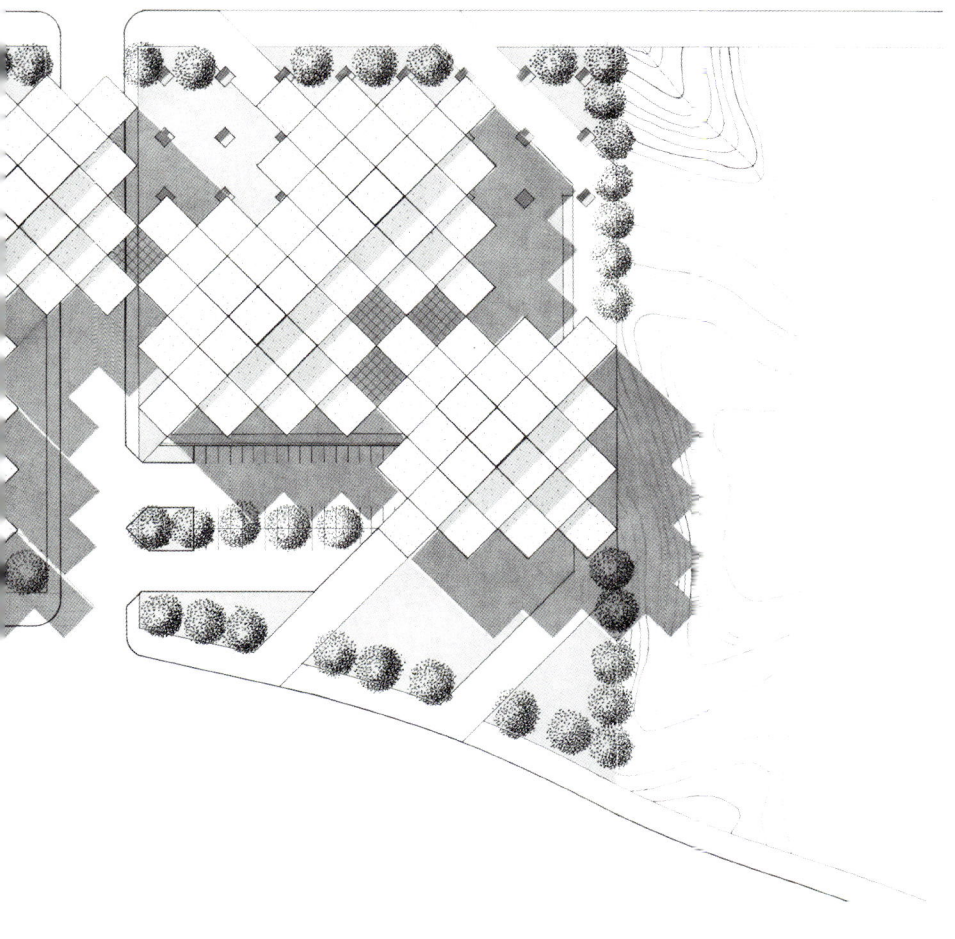

**Design 1978**
Tehran, Iran
1 million square feet
Poured-in-place concrete,
architectural bush-hammered
finish in neutral buff tones,
steel support cables, glass, clay
tile, acoustical ceilings, and
Persian carpet color accents

1  Site plan
2  Site model
3&4  Model views

The Pahlavi National Library, sponsored by the Shah of Iran, was to be part of a new civic complex for Tehran. Howey's concept for the competition project shown here is that of a powerful grove of towers rising from a great sloping terrace. The existing slope of the site is similar to the Campo in Sienna, Italy. In this case the space is accentuated by having the tower trunks, or cores, populate this plaza. The trunks form the entrances, circulation, and control systems at the plaza. Emerging above from the towers are the stepped floors of the library. The eleven towers, which join together to form the great structure, are symbolic of the many components of the library complex. The towers on the south part of the site contain the main library functions.

The towers to the north contain the administrative functions. The most separate tower houses the Center for Research in Iranology. Structurally, the great tower cores hold up cantilevered double-floor level supports at mid-height of the towers. A steel cable support system from above reduces the load, with the lower levels suspended from these giant supports. From a distance or from the air, the library's strong ziggurat form dominates. Unfortunately, the competition was abandoned when the Shah abdicated in 1979.

*with Carl Abbott, FAIA*

**59**

**Iran National Library
Competition**

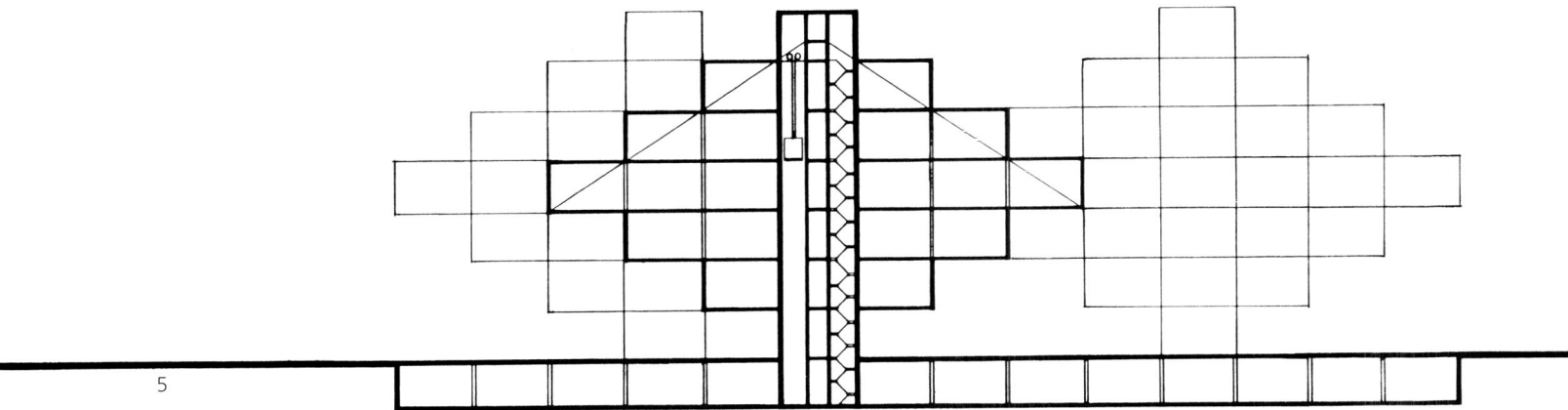

5

6

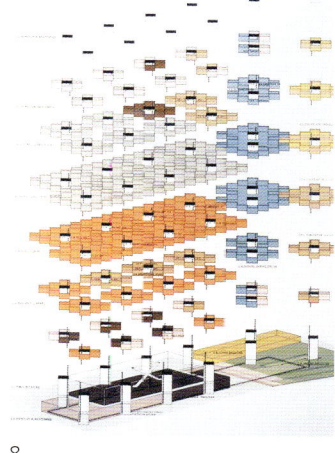

7

8

5 Section
6 Perspective
7 Model view
8 Schematic projection

1

MODULE VARIATIONS

ELEVATION          X MODULE PLAN

ELEVATION          Y MODULE PLAN

2

SECTION

BASIC MODULE PLAN

3

PLAN - 1/4"

ELEVATION

PLAN - 1/4"

ELEVAT

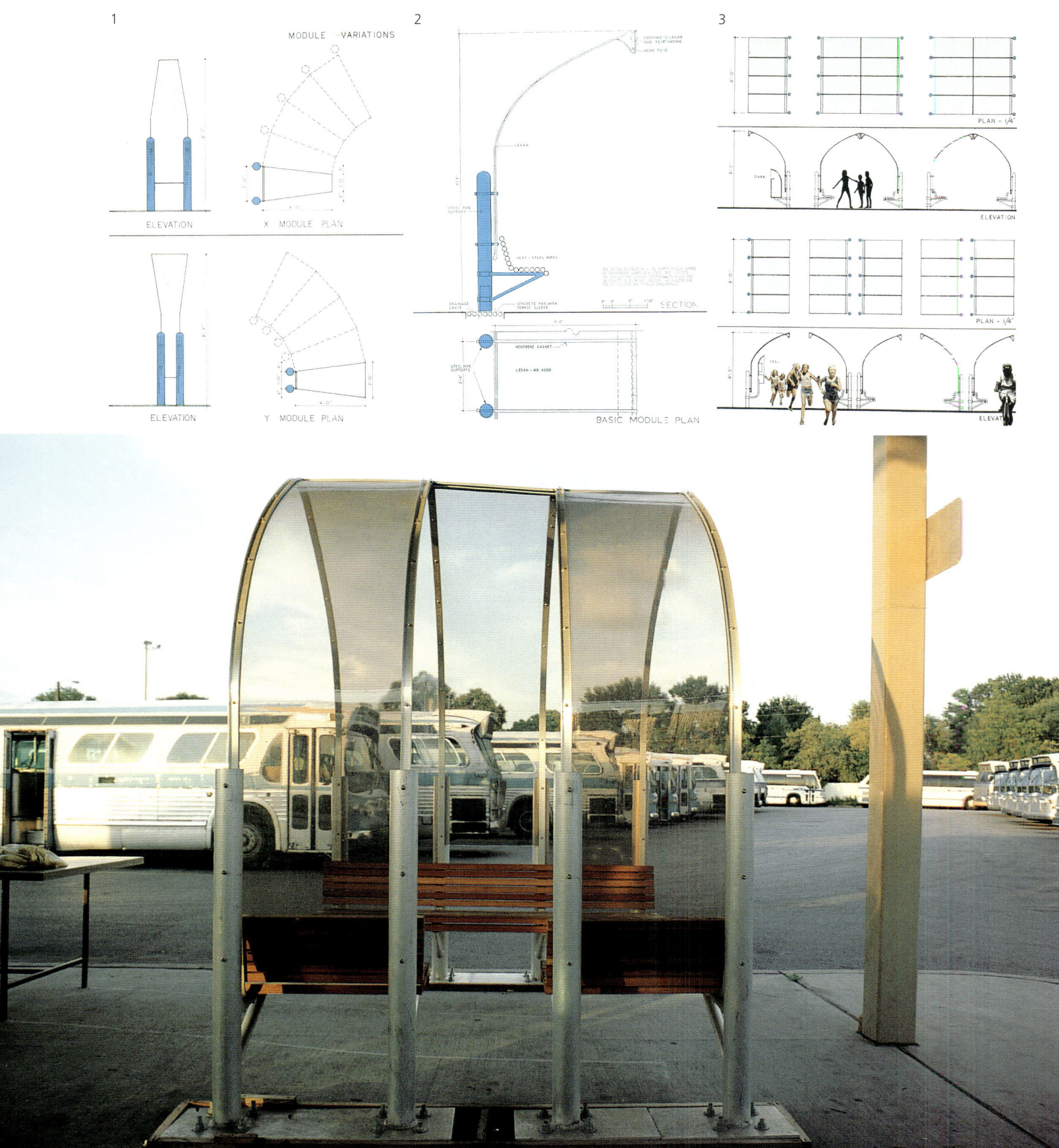

4

5

1 Plan/elevation single
2 Section/plan single
3 Plan/elevation multiple
4&5 Prototype
6&7 Model

This modular shelter was the winning entry in a competition held by the City of St. Petersburg, Florida. The program requirements were weather protection, maximum visibility for safety, and adaptability to change. The design consists of two basic materials: a shell of clear or tinted polycarbonate lexan, and steel supporting and accessory materials. Modules of these materials were designed to be bolted together and adapted to many different city sites. The basic module is a rectangle with "x" and "y" wedge-shaped variations in place. The variations allow for great freedom in shelter forms adaptable to bus shelters, parks, playgrounds, and malls. Landscape for each shelter is designed to act as buffer and definer, and consists of small-scale tropical trees and shrubs. The visual intent of this short-term "people" shelter is to add a recognizable public facility to the cityscape that is a simple and quiet statement.

*with Carl Abbott, FAIA*

# 60

## Prototype Shelter Competition

### Design/Construction 1977/1979

St. Petersburg, Florida
City of St. Petersburg
4 square feet
Custom fabricated, lexan and steel units, patented 1980

6

7

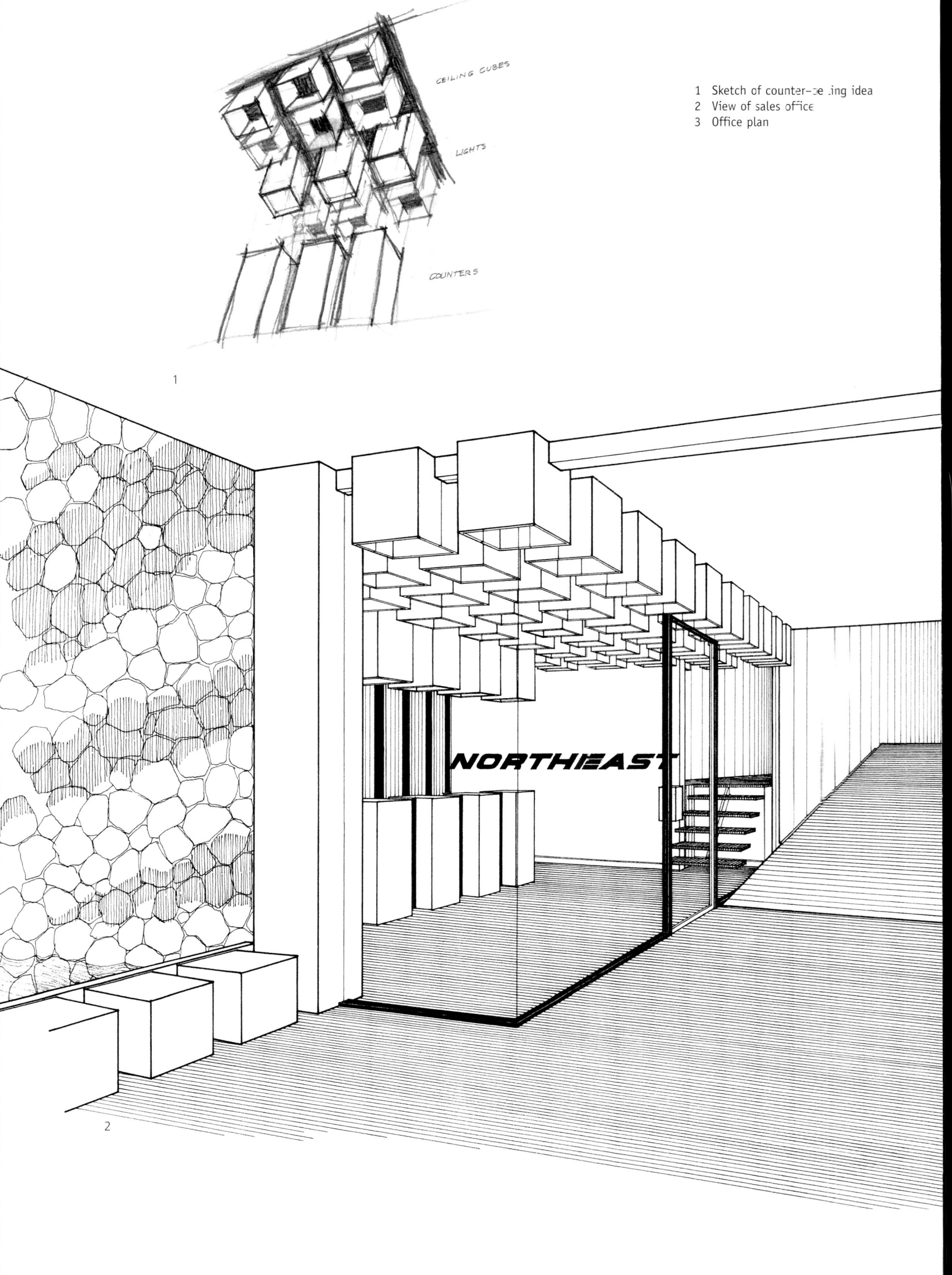

1 Sketch of counter-ceiling idea
2 View of sales office
3 Office plan

## Airline Ticketing Office

This project was for Howey's first national client, Northeast Airlines. The airline's Nassau office was to be located in an existing retail complex. Northeast, whose air routes stretched from Canada to the Bahamas, required instant recognition for its name.

In this design, floor-to-ceiling glass was used to immediately invite the passerby into the sales space. Above, a grid of ceiling cubes merges with the perimeter glass walls and expands into the public hall as seating units. Airline symbols and logos were wall-mounted. Oranges, yellows, whites, and wood tones were selected to reflect the casual island attitude of the Bahamas.

### Design 1968
Nassau, Bahamas
1,500 square feet

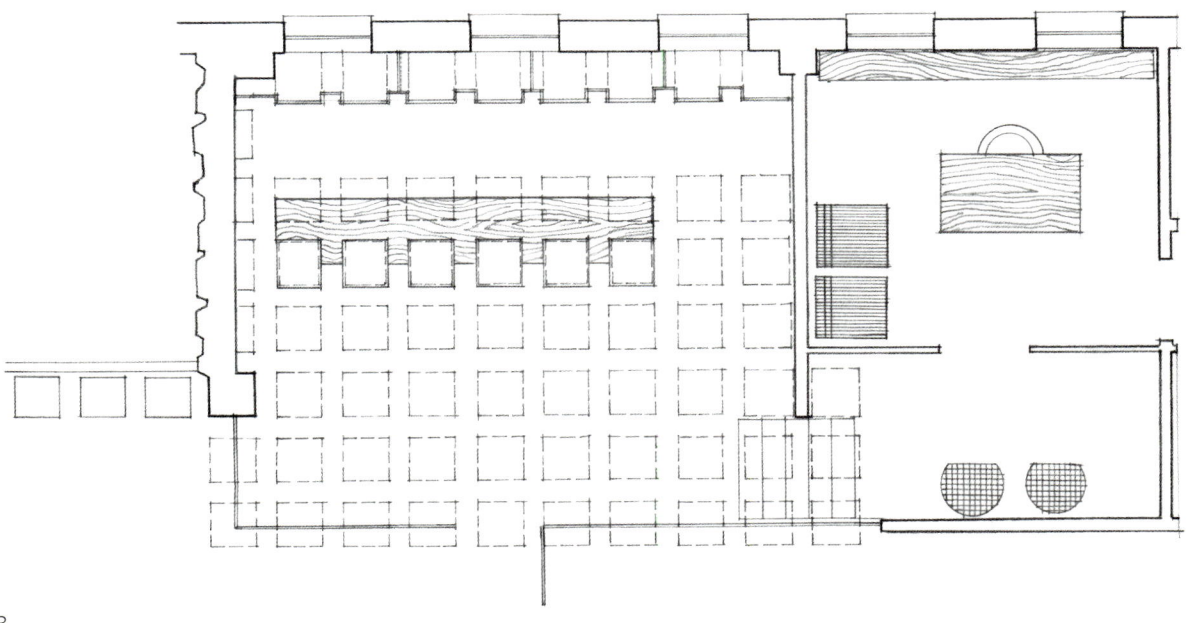

3

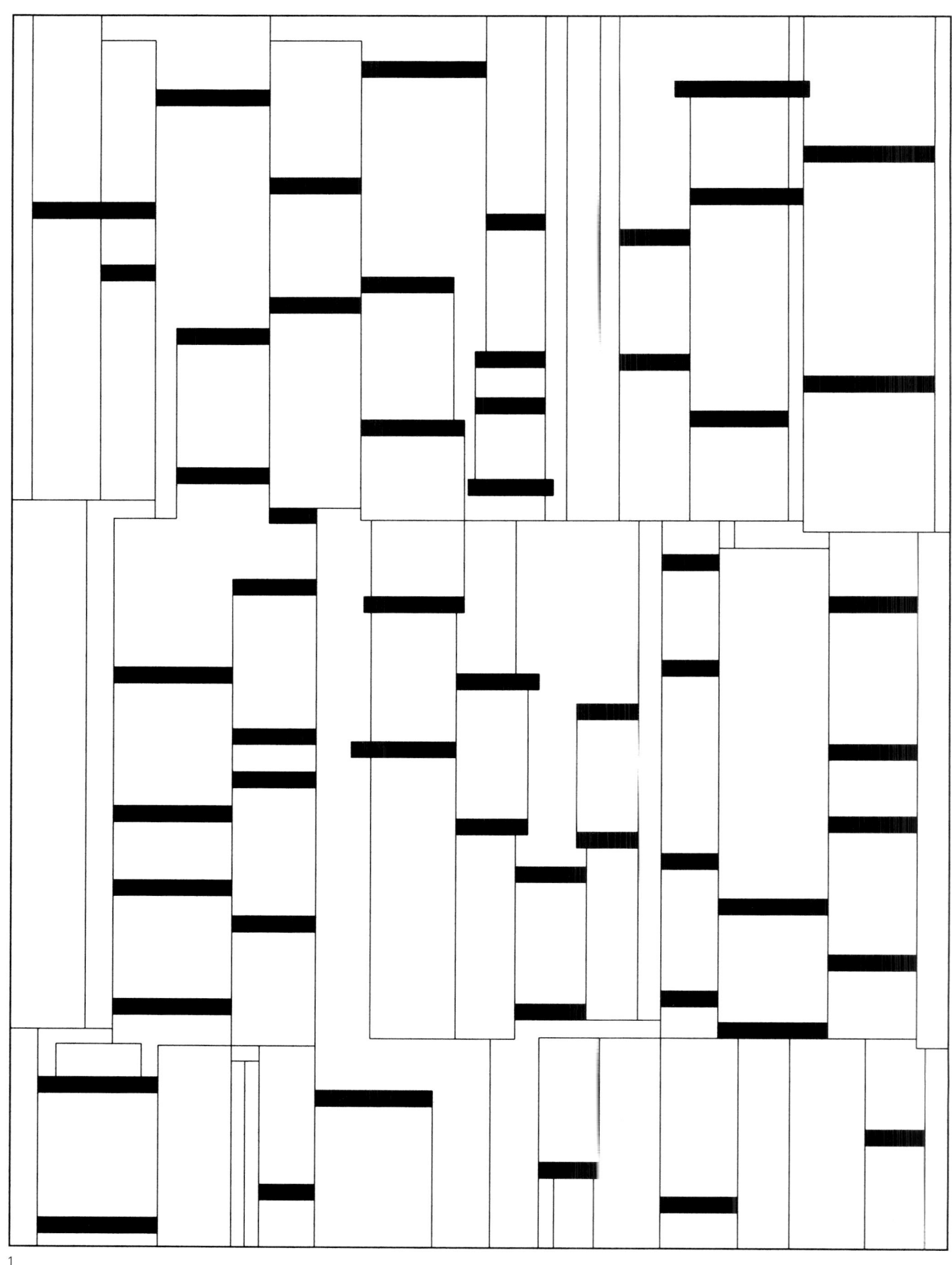

1

1 Inspiration for design
2 Aerial sketch

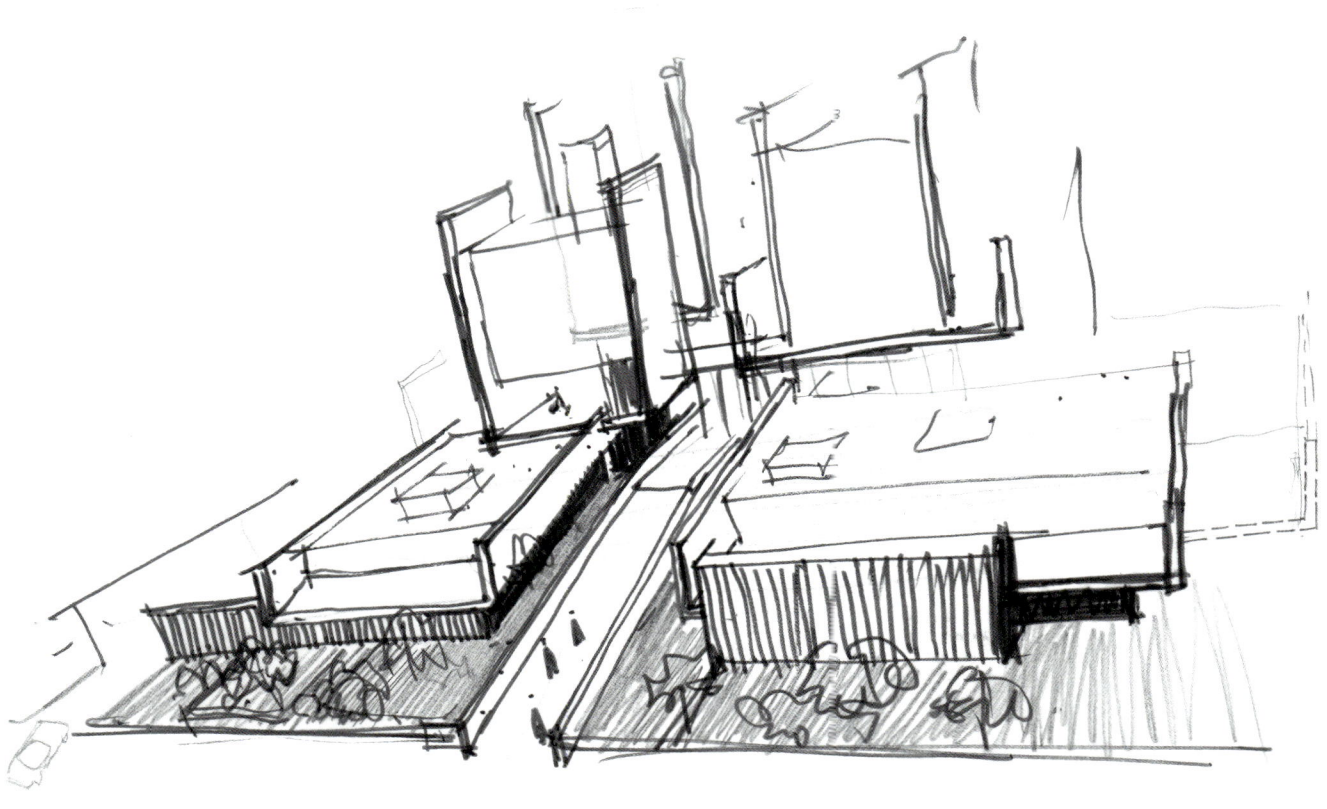

2

## Design 1966

Berkeley, California
180,000 square feet
Concrete foundation, precast
concrete channel floor and
roof system, drywall, glass,
bronze, and copper

## 62

## University Arts Center Competition

The 1.75-acre site for this national competition is bordered by busy streets on the north and south. On either side were residences with small offices in transition to commercial use. The program called for a university arts center incorporating seven galleries for traveling exhibitions, sculpture courts, a theater, and conference spaces accessible to walk-in students and the public. Howey took advantage of the changes in site grade by placing the lobby at midpoint where it would be accessed by entry ramps spanning lower outdoor sculpture courts located on both streets. The major galleries and conference center were placed next to the main lobby. Floor-to-ceiling gallery walls were segmented to create a rhythm of progression in each space. Access to the theater was a half-level down from the lobby, and service and support were at lower levels. Above were administration offices and smaller galleries with linear skylights incorporated in the precast channel concrete roof structure.

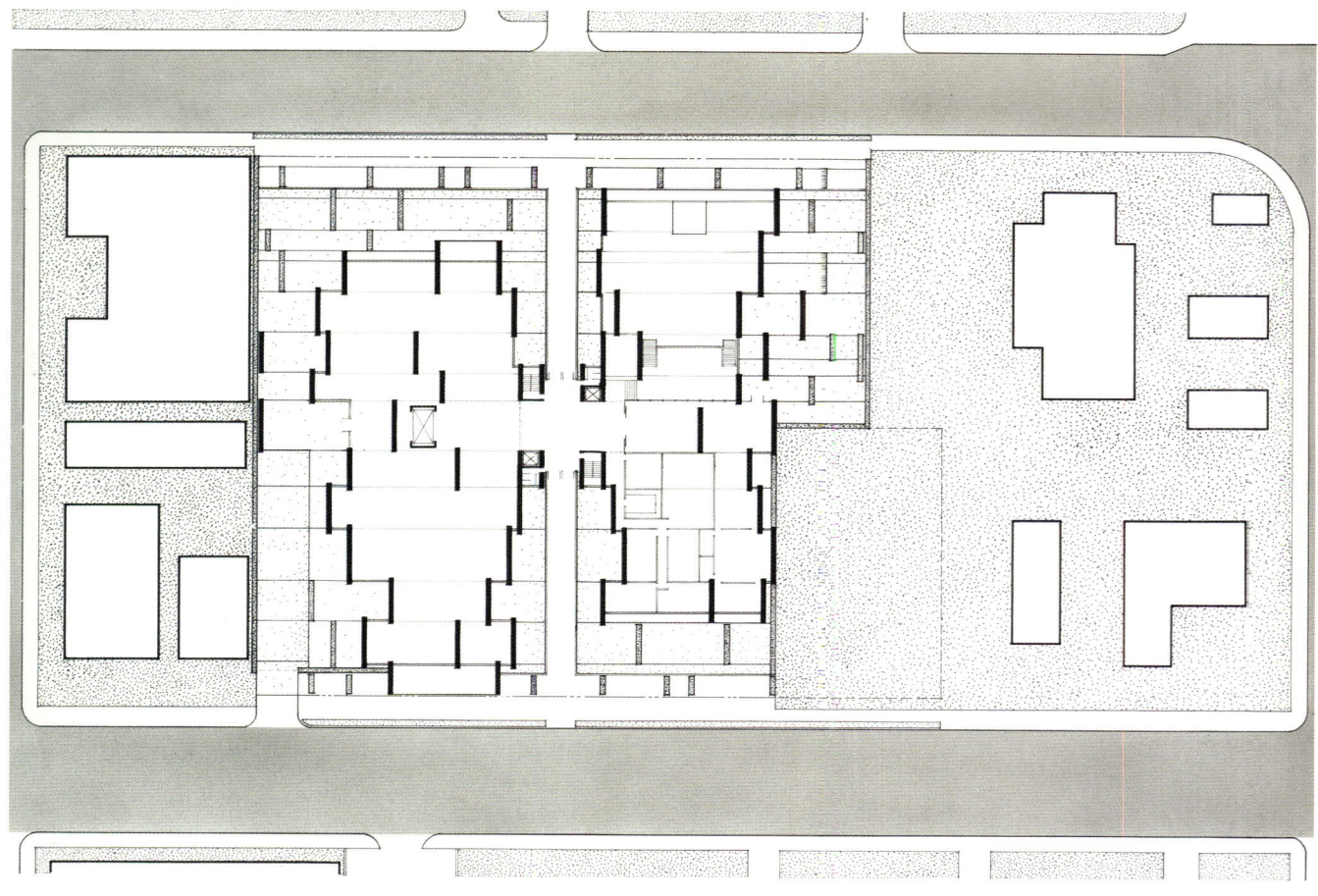

3

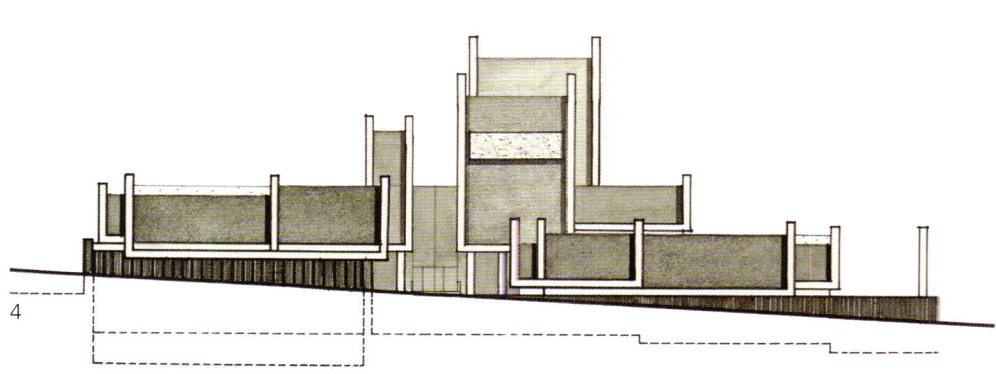

4

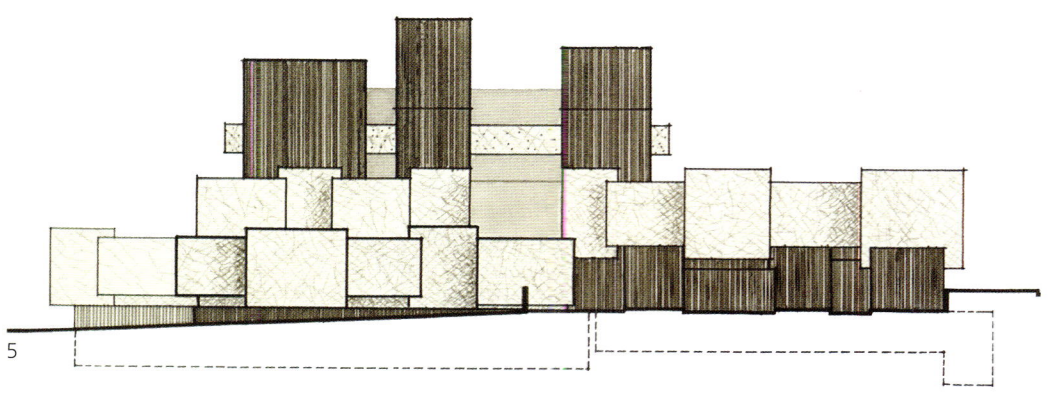

5

6

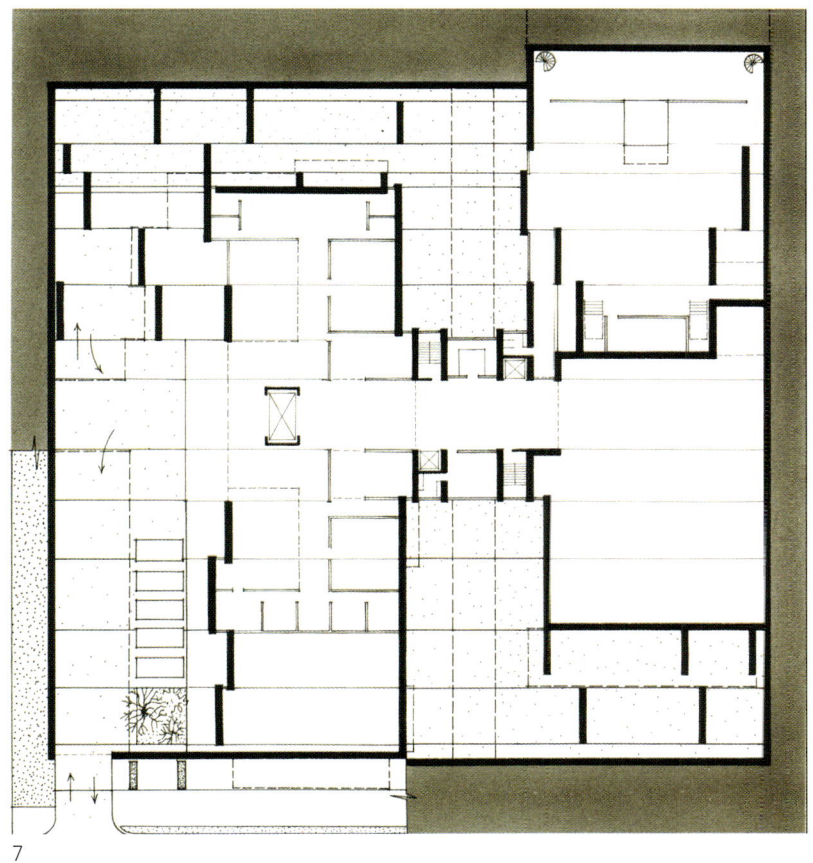

7

3  Site plan/main entry level
4  North elevation
5  East elevation
6  Second level balcony
7  Lower level plan

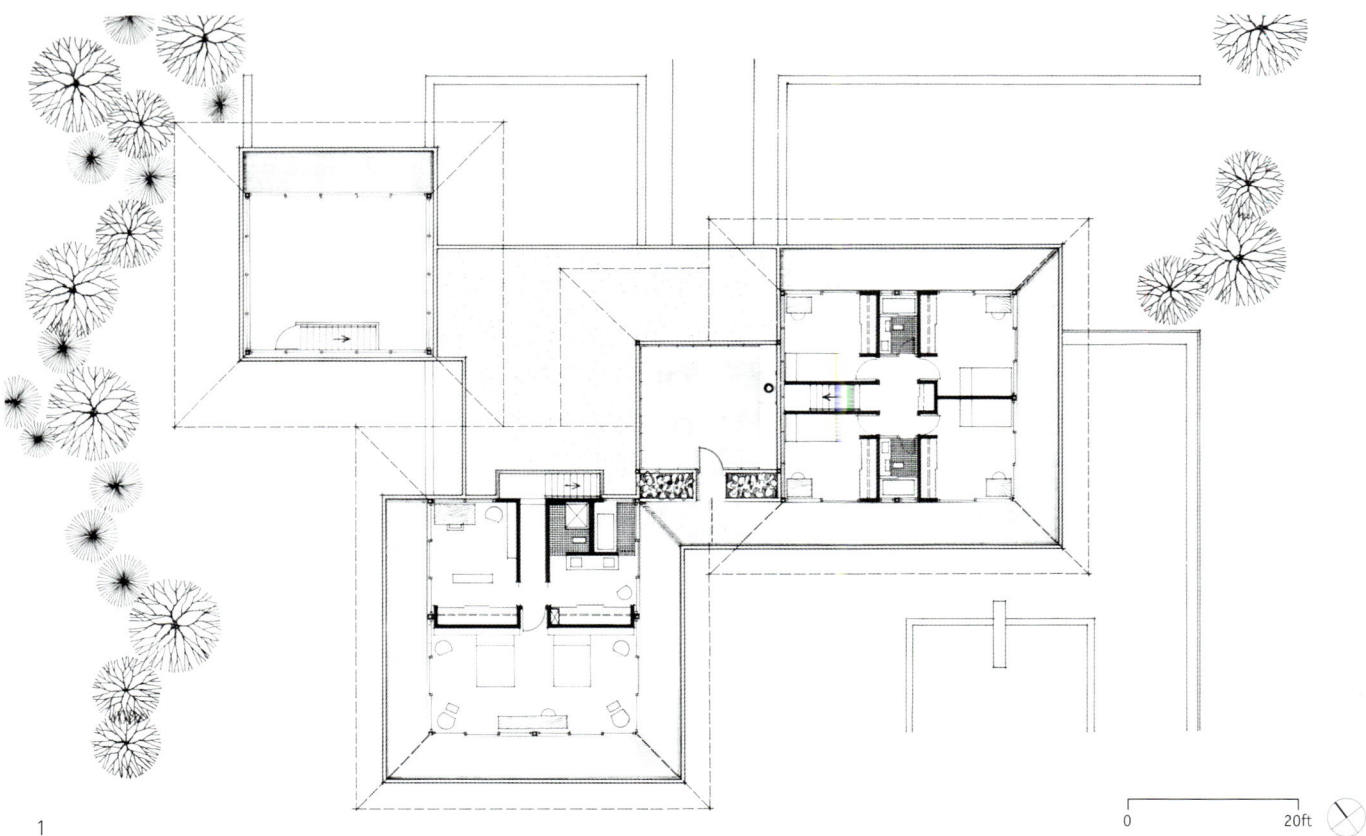

1

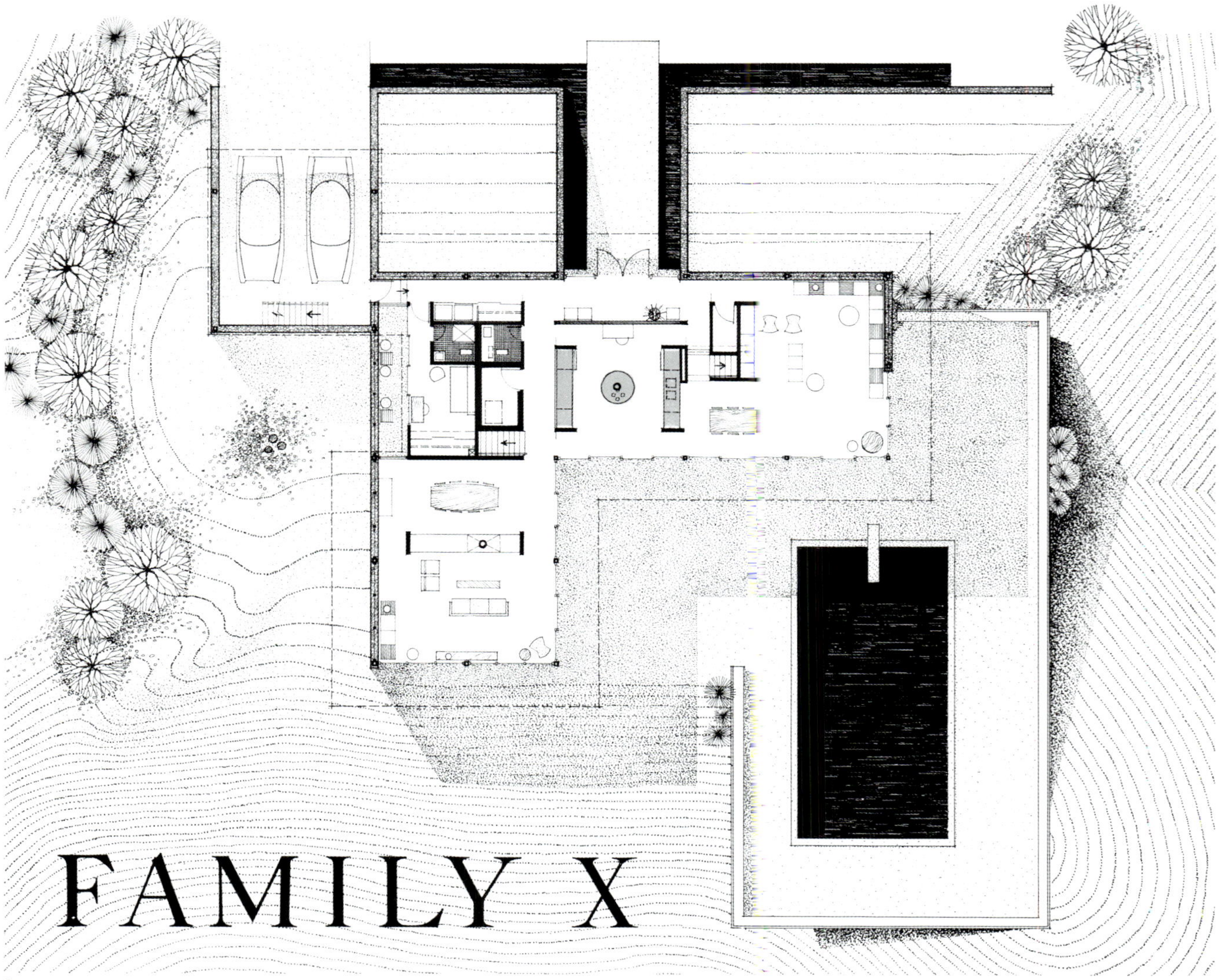

FAMILY X

2

## 63

**Architectural Competition**

1 Level 2 floor plan
2 Level 1 floor plan
3 Section
4 West elevation

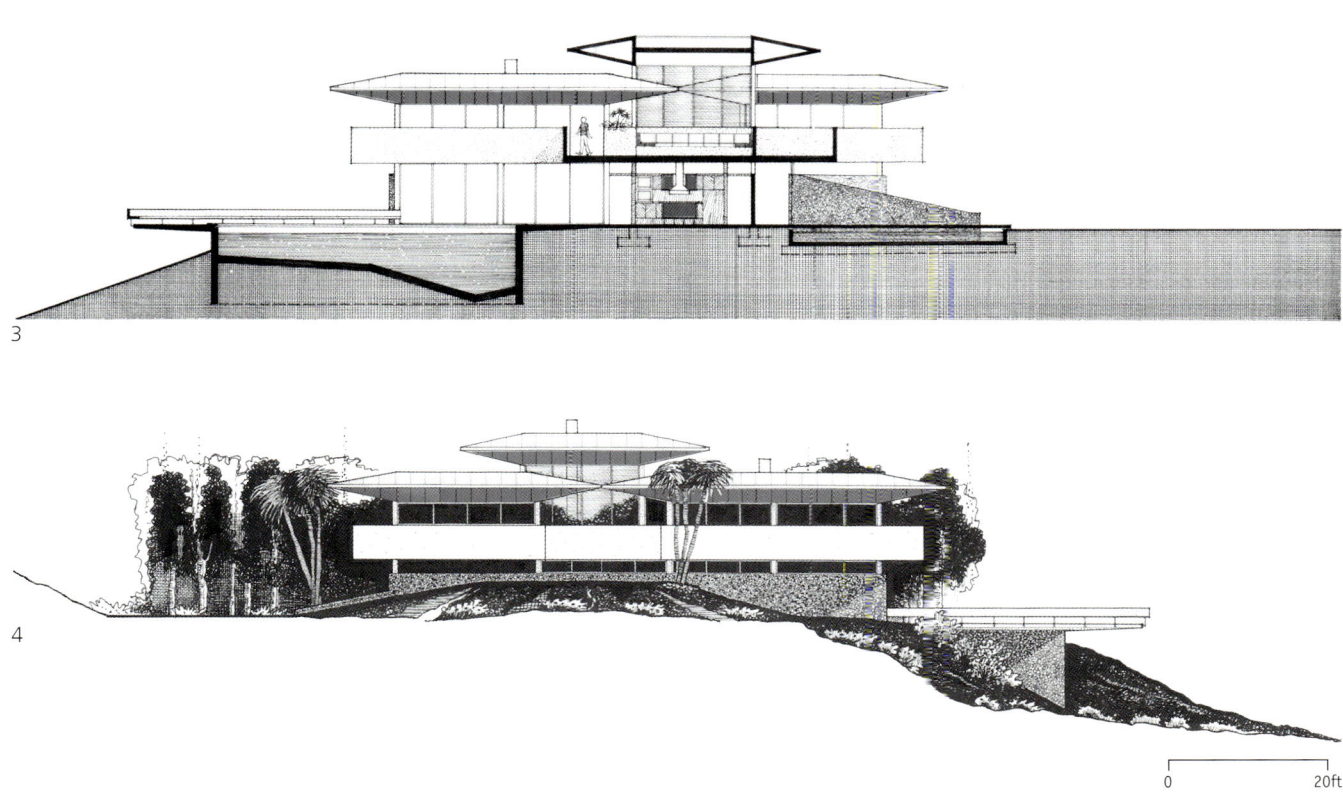

3

4

0                    20ft

### Design 1964

Hollywood, California
Mt. Olympus Corporation
7,000 square feet
Concrete, steel frames,
intermediate wood framing
with plywood diaphragms,
glass, stucco, aluminum,
and copper roofs

Prior to opening his Tampa office, Howey entered this international design competition sponsored by a California luxury homes developer. Three prototype residences programs were offered and a residence for a family of six was chosen. The site and its access road were located along a ridge at Mt. Olympus, offering spectacular views to Hollywood below. Howey's solution placed the house and pool facing the city just at the top of a steep incline rising above the city. The entry side of the property was earth-bermed for privacy. Above the main level is a series of pavilion roofs enclosing the second-level children's bedroom wing, master bedroom suite, and a future den. Below, the foyer and kitchen located in the knuckle of the L-plan, serve both the dining–family room and the formal dining–living spaces. A large terrace provided views and access to a pool. Above the terrace, a perimeter balcony and central rooftop gazebo completed the design.

APPENDIX

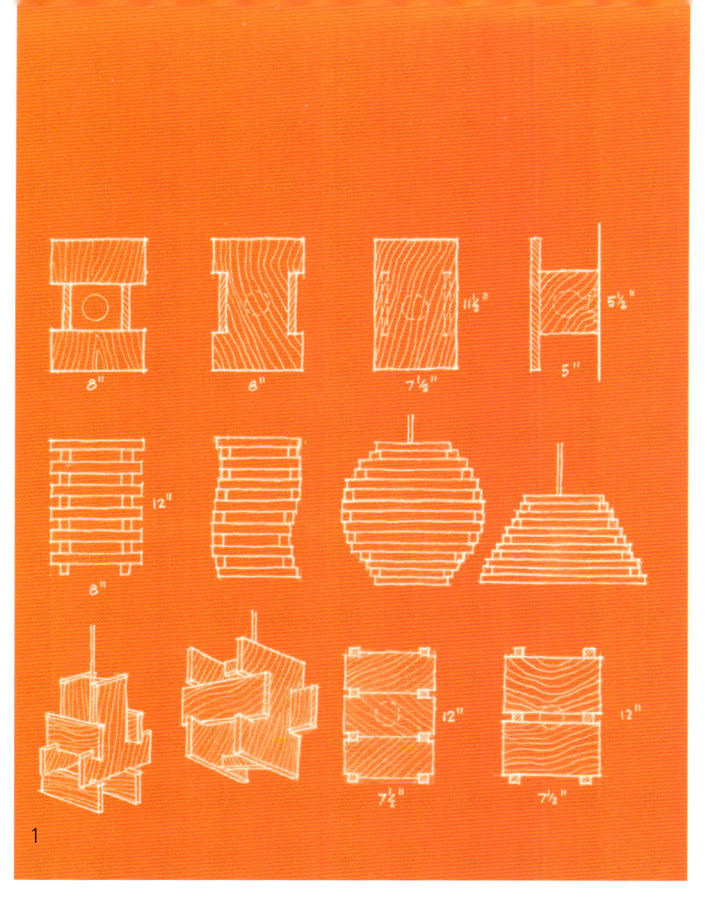

1

2

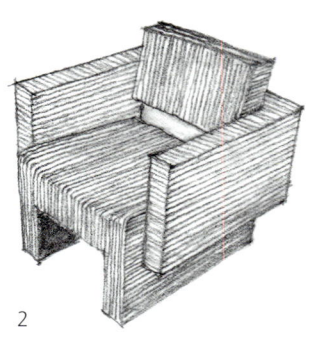

3

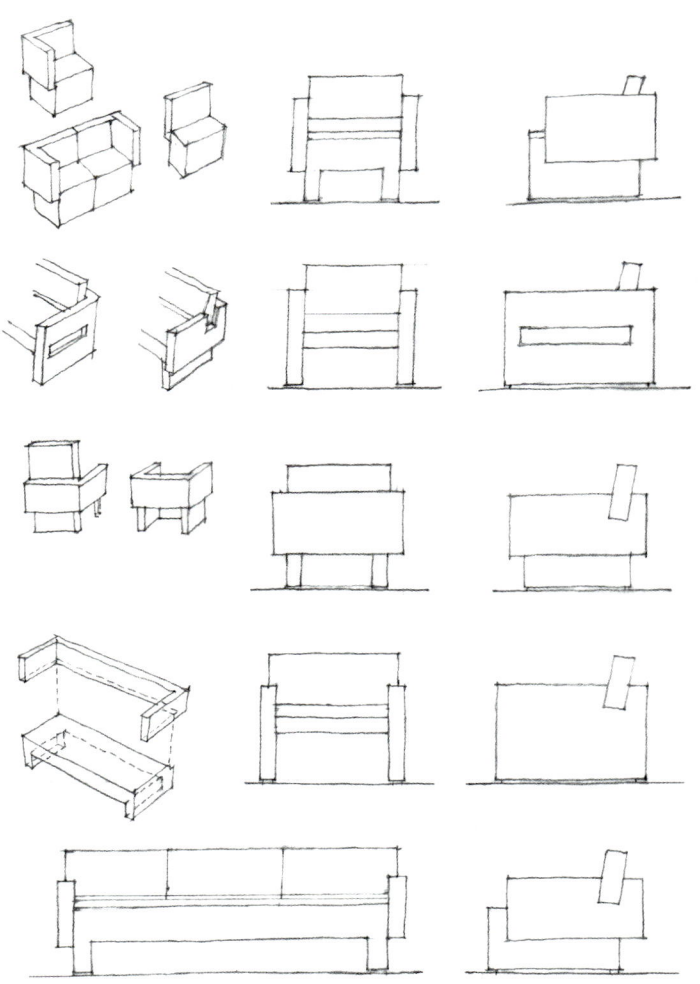

4

$4\frac{1}{2}$" ?

4" ?

$\frac{1}{2}$" PLYWOOD ?

12"

5"

5"

2" ?

TO BE DETERM'MED

SECTION WITH BACK CUSHION IN

1 Light fixture designs
2–5 Sofa chair designs
Following pages Furniture working drawings

# 64

## Product design

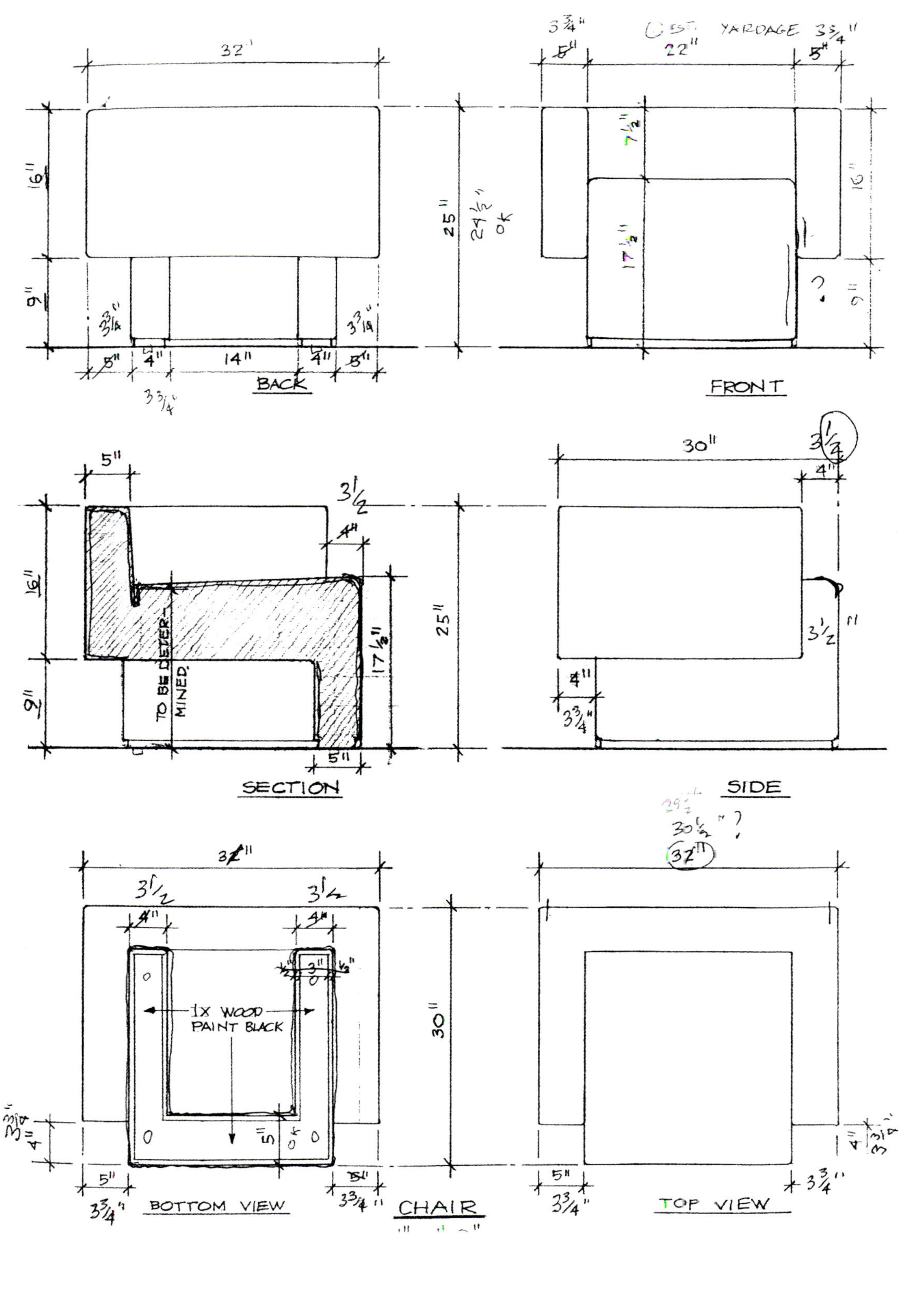


5

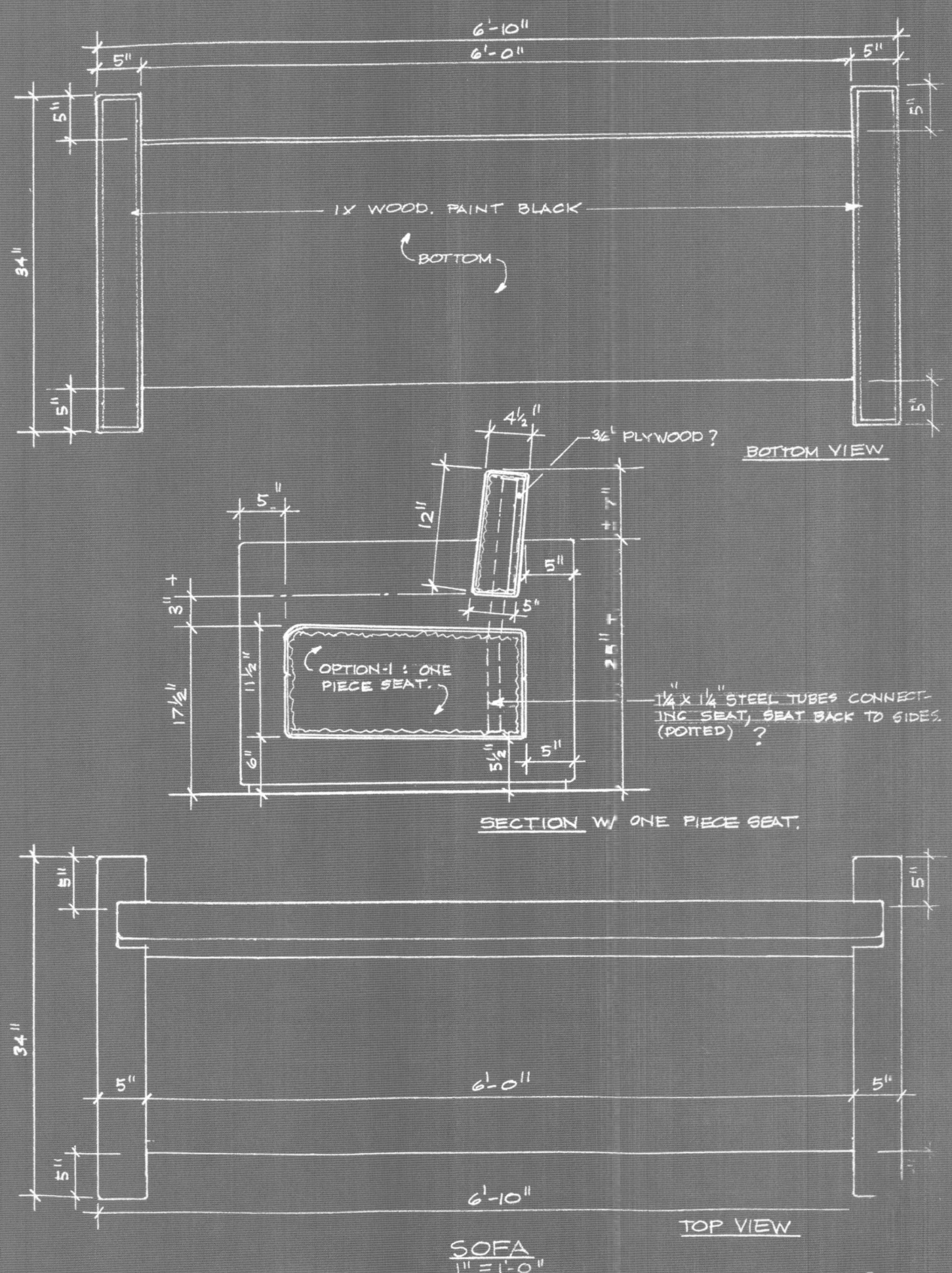

6'-10"
6'-0"
5"
5"
5"
5"

34"

1X WOOD. PAINT BLACK

BOTTOM

5"
5"

BOTTOM VIEW

4½"

3/4" PLYWOOD ?

5"

12"

5"

5"

5"

3"

OPTION-1 : ONE
PIECE SEAT.

1¼" X 1¼" STEEL TUBES CONNECT-
ING SEAT, SEAT BACK TO SIDES.
(POTTED) ?

17½"

11½"

6"

5½"

5"

SECTION W/ ONE PIECE SEAT.

5"
5"

34"

5"

6'-0"

5"

5"

5"

6'-10"

TOP VIEW

SOFA
1"=1'-0"

9-9-02

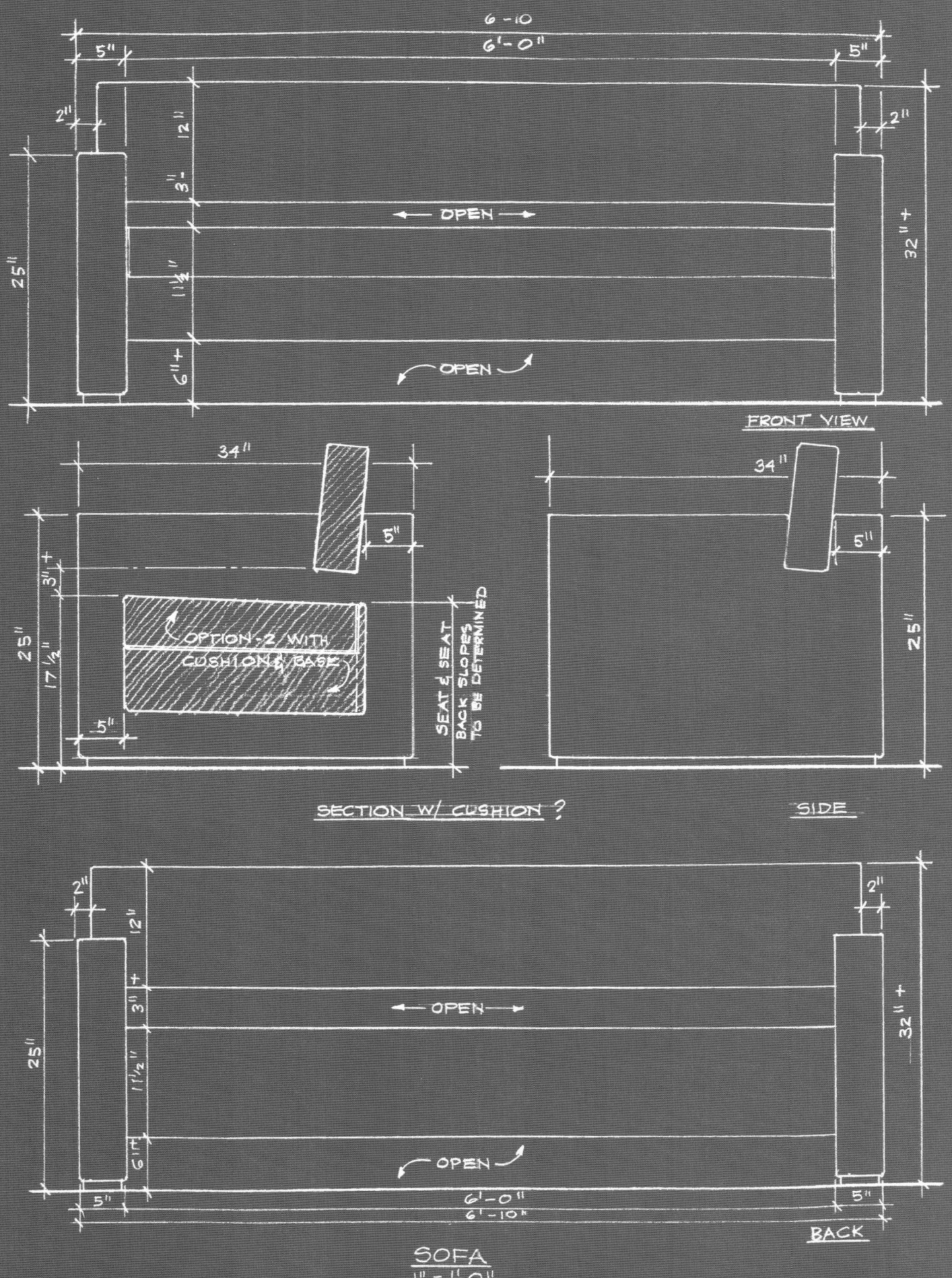

6'-10"
6'-0"
5"
2"
12"
3"
OPEN
25"
1 1/2"
32"+
OPEN
6"+
FRONT VIEW

34"
5"
+
3"
25"
17 1/2"
OPTION-2 WITH
CUSHION & BASE
SEAT & SEAT
BACK SLOPES
TO BE DETERMINED
5"

34"
5"
25"

SECTION W/ CUSHION ?

SIDE

2"
2"
12"
25"
3"
OPEN
1 1/2"
32"+
6"+
OPEN
5"
6'-0"
6'-10"
5"

BACK

SOFA
1" = 1'-0"

# Bio graphy

## John Howey

A design graduate of the Georgia Institute of Technology, John Howey worked for various architectural firms in Atlanta, New Orleans, the Tampa Bay area, and California before beginning his Tampa practice in 1965. In 1973, his firm incorporated and became one of the first businesses established in Tampa's old warehouse district. In 1980, his firm purchased and restored the 100-year-old brick warehouse where he continues to practice architecture today.

After graduating with Bachelor of Science and Bachelor of Architecture degrees, Howey completed his six-month military duty with the U.S. Army Corps of Engineers. Following that, he moved to Florida's Gulf Coast and became a registered architect. At this point, with his interest also in the West Coast, he traveled to Southern California with an extended stay in San Francisco. Here he experienced the work of the early California Modernists, such as Irving Gill, Rudolph Schindler, Bernard Maybeck, and the later Case Study architects' work. From this sojourn Howey acquired his lifelong interest in regional 20th-century American architecture. On his return to Florida and upon winning the 1964 AIA St. Petersburg Residential Competition, Howey moved to Tampa to establish his present practice.

He has published numerous articles and two books: *The Sarasota School of Architecture* (M.I.T. Press, 1995) and *Florida Architecture, A Celebration* (A.I.A., Florida, 2000). A touring exhibition sponsored by Selby Gallery based on the Sarasota book traveled the United States for four years and included tour appearances and lectures by Howey. He has been a visiting critic, lecturer, and/or adjunct professor at the New School of Architecture, San Diego; SCI-Arc, Los Angeles; the Universities of Utah, Florida, South Florida, Florida A & M, and Tennessee; and the Louisiana Technical Institute.

Howey has received numerous design awards and honors for his work. These include: an AIA Florida 2000 Millennium Award of Honor for Design; 1985 AIA Regional Award of Honor for Design; and Fellow of the American Institute of Architects in Design 1989. In 1988, a one-man exhibition of his completed projects, models, and drawings was held by the University of South Florida and New College in Sarasota. An exhibition of Howey's current work is planned by Selby Gallery, Sarasota, in 2006.

## 1964

Mt. Olympus Homes

    California

St. Petersburg residential competition

    St. Petersburg, Florida

Remodel for Dr Kenneth Everts

    Berkeley, California

## 1965

Residence for Mr and Mrs Thomas Lifsey

    Tampa, Florida

Office remodel for Maxwell Lopin

    Tampa, Florida

Remodel for Dr and Mrs Julian Stampa

    St. Petersburg, Florida

Residence for Mr and Mrs Payson Kennedy

    Atlanta, Georgia

University of California Arts Center competition

    Berkeley, California

John Howey office, 217 N. Franklin Street

    Tampa, Florida

Nursing home for Mr and Mrs Lynn Carr

    Tampa, Florida

Remodel for LM Anderson Dental Supply

    Tampa, Florida

New parking facilities for St. Petersburg Times

    St. Petersburg, Florida

Residence for Mr and Mrs Wayne Greenlee

    Tampa, Florida

Remodel of Lykes Ranch

    Brighton, Florida

Remodel of ticketing office for Pan American Airlines

    Tampa, Florida

## 1966

Apartment building for Mr and Mrs Kenneth Carithers

    Tampa, Florida

Remodel of 1100 W. Kennedy Building

    Tampa, Florida

Wishart law office

    Tampa, Florida

Wishart highrise apartments

    Tampa, Florida

Wishart garden apartments

    Tampa, Florida

# Chrono logy

## Chronological list of buildings and projects

Temple Terrace Lutheran Church
   Temple Terrace, Florida
Remodel of Bayview Hotel
   Tampa, Florida
University of Tampa Scandinavian Room
   Tampa, Florida

## 1967

Hillsborough County School projects
   Tampa, Florida
Remodel of Anderson Lumber Company
   St. Petersburg, Florida
Residence remodel for Dr and Mrs Burns Creighton
   Tampa, Florida
Residence remodel for Mr and Mrs Jack Holtzclaw
   Tampa, Florida
Residence remodel for Mr and Mrs Richard Swirbul
   Tampa, Florida
Remodel of Northeast Airlines ticket offices
   Tampa, Florida
Offices for Henry Monteau
   Tampa, Florida
Residence for Mr and Mrs John Bierley
   Tampa, Florida
Beach house for Mr and Mrs David McClean
   Sarasota, Florida
Remodel of restaurant for Mr and Mrs Zudar
   Tampa, Florida

## 1968

Residence remodel for Mr and Mrs David Von Thaden
   Tampa, Florida
200-bed Extended Care Hospital for Dr Anthony Spoto
   Tampa, Florida
Residence remodel for Mrs June Libby
   Brooksville, Florida
New canopy for Hawaiian Village and Mr Samuel Taub
   Tampa, Florida
Warehouse for Mr Louis Curry
   St. Petersburg, Florida
Remodel of Northeast Airlines ticket office
   Miami, Florida
Residence remodel for Dr and Mrs Stephen Speronis
   Tampa, Florida
Remodel of Northeast Airlines ticket office
   Nassau, Bahamas

Residence remodel for Dr and Mrs Carlos Barbas
   Tampa, Florida
Medical clinic for Dr Hector L Rivera
   Tampa, Florida
Nursery school for Mr and Mrs Charles T Davidson
   Tampa, Florida

## 1969

Madison Junior High School
   Tampa, Florida
Recreational motor park for Robert Bradley
   Hillsborough County, Florida
Remodel of law office for H Vincent Thorton
   Tampa, Florida
University of South Florida faculty office/classroom building
   Tampa, Florida
Yale math building competition
   New Haven, Connecticut
Beauty center for Karl and John Hines
   St. Petersburg, Florida
MacDill and Patrick Air Force Base renovations
   Tampa and Cocoa Beach, Florida

## 1970

US Post Office addition
   Arcadia, Florida
Medical Center renovations and additions for Dr Buddy Beville
   Tampa, Florida
Gandy Moorings marina for Dr and Mrs Stephen Speronis
   Tampa, Florida
Midway Bank remodel with Paul T Ward
   Tampa, Florida

## 1971

John Howey office, 308 Tampa Street
   Tampa, Florida
Mr and Mrs John Howey Watrous Street residence
   Tampa, Florida
Good Samaritan Hospital for Dr Richard Mayer
   Tampa, Florida
MacDill Air Force Base multi-family housing
   Tampa, Florida

## 1972

Additions to Monroe Junior High School
   Tampa, Florida

John Martin residence
Tampa, Florida

MacDill Air Force Base youth center
Tampa, Florida

Mr and Mrs John McPherson residence
Orlando, Florida

Edward Campbell CPA, office renovation
Tampa, Florida

Mr and Mrs Lee Ward residence
Tarpon Springs, Florida

## 1973

Louis Pappas restaurant
Tarpon Springs, Florida

Sagee Mountain Development for John Trinkle
Highlands, North Carolina

Plaza One shopping center
New Port Richey, Florida

## 1973–1977

Hillsborough County Maintenance Center
Ruskin and Riverview, Florida

## 1974

Bay Villa Townhouses
Tampa, Florida

Mr and Mrs Vance Smith residence
Tampa, Florida

US Post Office
Dunellon, Florida

US Post Office
Lakeland, Florida

## 1975

Model Cities Health Care Center
Tampa, Florida

Offices for Dr Albert Davis
St. Petersburg, Florida

Residence remodel for Mr and Mrs Dwight Emanuelson
Tampa, Florida

## 1976

Residence for Keith Brookins
Tampa, Florida

Residence for Mr and Mrs Michael Trocke
Tampa, Florida

Blanchard residence remodeling
Tampa, Florida

Bayside office building remodeling for Alfred Austin
Tampa, Florida

Jack Mayworth residence
Tampa, Florida

Biscayne West competition
Miami, Florida

Minnesota II National open competition
St. Paul, Minnesota

## 1977

City Hall Plaza
Tampa, Florida

St. John's Episcopal Church Courtyard
Tampa, Florida

Dr Charles Diminico office remodel
Tampa, Florida

Iran National Library competition
Tehran, Iran

St. Petersburg bus shelter competition
St. Petersburg, Florida

## 1978

Offices for Dr Allan Heitman
Largo, Florida

Residence for Mr and Mrs Ralph Lewis
St. Petersburg, Florida

Howard Zion residence
Tampa, Florida

Interbay Design Gallery
Tampa, Florida

Mr and Mrs Joel Healy residence
Tampa, Florida

Campus car wash center
Tampa, Florida

Silver Oaks Crowder Corporation
Tampa, Florida

AR Dick Williers, Jr residence
Tampa, Florida

## 1979

Steven Boynton apartment complex
Tampa, Florida

Edward S. Bolding and Land professional offices
Tampa, Florida

St. Petersburg Shelter competition

    St. Petersburg, Florida

George Gleason townhome development

    Tampa, Florida

Wayne Greenlee residence

    Tampa, Florida

## 1980

Nantahala Outdoor Center

    Wesser, North Carolina

Caradonna medical offices

    Tampa, Florida

101 S. Franklin Street building renovation

    Tampa, Florida

Mr and Mrs John Shuman residence

    Clearwater, Florida

Janus Landing commercial development

    St. Petersburg, Florida

## 1981

Dr and Mrs Giglio residence

    Port Richey, Florida

Mr and Mrs Ernest Garrison addition

    Tampa, Florida

Interbay Branch YMCA

    Tampa, Florida

Bartke's dinner theater

    Tampa, Florida

Dr Albert Davis medical office and residence

    St. Petersburg, Florida

Village Presbyterian church

    Tampa, Florida

Vietnam Memorial competition

    Washington, DC

## 1982

Constans residence

    Tampa, Florida

Wodrich residence

    Tampa, Florida

Mr and Mrs Roland Wilson residence restoration

    Tampa, Florida

Mr and Mrs Payson Kennedy residence

    Wesser, North Carolina

Fort Lauderdale Plaza competition

    Ft. Lauderdale, Florida

## 1983

Medical offices for Dr Robert Wharton

    St. Petersburg, Florida

Drs Harris and Fletcher medical offices

    Tampa, Florida

Flagship Bank drive-in tellers

    Tampa, Florida

Dr Stanley Moles residence

    Bellaire, Florida

City Government Springs project

    Tampa, Florida

Mr and Mrs Jordan-Holmes residence

    Tampa, Florida

Porter and Fletcher office park

    Tampa, Florida

Alphonso Brown houseboat

    Tampa, Florida

## 1984

Florida Vietnam Memorial competition

    Tallahassee, Florida

Mr and Mrs Sembler residence

    Clearwater, Florida

Mr and Mrs Luis Menendez residence

    Tampa, Florida

Luggage Services addition

    Tampa, Florida

Columbus Landscape competition

    Columbus, Indiana

United Chambers Insurance offices

    Tampa, Florida

## 1985

University of Florida Museum competition

    Gainesville, Florida

Mr and Mrs Charles Hay residence

    Sarasota, Florida

Mr and Mrs Carl Lindell residence

    Tampa, Florida

Lancaster and York development

    Safety Harbor, Florida

Mr and Mrs David Allison residence

    Alarka, North Carolina

Countresquire residential development

    Clearwater, Florida

Mr and Mrs Jack Whiteside residence

    Anna Maria Island, Florida

Albritton-Sessions law offices

    Tampa, Florida

Beckman, McAliley, and Schultz law offices

    Tampa, Florida

Residence remodel for Mr and Mrs Jurge Oggenfuss

    Tampa, Florida

Executive office center

    Tampa, Florida

## 1986

Ybor City Gateway competition

    Tampa, Florida

Hodges and Carle law offices

    Zephyrhills, Florida

Sunrise Shopping Center renovation and additions

    Hudson, Florida

Mr and Mrs Robert Carr residence, and Windsong Kenne s

    Tampa, Florida

Curlew Creek Bridge for Mr and Mrs John Shuman

    Clearwater, Florida

Sea Born School renovation

    Tampa, Florida

Bowen II Travel Service interior

    Tampa, Florida

## 1987

Vietnam Veterans Memorial competition

    St. Petersburg, Florida

Residence remodeling for Mr and Mrs Robert Neumeiste

    Tampa, Florida

National Car Rental offices

    Tampa, Florida

Warehouse for Henry Fernandez

    Tampa, Florida

Clock tower for Stan Good

    Tampa, Florida

Dayspring Episcopal conference center

    Ellenton, Florida

Gary Johnson fitness studio

    Tampa, Florida

## 1988

Addition for Lewis Hill offices

    Tampa, Florida

Addition for Henry Powers residence

    Tampa, Florida

## 1989

Bay Park Place condomiriums

    Tampa, Florida

2540, 2542, 2552 Palm Drive condominium units

    Tampa, Florida

Mr and Mrs Frank Seco De Lucena residence

    Shell Point, Florida

## 1990

Mr and Mrs James Wallace residence

    Manasota Key, Florida

2538, 2546, 2548 Palm Drive condominium units

    Tampa, Florida

## 1991

2544 Palm Drive condominium unit

    Tampa, Florida

## 1992

Governor's Island Competition

    New York

## 1993

Mr and Mrs Alexandre Georges residence

    Loire Valley, France

Embarcadero competition

    San Francisco, California

## 1994

Residence for Mr and Mrs Paul Whiting

    Longboat Key, Florida

Lincoln Elementary School

    Plant City, Florida

Stewart Joiner law offices

    Tampa, Florida

## 1995

Renovations to residence for Mr and Mrs Gene Gardner

    Hillsborough County, Florida

## 1997

John Howey office, 121 W. Whiting Street
　Tampa, Florida

Umbrella House restoration for Mr and Mrs Gary Stover
　Sarasota, Florida

## 1998

2550 Palm Drive condominium unit
　Tampa, Florida

Remodel of residence for Rose Diaz
　Tampa, Florida

## 1999

City Center renewal project
　Tampa, Florida

Additions to medical office for Dr Edward Linebaugh
　Tampa, Florida

Industrial building for Pallets Source of Tampa
　Tampa, Florida

Remodel of residence for Mr and Mrs Duncan Yull
　Sarasota, Florida

Artist studio for Rosa Linda Borcia
　Tampa, Florida

ATO fraternity house
　Tallahassee, Florida

## 2000

Golf course/residential development
　Zephyrhills, Florida

Ybor City service screen enclosures
　Tampa, Florida

TKTS competition
　New York, New York

The Gallery house for Mr and Mrs Jerry Holton
　St. Petersburg, Florida

## 2001

Tower 101 for Tampa Tower LLC
　Tampa, Florida

Remodeling and additions for Gator Gypsum
　Tampa, Florida

Office complex for Hillsborough County Bar Association
　Tampa, Florida

## 2002

YMCA Downtown fitness center addition
　Tampa, Florida

Residential complex for Donald Blair
　Tampa, Florida

## 2003

Florida bayfront residence for Mark Richens
　Islamorada, Florida

## 2004

Loft Apartments for Mr and Mrs Henry Fernandez
　Tampa, Florida

Warehouse renovation for Henry Fernandez
　Tampa, Florida

## 2005

Residence for Mr and Mrs William Roth
　Springhill, Florida

Residence additions for Mr and Mrs James Hatton
　Tampa, Florida

Hattricks Sports Bar renovations
　Tampa, Florida

# Collab
# orators

John S Philip

Richard Williams

Richard Redman

Beth Moberly

James Parks

Erin McDuffie

Clark MacKinnon

Max Strang

William Muse

Carlos Molnar

Robert Mercer

Michael Renaud

Hans Brunner

Gerald McCants

Patricia Titus

Laura Lake

Maria Howey

Peeti Sastrawaha

Dick Tilley

Geno Knowles

Rik Edmonds

John Mistretta

Glenda Cordova

Jeanette Knowles

Jorge Barrio

Charles Brink

Judy Nelson

Marvin Rand

John Cochran

William Rast

Eric Kuehlem

Leslie Robertson

Patrick McDonald

William Faschen

Lee Harvard

Hardee Williams

Jose Forns, Jr.

Nancy Robinson

Carl Abbott

Genevieve Dermer

Rick Rowe

Joan Farago

Stephen Sobieralski

Susan Greco

Elizabeth Kremmer

Barbara Gale

Jon Summers

John Jay

Carlos Ugarte

Gregg De Meza

Celeste Cotton

Richard Thurlby

Heidi Adams

Victor Colum

Robert Phillips

Sarah Burchill

Kathy Cannon

Barbara Apel

William C Henderson

Jennifer Parmer

Kenya Thenthem

# Awards

**Awards, Exhibitions, and Competitions**

## 2004

**AIA Gulf Coast Chapter Award**

Presidential Honor Award, Sarasota

## 2000

**AIA Regional Award**

President's Award for development of book

*Florida Architecture—A Celebration*

**AIA Regional 2000 Millennium**

Award of Honor for Design as one of Florida's top design

firms of the 20th century

**AIA Regional Award**

For 20th Century Decade Award winner, 1981–1990

**TKTS Competition**

New York

## 1995

**Selby Gallery Exhibition**

Curator, the work of the Sarasota School of Architects,

Sarasota

## 1994

**Embarcadero Competition**

San Francisco

## 1992

**Governor's Island Competition**

New York

## 1989

**AIA Regional Award**

Seco De Lucena Residence, Shell Point, Florida

**AIA Regional Award**

Bay Park Place Condominiums, Tampa

**American Institute of Architects**

Elevation to Fellowship, St. Louis

## 1988

**New College/University of South Florida Exhibition**

The Work of John Howey, Sarasota

## 1987

**AIA National Convention Design Exhibition**

101 S. Franklin Street Building, Orlando

## 1986

**AIA Florida/Caribbean Regional Award of Honor for Design**

Over an extended period of time, Tallahassee

## 1985

**AIA Regional Award**

Modular Transit Shelter, St. Petersburg

**AIA Regional Award**

101 S. Franklin Street Building, Tampa

**AIA Regional Convention Tour of Homes**

Williers Residence, Tampa

**AIA Tampa Bay Award**

Medal of Honor for Consistent Design Excellence, Tampa

**University of Florida Museum Competition**

Finalist, Gainesville

## 1984

**Florida Trust for Historic Preservation Award**

101 S. Franklin Street Building, Tampa

**AIA Tampa Bay Award**

Modular Transit Shelter, St. Petersburg

**AIA Tampa Bay Award**

Dr Wharton Medical Offices, St. Petersburg

**Hillsborough County Planning Commission Award**

Williers Residence, Tampa

**Hillsborough County Planning Commission Award**

Village Presbyterian Church, Tampa

## 1983

**Hillsborough County Planning Commission Award**

101 S. Franklin Street Building, Tampa

## 1982

**AIA Tampa Bay Award**

Hillsborough County Maintenance Facility, Riverview

**AIA Tampa Bay Award**

Kennedy Residence, Wesser, North Carolina

**AIA Tampa Bay Award**

City Hall Plaza, Tampa

**AIA Tampa Bay Award**

101 S. Franklin Street Building, Tampa

**AIA Tampa Bay Award**

Williers Residence, Tampa

**Tampa Preservation, Inc. Award**

101 S. Franklin Street Building, Tampa

## 1981

**National Vietnam Memorial Competition**

Washington, DC

**Tampa Community Design Center Tour of Homes**

Bay Villa Townhomes, Tampa

**AIA Regional Award**

Williers Residence, Tampa

## 1978

**AIA Tampa Bay Award**

Hillsborough County Maintenance Facility, Ruskin

**AIA Tampa Bay Award**

Blanchard Residence Renovation, Tampa

**AIA Tampa Bay Award**

Bay Villa Townhomes, Tampa

## 1977

**AIA Open Competition First Place Winner**

Prototype Shelter, St. Petersburg

**Iran National Library Competition**

Tehran, Iran

## 1976

**AIA Tampa Bay Award**

Louis Pappas Restaurant, Tarpon Springs

**Biscayne West Competition**

Miami

**AIA Tampa Bay Award**

Dr Davis Medical Offices, St. Petersburg

**National Open Competition**

Minnesota State Capitol Annex, St. Paul, featured
in 1978 Yale Architectural Calendar

**AIA Tampa Bay Award**

Bierley Residence, Tampa

## 1969

**National Open Competition**

Yale Math Building, New Haven

## 1965

**National Open Competition**

University of California Arts Center, Berkeley

## 1964

**AIA Open Competition First Place Winner**

Duval Residence, St. Petersburg

**National Open Competition**

Mt. Olympus Homes, California

## Selected Journals and Periodicals

'Winner, Local Architect's Contest,' *St. Petersburg Times*,
    8 March 1964, pp. 1F, 6F.

'Plan of the Week,' *St. Petersburg Times*, 31 October 1965, p. 3F.

Bierley Residence, *Florida Architect*, November/December 1970,
    pp. 24–25.

Louis Pappas Restaurant, *Florida Architect*, 1976.

A Review of Minnesota State Capitol Annex, Yale Alumni
    Calendar, 1978.

'Plaza is Popular Focal Point,' *Tampa Tribune*,
    28 December 1980.

Private Residence, *Florida Architect*, Fall 1981, p. 17.

Williers Residence, *Florida Builder*, October 1981.

Letter to Editor: 'Manhattan Highrises,' *New York Times*,
    November 1981.

'101 South Franklin Street Building,' *Florida Preservation News*,
    Winter 1984.

'John Howey Associates, Current Work,' *Centerline*, May 1984.

Modular Transit Shelter, *Florida Builder*, May 1985.

'Tampa City Hall Plaza,' *Sarasota Magazine*, June 1985.

'University of Florida Museum,' *Centerline*, June 1985.

'Modular Transit Shelter,' *Centerline*, Summer 1985.

'John Howey Associates: Where Preconceived Ideas Give Way
    to Diverse Designs,' *Florida Architect*, July/August 1985,
    pp. 30–35.

'101 S. Franklin Street,' *Florida Construction Industry*,
    August 1985.

'John Howey: Beyond Contemporary,' *Southern Homes/Tampa
    Bay*, Fall 1985, pp. 68–75.

'John Howey AIA,' *Centerline*, September 1985.

'101 S. Franklin Street,' *Florida Architect*, September/October 1985.

'101 S. Franklin Street,' *Florida Builder*, November 1985.

'Modular Transit Shelter,' *Florida Construction Industry*,
    November 1985.

'101 S. Franklin Street,' *Contact*, Winter 1985.

'Rising to the Heavens, Village Presbyterian Church,' *Suncoast
    Almanac*, 1986.

'From "Cigar City" to "Florida's Next Great City" ' *Florida
    Architect*, May/June 1987, pp. 38–39.

'John Howey: Geometer of Spaces,' *Florida Architect*,
    March/April 1988, pp. 18–20.

'Unbuilt Awards,' *Florida Architect*, July/August 1989, pp. 26–28.

'Unbuilt Award Winner Becomes Reality,' *Florida Architect*,
    November/December 1992, pp. 24–25.

'John Howey and Associates, Tower 101,' *Florida Architect*,
    Winter 2001, pp. 20–21.

## Articles

Ardren, Bob, 'New Shelter—Bay Park Place,' *Tampa Tribune*,
    17 June 1989.

Benbow, Charles, 'Old and New City Buildings in Conflict as
    Neighbors,' *St. Petersburg Times*, 1 June 1980, p. 1F.

Benbow, Charles, 'Architects Honored for Designs,'
    *St. Petersburg Times*, 4 October 1981, p. 3H.

Benbow, Charles, 'Architects and Builders' Group Recognizes
    Member's Excellence,' *St. Petersburg Times*, 21 November
    1982, p. 5F.

Benbow, Charles, 'Architects Gather to Honor their Own,'
    *St. Petersburg Times*, 1 April 1984, p. 1H.

Fulton, Pat, 'Remodeling Your Home,' *Tampa Tribune—Home
    and Design*, 16 November 1986.

Garrison, Rene, 'John Howey: Making Space that Endures,'
    *Tampa Tribune*, 2 January 1983, p. 1H.

Garrison, Rene, 'Tampa Firm Wins Design Awards,' *Tampa
    Tribune*, 2 June 1985, p. 1H.

Garrison, Rene, 'Where Architects Live—John Howey,' *Tampa
    Tribune—Home and Design*, 6 July 1986, p. 1H.

Garrison, Rene, 'Unbuilt Design Awards,' *Tampa Tribune*, 22 July
    1989, p. 1G, and 15 September 1989, p. 12G.

Graham, Lisa, 'Etc.,' *La Gaceta*, November 1981.

Lane, Elaine, 'Bringing the Outdoors In,' *Tampa Tribune—Florida
    Living*, 15 December 1968, p. 1.

Steele, Kathy, 'Building on Dreams,' *Tampa Tribune*,
    16 June 2002.

Wilborn, Paul, 'Whiting Street,' *Tampa Tribune—Florida Living*,
    16 November 1980, p. 1.

# Photography

**Credits**

| | | |
|---|---|---|
| 1 | Loft Apartments | Rudy Lopez |
| 2 | Tower 101 | George Cott, Rudy Lopez |
| 3 | Gallery House | George Cott |
| 4 | 2548 Bay Park Place | George Cott |
| 5 | Mountain Residence | Rudy Lopez |
| 6 | Medical Offices and Residence | George Cott |
| 7 | Bayview Hotel | Hans Brunner |
| 8 | Modular Apartments | |
| 9 | School of Nursing Dormitory | George Cott, John Howey |
| 10 | Umbrella House Restoration | Christian Korab, Rudy Lopez |
| 11 | Florida Bayfront Residence | John Howey, John Mistretta |
| 12 | Gulf Front Residence | George Cott |
| 13 | Embarcadero Competition | George Cott |
| 14 | Island House | John Howey |
| 15 | Coastal Residence | Marvin Rand |
| 16 | Beach Front Residence | George Cott |
| 17 | Island Residence | John Howey |
| 18 | Lake Residence | Steven Brooke |
| 19 | Louis Pappas Restaurant | George Cott |
| 20 | Bierley Residence | John Howey, George Cott, JR Beckenbach |
| 21 | Garden Apartments | John Howey |
| 22 | Residence Design Competition | JR Beckenbach |
| 23 | Country Residence | John Howey, John Mistretta |
| 24 | Bay Park Place | George Cott |
| 25 | 2538 Bay Park Place | John Howey, John Mistretta |
| 26 | Dayspring Conference Center | George Cott |
| 27 | Gilio Residence | John Howey |
| 28 | Museum Competition | George Cott |
| 29 | Williers Residence | Steven Brooke, George Cott |
| 30 | Residence Additions | Tony Lopez |
| 31 | Bay Villa Townhomes | George Cott, John Howey |
| 32 | Smith Residence | John Howey |
| 33 | Kennedy Residence One | JR Beckenbach, George Cott |
| 34 | Summer Residence | John Howey |
| 35 | Kennedy Residence Two | John Howey, George Cott, Rudy Lopez |
| 36 | Vietnam War Memorial Competition | George Cott, Rudy Lopez |
| 37 | Presbyterian Church | George Cott |
| 38 | Countresquire | John Howey |

Divider: Earth — Getty Images

Divider: Sky, Water, Flora — Dimension Photography

Divider: Urban — Tampa Bay Convention and Visitors Bureau

# Acknow ledgments

My appreciation is bicoastal, spanning from the Atlantic to the Pacific, beginning in Florida, with a stay in California, and ending up along the Gulf Coast:

To Paul Rudolph and Victor Lundy who opened my eyes to their Sarasota work.

To Irving Gill, Rudolph Schindler, John Lautner and the Case Study Group whose designs I experienced along the Southern California coast.

And finally, to my wife, Maria, whose Midwest sensibilities have sustained me in my architectural journey.

John Howey